Read

Houghton
Mifflin
Harcourt

JOURNEYS
COMMON CORE

Program Authors

James F. Baumann · David J. Chard · Jamal Cooks
J. David Cooper · Russell Gersten · Marjorie Lipson
Lesley Mandel Morrow · John J. Pikulski · Héctor H. Rivera
Mabel Rivera · Shane Templeton · Sheila W. Valencia
Catherine Valentino · MaryEllen Vogt

Consulting Author

Irene Fountas

Cover illustration by Mike Wimmer.

JOURNEYS
COMMON CORE

Unit 1

Unit 2

Hound Dog True
REALISTIC FICTION
by Linda Urban

Unit 3

Unit 4

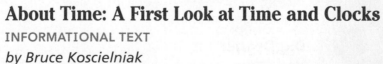

About Time: A First Look at Time and Clocks
INFORMATIONAL TEXT
by Bruce Koscielniak

Unit 5

Welcome, Reader!

You are about to set out on a reading journey that will take you from a cloud forest expedition for tree kangaroos to a deserted island where a boy joins forces with a wild horse to survive. Along the way, you will learn amazing things as you become a better reader.

Your reading journey begins in a school that is unlike any you have ever seen.

Plenty of other reading adventures lie ahead. Just turn the page!

Sincerely,

The Authors

unit 1

Vocabulary in Context

TARGET VOCABULARY

specialty
disturbing
collapsed
squashing
shifted
numb
staggered
struggled
wobbled
interrupted

Vocabulary Reader

Context Cards

L.5.6 acquire and use general academic and domain-specific words and phrases

16

① specialty

A schoolroom may be set up for one skill, or specialty. In this room, students use computers.

② disturbing

Loud noises are disturbing students working in the library. Please be courteous.

③ collapsed

After a hard practice, you might find a tired team collapsed onto benches in the gym.

④ squashing

It's not unusual to see students squashing, or pressing, clay into shapes in the art room.

Go Digital

▶ Study each Context Card.

▶ Use a dictionary or a glossary to verify the meanings of the Vocabulary words.

5 shifted

These students shifted, or moved, their attention to the first question on the test.

6 numb

Wear mittens on cold, numb hands. When your fingers warm up you will feel them.

7 staggered

Wearing heavy backpacks, these students staggered unsteadily to class.

8 struggled

These science students struggled to make their difficult chemistry experiment work.

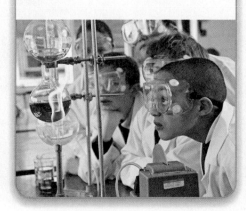

9 wobbled

This girl held her stack of books steady when it wobbled. She kept it from falling over.

10 interrupted

This band teacher interrupted, or briefly stopped, the band to ask them to start over.

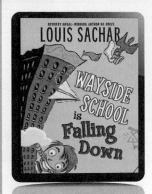

Read and Comprehend

 Go Digital

✓ TARGET SKILL

Story Structure As you read "A Package for Mrs. Jewls," keep track of the story's setting, characters, and plot. Look for the main character's problem, or **conflict**, the **events** surrounding the conflict, and the **resolution** of the conflict. These elements make up the story's overall structure, or organization. Use a graphic organizer like this one to record the important parts of the story.

Setting	Characters
Plot	
Conflict: Events: Resolution:	

✓ TARGET STRATEGY

Summarize As you read "A Package for Mrs. Jewls," pause now and then to **summarize**, or retell the important parts of the story in your own words.

 COMMON CORE **RL.5.2** determine theme from details/summarize; **RL.5.5** explain how chapters, scenes, or stanzas fit together to provide the overall structure

18

Experiments

Why do pencils fall down instead of up? How do rockets stay in space? Physical science, the study of nonliving matter, seeks to answer these kinds of questions. Physical science investigates how objects and various forces, such as energy, interact.

In "A Package for Mrs. Jewls," Mrs. Jewls's class is learning about gravity. Gravity is the force that pulls objects toward Earth's center. To demonstrate gravity in action, Mrs. Jewls has the students perform experiments, or tests used to prove whether ideas are correct. As you read the story, you will learn about gravity, too.

ANCHOR TEXT

✅ TARGET SKILL

Story Structure Examine details about setting, characters, and plot.

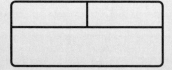

✅ GENRE

Humorous fiction is a story that is written to entertain. As you read, look for:

- ▶ funny or unusual characters and events
- ▶ dialogue that contains jokes or dual meanings
- ▶ an unexpected resolution to the story's conflict

COMMON CORE **RL.5.5** explain how chapters, scenes, or stanzas fit together to provide the overall structure; **RL.5.6** describe how a narrator's or speaker's point of view influences how events are described; **RL.5.10** read and comprehend literature

 Go Digital

MEET THE AUTHOR

Louis Sachar

While working as an elementary school aide, Louis Sachar wrote some stories and read them to his students. The kids loved his stories, and he's been writing ever since. Sachar says, "I want kids to think that reading can be just as much fun, or more so, than TV or video games or whatever else they do."

MEET THE ILLUSTRATOR

Bruce MacPherson

Bruce MacPherson's illustrations have appeared in newspapers and magazines nationwide. Although his own children are now grown, he loves illustrating for kids. His humorous, colorful artwork has appeared in the books *Josefina Javelina* and *Thank You, Aunt Tallulah!*

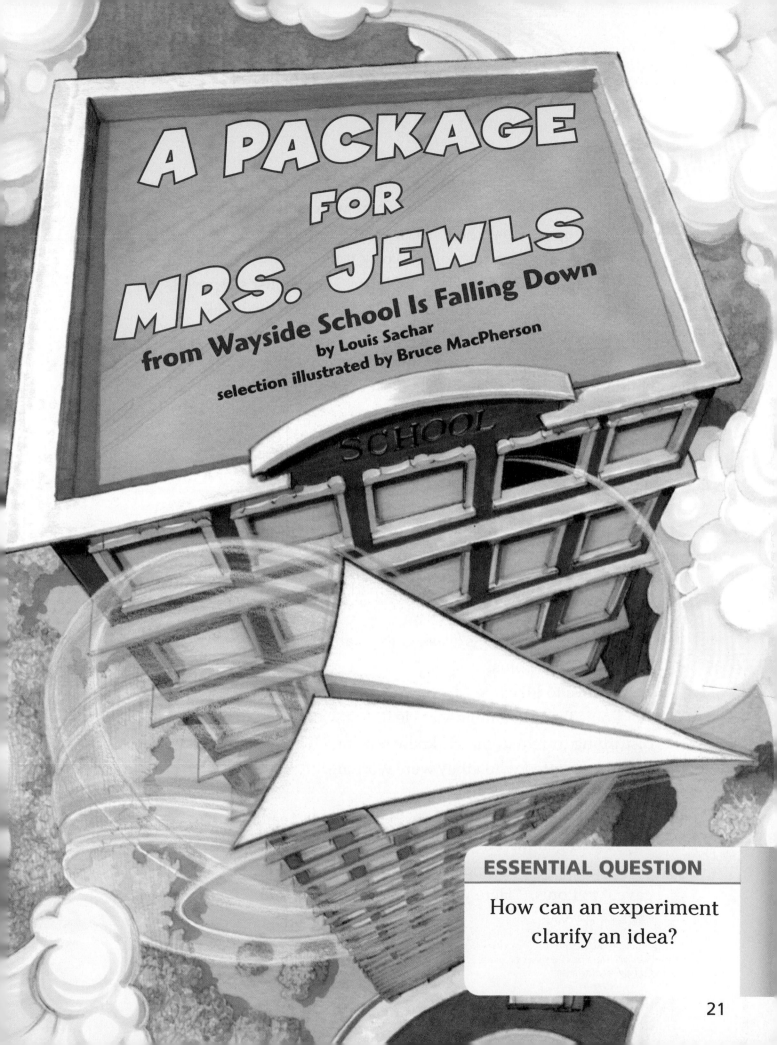

A PACKAGE FOR MRS. JEWLS

from Wayside School Is Falling Down

by Louis Sachar

selection illustrated by Bruce MacPherson

ESSENTIAL QUESTION

How can an experiment clarify an idea?

Louis, the yard teacher, frowned.

The school yard was a mess. There were pencils and pieces of paper everywhere. How'd all this junk get here? he wondered. Well, I'm not going to pick it up!

It wasn't his job to pick up garbage. He was just supposed to pass out the balls during lunch and recess, and also make sure the kids didn't kill each other.

He sighed, then began cleaning it up. He loved all the children at Wayside School. He didn't want them playing on a dirty playground.

As he was picking up the pencils and pieces of paper, a large truck drove into the parking lot. It honked its horn twice, then twice more.

Louis ran to the truck. "Quiet!" he whispered. "Children are trying to learn in there!" He pointed at the school.

A short man with big, bushy hair stepped out of the truck. "I have a package for somebody named Mrs. Jewls," he said.

"I'll take it," said Louis.

"Are you Mrs. Jewls?" asked the man.

"No," said Louis.

"I have to give it to Mrs. Jewls," said the man.

Louis thought a moment. He didn't want the man disturbing the children. He knew how much they hated to be interrupted when they were working.

"I'm Mrs. Jewls," he said.

"But you just said you weren't Mrs. Jewls," said the man.

"I changed my mind," said Louis.

The man got the package out of the back of the truck and gave it to Louis. "Here you go, Mrs. Jewls," he said.

"Uhh!" Louis grunted. It was a very heavy package. The word FRAGILE was printed on every side. He had to be careful not to drop it.

The package was so big, Louis couldn't see where he was going. Fortunately, he knew the way to Mrs. Jewls's class by heart. It was straight up.

Wayside School was thirty stories high, with only one room on each story. Mrs. Jewls's class was at the very top. It was Louis's favorite class.

He pushed through the door to the school, then started up the stairs. There was no elevator.

There were stairs that led down to the basement, too, but nobody ever went down there. There were dead rats living in the basement.

The box was pressed against Louis's face, squashing his nose. Even so, when he reached the fifteenth floor, he could smell Miss Mush cooking in the cafeteria. It smelled like she was making mushrooms. Maybe on my way back I'll stop by Miss Mush's room and get some mushrooms, he thought. He didn't want to miss Miss Mush's mushrooms. They were her specialty.

He huffed and groaned and continued up the stairs. His arms and legs were very sore, but he didn't want to rest. This package might be important, he thought. I have to get it to Mrs. Jewls right away.

He stepped easily from the eighteenth story to the twentieth. There was no nineteenth story.

Miss Zarves taught the class on the nineteenth story. There was no Miss Zarves.

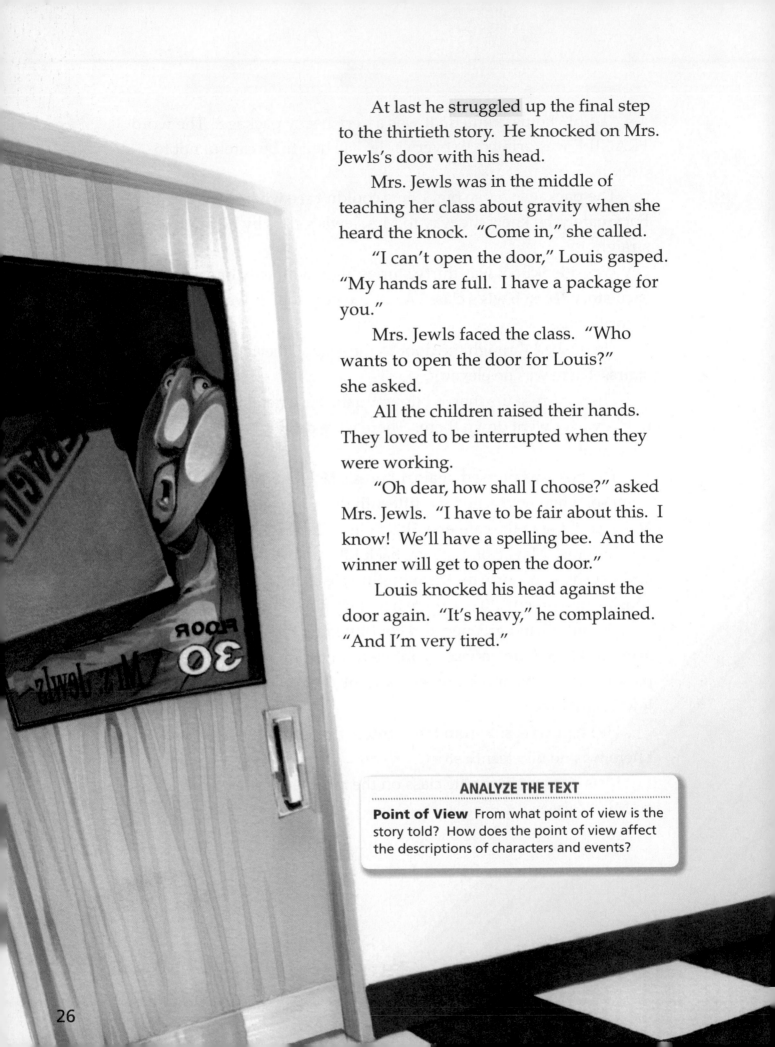

At last he struggled up the final step to the thirtieth story. He knocked on Mrs. Jewls's door with his head.

Mrs. Jewls was in the middle of teaching her class about gravity when she heard the knock. "Come in," she called.

"I can't open the door," Louis gasped. "My hands are full. I have a package for you."

Mrs. Jewls faced the class. "Who wants to open the door for Louis?" she asked.

All the children raised their hands. They loved to be interrupted when they were working.

"Oh dear, how shall I choose?" asked Mrs. Jewls. "I have to be fair about this. I know! We'll have a spelling bee. And the winner will get to open the door."

Louis knocked his head against the door again. "It's heavy," he complained. "And I'm very tired."

ANALYZE THE TEXT

Point of View From what point of view is the story told? How does the point of view affect the descriptions of characters and events?

26

"Just a second," Mrs. Jewls called back. "Allison, the first word's for you. Heavy."

"Heavy," said Allison. "H-E-A-V-Y. Heavy."

"Very good. Jason, You're next. Tired."

"Tired," said Jason. "S-L-E-E-P-Y. Tired."

Louis felt the package slipping from his sweaty fingers. He shifted his weight to get a better grip. The corners of the box dug into the sides of his arms. He felt his hands go numb.

Actually, he *didn't* feel them go numb.

"Jenny, package."

"Package," said Jenny. "B-O-X. Package."

"Excellent!" said Mrs. Jewls.

Louis felt like he was going to faint.

At last John opened the door. "I won the spelling bee, Louis!" he said.

"Very good, John," muttered Louis.

"Aren't you going to shake my hand?" asked John.

Louis shifted the box to one arm, quickly shook John's hand, then grabbed the box again and staggered into the room.

"Where do you want it, Mrs. Jewls?"

"I don't know," said Mrs. Jewls. "What is it?"

"I don't know," said Louis. "I'll have to put it down someplace so you can open it."

"But how can I tell you where to put it until I know what it is?" asked Mrs. Jewls. "You might put it in the wrong place."

So Louis held the box as Mrs. Jewls stood on a chair next to him and tore open the top. His legs wobbled beneath him.

"It's a computer," exclaimed Mrs. Jewls.

Everybody booed.

"What's the matter?" asked Louis. "I thought everyone loved computers."

"We don't want it, Louis," said Eric Bacon.

"Take it back, Jack," said Terrence.

"Get that piece of junk out of here," said Maurecia.

"Now, don't be that way," said Mrs. Jewls. "The computer will help us learn. It's a lot quicker than a pencil and paper."

"But the quicker we learn, the more work we have to do," complained Todd.

"You may set it over there on the counter, Louis," said Mrs. Jewls.

Louis set the computer on the counter next to Sharie's desk. Then he collapsed on the floor.

ANALYZE THE TEXT

Story Structure Why does Louis collapse to the floor? What story details explain the reason?

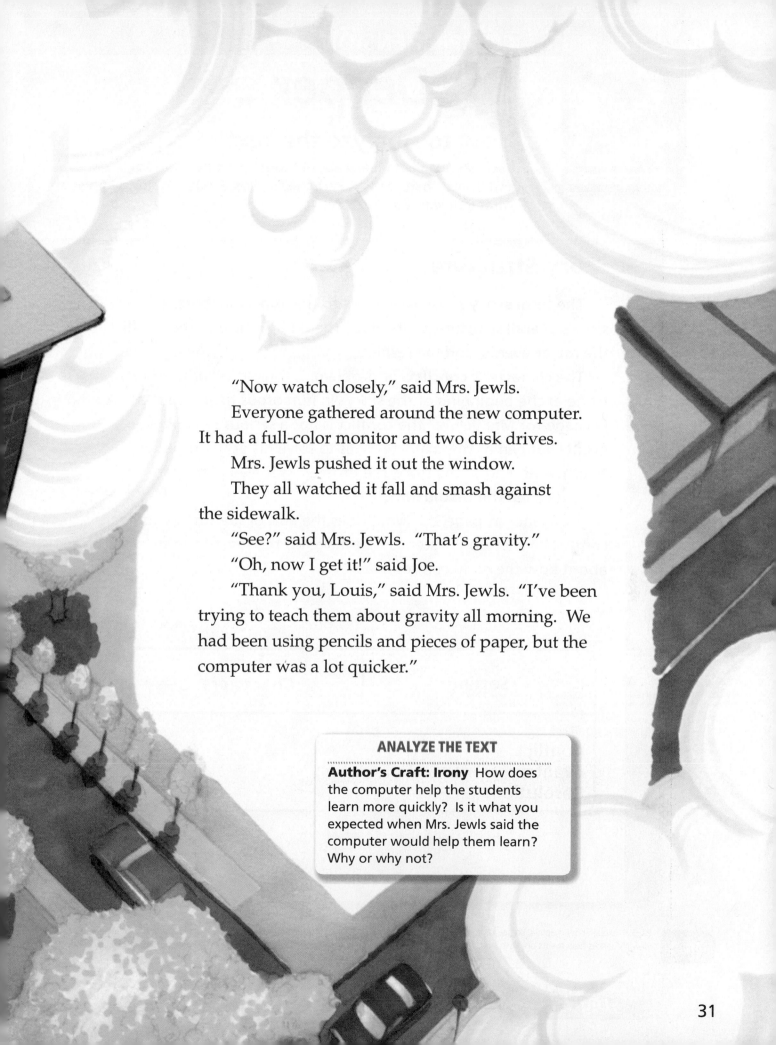

"Now watch closely," said Mrs. Jewls.

Everyone gathered around the new computer. It had a full-color monitor and two disk drives.

Mrs. Jewls pushed it out the window.

They all watched it fall and smash against the sidewalk.

"See?" said Mrs. Jewls. "That's gravity."

"Oh, now I get it!" said Joe.

"Thank you, Louis," said Mrs. Jewls. "I've been trying to teach them about gravity all morning. We had been using pencils and pieces of paper, but the computer was a lot quicker."

ANALYZE THE TEXT

Author's Craft: Irony How does the computer help the students learn more quickly? Is it what you expected when Mrs. Jewls said the computer would help them learn? Why or why not?

Dig Deeper

How to Analyze the Text

Use these pages to learn about Story Structure, Point of View, and Irony. Then read "A Package for Mrs. Jewls" again to apply what you learned.

Story Structure

The term **story structure** refers to the important parts of a story's overall structure, or its plot. These parts include the conflict, the major events, and the resolution.

The character's **conflict**, or problem, is usually introduced in a scene at the beginning of the story. In humorous fiction such as "A Package for Mrs. Jewls," the conflict is not a serious one. Funny events happen as the character tries to solve his or her problem. Near the ending of the story, the problem is solved. This part of the story is called the **resolution.**

Look back at page 25. What does the author identify as Louis's conflict? What do the scenes that make up the rest of the story tell about how the conflict is resolved?

Setting	Characters
Plot	

Conflict:
Events:
Resolution:

RL.5.5 explain how chapters, scenes, or stanzas fit together to provide the overall structure; **RL.5.6** describe how a narrator's or speaker's point of view influences how events are described; **RL.5.10** read and comprehend literature; **RF.5.4a** read on-level text with purpose and understanding

Point of View

Point of view refers to who is telling the story. When a narrator is an observer, the point of view is **third person.** Sometimes a third-person narrator shares only one character's thoughts and feelings. This point of view is called **third-person limited.** When a third-person narrator shares the thoughts and feelings of all of the characters, the point of view is **third-person omniscient.** Revisit "A Package for Mrs. Jewls," and think about what the narrator shares about the characters. From which point of view is the story told?

Author's Craft: Irony

Authors sometimes use irony to add humor to a story. **Irony** occurs when something happens that is the opposite of what readers expect. The ending of "A Package for Mrs. Jewls" is an example of irony. After Louis has struggled to carry the heavy package up to the thirtieth floor, being careful to keep it safe, Mrs. Jewls simply tosses it out the window.

FRAGILE
handle with care

Your Turn

RETURN TO THE ESSENTIAL QUESTION

Turn and Talk

Review the selection to prepare to discuss this question: *How can an experiment clarify an idea?* With a partner, take turns explaining your response to the question. Give evidence from the text to support your points.

Classroom Conversation

Continue your discussion of "A Package for Mrs. Jewls" by explaining your answers to these questions:

1 Why is the school yard a mess at the beginning of the story?

2 What do you learn about Louis's character from the way he responds to his conflict?

3 What clues might have helped you predict the story's ending?

ANALYZE HUMOR

Chart It An unusual setting, unexpected character dialogue and actions, and funny events all create humor in "A Package for Mrs. Jewls." With a partner or a small group of classmates, make a T-Map. In the left column, list examples of humor from the story. In the right column, explain why each is funny.

WRITE ABOUT READING

Response Would "A Package for Mrs. Jewls" be as funny if it were told from another point of view? Does knowing Louis's thoughts and feelings add to your enjoyment of the story? Write a paragraph explaining how the point of view affects the way you see the characters and events. Use quotations and other text evidence from the story to support your opinion.

This package might be important!

Writing Tip

Provide several strong examples from the story to support your opinion. Use transitional words and phrases to show how the examples are related to your main point.

COMMON CORE **RL.5.6** describe how a narrator's or speaker's point of view influences how events are described; **W.5.1c** link opinion and reasons using words, phrases, and clauses; **W.5.9a** apply grade 5 Reading standards to literature; **SL.5.1a** come to discussions prepared/ explicitly draw on preparation and other information about the topic

Lesson 1

READERS' THEATER

Questioning Gravity *

by Katie Sharp

✓ GENRE

Readers' theater is a text that has been formatted for readers to read aloud.

✓ TEXT FOCUS

An **interview** uses a question-and-answer format to give information in a person's own words.

Cast

Dr. Gene E. Us

Alex

Sara

Ed

Dr. Gene E. Us: Greetings students! I hope I'm not disturbing your work.

Alex: Who are you?

Dr. Gene E. Us: That's a great question. And it tells me I have come to the right class. Good scientists always ask questions.

Sara: So, who are you and why are you here?

RI.5.10 read and comprehend informational texts

COMMON CORE

Dr. Gene E. Us: Ah . . . another scientist! My name is Dr. Gene E. Us, and my specialty is science. Your teacher asked me to come here to answer your science questions. Ask me anything!

Ed: Yesterday, I was carrying a big stack of books home from the library. There were so many that the top one wobbled and crashed to the ground. Then I staggered and fell trying to catch it. That got me thinking. If the Earth has such strong gravity, why isn't everything in space falling onto Earth and squashing us?

Dr. Gene E. Us: Ah, when I was your age, I struggled with that question, too. You see, gravity gets weaker with distance. But without any gravity, the Moon would fly off into space and we might never see it again. It makes me numb just thinking about it.

Sara: All this talk about Earth and the Moon makes me wonder something. Where did the planets come from in the first place?

Dr. Gene E. Us: Another good question! Most scientists believe that about 4.6 billion years ago, dust and gas came together to form a huge cloud. They came together because of our good friend gravity. At first the core of the cloud started to spin around slowly. But as the cloud collapsed, the core spun faster and faster and eventually became the Sun. The stuff left over cooled and became the planets, asteroids, and other objects in space.

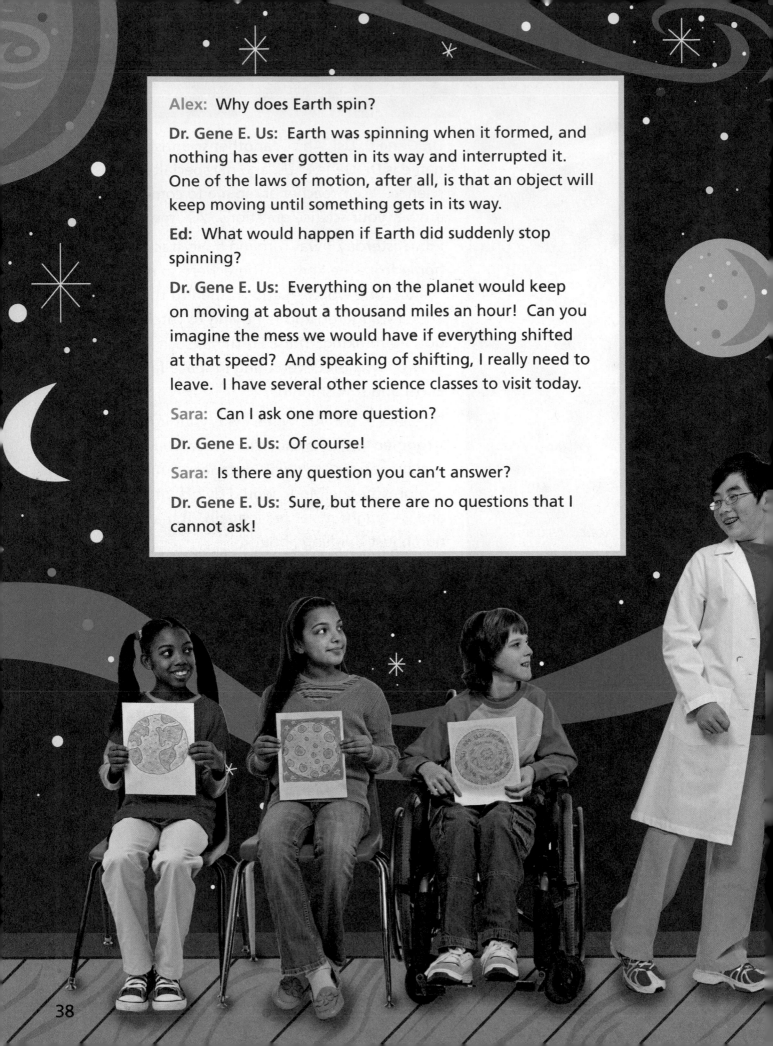

Alex: Why does Earth spin?

Dr. Gene E. Us: Earth was spinning when it formed, and nothing has ever gotten in its way and interrupted it. One of the laws of motion, after all, is that an object will keep moving until something gets in its way.

Ed: What would happen if Earth did suddenly stop spinning?

Dr. Gene E. Us: Everything on the planet would keep on moving at about a thousand miles an hour! Can you imagine the mess we would have if everything shifted at that speed? And speaking of shifting, I really need to leave. I have several other science classes to visit today.

Sara: Can I ask one more question?

Dr. Gene E. Us: Of course!

Sara: Is there any question you can't answer?

Dr. Gene E. Us: Sure, but there are no questions that I cannot ask!

Compare Texts

TEXT TO TEXT

Compare Texts About Learning Talk with a partner about the similarities and differences between "A Package for Mrs. Jewls" and "Questioning Gravity." Then work together to write a paragraph about the purpose and the message of each text.

TEXT TO SELF

Describe a Scene The author of "A Package for Mrs. Jewls" uses third-person limited point of view to tell a humorous story. Write about a time when something extraordinary happened to you. Then explain how a different point of view might have changed your story.

TEXT TO WORLD

Research a Science Question The students in "Questioning Gravity" learn some surprising scientific facts. Create a list of questions you would ask Dr. Gene E. Us if you had a chance. Then choose one and use print and digital sources to find an answer to it. Share your findings with the class.

1. Why is the sky blue?

2. Why is

COMMON CORE **RL.5.1** quote accurately when explaining what the text says explicitly and when drawing inferences; **RI.5.7** draw on information from print and digital sources to locate answers or solve problems; **W.5.3a** orient the reader by establishing a situation and introducing a narrator or characters/organize an event sequence; **W.5.10** write routinely over extended time frames and shorter time frames

Grammar

What Is a Sentence? A **sentence** is a group of words that expresses a complete thought. To be complete, a sentence must have both a subject and a predicate. The **simple subject** is the word or words that name the person or thing the sentence is about. The **simple predicate** is the main word or words that tell what the subject is or does.

Complete Sentences
simple subject   simple predicate A large truck entered the parking lot.
simple subject   simple predicate A teacher ran to the truck.

A group of words that does not express a complete thought is a **fragment.**

Sentence Fragments
A package for Mrs. Jewls. (does not tell what the subject does)
Handed the package to a teacher. (does not tell who did the action)

Try This! **Identify each of the following as a sentence or a fragment. List on a sheet of paper the simple subject and the simple predicate in each complete sentence. Then rewrite each fragment as a complete sentence.**

1 Carrying a heavy package up the stairs.

2 The teacher knocks on the door with his head.

3 The happy students compete in a spelling bee.

Always check the sentences you write to make sure they are complete. Fix any fragments you find. Sometimes you can fix a fragment by adding it to a complete sentence.

Complete Sentence	Fragment
Mrs. Jewls put her hands on the computer.	Shoved it out the window.

Complete Sentence + Fragment

Mrs. Jewls put her hands on the computer and shoved it out the window.

 Connect Grammar to Writing

As you revise your short story this week, make sure each sentence contains a subject and a predicate. Change any fragments you find into complete sentences.

W.5.3a orient the reader by establishing a situation and introducing a narrator or characters/organize an event sequence; **W.5.3b** use narrative techniques to develop experiences and events or show characters' responses; **W.5.3d** use concrete words and phrases and sensory details; **W.5.3e** provide a conclusion

Narrative Writing

✅ **Ideas**   In "A Package for Mrs. Jewls," the author's words and details bring the story events to life. For example, Louis *huffed* and *groaned* up the stairs. You can make your **short story** more clear and lively by adding sensory details and strong, active verbs.

Eduardo drafted a short story about someone accomplishing a difficult task. Later, he included vivid details to add more action and interest to his story.

Writing Traits Checklist

✅ **Ideas**
Did I tell the events clearly, using specific details?

✅ **Organization**
Does each event help build the story structure?

✅ **Sentence Fluency**
Did I use complete sentences?

✅ **Word Choice**
Did I use strong, active verbs and sensory details?

✅ **Voice**
Do my words help reveal the mood of the story?

✅ **Conventions**
Did I use correct spelling, grammar, and punctuation?

Revised Draft

Aldo's basement was a mess. Last week, he
had been ~~working with wood.~~ ^sawing and hammering furiously.

^scraps and sawdust
~~Scraps of~~ wood had scattered everywhere.

~~Sawdust everywhere.~~ Now paint was ~~getting~~ ^splattering

all over the floor as Aldo ~~tried to finish~~ ^raced to complete

his project. The school's Medieval Fair was

tomorrow, and he had promised to bring in

a big surprise.

Aldo's Surprise

by Eduardo Martinez

Aldo's basement was a mess. Last week, he had been sawing and hammering furiously. Wood scraps and sawdust had scattered everywhere. Now paint was splattering all over the floor as Aldo raced to complete his project. The school's Medieval Fair was tomorrow, and he had promised to bring in a big surprise. After four hours of painting, Aldo stood back to admire his creation. He had built a model of a medieval castle, complete with a drawbridge that really worked and two tall turrets. In the morning, he'd be ready to reveal his masterpiece to the world. Suddenly, Aldo saw a slight problem. His wood-and-cardboard castle was much too big to fit up the stairs!

Aldo could not believe he had missed such a crucial detail. He knelt in front of the castle and examined it from every angle. He peered at the basement door. He did not see a solution to his problem and felt heartbroken at the idea of having to take the castle apart and reassemble it upstairs. Resigned, Aldo stood up, and his elbow knocked against the castle, pulling it loose from the plywood base. Now he could turn it sideways and take it upstairs, and then reattach the board! Things were looking up again.

Reading as a Writer

Which sensory details and strong verbs make Eduardo's story come alive? Where can you add details and strong verbs to your own narrative writing?

In my final copy, I added sensory details and strong, active verbs.
I also combined fragments to form complete sentences.

Vocabulary in Context

☑ **TARGET VOCABULARY**

discomfort

primitive

interior

honored

secretive

immersed

bungled

contagious

brandishing

imprinted

Vocabulary Reader

Context Cards

COMMON CORE

L.5.4a use context as a clue to the meaning of a word or phrase

---

1 discomfort

The discomfort of lying in a sleeping bag on the ground can lead to a poor night's sleep.

2 primitive

Camp cabins are usually primitive, or very rough and simple.

3 interior

The interior of a tent or cabin is a good place for campers to store supplies.

4 honored

To feel honored is to feel proud to be given special recognition or opportunity.

Go Digital

▶ Study each Context Card.

▶ Use context clues to determine the meaning of each Vocabulary word.

5 secretive

A team may act **secretive** during a game to prevent opponents from knowing their strategy.

6 immersed

These students are **immersed** in a favorite book. They are thinking about little else.

7 bungled

This football player **bungled** the catch and missed the ball.

8 contagious

They tried to stay quiet, but these campers found their laughter was **contagious**.

9 brandishing

These soccer players are **brandishing** the trophy they won.

10 imprinted

This coin is **imprinted** with the image of a royal crown.

Read and Comprehend

☑ TARGET SKILL

Theme The author of a play wants to tell a good story. In most cases, he or she also wants to convey a **theme,** or a message about life or people. As you read "A Royal Mystery," pay attention to what the characters say, what happens in the story, and any character actions or reactions. Which details in the play suggest a message or theme? Use this graphic organizer to record key details that help you determine the play's theme.

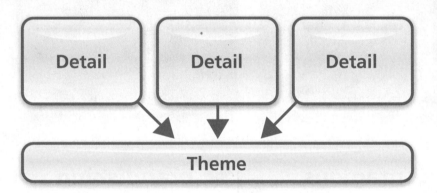

| Detail | Detail | Detail |

Theme

☑ TARGET STRATEGY

Question As you fill in your graphic organizer, ask yourself **questions** about the play. Asking questions can lead to a deeper understanding of the author's ideas. Questioning also helps you identify what you would like to know more about.

Performance and Visual Arts

The arts provide many different ways for people to express their ideas and feelings. In the performing arts, performers communicate directly with an audience. They might dance, play music, or act in a play. The visual arts involve something that the audience can watch or look at. Visual artists paint murals, direct movies, and create sculptures, to name just a few examples.

The selection you are about to read, "A Royal Mystery," is a play. As you read, keep in mind that the story is meant to be performed. Visualize actors moving around a stage and speaking the dialogue. What kinds of costumes might they wear? What would the set look like? Bring the performance to life in your imagination!

ANCHOR TEXT

A Royal Mystery

✓ TARGET SKILL

Theme Study the characters to determine the play's theme, or central message.

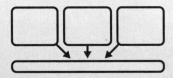

✓ GENRE

A **play** is a story that can be performed for an audience. As you read, look for:

- ▶ text that consists mainly of dialogue
- ▶ characters' actions and feelings that are shown through dialogue
- ▶ stage directions and descriptions of settings

COMMON CORE **RL.5.2** determine theme from details/summarize; **RL.5.5** explain how chapters, scenes, or stanzas fit together to provide the overall structure; **RL.5.10** read and comprehend literature

 Go Digital

MEET THE ILLUSTRATOR

Jessica Secheret

Jessica Secheret began drawing and painting at a very young age. "I had strange buddies that were always with me—felt pens, colored pencils, brushes, and paint," the artist says. Today she lives and works at her studio in Paris, France. She says that drawing for magazines and books allows her to do what she loves: put her imagination on paper.

A Royal Mystery

by Audrey Carangelo

illustrated by Jessica Secheret

ESSENTIAL QUESTION

How can art and performance help people understand a text?

49

Camp Katahdin, a summer camp for girls and boys from seven to twelve years old, is located deep in the woods and far from any towns or cities. There are miles of nature trails, horseback riding and jumping arenas, and a wide, deep lake.

Characters:

- Misty   • Althea   • Rena
- Narrator   • Julio   • Gerard

Scene I

Setting: A tent platform at Camp Katahdin

Misty: Althea! Good to see you back at camp.

Althea: You too, Misty! Hope you don't mind that I have a new tentmate this year.

Misty: (*laughing*) No problemo! I'm sorry for being such a klutz last year! I probably cost you the trophy. I think I had problems with just about every event!

Althea: We can't all be good at everything! I'm hoping my new roomie will know how to ride a horse, unlike someone I know.

Misty: (*a little offended*) Hey, canoe-tipping doesn't help tentmates win a tournament either.

Althea: (*sheepishly*) Oh, yeah, I sort of forgot about that.

Misty: So, where is your new tentmate?

Althea: I guess she's not here yet. Keep your fingers crossed that she's not scared of horses!

Rena: (*stepping into the tent, lugging two heavy suitcases*) Good day! Good day!

Althea: Hey! Welcome, tentmate!

Rena: (*tossing matching leather luggage onto a cot*) Umph! Gerard has packed these so heavily! And I've had to carry them myself!

Misty: (*whispering and rolling her eyes*) Uh-oh! Fancy matching luggage? That's not a good sign—but never judge a book by its cover, right?

Althea: (*eyeing the new girl warily*) Hi, I'm Althea. That's a lot of stuff there.

Misty: And I'm Misty, Althea's tentmate from last year.

Rena: Wonderful to meet you both! My name is Rena. (*looking around the tent, confused*) May I ask where the closets might be?

Althea: (*pointing to an army trunk*) You're looking at it! You ride horses?

Rena: Certainly. I'm a champion jumper. And where is the bed? I don't see one.

Althea: (*pointing to a cot*) So you can ride! Any other sports?

Rena: I've won a few archery contests. And, excuse me, . . . restrooms?

Althea: (nodding toward the open tent flap) Next to the showers. Impressive, Rena. I think we'll get along fine! Come on, it's time for lunch. To the mess tent!

Rena: The what?

Misty: Mess tent. It's where we eat.

Rena: Where we eat? Are you quite certain?

Althea: (*teasing and mimicking Rena's tone*) Yes. Quite. (*The girls exit, with Rena holding the flap back gingerly as she steps through.*)

51

Setting: Later that evening at the entrance of the girls' tent

Narrator: The girls return to the tent, struggling under the weight of several mattresses.

Rena: I can't thank you enough for locating these extra mattresses.

Althea: (*swinging the mattresses*) No prob. Let's swing them up there. One, two, three—heave!

Rena: Earlier, I tried out that silly cot. It filled me with such discomfort that I'm sure I will never be able to fall asleep.

Althea: Don't worry. Lots of campers grab extra mattresses the first night.

Rena: Really?

Althea: Well, not six—but still.

Rena: Would you like one?

Althea: Nah, I'm good. Let's try and get some sleep now. We need to be on our game tomorrow. A perfect bull's-eye every time, right? (*shooting an imaginary bow*)

Scene III

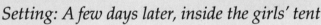

Setting: A few days later, inside the girls' tent

Narrator: Rena is trying to adjust to camp life, as both girls get to know each other better.

Rena: (*entering the tent*) Ohhhh. I do so hate camping! The showers are absolutely primitive.

Althea: (*laughing*) That's all part of camping, right?

Rena: I wouldn't know.

Althea: I don't get why you're here, Rena. You don't seem like a summer camp kind of girl.

Rena: (*shrugging her shoulders*) I suppose you're right. This was Gerard's idea. He believes that I should meet more young people my age.

Althea: Who's Gerard?

Rena: He's . . . just Gerard. That's all. (*seeing Althea's frustration*) Well, fine then. Gerard is my temporary guardian. My parents are away for a bit, and I miss them terribly. There! Are you happy?

Althea: Whoa. Sorry, Rena. I didn't mean to upset you.

Rena: I would prefer not to talk about it. (*pauses*) So, why don't you show me more of the camp? I'd like to see those horse stables now.

Scene IV

Setting: Later the same day in the interior of a horse stable

Narrator: Inside the cool stable, it smells of horses and fresh hay. Sunlight filters through a row of windows as the girls visit Charger, Althea's favorite horse.

Rena: (*stepping inside and looking around*) It's so peaceful here. (*excitedly*) Oh, what a beautiful Appaloosa! I love their spotted markings, don't you?

Althea: I thought you'd like Charger. He's really smart, and just wait 'til you ride him! So, do you get to ride much where you're from? Where are you from anyway?

Rena: A city in the North.

Althea: New York? Boston?

Rena: (*interrupting*) . . . the Northwest.

Althea: Seattle? Vancouver? You're Canadian! Yeah, that makes sense with your strange accent.

Rena: Accent?

Althea: Yeah, like now. (*mimicking Rena*) Whatever do you mean by accent? (*seeing Rena's irritation*) Sorry. So, where'd you say you're from?

Rena: We move frequently. (*She looks uncomfortable.*)

Althea: Fine. Changing subject now! So, are you really a champion horse jumper?

Rena: I've been riding almost my entire life. I suppose I have quite a few trophies.

Althea: (*Her eyes light up.*) You know of the Tournament of Champions, right?

Rena: No, I've never heard of it. (*teasing*) Only every day since I stepped into the tent!

Althea: Funny. So, listen, we can get a higher team score if you jump Charger. I'll enter the softball throw instead.

Rena: I would be honored to jump Charger. And don't worry, Althea, I vow to help you win that trophy this year.

Althea: Super! But for now, we've won the honor of mucking out the horse stalls. (*handing Rena a pitchfork*)

Rena: Excuse me? Did you say muck out? (*sputtering*) Please say you're joking! What's that odor?

Althea: Just part of camping!

Setting: Early morning in the last week of summer camp

Narrator: The campers are preparing for the day's tournament events. Althea rests on her cot, reading a book of fairy tales.

Althea: (*to herself*) That's it! Now I know why Rena is being so secretive.

Rena: (*entering the tent*) Is that right? First of all, I don't have secrets. I simply choose not to share certain things.

Althea: Sorry. I didn't mean to offend you. I'm just trying to figure you out.

Rena: Figure me out? (*angrily*) Perhaps you should figure yourself out! For example, why is it so important for you to win some silly trophy? Oh, dear! Forgive me for shouting. That was very rude.

Althea: You weren't exactly shouting.

Rena: I must run now. (*picking up a towel*) I promised that I would take swimming lessons, but now I'm late.

Althea: Wait, Rena. I know you hate swimming and that you're only taking lessons because you said you'd help me win.

Rena: Well, I also hate breaking promises. (*looking hurt*) I must ask, though, what do you mean, help you win? Have I made the mistake of assuming that we are a team?

(*Rena exits.*)

ANALYZE THE TEXT

Characterization How are Althea and Rena alike and different? What does the author do to show readers that Althea and Rena have distinct personalities?

55

Scene VI

Setting: In the girls' tent later that same morning

Narrator: Rena walks into the tent still wearing her swimming cap. Althea looks up from her reading. She's still immersed in the book of fairy tales.

Althea: Enjoy the lake?

Rena: Lake? Is that what you call that dreadful little mudhole? As soon as I change, I'm going to saddle Charger and practice jumping. Would you care to come?

Althea: Yeah, but I have the canoe race this afternoon. I'm resting up for the big competition.

Rena: Althea! I nearly forgot. I'm so happy you reminded me. Of course, I'll be there for your race. We shall win this tournament *together*.

Althea: (*her face lights up*) Really? I thought you still might be angry. You told me to figure myself out and . . .

Rena: (*interrupting*) And have you figured yourself out?

Althea: I think so.

Rena: Well, I'm ready to listen.

Althea: Okay, so I don't have anything that I'm good at back home. Here, I'm good at stuff—well, except canoeing. If I take home the camp trophy, then I can remember I'm good at something, even when I'm not here. Does that make any sense?

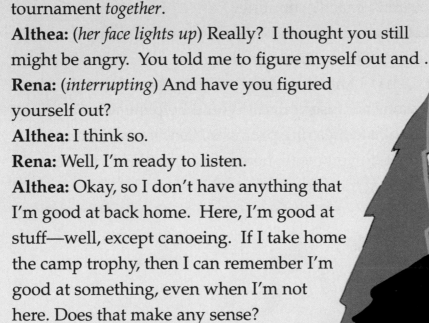

ANALYZE THE TEXT

Elements of Drama Every scene in this play begins with a note about the setting. Why is this information important to your understanding of the text?

Rena: It makes perfect sense. And you thought of all that while I was swimming? (*teasing*) There may be hope for you after all. (*sneezing*) Achoo! I knew that nasty water was five degrees too— *ACHOO!*—chilly.

Althea: (*throwing a pillow*) Toughen up, girl! We have a tournament to win!

Scene VII

Setting: The lake at Camp Katahdin

Narrator: The canoe race is under way. The shore is lined with cheering campers. Julio, a camp counselor, is announcing the race.

Julio: (*excitedly*) It's a close race, campers! Althea is holding on to second place! Oh, no! She bungled the turn! Althea slips back to fourth. Wait—here comes Misty, now pulling into second place!

Rena: Go, Althea!

Julio: Althea's digging those paddles in! She's neck and neck with Kara. Wait! Kara has dropped back and Althea has moved into third place!

(*The crowd on the beach shouts as the canoes race toward the finish line.*)

Rena: You can do it, Althea!

Julio: What a race! At the finish line, it's Jai in first place! Misty takes second, and by a matter of inches, Althea has placed third! Great job, everyone!

(*Rena runs to congratulate Althea.*)

Rena: You did it!

Althea: Did what? I didn't win the race.

Rena: Well, you did your best, and that's what counts. We can still win the tournament.

Althea: (*glumly*) Yeah, but . . .

Rena: Absolutely no buts! You told me the same thing when I placed third at the track meet.

Althea: (*brightening*) We got a good lead when you earned the top jumping score with Charger.

Rena: And your winning softball throw added several points!

Althea: (*excitedly*) So, if we place first and second in the archery contest tomorrow, we could still win the tournament!

Rena: Your competitiveness is certainly contagious!

Althea: Last one to the mess tent gets stable duty!

Rena: (*laughing*) I adore how you make everything a contest!

Scene VIII

Setting: Evening in the girls' tent

Narrator: Tomorrow is the last day of camp and the last day of the tournament. Althea is determined to solve the mystery that surrounds Rena. She has pocketed a few peanuts from the mess tent.

(*Althea slips one peanut beneath Rena's six mattresses.*)

Rena: (*entering the tent holding her toothbrush*) I'm terribly excited about tomorrow! I may not sleep at all!

Althea: Same here. But the sooner we sleep, the sooner we win! So, lights out!

Narrator: Rena tosses and turns in her bunk all night. Meanwhile, Althea stays awake to see if Rena falls asleep. Morning arrives at last.

Rena: OWWWW! I feel as if I've slept on top of a boulder the size of Mount Rushmore.

Althea: Yes! It worked!

Rena: What worked?

(*Althea digs under Rena's mattresses until she finds what she is looking for—a peanut.*)

Althea: (*brandishing the peanut*) This! This worked. I put it under your mattress last night, and you felt it! You felt this tiny peanut through *six* mattresses.

Rena: I don't understand. Why would you want to torture me in such a way?

Althea: Torture? I'm investigating a mystery! I'm trying to get to the bottom of, well, I'm . . .

Rena: Torturing me.

Althea: Okay, well, sorry about that part. But you'll be really happy to learn what I found out.

Rena: (*sarcastically*) Happy? Oh, wonderful! Please, tell me. (*rubbing her sore leg*) What did you find out?

Althea: Well, m'lady, this peanut—this insignificant legume—proves beyond a shadow of a doubt, that you are a descendant of kings and queens! Royalty! I'm talking a *princess*!

Rena: A princess? Whatever do you mean?

Althea: It's all right here. Listen (*reading from the book*):

. . . those of royal blood are sensitive to the slightest chills and faintest odors. They speak with formality and refinement. Their sensitivity is such that they may detect a tiny pea below twenty mattresses. In these ways and more, royalty and their descendants are different from the common population.

Rena: Are you saying . . . ?

Althea: Think about it. Stinky stables. Chilly lake. The way you speak, and now the peanut!

Rena: (*musing*) Could this be true? And if so, then what shall I do?

Althea: What you shall do is join me on the battlefield so we can win the tournament!

Rena: Althea, look at this bruise! I can't compete with such an injury!

Althea: Nonsense! A princess must rise above a mere bruise. So, get a move on!

(*Both girls exit.*)

Scene IX

Setting: Later that day, on a wooded trail leading from the archery field to the girls' tent

Narrator: Rena and Althea carry the trophy, struggling under its enormous weight.

Rena: The bull's-eye you shot was positively amazing!

Althea: Well, Princess, your last arrow split *my arrow* in half—that's *royally* amazing!

Narrator: Before the girls reach their tent, Rena spots Gerard standing near a limousine.

Rena: Gerard! Come and meet Althea.

Gerard: (*smiling and eyeing the trophy*) Brava, Miss Rena! But now, I must deliver a message that I believe you'll find quite important. (*handing her a small envelope*)

Narrator: Rena reads the note.

Rena: (*reading*) "Darling Rena, we regret that you have heard from us so infrequently of late. Much has happened in our tiny kingdom of Corelia. Quite recently, your father and I were named to succeed your great-uncle as rulers. It is time for us all to be together again. Gerard will accompany you on your journey. We count the hours until you arrive."

Narrator: Rena pulls a necklace from the envelope. From a chain hangs a golden disk imprinted with a regal lion.

Althea: (*looking puzzled*) Hey, look at this! (*pulling a delicate gold chain from her shirt*) My aunt sent this to me when I was five. . . .

Rena: Oh, my. Then this means . . . ?

Gerard: (*looking at his watch*) Ladies, a plane awaits! This conversation must continue at another time.

Rena: (*laughing*) Goodbye, Princess!

Althea: Goodbye yourself! I better see you here next year. I'll have solved another royal mystery by then!

The End

ANALYZE THE TEXT

Theme How do Althea and Rena respond to challenges in this play? How does each character's response relate to the play's theme?

Dig Deeper

How to Analyze the Text

Use these pages to learn about Theme, Elements of Drama, and Characterization. Then read "A Royal Mystery" again to apply what you learned.

Theme

Like any other work of fiction, a play often conveys an important message about life to its audience. This message, or **theme,** is revealed mostly through a play's characters. The changes they undergo, the ways in which they react to conflict, and the lessons they learn all help reveal a play's theme.

In "A Royal Mystery," the relationship between Rena and Althea changes. As they work together toward their goal, they learn to appreciate each other's unique qualities. What other text evidence and details about Rena and Althea help you identify the play's theme? What lesson can you learn from their experiences?

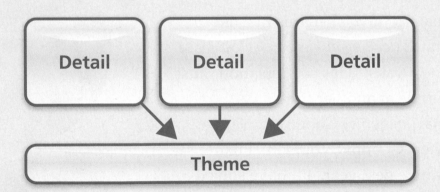

COMMON CORE **RL.5.2** determine theme from details/summarize; **RL.5.3** compare and contrast characters, settings, or events, drawing on details; **RL.5.5** explain how chapters, scenes, or stanzas fit together to provide the overall structure; **RL.5.10** read and comprehend literature; **RF.5.4a** read on-level text with purpose and understanding

Elements of Drama

Plays are divided into **scenes,** which are like the chapters in a book. The scenes fit together to create the structure of the plot. For example, in Scene II, Rena and Althea struggle back to their tent with extra mattresses for Rena's cot. At first, the audience is not sure how this event connects to the overall plot. However, in Scene VIII, the mattresses become important when Althea uses them to prove that Rena is a princess.

Characterization

Characterization refers to the ways in which an author shows what a character is like. In "A Royal Mystery," the author reveals Althea's competitive nature through her dialogue in Scene I. Althea is still disappointed that she didn't win the trophy last year, but she intends to win it this year. The author also sets up a contrast between Althea and Rena. How are these characters similar and different? What do you learn about each one by comparing and contrasting them?

Your Turn

Turn and Talk Review the selection to prepare to discuss this question: *How can art and performance help people understand a text?* As you discuss, take turns reviewing and elaborating on each other's key points. Use text evidence to support your ideas.

Classroom Conversation

Continue your discussion of "A Royal Mystery" by explaining your answers to these questions:

1. How does the dialogue in Scene I help the audience understand the setting of the play?

2. How do the stage directions help you visualize the action?

3. Which of the illustrations are most helpful in bringing the play's characters to life? Why?

ANALYZE THE PLAY'S ENDING

List Clues In "A Royal Mystery," several clues foreshadow Rena's identity as a princess before it is finally revealed. With a partner, review Scenes VI through IX of the play. List dialogue and events that hint at the outcome of the play. Be sure to record specific quotations and examples on your list. Present your ideas to the class.

WRITE ABOUT READING

Response "A Royal Mystery" is divided into nine scenes. By the end of the last scene, the mystery introduced at the beginning has been solved. How does each scene move the plot forward? Write two paragraphs in which you explain how all the scenes together create a complete story. Be sure to provide specific evidence from the text.

Writing Tip

State your main idea at the beginning of your first paragraph. Write in complete sentences so that your readers understand your explanation.

COMMON CORE RL.5.5 explain how chapters, scenes, or stanzas fit together to provide the overall structure; W.5.9a apply grade 5 Reading standards to literature; W.5.10 write routinely over extended time frames and shorter time frames; SL.5.1a come to discussions prepared/ explicitly draw on preparation and other information about the topic; SL.5.1c pose and respond to questions, make comments that contribute to the discussion, and elaborate on others' remarks

The Princess and the Pea

by Annie Dalton

Embroideries by Belinda Downes

ONCE THERE WAS A PRINCE who was as handsome as any prince could be. But he was also a persnickety prince—the kind of young man who likes everything just so. And he got it into his head that he could only marry a real princess. He knew perfectly well that a real princess is as rare as a unicorn, but this didn't put him off, not at all.

"I'll just search high and low until I find one," he said cheerfully.

So with two friends for company, off he rode into the wide world to find a real princess to be his bride. Now, on his travels, as you'd expect, the prince met dozens and dozens of princesses. But whenever he made up his mind to marry one, right at the last minute he'd change his mind again and decide that this princess wasn't a real one after all.

His friends couldn't understand him.

"But the last one was perfect," they cried. "Hair like moonlit silk. Eyes like big blue pansies. What didn't you like? Her dancing?"

"Of course not," sighed the prince. "She's as graceful as a swan."

"Was it her handwriting then? Or her manners?"

"Her handwriting is miles better than mine," said the prince, gloomily. "So are her manners."

"You hate her voice, is that it?"

"How could I," sighed the prince. "Her voice is as soft as a dove's. Exactly how a princess's voice should be." And he buried his head in his hands.

"Then why won't you marry her?" cried his friends.

"Because I can't be sure she is a real princess," the prince explained.

So the prince and his companions rode sadly home.

"If I can't marry a real princess, then I won't marry at all," he told his mother, the queen.

That night a terrible storm blew up. Lightning crackled across the sky. Thunder boomed. The wind howled, and rain battered the windows.

68

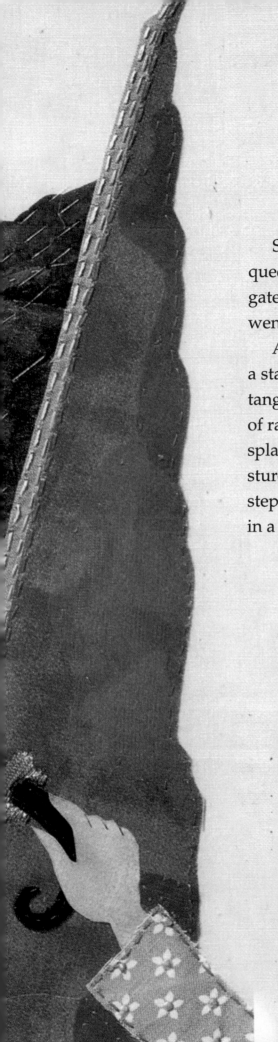

Suddenly, between crashes of thunder, the queen heard a firm tap-tapping at the palace gates, so she threw on her dressing gown and went to see who it could be.

A girl was standing outside. And what a state she was in! The wild weather had tangled her dark curls into a big bush. Rivers of rainwater streamed off her shoulders and splashed off her torn stockings, filling her sturdy little boots to overflowing. And every step she took made a sad squelch, like a frog in a ditch. Squish. Squash.

The queen nearly fainted when this sorry-looking creature said she was a princess who had lost her way in the storm and asked to stay the night.

She sounds unusually firm for a princess, thought the queen. Not a bit like a dove.

The girl wasn't especially graceful either, but marched sturdily across the threshold in her soggy boots—*squish, squash*—and hung her dripping knapsack on the hook in the hall, just as if she lived there!

Maybe you are a princess and maybe you aren't, young lady, thought the queen. But you won't fool me for long. And she asked the girl to sign the visitors' book to see if she had the proper handwriting for a princess. But the girl shivered so hard that the ink splurted out of the pen in one big blot.

"Never mind, some soup will warm you up," said the cunning queen. And she heated some cabbage soup left from the servants' supper and gave it to the girl with a lump of stale bread.

Instead of nibbling daintily like a princess should, the girl sat down at the kitchen table and hungrily spooned up every last drop. She even polished the bowl clean with her crust. When she'd finished, there was a splash of soup on her nose.

"That was the best soup I have ever tasted," she sighed.

"Hmm, maybe it is and maybe it isn't. But we'll settle this business once and for all," muttered the queen. For she knew a thing or two about princesses, if only her clever son had bothered to ask.

So the queen hurried along to the spare bedroom. She whisked all the sheets and blankets off the bed, and off came the mattress too. Then she took a dried pea out of her pocket, placed it in the middle of the bed, and put the mattress back on top.

Then on top of the first mattress, the queen piled another mattress, and another, until the bed was twenty mattresses high!

Next she collected up all the spare quilts in the palace; some with stripes, some with polka dots, and some which badly needed to go to the laundry. But when she counted them, they came to twenty exactly. The queen stacked all twenty quilts on top of the twenty mattresses until the bed swayed about like a ship at sea.

At last the girl took off her boots and clambered sleepily onto this huge high swaying bed, and the queen blew out the candle—*snuff*—and left her alone for the night.

Next morning the queen asked if she had slept well.

But the poor girl was as pale as a ghost.

"Not a wink, I'm afraid," she complained. "Something was sticking into me all night. Look—I'm bruised all over!"

When the queen saw that the girl had felt a tiny pea digging into her through twenty mattresses and twenty quilts, she knew she must be a real princess after all, and ran to tell her son that the search was over.

"Only a real princess has skin so delicate," she told him.

"A real princess at last!" he gasped. "Then if she likes me, we'll marry at once!

So the prince married the princess. After the wedding was over the pea was put on show in the Royal Museum.

And if you don't believe me, then go and see it for yourself.

Compare Texts

Compare Texts with Similar Themes With a partner, identify the themes of "A Royal Mystery" and "The Princess and the Pea." List details from each text that support your analysis of the theme. Then discuss the ways in which the messages of both selections are the same and different. Summarize your comparison for the class.

Write a Scene Recall a time when you worked with a partner or a group to accomplish a goal. Perhaps you helped clean up a park or raise funds for a cause. Think about how to present your experience in the form of a play, and then write one scene. Use "A Royal Mystery" as a guide for writing stage directions and dialogue. Share your scene with a partner and discuss how each of you dramatized your ideas.

Compare Varieties of English You might notice that people in your family or group of friends have certain ways of speaking that are unique to them. A person's speech can reflect his or her background, ethnicity, personality, or even geographical location. Think about the ways in which Rena and Althea speak in "A Royal Mystery." Work with a small group to compare and contrast each character's way of speaking and what it reveals about her.

COMMON CORE **RL.5.2** determine theme from details/summarize; **RL.5.3** compare and contrast characters, settings, or events, drawing on details; **RL.5.9** compare and contrast stories in the same genre on their approaches to themes and topics; **L.5.3b** compare and contrast varieties of English in stories, dramas, or poems

Grammar

What Are the Four Kinds of Sentences? A sentence that tells something is a **declarative sentence.** It ends with a period. A sentence that asks something is an **interrogative sentence.** It ends with a question mark. A sentence that expresses strong feeling is an **exclamatory sentence.** It ends with an exclamation point. A sentence that gives an order is an **imperative sentence.** It ends with a period.

Example	Kind of Sentence
period We will win the contest.	declarative
question mark How long should we practice?	interrogative
exclamation point We should practice until we're perfect!	exclamatory
period Start practicing.	imperative

Try This! **Work with a partner. Read aloud each sentence below. Then tell which kind of sentence it is and explain how you know.**

1. Come and watch me in the canoe race.

2. What time does it begin?

3. It takes place at two o'clock down at the lake.

4. I can't wait to see you win!

You know that there are four kinds of sentences and that each kind does a different job. Using a variety of sentence types can make your writing more lively and interesting.

One Sentence Type	Varied Sentence Types
It would be great if you could listen to my story about what happened at camp. At first, Rena seemed like an ordinary camper. I was wrong. I noticed many clues and finally put it all together. No one ever would have guessed that she was a princess.	Listen to what happened at camp. At first, Rena seemed like an ordinary camper. I was totally wrong about that! I noticed many clues and finally put it all together. Who would ever have guessed that she was a princess?

 Connect Grammar to Writing

When you revise your description, vary the kinds of sentences in your writing. Using a variety of sentence types will help you hold the interest of your audience. Be careful not to overuse exclamatory sentences.

W.5.3b use narrative techniques to develop experiences and events or show characters' responses; **W.5.3d** use concrete words and phrases and sensory details; **W.5.5** develop and strengthen writing by planning, revising, editing, rewriting, or trying a new approach; **W.5.10** write routinely over extended time frames and shorter time frames

Narrative Writing

✔ **Voice** The author of "A Royal Mystery" creates a mood of excitement by describing the action during the athletic competitions at the summer camp. A good **description** describes events in vivid ways to highlight the narrator's or main character's experiences and feelings.

Natalie drafted a description about a memorable summer camp experience. Later, she added words and phrases to give the reader a clearer sense of her feelings about it.

Writing Traits Checklist

✔ **Ideas**
Did I use vivid details to describe the setting?

✔ **Organization**
Did I present the details in an order that makes sense?

✔ **Sentence Fluency**
Did I use varied sentence types?

✔ **Word Choice**
Did I use sensory words?

✔ **Voice**
Do my words reveal an attitude or feeling about the place?

✔ **Conventions**
Did I use correct spelling, grammar, and punctuation?

Revised Draft

Each stroke of my canoe paddle created

a dark swirl in the water. The air ~~was~~ _^sludgy_ _^warm, sticky_

~~warm and sticky. It was full of~~ _humming with_

Ugh!
mosquitoes. ^It smelled like rotten eggs~~.~~ _!_

My nature group was exploring the

Oxbow Nature Reserve with Terry, our guide.

The Bog Slog

by Natalie Sheng

Each stroke of my canoe paddle created a dark swirl in the sludgy water. The warm, sticky air was humming with mosquitoes. Ugh! It smelled like rotten eggs!

My nature group was exploring the Oxbow Nature Reserve with Terry, our guide. The area was once a lake that is slowly becoming land. What does that make it now? It is a swamp and a frustrating place for canoeing.

"Don't go near the shore!" called Terry. Too late! My friend Erin and I were already stuck.

We got out to free the canoe, and our feet sank into the muddy bottom. As we slogged through mud up to our knees, we truly understood what it means to feel "bogged down." We now call that unforgettable summer-camp field trip The Bog Slog.

Reading as a Writer

What words help you know how Natalie feels about her setting? How can you change your description to make your feelings clear?

In my final paper, I added sensory words that showed my attitude. I also added different sentence types.

debate

prodded

gradually

decorated

beckoned

scanned

inflated

stalled

shaken

hesitated

Vocabulary
Reader

Context
Cards

L.5.6 acquire and use general academic and domain-specific words and phrases

80

Vocabulary in Context

1 debate

This class held a debate to discuss which project helps their school the most.

2 prodded

No one needed to be prodded, or pushed, to buy an item at this class bake sale.

3 gradually

The graph shows that gradually, or little by little, the class will get funds for a field trip.

4 decorated

Students decorated this room with crepe paper and balloons for the graduation ceremony.

▶ Study each Context Card.

▶ Break the longer words into syllables.
Use a dictionary to check your work.

5 beckoned

The cheerleaders beckoned, or signaled, the fans to join them in a cheer for the team.

6 scanned

This library aide scanned the shelves, looking carefully for a certain book.

7 inflated

This student inflated balloons to decorate the classroom for a party.

8 stalled

When traffic in the halls has stalled, a hall monitor may need to move people along.

9 shaken

Although shaken by the height of the microphone, this boy gave a good speech.

10 hesitated

This student hesitated, or hung back, before she tried to answer her teacher's question.

Read and Comprehend

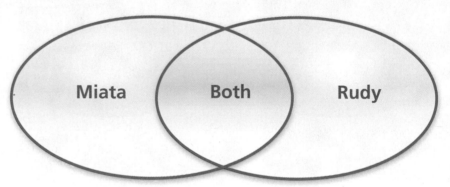

✓ **TARGET SKILL**

Compare and Contrast When you **compare,** you find similarities. When you **contrast,** you identify differences. In the story "Off and Running," Miata and Rudy, the two main characters, are alike in some ways and different in others. As you read the story, compare and contrast their behaviors and thoughts. Use a graphic organizer like this one to help you.

Miata   Both   Rudy

✓ **TARGET STRATEGY**

Infer/Predict When you **infer,** you understand something that is not stated directly. When you **predict,** you use clues to make logical guesses about what might happen in the future. As you read "Off and Running," use details from the text to infer what the characters think and feel and to predict their future actions.

RL.5.1 quote accurately when explaining what the text says explicitly and when drawing inferences; **RL.5.3** compare and contrast characters, settings, or events, drawing on details

Politics

Every two years, American voters choose people to represent them in local, state, or federal government. The candidates who want these positions first run a campaign. They make speeches, debate with other candidates, and get to know as many people as possible. If they win, they help pass laws and make decisions that affect the lives of American citizens.

In "Off and Running," the characters Miata and Rudy want to take part in student government. They want to influence how their school is run and what the students do. Each of them has specific ideas and a unique personal style. Their classmates must decide who will make the best leader.

ANCHOR TEXT

✅ TARGET SKILL

Compare and Contrast
Examine how two or more characters or ideas are alike and different.

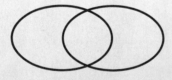

✅ GENRE

Realistic fiction includes characters and events that are like people and events in real life. As you read, look for:

▶ realistic characters and events

▶ characters' feelings that seem believable

▶ challenges and conflicts that might exist in real life

COMMON CORE **RL.5.3** compare and contrast characters, settings, or events, drawing on details; **RL.5.4** determine the meaning of words and phrases, including figurative language; **RL.5.10** read and comprehend literature

MEET THE AUTHOR
Gary Soto

When Gary Soto was a boy, living in Fresno, California, he thought he would grow up to study dinosaurs, but instead, when he was in college, he discovered poetry and started writing poems of his own; he has been a writer ever since. He decided to write for young people in his first collection of short stories, *Baseball in April*, because he recognized a need to give young Mexican Americans stories about their culture and their neighborhoods. Mr. Soto gets ideas for his poems and stories from his own experiences, his Mexican American heritage, and his vivid imagination.

MEET THE ILLUSTRATOR
Eric Velasquez

Growing up in Harlem, a New York City neighborhood, Eric Velasquez loved taking art classes and remembers being influenced by the culture around him and encouraged by his mother, who recognized his love for drawing. He advises young people who would like to become artists to "draw, draw, draw, paint, paint, paint, read, read, read." He also loves old movies, which have inspired many of his illustrations.

Off and Running

by Gary Soto

selection illustrated by Eric Velasquez

ESSENTIAL QUESTION

Why is determination a good quality for a politician to have?

85

Miata Ramirez is running for fifth-grade class president with her best friend, Ana, as her running mate; also running is Rudy Herrera with his friend Alex. Miata has good ideas to improve the school, but Rudy is funny and popular; it will be a close race, and both students try to convince their classmates to vote for them when election speeches are held in front of the entire class.

Miata scanned the audience sitting on the floor in the multipurpose room, which was still decorated with banners for the sixteenth of September, Mexican Independence Day. The heads of the fifth-graders wagged like apples on a branch. Miata was nervous about the debate. But this was her big chance to tell the students why they should vote for her and not for Rudy.

Miata looked at Rudy sitting next to her. She could see that he was chewing gum, which was against school rules. He was smacking his lips and waving to the boys in the audience.

Blowing a bubble, Rudy turned to Miata. The bubble grew as large as a fist and popped like a fist in a baseball glove. He laughed and asked, "You want some gum?"

"No, it's against school rules," Miata said. "I'm not going to get in trouble just before elections."

"Oh yeah, that's right," Rudy said. He swallowed the bubble gum and opened his mouth like an alligator's. His throat blared "Ahhhhhhhhhh." He closed his mouth and said, "See, it's all gone."

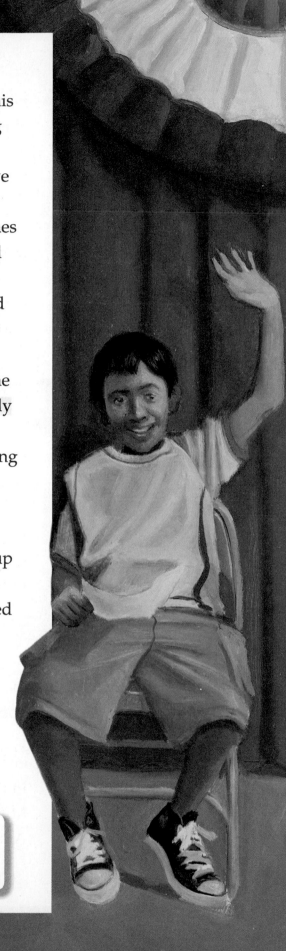

"That's ugly, Rudy." Miata grimaced.

Rudy shrugged his shoulders. He turned his attention to the audience. Someone was yelling at Rudy to ask if he wanted to exchange his sandwich for a burrito during lunch. Rudy gave him a thumbs-up response.

Miata's nervous knees shivered, and the lines on her palms ran with sticky sweat. She looked down at the five MIATA AND ANA badges on the front of her blouse. Earlier they had seemed so neat, but now they just got in her way.

"People—fifth-graders—let's settle down," Mrs. Castillo, the vice principal, yelled above the noise. She repeated her command and gradually the bobbing heads stopped moving.

"Yeah, let's knock it off," Rudy yelled, getting to his feet. His gaze locked on two boys who were pushing each other. "Carlos, leave Jaime (HI meh) alone. Save it for the playground."

Carlos stopped shoving his friend and sat up as straight as an angel, which he was not.

"That's better," Rudy said. He then returned to his seat.

"Thank you, Rudy," Mrs. Castillo said.

"No problem," he said.

Mrs. Castillo turned to Miata and, with a smile, said sweetly, "We're going to hear from Miata first. She's in room six. Let's hear what she has to say."

ANALYZE THE TEXT

Idioms Find the idiom Rudy uses when he speaks to the students. What does it mean?

There was light applause as Miata rose from her chair and approached the podium. She climbed onto a box that was set there for her. She adjusted the microphone.

"Good morning," Miata said.

"It's almost afternoon," Carlos yelled.

Miata looked at the clock on the wall and then at Carlos. She decided to ignore him. She continued with a bright chime in her voice. "I'm seeking your votes next Tuesday. I want to be your president."

"President of the United States?" Carlos yelled through the funnel of his hands.

With that, Mrs. Castillo, now stern faced, shook a finger at him. He returned to sitting as straight as an angel.

Miata breathed in as she gathered strength. She inflated her lungs and boomed, "If elected, I plan to beautify the school grounds. I want to get rid of all that *cholo* graffiti and put some flowers in by our fifth-grade rooms."

Some of the students, mostly girls, applauded.

"I'm sure you're tired of a *cochino*[1]-looking (koh CHEE noh) school," Miata boomed even louder.

There was more applause, but not enough to make Miata confident. She eyed Ana in the audience. Ana hadn't clapped that hard. Miata clicked her tongue and thought, Come on, Ana, let's get with it.

[1] *cochino*: dirty

"Those are good ideas," Ana remarked, not too bravely. She looked around at the audience. No one was applauding.

Miata paused, somewhat shaken. She had practiced with Ana on the school grounds, but now behind the podium the words didn't seem as powerful.

"I plan to get parents involved," Miata continued. "I want them to help with the cleanup."

Only one student applauded. It was Carlos. He was applauding as hard as rain on a car roof. He wouldn't stop until Mrs. Castillo beckoned him with a finger. He was being called out of the room. He rose to his feet and said, "I'll vote for you, Miata. You're nicer." Then, looking at Rudy, Carlos stepped over his classmates sitting on the floor. "Nah, I better vote for Rudy. I owe him a quarter." He was prodded from the multipurpose room toward the principal's office.

"Just think," Miata said, her voice weak. She was losing her confidence. "We can put some really nice azaleas and pansies outside our windows. The walls will be all clean, not like they are now." She looked at her scribbled notes, then up toward the audience. "It'll be work, but we can do it."

The audience scrunched up their faces.

"And I have plans for a school trip," Miata countered quickly, sensing that she was losing her listeners. "And I have a fund-raising idea for how we can get computers."

The audience yawned. Two posters that said VOTE FOR MIATA AND ANA sank down.

"I have a question," a boy said, his hand as tall as a spear.

"Yes."

"Are we gonna get paid to work?" His face was lit with a grin. He knew he was being silly.

"No, we're not getting paid. It's for our school."

The students muttered but applauded lightly. A few of the posters went up again in a rattle but quickly sank down.

"Please think of me when you vote on Tuesday," Miata said. Her voice was now as faint as a baby bird's chirp.

She sat down, exhausted. She wanted to shake her head in defeat but knew that she had to sit up bravely. She waved at the audience, but only a few students waved back. Not one of them was a boy.

Then Rudy stood up. He approached the podium and leaped up onto the box.

"Hey, I like this," he laughed. As he held on to the podium, he wobbled the box and said, "It's like a skateboard!"

The audience laughed. From where she sat, Miata could see that more than one boy was chewing bubble gum.

Rudy then became serious. He looked at Miata and said, "She's got some ideas. Miata would make a good prez, but I think I would make a truly great one."

The audience laughed.

"And you know why?" Rudy asked.

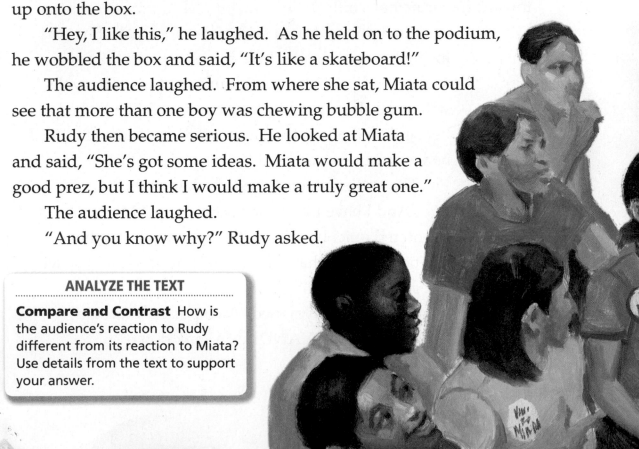

ANALYZE THE TEXT

Compare and Contrast How is the audience's reaction to Rudy different from its reaction to Miata? Use details from the text to support your answer.

"Why?" some of the boys in the audience repeated.

Rudy turned a cupped ear to the audience. "I can't hear you."

"Why?" yelled a mixed group of boys and girls.

"Still can't hear you." Rudy smiled.

"*Why*?" the entire audience yelled.

Rudy nodded his head, smiling. He had their attention. "It's because . . . I'm going to work to get us more recess time."

The audience applauded and chanted, "More recess! More recess! More recess!"

"Yeah, *gente!*[2] (HEHN teh) Instead of just fifteen minutes, I'm going to ask the principal for twenty—at least! Maybe even half an hour, homeboys!"

[2] *gente*: people

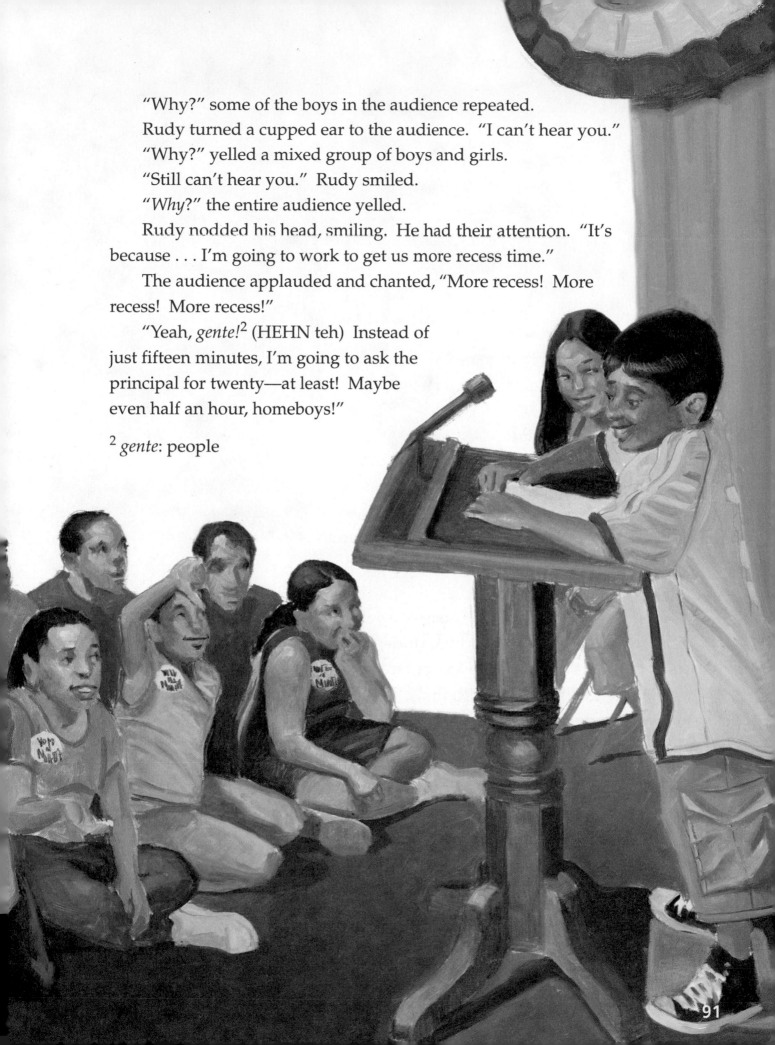

91

"Why not an hour?" someone yelled from the audience.

"We can't push our luck, dude," Rudy responded.

Miata wanted to cover her face. It was obvious that the audience was siding with Rudy.

Rudy raised his hands and asked for silence.

"Plus," he continued as he slowly scanned the audience. "Plus I'm going to ask for Ice Cream Day every day. Not just on Fridays."

The audience roared as Rudy wobbled the box and then jumped off. He returned to his seat, pushing a fresh piece of bubble gum into his mouth.

"You got good ideas," Rudy said with confidence. "Good luck. *Buena suerte*." (BWEH nah SWER teh) He extended a hand.

"Yeah, thanks. I'll need it," Miata said in a whisper as she stood up and shook Rudy's hand, which was as cool as a lizard's. "Good luck to you, too, Rudy."

After the debate, the students returned to their classrooms. Miata tried to put on a good face. Most of the girls knew that Rudy was a joker. They knew he could never get that extra five minutes of recess or Ice Cream Day five days a week. But the boys might believe him. Miata needed a new strategy.

ANALYZE THE TEXT

Formal and Informal Language
Does Miata speak formally or informally in her speech? How is her way of speaking different from Rudy's?

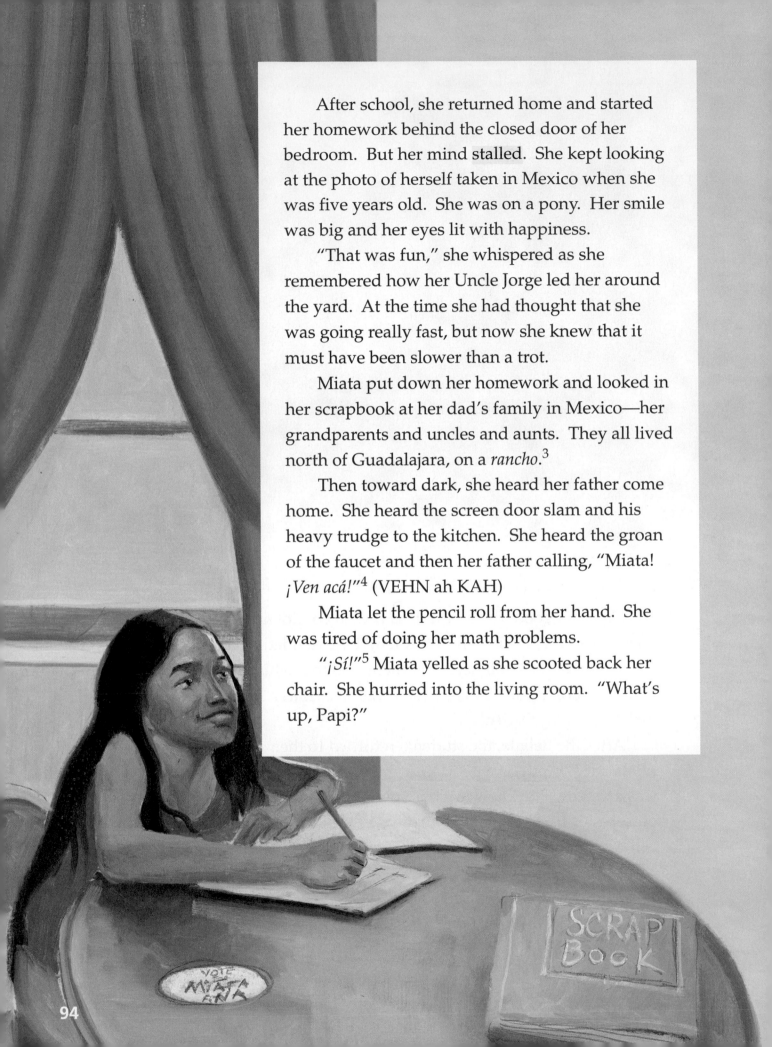

After school, she returned home and started her homework behind the closed door of her bedroom. But her mind stalled. She kept looking at the photo of herself taken in Mexico when she was five years old. She was on a pony. Her smile was big and her eyes lit with happiness.

"That was fun," she whispered as she remembered how her Uncle Jorge led her around the yard. At the time she had thought that she was going really fast, but now she knew that it must have been slower than a trot.

Miata put down her homework and looked in her scrapbook at her dad's family in Mexico—her grandparents and uncles and aunts. They all lived north of Guadalajara, on a *rancho*.[3]

Then toward dark, she heard her father come home. She heard the screen door slam and his heavy trudge to the kitchen. She heard the groan of the faucet and then her father calling, "Miata! *¡Ven acá!*"[4] (VEHN ah KAH)

Miata let the pencil roll from her hand. She was tired of doing her math problems.

"*¡Sí!*"[5] Miata yelled as she scooted back her chair. She hurried into the living room. "What's up, Papi?"

"I found something at work."

"What?"

"A most unusual thing."

"What is it? Tell me."

He was holding a small white box in his hand.

"It scared me when I found it." Her father's face was dark with worry and dust from his long hours at work.

Miata furrowed her brow. She was curious.

Slowly her father lifted the lid from the box. Miata peeked in, standing on her tiptoes. In it stood an adult index finger that was as gnarled as a root. She eyed her father and clicked her tongue.

"Where do you think it came from, *mi'ja*[6] (ME hah)?" her father asked seriously. He petted the finger with his free hand.

"From your left hand, Papi," Miata answered, hands on her hips. "That's where it came from."

A sudden smile brightened his face. He wiggled the finger in the box and screamed, "*Ay*,[7] (EYE) it's coming alive. I better put it down the garbage disposal." He ran into the kitchen laughing, and Miata followed her father. But he only got himself another glass of water.

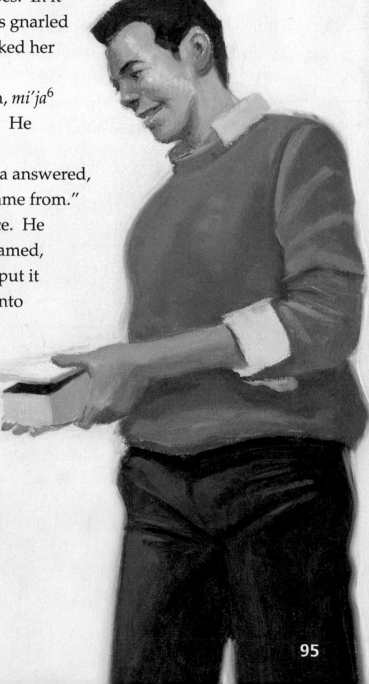

[3] *rancho*: ranch or large farm

[4] *¡Ven acá!*: Come here!

[5] *¡Sí!*: Yes!

[6] *mi'ja*: my dear; my daughter

[7] *Ay*: Uh-oh

"Dad?" Miata asked, taking his large work-stained hand into hers.

"Yeah, *mi'ja*." He wiped his mouth with the back of his free hand.

"Do you think I should run for office?" She hesitated and then continued. "I mean, I'm not as popular as Rudy or his friend Alex."

"Well, popularity is one thing, but service is another. ¿*Entiendes?*" [8] (ehn TYEHN dehs)

Miata shook her head. She was confused.

"I mean, it's OK to have a lot of people who like you, but it's far better to help people, to get things done." He gave her a light hug. "Don't worry. Just go for it. If it doesn't happen, *pues*,[9] (PWEHS) you can still do good."

Miata liked that. She had plans for the school, and they were good ones.

[8] ¿*Entiendes?*: Do you understand?
[9] *pues*: then

Consider This

Like the characters Miata and Rudy in "Off and Running," some students decide to run for office in school elections, and some students like it so much that they decide to follow a career in politics when they grow up. Why not participate in a school election and see if you have what it takes to be a successful politician?

Running for office in a school election has many of the same elements of city, state, or national elections, just on a smaller scale. School elections can also be a good way to see if your strengths are a good fit for the expectations of a campaign and a career in public service. Above all else, you need to have a passion for working with people and a strong desire to make your community a better place to live and work.

In a school election you will develop a platform, or important items that you will accomplish once you are elected to office; this is something to make final before your campaign begins because changing your platform mid-campaign might confuse your classmates. If you are voted into office, students will be watching to see if you follow through on your platform promises.

To run a successful campaign, you will need volunteers to help carry out your campaign strategy, which is your plan for promoting yourself and your platform. The following questions can be useful when developing a campaign strategy: Will you make campaign buttons, banners, or posters? What will your campaign slogan be? Where and when will you give speeches? Will you debate your opponent? If you anticipate a debate, get friends and volunteers to help you practice by playing the roles of audience members and your opponent.

Finally, a school election can help you consider your strengths and whether they are a good fit for a political career. Running for office will be easier if you like interacting with people and you are comfortable speaking in front of a crowd. Candidates also need to have good listening skills so they can respond to questions effectively; once in office, strong speaking and listening skills will help you listen to many points of view and share your opinions and decisions with others.

Participating in a school election can help you realize that you have the skills and the desire to make a difference in people's lives. Will your next campaign be for city mayor? It could happen sooner than you think; check your local laws to be sure, but many towns allow citizens to run for office when they are 17. As long as you are 18 by the date of the general election, and you receive the most votes, you could be mayor while you are still in high school!

Dig Deeper

How to Analyze the Text

Use these pages to learn about Compare and Contrast, Idioms, and Formal and Informal Language. Then read "Off and Running" again to apply what you learned.

Compare and Contrast

In the story "Off and Running," Miata and Rudy are realistic characters who approach the same goal in different ways. Their personalities are shown through what they say and do.

When you **compare and contrast,** you look for details that show how characters or ideas in a text are the same and different. To compare characters, think about what the characters say, what they do, and how they feel. Comparing and contrasting characters helps you understand their unique traits and motivations.

Look back through the story to find text evidence about Miata and Rudy. What similarities and differences between the two characters do you discover?

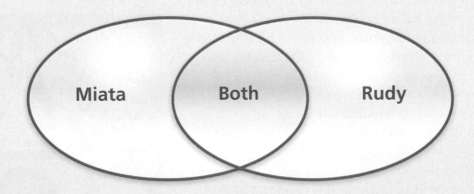

Miata   Both   Rudy

RL.5.3 compare and contrast characters, settings, or events, drawing on details; **RL.5.4** determine the meaning of words and phrases, including figurative language; **RL.5.10** read and comprehend literature; **RF.5.4a** read on-level text with purpose and understanding; **L.5.3b** compare and contrast varieties of English in stories, dramas, or poems; **L.5.5b** recognize and explain the meaning of idioms, adages, and proverbs

Idioms

To make dialogue more realistic and lively, authors may include **idioms,** or phrases with meanings that differ from the literal meanings of the words. Look back at page 92. Rudy says, "We can't push our luck." Real fifth graders might use this idiom when talking to each other. It means, "We can't be too greedy, or we won't get anything."

Formal and Informal Language

Miata's speech includes **formal** phrases such as *I'm seeking your votes* and *I plan to beautify the school grounds.* In contrast, Rudy uses **informal** slang words such as *dude* and *homeboys.* What differences between Miata and Rudy are revealed through their dialogue? What does their use of some Spanish terms tell you about both characters?

Your Turn

RETURN TO THE ESSENTIAL QUESTION

Turn and Talk Review the selection to prepare to discuss this question: *Why is determination a good quality for a politician to have?* As you discuss, take turns reviewing and explaining each other's key ideas. Use text evidence to support your opinion.

Classroom Conversation

Continue your discussion of "Off and Running" by explaining your answers to these questions:

1. How does Miata show determination in the story?

2. How are some of the obstacles that Miata faces similar to those faced by real politicians?

3. Do you agree with the advice Miata's father gives her? Why?

ANALYZE DIALOGUE

Make a List Authors include dialogue in their stories for many reasons. In "Off and Running," the dialogue makes the characters sound like real fifth graders. Gary Soto also uses what characters say in order to show some of their feelings. List examples of good dialogue from the story. Explain how each example makes the speaker seem realistic or shows what he or she is feeling.

Response Think about what Miata and Rudy say in their speeches. If you were a member of the fifth-grade class in "Off and Running," which candidate would you vote for? Why? Write a paragraph in which you compare and contrast the two characters and state your choice for class president. Include an explanation of why you would vote for this student. Support your reasons with details and quotations from the story.

Writing Tip

State your opinion at the beginning of your response. Organize your reasons by presenting the strongest ones first. Support each with details and evidence from the story. Remember to end your paragraph with a strong concluding statement.

COMMON CORE **RL.5.1** quote accurately when explaining what the text says explicitly and when drawing inferences; **RL.5.3** compare and contrast characters, settings, or events, drawing on details; **W.5.1a** introduce a topic, state an opinion, and create an organizational structure; **W.5.1b** provide logically ordered reasons supported by facts and details; **W.5.1d** provide a concluding statement or section; **W.5.9a** apply grade 5 Reading standards to literature

PERSUASIVE TEXT

VOTE FOR ME!

by Pamela Zarn

A class election debate is not the only method candidates have to convince other students to vote for them. If you have hesitated to run for office because public speaking leaves you feeling shaken, or if you feel your campaign efforts have stalled, try creating election advertisements to catch people's interest.

Posters are a great way to advertise your strengths. Use short sentences and bold, clear lettering so that your message can be easily scanned by students as they pass on the way to class. Posters are also a great way to reach those students who may need to be beckoned or prodded into going to the polls to vote.

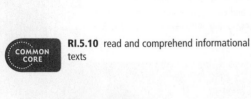

Read the campaign posters below and on page 104. Think about how the candidates' posters persuade you to vote for them. How do the techniques differ from a commercial on television?

The candidate provides a call to action. It is short and punchy. A few words are better than a paragraph.

The poster is decorated with an eye-catching image of a pizza, which helps to associate the candidate with something kids like.

She makes a generalization.

She makes a promise. You should ask yourself if it is an exaggerated promise.

She asks a question with emotional appeal. Most ads want you to feel before you think.

IF YOU LIKE PIZZA, VOTE NATASHA!

Everybody loves pizza! Wouldn't you like pizza for lunch EVERY day? If you vote for Natasha, our cafeteria will never be without pizza again!

He begins with a short, eye-catching campaign slogan. The easier it is to remember, the better.

The candidate's poster includes inflated balloons in the school colors for emotional appeal.

He gives supporting examples of his strengths. Always check to see if the information in ads is true.

He lists his strengths.

He makes a promise. His promise is one that will make students feel good about him.

VOTE JARED

HE HAS WHAT IT TAKES!

- Leadership: soccer team co-captain
- Communication: member of student-teacher council
- Action: leader in the class fund-raiser

I will listen to fifth graders and do what it takes to get what they want!

Whom would you vote for?
Did one of these posters catch your eye right away, or did you gradually decide which candidate you favor?

Compare Texts

Compare Messages With a partner, determine the theme of "Off and Running" and the main idea of "Vote for Me!" Talk about the points both authors make about campaigning and true leadership. Then discuss how each author conveys his or her thoughts about how to be a good political candidate.

Recognize Exaggerated Statements Many candidates running for office exaggerate what they will do when elected. In "Off and Running," which candidate exaggerates what he or she will do? Write a brief campaign speech for class president, telling what you would do if elected and why classmates should vote for you. Deliver your speech to a small group. Speak clearly, at an understandable pace. Remember to use formal language when making your points.

Research Political Leaders The candidates in "Off and Running" want to take a leadership role in their school. With a partner, use print and digital sources to gather information about two important political leaders. Then compare and contrast examples of their leadership.

Go Digital

COMMON CORE

RL.5.2 determine theme from details/summarize; **RI.5.7** draw on information from print and digital sources to locate answers or solve problems; **SL.5.4** report on a topic or text, or present an opinion/speak clearly at an understandable pace; **SL.5.6** adapt speech to contexts and tasks, using formal English when appropriate to task and situation

Grammar

What Is a Compound Sentence? A **compound sentence** is a sentence made up of two shorter sentences joined by a comma and the **conjunction** *and, but,* or *or.* Each part of a compound sentence has its own **complete subject** and **complete predicate.**

Compound Sentences

complete   complete   complete   complete
subject   predicate   subject   predicate

Miata sits quietly, but her opponent yells to the crowd.

In each part of a compound sentence, a present-tense verb and its subject must agree in number. This agreement is known as subject-verb agreement.

plural   plural form singular singular form
subject of verb   subject   of verb

Two boys scuffle, and Rudy hollers at them.

Try This! **Find the errors in these compound sentences. Which do not contain proper subject-verb agreement? Where should commas be placed? Write the sentences correctly on another sheet of paper.**

❶ Miata presents her plan and students clap.

❷ Ana and Carlos disappoints Miata and she feels sad.

❸ Some boys chew gum but no one stop them.

In your writing, you might find pairs of sentences that are related in some way. Try combining the sentences using a comma and the conjunction *and*, *but*, or *or*.

Related Sentences

Several girls supported Jeanne.

Eddie was popular with almost everyone.

Compound Sentence

Several girls supported Jeanne, but Eddie was popular with almost everyone.

 Connect Grammar to Writing

As you revise your dialogue piece this week, look for related sentences that you can rewrite as compound sentences, using a comma and the conjunction *and*, *but*, or *or*. Be sure to use proper subject-verb agreement.

W.5.3a orient the reader by establishing a situation and introducing a narrator or characters/organize an event sequence; **W.5.3b** use narrative techniques to develop experiences and events or show characters' responses; **W.5.5** develop and strengthen writing by planning, revising, editing, rewriting, or trying a new approach; **W.5.10** write routinely over extended time frames and shorter time frames

Narrative Writing

✓ **Word Choice** Good **dialogue** in a narrative sounds natural and expresses the personalities and feelings of the characters who are speaking. Dialogue can make your narrative more realistic.

Brad drafted a narrative in which two or more characters provoke a reaction in each other. Later, he changed some words to make the dialogue sound more natural. Use the Writing Traits Checklist below as you revise your writing.

Writing Traits Checklist

✓ **Ideas**
Does the dialogue reveal a problem or conflict?

✓ **Organization**
Do the words of one speaker cause a reaction in another?

✓ **Sentence Fluency**
Does the dialogue have a natural flow?

✓ **Word Choice**
Did I choose words that make events and feelings clear?

✓ **Voice**
Do the speakers' words reveal their traits?

✓ **Conventions**
Did I use correct spelling, grammar, and punctuation?

Revised Draft

"Writing history skits is a blast!"
~~"You will enjoy writing skits,"~~ said Ms. Ghose,

the fifth-grade social studies teacher.
"In your dreams,"
~~"I don't think I will like it much,"~~ muttered

Evan as he sat down with his group. He could

see that he would have to be the leader.

History Superhero

by Brad Baumgartner

"Writing history skits is a blast!" said Ms. Ghose, the fifth-grade social studies teacher.

"In your dreams," muttered Evan as he sat down with his group. He could see that he would have to be the leader. "Okay, let's decide who we'll be. How about George and Martha Washington?"

"That is so pathetic," said Derek, who thought everything was pathetic and who rarely smiled. Kalil yawned. Nothing interested him except superheroes. Jolene sketched in her notebook and didn't look up.

"Wait!" said Evan. "How about making George a superhero with secret powers that no one knows about, not even Martha? Jolene could be Martha, and Kalil could be George."

"Okay," said Kalil. "I could go with that." Jolene stopped sketching and looked up. Best of all, Derek actually smiled. Maybe Ms. Ghose had been right—it was starting to look like writing the history skit would be a blast after all!

Reading as a Writer

How does Brad show his characters' personalities? What kinds of dialogue could help your narrative show more about your characters?

In my final paper, I changed my characters' dialogue to sound more realistic. I also used a comma and the conjunction *and* to combine sentences.

Vocabulary in Context

☑ TARGET VOCABULARY

competition
identical
routine
element
intimidated
unison
recite
qualifying
uniform
mastered

Vocabulary Reader

Context Cards

 L.5.6 acquire and use general academic and domain-specific words and phrases

1 competition
A contest between evenly matched teams makes for an exciting competition.

2 identical
The clothing worn by members of a team is often exactly alike, or identical.

3 routine
This coach is explaining a routine, or set course of action, that the team must learn.

4 element
Speed is an important part, or element, of many team sports, such as hockey.

Go Digital

▶ Study each Context Card.

▶ Make up a new context sentence that uses two Vocabulary words.

5 intimidated

Smaller players might be intimidated, or frightened, by larger players.

6 unison

These rowers must work in unison to win. They must move their oars as one.

7 recite

Cheerleaders recite a cheer to urge the team to win. Then they shout out another.

8 qualifying

This team won three earlier races, qualifying them to take part in the finals.

9 uniform

Professional baseball fields are uniform in size. Bases are always ninety feet apart.

10 mastered

The medals these girls won show that they have mastered their athletic skills.

Read and Comprehend

☑ TARGET SKILL

Sequence of Events Sequence is a text structure that nonfiction authors can use to organize their information. In a sequence structure, events are described in chronological order. As you read "Double Dutch," look for time-order words and phrases, such as *years ago, first,* and *Friday*. Use a graphic organizer like this one to help you keep track of events and understand how they are related.

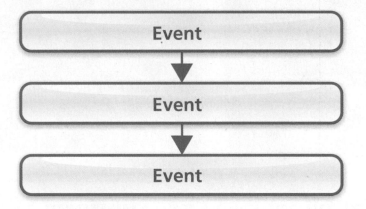

Event

↓

Event

↓

Event

☑ TARGET STRATEGY

Monitor/Clarify As you read "Double Dutch," **monitor**, or pay attention to, your understanding of the text. If something does not make sense, stop to **clarify** it, or make it clear.

 RI.5.3 explain the relationships between individuals/events/ideas/concepts in a text.

Physical Fitness

Jumping rope can be a great way to keep fit. Double Dutch is a game of jump rope with a twist. There are two ropes, and each is turned in a different direction. A double Dutch team has at least three or four members, including two rope turners and one or two jumpers. Within the ropes, the jumpers may do the same moves or different ones. The turners may recite rhymes to help keep the jumpers moving in the same rhythm.

As you will see while reading the selection, being on a double Dutch team does more than keep the members in good shape. They also learn lessons about teamwork, discipline, and competition.

ANCHOR TEXT

DOUBLE DUTCH
A Celebration of Jump Rope, Rhyme, and Sisterhood

VERONICA CHAMBERS

 TARGET SKILL

Sequence of Events
Identify the time order in which events take place.

 GENRE

Narrative nonfiction
tells about real people, things, events, or places. As you read, look for:

▶ events presented in time order

▶ factual information that tells a story

▶ pictures of people and events mentioned in the text

COMMON CORE **RI.5.10** read and comprehend informational texts; **RF.5.4a** read on-level text with purpose and understanding

Go Digital

MEET THE AUTHOR

Veronica Chambers

Veronica Chambers was born in Panama. When she was five, she moved to New York City, where she got her first library card and learned to jump double Dutch. She loves to travel and learn new languages. She can speak English, Spanish, Japanese, and French. Her books for young people include novels about best friends Marisol and Magdalena, and the biography *Celia Cruz, Queen of Salsa*. Chambers receives lots of e-mail each day, but she still prefers to write letters.

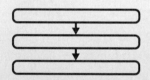

DOUBLE DUTCH

A Celebration of Jump Rope, Rhyme, and Sisterhood

by Veronica Chambers

ROCKETT GIRLS

It's early Saturday morning, and five girls gather in the gymnasium of Reed Junior High School in Central Islip, Long Island. They are a multiracial group: white, black, and brown, but each girl is dressed in a matching red tracksuit. When they jump into the double-Dutch ropes, each head bobs with an identical ponytail. They are a team. And what's more, each girl, averaging only thirteen years old, knows what it's like to be a winner. The Snazzy Steppers, as this team is called, are the New York City champions. They are also ranked fifth in the world.

As they unfold their ropes and begin to jump, they are intensely silent. They don't sing songs; they don't recite rhymes. Peggy and Debbie jump in to rehearse their doubles routine. They move in unison, which isn't easy, and they execute even the most complex moves with a uniform grace. It's as if they were rowers on the same boat, their arms and legs slicing and curving together. The two turners offer up tips and criticism. "Don't go faster than the rope," Lanieequah reminds her teammates. Sometimes, the entire team catches a case of the giggles, prompting their coach to insist they focus harder. "I'm not laughing," Peggy mutters. "Yes, you were," whispers Debbie. "I smile and then you laugh."

In the ropes, it seems that the Steppers defy gravity. They do handstands and back-flips. They bend to touch their feet and kick their legs as high as Radio City Rockettes. But they are something even better. They are astronauts of the asphalt, rocket girls limited only by their imagination and their unbelievably limber, athletic bodies.

Coach Rockett

Life for the Snazzy Steppers wasn't always so sweet. It was only five years ago that these girls couldn't jump double Dutch at all. Their coach, David Rockett, started the team eight years ago when he became frustrated with the lack of positive activities for kids in the public school where he teaches. "One recess, I was looking out the window of my classroom," says Coach Rockett. "Some of the kids were doing double Dutch on the playground. I was fascinated by the call-and-response element, the rhythms, and the movement." The very next day, Rockett went to the local hardware store and bought a couple hundred yards of clothesline. He made a flyer inviting students to form a double-Dutch team. Forty girls showed up!

Coach Rockett was thrilled but intimidated. Most of the girls had no double-Dutch experience. He'd have to teach them; but first, he had to learn himself! No small feat for a forty-something white guy from the 'burbs. But Coach Rockett was determined to see his girls fly. He visited other schools and playgrounds, asking kids for lessons. He studied books about jump rope and scanned the Internet for competition tips and news. In just a few short months, he had mastered the game. Coach Rockett even wrote a song to help teach his girls how to jump:

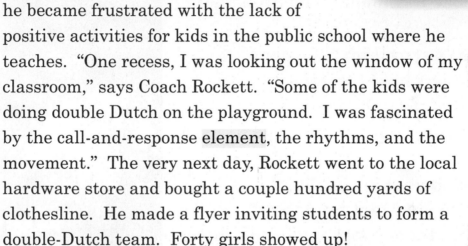

ANALYZE THE TEXT

Sequence of Events What are the steps Coach Rockett took to create a double-Dutch team? List the steps in sequential order.

My name is Franny.
I'm the rainbow frog.
Inside the ropes
I'm a double-Dutch star!

Bring three friends together,
who share the same dream.
Two turners and one jumper
make a winning jump-rope team!

Let's start with two ropes,
turners hold the ends.
Don't drop the ropes,
or you'll have to start again.

Bend your knees slightly,
with your feet set apart.
Spin those ropes round and round,
you're off to a good start.

Can you imagine an eggbeater
as it spins round and round?
That's how the ropes look
as they slap on the ground.

Come gather around, friends.
We're going to have some fun
singing and jumping
double Dutch.

Coach Rockett taught the girls all he knew, and then they attended their first competition in Harlem. The girls were pulverized. Back in Central Islip, it had seemed that they were so talented! Everyone at Reed Junior High School was impressed by the way they could do flips and somersaults in the rope. Sure, at home, the Snazzy Steppers were so baaaaad, they were good, but the teams in Harlem were faster, bolder, smoother, and sassier. The girls left Harlem with no trophies and their confidence ripped to pieces. "It was the most painful thing to watch. They thought they were all that," remembers Coach Rockett. "Then they saw double Dutch for the first time. The girls hid in the bathroom at the competition, feigning illness. They were so scared. They knew they were one of the weakest teams in the league."

ANALYZE THE TEXT

Narrative Pacing How does the addition of dialogue affect the pacing of the text?

I had a little puppy.
His name was Tiny Tim.
I put him in the bathtub,
to see if he could swim.

He drank all the water,
he swallowed a bar of soap.
Next thing you know,
it was halfway down his
throat.

In jumps the doctor.
In jumps the nurse.
In jumps the lady with
the alligator purse.

Out jumps the doctor.
Out jumps the nurse.
Out jumps the lady with
the alligator purse.

ANALYZE THE TEXT

Rhythm Notice the rhythm, or the way words are stressed, in the poem above. Why is rhythm important in double-Dutch rhymes? How do the double-Dutch rhymes add to the text?

The Snazzy Steppers were down but by no means out. Each year, they returned to competition a little stronger. First, they won fifth place, then fourth, then third, then second. Finally, after a lot of hard work, they grabbed the number-one spot in New York City, qualifying for the world championships. They've been flying high ever since. They've also become the best of friends. "It's a funny math," says Coach Rockett. "In double Dutch, one plus one plus one doesn't equal three. One plus one plus one equals one. You have to be tight. If you and I are turning and we have even the tiniest bit of animosity toward each other, it comes out on the ropes. You're trying to get kids to care about each other, to learn about each other, to nurture each other. When it works—when a team comes together—it makes for a powerful group of young women."

Each of the Snazzy Steppers has her favorite element of competition:

"Speed is my favorite thing. The challenge of it," says Debbie.

"Freestyle. It's where you get to express yourself," says Erika.

"My favorite thing is . . . the trophies!" says Katelyn.

"My best moment was when I learned the karate kick, when I was in the third grade. It's such an easy trick, but it was my first trick. The first time I ever showed some style in the rope," says Peggy.

"I'm the only girl on the team who came in knowing street double Dutch. It's different from competitive jumping. In street rope, you jump long and fast. In competition, you're slowing down the rope so you can catch the trick. It was almost harder than learning from scratch. My style had to change," says Lanieequah.

DOUBLE DUTCH IS . . .

"...**fearlessness.** The audacious willingness to jump in and mix things up when life is sweeping over you from all sides in incessant, overwhelming waves. The skill—ultimately, the thrill—is not in stopping the flow, but in keeping pace with rhythm."

—Lynette Clementson,
reporter for the *New York Times*

"... **confidence** in motion. Double Dutch is bodies in motion, not decoration: strong, glorious, exultant.

Double Dutch is glorious."

—Peggy Orenstein,
award-winning author of *School Girls*

Dig Deeper

How to Analyze the Text

Use these pages to learn about Sequence of Events, Narrative Pacing, and Rhythm. Then read "Double Dutch" again to apply what you learned.

Sequence of Events

Nonfiction authors often use a text structure known as **sequence** to organize their information. Events are presented in chronological order, or the order in which they happened. To describe the relationships between events in a sequence, authors may include words and phrases such as *first, then*, and *years ago*. Sometimes authors skip over certain events in order to keep the story moving. In these instances, readers can use text clues to make **inferences,** or to figure out what has happened on their own.

In "Double Dutch," the author uses a sequence of events to tell the story of the Snazzy Steppers. The arrangement of the events in time order helps readers understand how the events are connected. Look back through the selection. In what order do the important events happen, and how are they related?

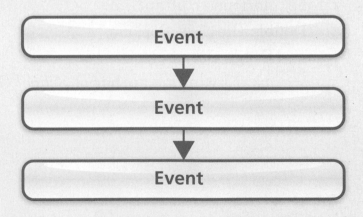

RI.5.3 explain the relationships between individuals/events/ideas/concepts in a text; RI.5.10 read and comprehend informational texts; RF.5.4a read on-level text with purpose and understanding

Narrative Pacing

Even though "Double Dutch" is nonfiction, it has a narrative structure, meaning it is told like a story. To keep the reader's attention, the author varies the **pacing** of the narrative, or the rate at which it moves along. To slow the pace, the author adds details, such as dialogue. To speed up the narrative, the author leaves out descriptive details or skips over less important events.

Rhythm

In "Double Dutch," the author includes some of the poems that jumpers use to keep time. These poems have a strong **rhythm,** or beat, formed by stressing certain syllables. Reading these poems aloud or silently helps readers feel as if they are jumping rope, too.

Your Turn

Turn and Talk Review the selection to prepare to discuss this question: *How can being active in sports improve someone's attitude?* As you discuss, ask questions to make sure you understand your partner's ideas. Give examples from text evidence and your own life to clarify your points.

Classroom Conversation

Continue your discussion of "Double Dutch" by using text evidence to explain your answers to these questions:

1. In what ways do members of the Snazzy Steppers benefit from their activity?

2. Why did Coach Rockett start the team?

3. Why does the author include direct quotations from team members?

TALK ABOUT WORDS

Analyze Author's Word Choice The author uses strong, descriptive words and phrases to help readers picture the events and understand the girls' feelings. With a partner, choose a passage from the narrative that you think is especially vivid. Discuss which words and phrases help you picture the events or understand how the Snazzy Steppers feel.

WRITE ABOUT READING

Response The Snazzy Steppers went from being one of the worst double Dutch teams in the league to being the best. How did they accomplish this feat? Write a paragraph explaining how hard the Snazzy Steppers worked to become champions. Include quotations and other text evidence to support your explanation.

Writing Tip

Conclude your explanation with one or two sentences summarizing your main idea.

COMMON CORE **RI.5.1** quote accurately when explaining what the text says explicitly and when drawing inferences; **W.5.2e** provide a concluding statement or section; **W.5.9b** apply grade 5 Reading standards to informational texts; **SL.5.1a** come to discussions prepared/explicitly draw on preparation and other information about the topic; **SL.5.1c** pose and respond to questions, make comments that contribute to the discussion, and elaborate on others' remarks

POETRY

COMMON CORE RL.5.10 read and comprehend literature

SCORE!

Winning is not the only element of sports. Many people love to watch a pair of figure skaters spinning in unison. Some are awed by the precision of a gymnast's balance beam routine. For others, teamwork on the basketball court brings them the greatest satisfaction.

Though no two athletes are identical, they all share one thing: the love of sports. The following poems celebrate the joy, beauty, and sportsmanship of athletics in its many forms.

Good Sportsmanship

by Richard Armour

Good sportsmanship we hail, we sing,
It's always pleasant when you spot it.
There's only one unhappy thing:
You have to lose to prove you've got it.

This poem by Jane Yolen shows that karate is much more than a competition. Those who have mastered karate must also have grace and discipline, and they must know how to use their skill wisely.

Karate Kid

by Jane Yolen

I am wind,
I am wall,
I am wave,
I rise, I fall,
I am crane
In lofty flight,
Training that
I need not fight.

I am tiger,
I am tree,
I am flower,
I am knee,
I am elbow,
I am hands
Taught to do
The heart's commands.

Not to bully,
Not to fight,
Dragon left
And leopard right.
Wind and wave,
Tree and flower,
Chop.
       Kick.
             Peace.
                  Power.

Deanie McLeanie

by Walter Dean Myers

Deanie McLeanie is a basketball genie
Six foot seven from his sneakers to his beanie

He wears a fourteen jersey and a fifteen shoe
And there's nothing on the court that the kid can't do

He can scoop, he can loop
He can put it through the hoop

He can ram, he can slam
He can do the flying jam

He can tap, he can rap
He can snatch it with a slap

He can dunk, he can plunk
He can stop and make the junk

He can shake, he can bake
He can lose you with a fake

He can pin, he can win
He can do the copter spin

Cause Deanie McLeanie's a basketball genie
Six foot seven from his sneakers to his beanie

He wears a fourteen jersey and a fifteen shoe
And there's nothing on the court that the kid can't do.

WRITE A SPORTS POEM

Write a poem based on a memory of a sporting event you participated in or watched. Think about the feelings you had. Perhaps you felt intimidated by an opponent or excited when your favorite team won a qualifying event. As you write, use the poems in this lesson for inspiration. Include rhyme, repetition, or a uniform rhythm to emphasize emotion and action. Recite your poem to a friend when you are finished.

Compare Texts

TEXT TO TEXT

Compare Portrayals of Athletes Choose a poem from "Score!" and a passage from "Double Dutch" that describe the movements of athletes. Discuss how the pictures they create in your mind are the same and different. In your comparison, focus on the word choice and the kinds of images used by each writer. Use quotes from both texts to support your thoughts.

TEXT TO SELF

Write a Poem You have read several poems relating to sports and athletes. Write a poem or song about your favorite free-time activity. Use rhyme, rhythm, and sound to show how you feel about the activity. Remember that rhyme is a sound device that can create rhythm or a certain feeling.

TEXT TO WORLD

Summarize a Newspaper Article "Double Dutch" originally appeared as an article in the *New York Times*. Look through a local newspaper and choose an article that interests you. Note the main ideas and supporting ideas in the article, and summarize those points for a classmate.

COMMON CORE **RL.5.1** quote accurately when explaining what a text says explicitly and when drawing inferences; **RI.5.2** determine two or more main ideas and explain how they are supported by details/summarize; **W.5.10** write routinely over extended time frames and shorter time frames

Grammar

What Are Common and Proper Nouns? When you talk or write about a general person, place, or thing, you use a **common noun.** When you talk or write about a particular person, place, or thing, you use a **proper noun.** Capitalize every proper noun.

Common Nouns	Proper Nouns
boy	Al Moniz
street	Century Boulevard

The name of an organization is a proper noun. Capitalize every important word in the name. Some organizations use a name made up of **initials,** or the first letter of each important word. If a name made from initials can be read as a word, it is called an **acronym.** Acronyms and other names made of initials are written with all capital letters. An **abbreviation** is a shortened form of a word. An abbreviation of a proper noun begins with a capital letter and usually ends with a period.

Name of organization	Uptown Jump Rope Club
Organization initials	SCA (Sports Clubs of America)
Acronym	NATO [NAY toh] (North Atlantic Treaty Organization)
Abbreviation	Mr. (Mister)

Try This! **With a partner, find in the following sentences a common noun, a proper noun, the name of an organization, a name made up of initials, and an acronym.**

❶ My sister wants to work for NASA or the FBI.

❷ She is a member of the Lubbock Junior Scientists Club.

❸ Her hero is Sally Ride.

You have learned to capitalize important words in names of organizations. You also have learned to capitalize all letters in acronyms and names made of initials. When you proofread your work, make sure you have written these items correctly. Remember to capitalize proper nouns such as street names, as well.

Incorrect Capitalization	Correct Capitalization
Wed., oct. 8 7:00 P.M.	Wed., Oct. 8 7:00 P.M.
Come to a lecture by dr. Roberta price of the American double dutch Association. You may know it by its acronym, Adda. Dr. price has appeared many times on programs on Pbs, the Public Broadcasting system.	Come to a lecture by Dr. Roberta Price of the American Double Dutch Association. You may know it by its acronym, ADDA. Dr. Price has appeared many times on programs on PBS, the Public Broadcasting System.

 ## Connect Grammar to Writing

As you revise your fictional narrative next week, look for proper nouns of all kinds. If you find a proper noun that you have not capitalized, rewrite it with correct capitalization.

Narrative Writing

Reading-Writing Workshop: Prewrite

☑ **Ideas** Good writers explore their topic before they write a draft. As you prepare to write your **fictional narrative,** ask yourself questions such as *Who? Where? What?* Write down words and phrases that you might build into a story.

Chermaine decided to write about a school event. While thinking about her topic, she made notes about her characters, setting, and events. Later, she organized her ideas into a story map. Use the Writing Process Checklist below as you prewrite.

Writing Process Checklist

▶ **Prewrite**

☑ Do I have enough ideas for a story?

☑ Who are my characters?

☑ Where and when does my story take place?

☑ What are the most important events?

☑ Did I include a problem and a solution?

Draft

Revise

Edit

Publish and Share

Exploring a Topic

Who?
- two basketball teams

Where?
- school playground
- basketball court

What?
- argue about using the hoop
- compete in the playoff game

Story Map

Characters	Setting
Elly and her team: good kids Ike and his team: bullies	School playground and basketball court

Plot

Problem: Some players can't practice because bullies hog the basketball hoop.

Event 1: Elly is chosen to lead the class team.

Event 2: Ike's team won't let them use the hoop.

Event 3: Elly's team ∧ secretly practices every evening.

Solution: Elly's team wins the big game.

Everyone is surprised! ∧

Reading as a Writer

How did Chermaine's story map help her develop new ideas? What ideas could you add to your story map?

I got some new ideas as I was making my story map. I started adding details about the plot.

Vocabulary in Context

ELISA'S DIARY

WORDS FREE AS CONFETTI

☑ **TARGET VOCABULARY**

opponents
brutal
supposedly
gorgeous
embarrassed
obvious
typically
preliminary
sweeping
officially

Vocabulary Reader

Context Cards

JOURNALS OF THE WEST

COMMON CORE **L.5.4c** consult reference materials, both print and digital, to find pronunciation and determine or clarify meaning

1 opponents

There must be at least two opponents, or rivals, in any competition.

2 brutal

Harsh, or brutal, weather can make running on the field very difficult.

3 supposedly

A school is supposedly, or thought to be, where children learn about the world.

4 gorgeous

Male parrots have gorgeous feathers. The rich colors help them compete for mates.

Go Digital

▶ Study each Context Card.

▶ Use a dictionary or a glossary to help you pronounce the Vocabulary words.

---

5 embarrassed

Don't be embarrassed or ashamed if you have tried your best but failed to win.

---

6 obvious

A clear photo of the finish line makes the winner of the race obvious.

---

7 typically

Plants compete for light. Typically, or usually, those that get more light grow faster.

---

8 preliminary

When strangers meet, shaking hands may be the preliminary, or first, thing they do.

---

9 sweeping

The winner of the election made a broad, sweeping gesture to thank her supporters.

---

10 officially

The judges officially declared this lamb to be the winner of the first-place blue ribbon.

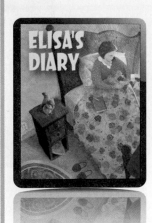

Read and Comprehend

 Go Digital

☑ TARGET SKILL

Theme As you read "Elisa's Diary," look for the **theme,** or central message, of the story. The main character's behavior often provides clues to the theme. Use this graphic organizer to record Elisa's qualities, motives, and actions. These details will help you determine the theme.

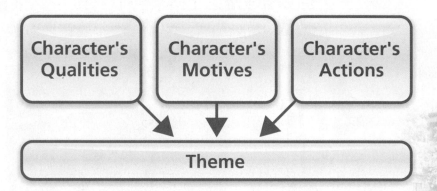

Character's Qualities →

Character's Motives →

Character's Actions →

Theme

☑ TARGET STRATEGY

Visualize When you **visualize,** you use details in the text to form vivid mental pictures of the characters, settings, and events. As you read "Elisa's Diary," pause now and then to visualize what is happening. Use your mental pictures to help you understand the story's meaning.

PREVIEW THE TOPIC

Language and Expression

Language conveys more than just facts. We use words to express our feelings, to share our experiences, and to make our friends laugh. People who speak the same language can get to know each other easily. People who don't may struggle to understand each other.

In the story you are about to read, Elisa has just moved to the United States. She has plenty of thoughts and feelings, but she feels awkward expressing them in English. When she starts school, she must find a way to overcome this language barrier and adjust to her new home.

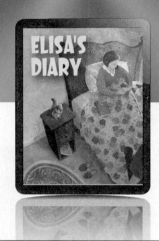

☑ **TARGET SKILL**

Theme Examine the main character's actions and response to problems to help you determine the story's theme, or message.

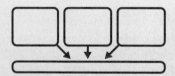

☑ **GENRE**

Realistic fiction includes characters and events that are like people and events in real life. As you read, look for:

▸ challenges and conflicts that might happen in real life
▸ characters' feelings that seem believable

COMMON CORE RL.5.2 determine theme from details/summarize; **RL.5.10** read and comprehend literature

MEET THE AUTHOR
Doris Luisa Oronoz

After Doris Luisa Oronoz and her family moved from Puerto Rico to the United States, her children went through experiences and feelings very similar to those that Elisa goes through. Oronoz has said that although this story is not based on real events, the emotions of Elisa's character are drawn from her memory. They are a meditation on the joys and difficulties children encounter when they move to a new place.

MEET THE ILLUSTRATOR
Byron Gin

Byron Gin lives near Chicago, Illinois, with his wife and two cats, Bear and Kathe. Born in California, Gin worked as an illustrator and printmaker before becoming a full-time painter. One group of his paintings, *Street Series*, captures people Gin has glimpsed while walking through downtown Chicago.

ELISA'S DIARY

by Doris Luisa Oronoz
Illustrated by Byron Gin

ESSENTIAL QUESTION

How can overcoming a challenge change someone's life?

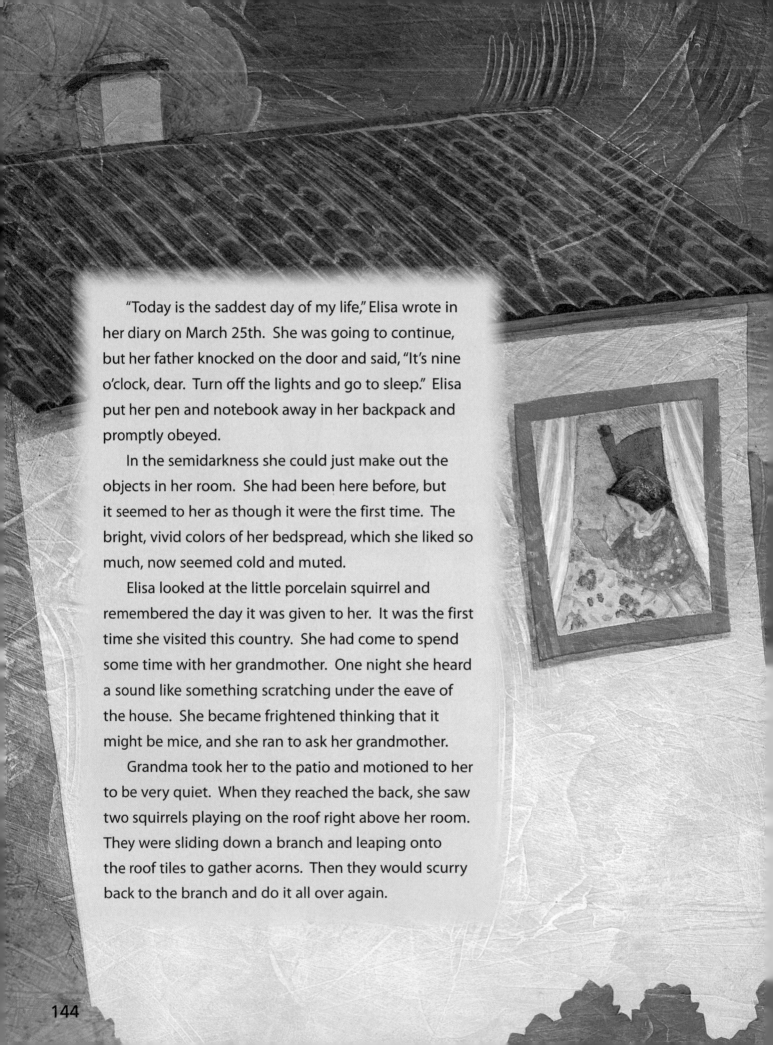

"Today is the saddest day of my life," Elisa wrote in her diary on March 25th. She was going to continue, but her father knocked on the door and said, "It's nine o'clock, dear. Turn off the lights and go to sleep." Elisa put her pen and notebook away in her backpack and promptly obeyed.

In the semidarkness she could just make out the objects in her room. She had been here before, but it seemed to her as though it were the first time. The bright, vivid colors of her bedspread, which she liked so much, now seemed cold and muted.

Elisa looked at the little porcelain squirrel and remembered the day it was given to her. It was the first time she visited this country. She had come to spend some time with her grandmother. One night she heard a sound like something scratching under the eave of the house. She became frightened thinking that it might be mice, and she ran to ask her grandmother.

Grandma took her to the patio and motioned to her to be very quiet. When they reached the back, she saw two squirrels playing on the roof right above her room. They were sliding down a branch and leaping onto the roof tiles to gather acorns. Then they would scurry back to the branch and do it all over again.

Since there were no squirrels in her country, this was a new experience. She enjoyed watching the squirrels so much that when her vacation was over, Grandma bought her a squirrel figurine and put it on her night table.

"It will be right here waiting for you when you get back."

"I'll be back soon, Grandma. I love this place. Maybe some day I'll come and live with you."

But that was then and this is now.

"Who needs squirrels?" she asked herself.

She closed her eyes and breathed deeply. She was exhausted. It had been a long day that for some reason had gone slowly. That morning she had been in Puerto Rico, and now she was in the United States of America. Except that this time, supposedly, it was forever. A tear rolled down her cheek and landed on the pillow.

Elisa was ten years old, and her brother Francisco was twelve. At least if they were going to go to the same school, she would have felt protected, but they weren't. And of course, boys at that age typically don't want anything to do with their little sisters anyway.

"He's unbearable," she thought aloud. Just then, her brother came in.

"Who's unbearable?" asked Francisco.

"You," answered Elisa, holding nothing back.

"Oh? Why is that?" asked her brother, surprised.

"Because you leave me alone all day while you're out running around."

"It's obvious that you're afraid to go out," answered her brother. "Look, I've met some neighbors, and they're nice."

"And in what language do you speak to them, huh?"

"Well, in English."

"I can imagine the crazy things you come up with."

"But at least I try," retorted her brother. "What you have to do is make an effort. If they don't understand me, I talk with my hands until something happens."

"I write well in English, and when I read, I understand a lot. But now, when they speak to me, I don't understand a word."

"Listen, the woman who lives in the house on the corner—"

"Which one?" interrupted Elisa.

"The one who gave me two dollars to take care of her cat."

"What about her?"

"She told me that she used to listen to the news on the radio and got used to hearing English that way. Then, little by little, she understood English better and better."

"I don't like the radio," declared Elisa.

"Turn on the TV, then, but not to those lovey-dovey soaps in Spanish and all that silly stuff you like."

"What do you want me to watch, then?"

"Things from here, like baseball, football . . ."

"Football is brutal. I despise sports!"

"Oh well, if you'd rather be ignorant . . ."

"O.K., forget it."

ANALYZE THE TEXT

Dialogue What does the dialogue between Elisa and Francisco reveal about each character? What makes it realistic?

Elisa regretted ever having wanted to be in the same school as her know-it-all brother. She'd have to solve her problem on her own, but how?

The summer came to an end, and the school year commenced. That's when she met José. That day she wrote in her diary,

I met a student from Guatemala. He's very quiet, and he spends all his time with his head down, drawing in a notebook. He has sad, dark eyes. I thought he was going to talk to me once, but he didn't. He just smiled and kept on drawing.

She read what she had written and added, "I think I'm going to like this school after all."

The fact is that she didn't like the school one bit. The second day of classes, the English teacher called her name, which sounded more like "Alisha" than "Elisa." She got up from her desk expecting a disaster, and that's exactly what happened. She was asked a question that she didn't understand. When it was repeated, she understood even less. She was so nervous that she could only stammer a few syllables "*eh, ah, ah, uh.*" She couldn't continue, and she collapsed in her seat in front of those forty faces—her opponents—some disbelieving, some mocking. How embarrassing!

Around noon, José's turn came. He got up, and he spoke shyly of the customs and traditions of his country. He mentioned the quetzal—a bird with soft feathers, a green crest, and a red chest. He told how this gorgeous bird was the symbol of power for the Maya and that today it is officially the national bird of Guatemala. Finally, he showed them a color drawing and told them proudly that the quetzal on the Guatemalan flag was an emblem of national liberty.

Everyone clapped. He sat down, and, as always, he put his head down and went back to drawing.

In the afternoon each student wrote a composition. Elisa wrote about her home, Puerto Rico. Like José, she described its customs and traditions and explained the symbolism of Puerto Rico's shield—a lamb, the emblem of peace and fraternity, appears in the green center. Above the lamb is a bundle of arrows, symbols of the creative force, and above the arrows is a yoke, which represents the joining of forces necessary to attain success. She thought it turned out pretty well, but writing was one thing and talking was another.

That night she didn't open her diary because she was tired of complaining, even if it was only to her diary.

The next morning Elisa smiled for the first time since classes had started. She got a good grade on her composition. She wanted to show it to everyone so that they'd see that she wasn't so dumb, but she didn't do it. Maybe she'd show it to José, though. Yes, to him. So during recess she called to him and proudly showed him her paper. He looked at it and, lowering his eyes, he said with a brief smile, "Congratulations."

"Thanks." said Elisa. "And how did you do?"

"O.K."

"No doubt you got an A and you don't want me to be embarrassed."

"No, it's not that, Elisa. It's that...I picked up English by listening. You know, 'on the street.' I never took English in school. I write it like I hear it, and everything comes out wrong."

Elisa read the paper that he handed her, and in one sweeping glance, she saw what he meant. She didn't know what to say.

"But you speak it very well," Elisa tried to console him.

"Speaking is one thing and writing is another."

"And vice-versa," said Elisa.

"And the opposite."

"And the other way around."

They laughed so hard that the rest of the kids came over to see what was so humorous, but they didn't tell anyone their secret. That afternoon, they made a deal. She would assist him with writing, and he, in turn, would help her with pronunciation.

Twelve years later, Elisa was getting ready for work. She pulled down a box of shoes from the top shelf of her closet. In the rush, several things fell on top of her. One of them was her old diary. It fell open to the last page. She picked it up and read.

Today I received my high school diploma. When I looked at myself in the mirror with my cap and gown and my gold honors tassels, I remembered the little girl who arrived here confused, scared, and sad. I'm happy now.

ANALYZE THE TEXT

Theme What is the theme of the story? How does Elisa's change over the course of the story support the theme?

She put away the notebook, got dressed, and headed for work. When she entered the classroom, her students looked at her—some shy, some confused, some scared. She saw those sad, preliminary, first-day-of-school looks that she knew so well.

She opened her lesson planner, thought a moment, and then shut it. She stood up and wrote on the board, "The joining of forces."

Then she said, "I'm going to tell you the story of a quetzal that came down to the plain with the gentleness of a lamb, and a lamb that soared to great heights on the wings of a quetzal."

ANALYZE THE TEXT

Sequence of Events Why does the author end the story by jumping ahead in time to show Elisa as a teacher? What impact does this change in sequence have on the story?

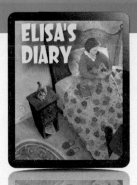

Dig Deeper

How to Analyze the Text

Use these pages to learn about Theme, Dialogue, and Sequence of Events. Then read "Elisa's Diary" again to apply what you learned.

Theme

Short stories such as "Elisa's Diary" convey a **theme**, or a message or lesson that the author wants readers to know. This message is often revealed through the main character's actions—especially how he or she reacts to conflict.

In "Elisa's Diary," the main character, Elisa, faces a conflict. The beginning of the story shows her first attempt at handling her problem. By the end of the story, she has a completely different response. How do her actions show her change of heart? How does this change reveal the theme of the story?

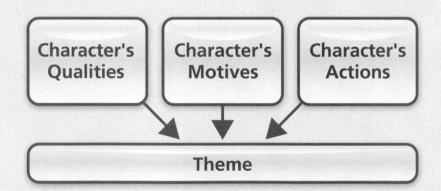

| Character's Qualities | Character's Motives | Character's Actions |

Theme

RL.5.2 determine theme from details/summarize; **RL.5.5** explain how chapters, scenes, or stanzas fit together to provide the overall structure; **RL.5.10** read and comprehend literature; **RF.5.4a** read on-level text with purpose and understanding

Go Digital

Dialogue

Authors use **dialogue,** or the words characters say, to show what characters are like. The dialogue on page 147 includes dashes and ellipses. Dashes (—) signal that one character is interrupting another one. Ellipses (…) indicate that a character's voice is fading away, often before a thought is completed. This punctuation helps make the characters' speech sound more realistic.

Sequence of Events

On page 151, the story's setting moves ahead twelve years from the time when the main action takes place. This jump in **sequence,** or the order of events, allows the author to show a scene with Elisa as an adult, teaching her own classroom of students. By providing this ending to the story, the author affirms that Elisa's conflict has been resolved. The story's overall structure is completed.

Your Turn

RETURN TO THE ESSENTIAL QUESTION

 With a partner, review the selection to prepare to discuss this question: *How can overcoming a challenge change someone's life?* Share your ideas with other pairs of students. Support your ideas using text evidence.

Classroom Conversation

Continue your discussion of "Elisa's Diary" by explaining your answers to these questions:

1 Is Elisa a believable character? Why or why not? What text evidence supports your opinion?

2 What do you think is the hardest part of learning a new language?

3 What does the end of the story show about Elisa's character?

COMPARE STORY SETTINGS

Discuss It In "Elisa's Diary," readers see Elisa in two settings, at home and at school. With a partner, use the details in the story to compare and contrast these two settings. Then discuss how Elisa acts, feels, and thinks in each place. Share what you learn about Elisa's character from the differences and similarities you find.

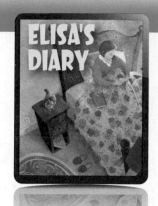

Response A conflict in a character's past may affect his or her future. Write a paragraph explaining the conflict that Elisa faces in the story. Tell how she overcomes it. Also include your opinion about how this conflict may have influenced Elisa's choice of career. Support your points with quotations, details, and other text evidence.

Writing Tip

Write a topic sentence that identifies the main idea of your paragraph. Then present your supporting details in the sentences that follow.

COMMON CORE **RL.5.3** compare and contrast characters, settings, or events, drawing on details; **W.5.1a** introduce a topic, state an opinion, and create an organizational structure; **W.5.10** write routinely over extended time frames and shorter time frames; **SL.5.1a** come to discussions prepared/explicitly draw on preparation and other information about the topic; **SL.5.1c** pose and respond to questions, make comments that contribute to the discussion, and elaborate on others' remarks

POETRY

WORDS FREE AS CONFETTI

RL.5.10 read and comprehend literature

WORDS FREE AS CONFETTI

BY PAT MORA
ILLUSTRATED BY ALESSANDRA CIMATORIBUS

Come, words, come in your every color.
I'll toss you in a storm or breeze.
I'll say, say, say you,
taste you sweet as plump plums,
bitter as old lemons.
I'll sniff you, words, warm
as almonds or tart as apple-red,
feel you green

and soft as new grass,
lightwhite as dandelion plumes,
or thorngray as cactus,
heavy as black cement,
cold as blue icicles,
warm as *abuelita's* yellowlap.
I'll hear you, words, loud as searoar's
purple crash, hushed

as *gatitos* curled in sleep,
as the last goldlullaby.
I'll see you long and dark as tunnels,
bright as rainbows,
playful as chestnutwind.
I'll watch you, words, rise and dance and spin.
I'll say, say, say you
in English,
in Spanish,

I'll find you.
Hold you.
Toss you.
I'm free too.
I say *yo soy libre*,
I am free
free, free,
free as confetti.

Compare Texts

TEXT TO TEXT

Compare Texts About Language "Elisa's Diary" and "Words Free as Confetti" share the topic of language. With a partner, discuss how the views of language are the same or different in each text. Make a list of quotes and examples from the texts to support your thoughts. Then share a summary of your key points with the class.

TEXT TO SELF

Write About a Challenge In "Elisa's Diary," the main character overcomes a challenge in order to be successful. Think of a challenge you have overcome. Write a short composition describing the challenge, your feelings about it, and what you learned.

TEXT TO WORLD

Compare Themes Find the poem's theme by thinking about its title and the reason the poet compares words to confetti. What is confetti like? What images does the poet create with words? Then use what you've learned to state the poem's theme. Compare that theme to the message "Elisa's Diary" conveys. Explain how these messages can be useful around the world.

Go
Digital

COMMON CORE **RL.5.1** quote accurately when explaining what the text says explicitly and when drawing inferences; **RL.5.2** determine theme from details/ summarize; **RL.5.9** compare and contrast stories in the same genre on their approaches to themes and topics; **W.5.10** write routinely over extended time frames and shorter time frames; **SL.5.1a** come to discussions prepared/explicitly draw on preparation and other information about the topic

Grammar

 Go Digital

How Are Plural Nouns Formed? A noun that names only one person, place, or thing is a **singular noun**. A noun that names more than one person, place, or thing is a **plural noun**. Most plural nouns are formed by adding *-s* or *-es*. Some are formed in other ways and need to be memorized.

Singular Nouns	Plural Nouns
Robin made one shot in the first half.	She made a total of five shots in both halves.
The coach spoke at a rally.	The coaches spoke at rallies.
The man runs like a deer.	The men run like deer.

A **collective noun** names a group of people, animals, or things that act as a unit. A collective noun is treated as a singular noun, unless it names more than one group or collection.

singular collective noun

Our local team wins the tough games.

plural collective noun

Our local teams win the tough games.

 **Try This!** **Copy each sentence onto a sheet of paper. Change the underlined singular nouns to plural nouns.**

1 The new <u>student</u> greeted the teachers.

2 During recess, friends sat on the <u>bench</u>.

3 The frisky <u>squirrel</u> gathered acorns.

4 The new books are on the <u>shelf</u>.

You have learned how to use singular and plural nouns to show exactly what you mean. Using exact nouns in your writing will create clear pictures for your readers. It also will help make your writing interesting and easy to understand.

Less Exact Noun	More Exact Noun
A fan brought his pet to the track meet.	A fan brought his iguana to the track meet.

 ## Connect Grammar to Writing

As you revise your fictional narrative, add exact nouns that will make your descriptions easy for readers to understand. Remember that exact nouns can be singular or plural. They create clear pictures in your writing.

W.5.3a orient the reader by establishing a situation and introducing a narrator or characters/organize an event sequence; **W.5.3b** use narrative techniques to develop experiences and events or show characters' responses; **W.5.3d** use concrete words and phrases and sensory details; **W.5.3e** provide a conclusion; **W.5.5** develop and strengthen writing by planning, revising, editing, rewriting, or trying a new approach

Narrative Writing

Reading-Writing Workshop: Revise

✔ **Voice**   When you revise a **fictional narrative,** use dialogue to give characters their own distinct voices and to show what they are like. What characters say and how they say it can reveal their feelings and personalities.

Chermaine drafted her story, using the story map she had made. Later, as she revised the story, she added dialogue to bring her characters to life and make her story more realistic.

Writing Process Checklist

Prewrite

Draft

▶ **Revise**

- ✔ **Did I create distinctive voices for my narrator and each of my characters?**
- ✔ **Did I include only events that are important to my plot?**
- ✔ **Did I use natural-sounding dialogue and exact details?**
- ✔ **Did I include a variety of sentence types?**
- ✔ **Did I pace my narrative effectively?**
- ✔ **Did I provide a strong conclusion?**

Edit

Publish and Share

Revised Draft

"I can't believe those losers won," Ike moaned. He looked stunned.

∧ ~~When Mrs. Mack's class won the Grade 5 Basketball Playoff, the other team looked~~ He and his team ~~stunned. They~~ had never fought so hard in their lives. With only two minutes left in the game, the score had been tied. Ike was dribbling the ball when elly managed to steal and shoot it. ~~She turned and shot~~ from the middle of the court—a three-point shot!

164

Beating the Basketball Bullies

by Chermaine Jones

"I can't believe those losers won," Ike moaned. He looked stunned. He and his team had never fought so hard in their lives. With only two minutes left in the game, the score had been tied. Ike was dribbling the ball when Elly managed to steal it and shoot from the middle of the court—a three-point shot! From that moment on, it was no contest. Elly's team won the Grade 5 Basketball Playoff, and the crowd went wild.

It was not the outcome the students in the stands had expected. They knew Ike and his team had hogged the practice court at recess every day and tried to intimidate the other fifth-grade team.

"Practice won't help you guys, anyway," Ike had sneered at the other team.

But Elly and her players hadn't been discouraged. They had practiced at the city gym every evening instead, and they had kept their spirits up. As the winning team walked off the court, Elly grinned. "Hey, Ike," she yelled. "Better luck next year!"

Reading as a Writer

What did you learn about the characters from the dialogue? Where can you add dialogue to give your characters a voice?

In my final story, I added dialogue to give my characters a voice. I also capitalized proper nouns.

Read the passage "Hannah's Trip to Space." As you read, stop and use text evidence to answer each question.

Hannah's Trip to Space

The Trip Begins

Today was the big day. Hannah and her class were taking a field trip to Space Center Houston, the visitors' center of NASA's Johnson Space Center, at last. Hannah was the first student to board the bus. Although she lived in Houston, this would be her first visit to the Space Center. She was eager to see the exhibits and learn more about the kinds of work done there. Like many students, Hannah thought she might like to be a scientist. She thought having a job that involved studying outer space would be an amazing experience.

Hannah looked out the window as the bus slowed and made a right turn into the Space Center. The driver pulled up to the front doors and opened the door of the bus. As Hannah stepped off the bus, she exclaimed to her friends, "I am *so* ready to go inside!"

As soon as she stepped into the building, Hannah saw something that made her smile. The person taking visitors' tickets was dressed in a real NASA jumpsuit. It seemed so official!

Inside the Space Center

To her right, Hannah saw a huge play area called the Kids Space Place. It looked like a play center at a fast-food restaurant. Hannah feared it might be a bit babyish. Upon entering the area, though, she realized that it was going to be a real adventure and a great learning experience. Her friend Ryan was also impressed. "Come on, Hannah," he said eagerly. "I bet we can land the model space shuttle all by ourselves."

"Of course we can do it!" Hannah said.

---

1 How does the narrator's point of view affect the way events are described in this passage?

Hannah entered the model and lay down face-up on the seat at the space shuttle controls, as a real astronaut might have done. She concentrated on the monitor above her. Ryan headed into another area, the command center. It was just like the actual command center where scientists had communicated with astronauts during space missions.

RL.5.2 determine theme from details/summarize; **RL.5.3** compare and contrast characters, settings, or events, drawing on details; **RL.5.5** explain how chapters, scenes, or stanzas fit together to provide the overall structure; **RL.5.6** describe how a narrator's or speaker's point of view influences how events are described

Hannah and Ryan could see each other on monitors and talk through microphones. Working together, they followed the procedure for landing the shuttle. When they succeeded, they congratulated each other and celebrated, just as they knew real astronauts and mission control would have done. The model shuttle had never left the ground, but Hannah and Ryan were proud that they had succeeded in meeting the challenge they had set for themselves.

 2 What does Hannah's response to the challenge of landing the model shuttle reveal about her?

Next, it was time to see the Living in Space demonstration. Hannah and her classmates filed onto the metal bleachers to watch the show. There in front of them was what looked exactly like the inside of a space station. A man who introduced himself as a Mission Briefing Officer walked onto the stage. He began by telling the audience about the International Space Station, called the ISS for short.

He explained that fifteen countries worked together over a period of ten years to build the space station. Now the huge station has more living space than a large house with five bedrooms. Hannah was surprised to hear that it even has a gymnasium. More than 200 astronauts from many nations have traveled to the space station and lived there while performing experiments in the labs or taking spacewalks to do work outside the station.

Next, the Mission Briefing Officer explained that he needed some volunteers to demonstrate how astronauts would live, eat, sleep, and work while at the station. Hannah eagerly raised her hand and was overjoyed when she was chosen. She hurried up to the stage with one of her classmates. Together, they demonstrated how daily activities would be completed in space.

The Mission Briefing Officer showed the audience a bed used in space. It didn't look like a normal bed, though. With Hannah's assistance, he showed the audience how an astronaut would use straps to stay in it. Hannah even had to strap her head to the pillow!

The other volunteer demonstrated how astronauts would eat. They would use magnets to attach their knives and forks to a tray to keep them from floating away. Hannah had not realized how difficult it would be to carry out normal routines in space.

3 How are the settings and the events that take place in the Living in Space demonstration and the Kids Space Place similar and different?

After the demonstration, the class visited a full-size model of a space shuttle. It was huge! Inside the flight deck, they saw what real astronauts might have seen when they would fly. Thousands of switches and buttons lined the walls. Hannah couldn't imagine having to learn the purpose of each one.

The Tram Tour

The final part of the field trip was a field trip in itself! The class boarded a tram for a tour of the Space Center. The tram stopped first at Hangar X. Everyone got off the tram and filed into the huge storage facility. There the group saw real space vehicles that were used in the past. The class also visited Memorial Grove, where an oak tree has been planted for each astronaut who has died during a space mission.

The last stop of the day was Rocket Park, where Hannah was excited to see a real Saturn V rocket. The rocket is about thirty-six stories high, taller than the Statue of Liberty. It weighs over six million pounds. Hannah learned that Saturn V rockets had flown twelve historic space missions for the Apollo program, including taking astronauts to the moon. She was thrilled to see one of these gigantic spacecrafts up close.

When the tour ended, the class walked past the Astronaut Gallery. Behind the glass cases were space suits that had been worn by real astronauts. As Hannah looked at them, she imagined herself working alongside the scientists who studied space. "Maybe they'll be sending astronauts back into space by the time we're scientists, Hannah," Ryan said, coming to stand next to her.

"Maybe we'll *be* those astronauts!" Hannah said. "You never know."

4 How do all three sections of the passage fit together and help develop the passage's theme?

Unit 2

☑ TARGET VOCABULARY

dwarfed

presence

procedure

outfitted

transferred

calculate

snug

perch

enthusiastic

beaming

Vocabulary
Reader

Context
Cards

L.5.6 acquire and use general academic and domain-specific words and phrases

170

Vocabulary in Context

1 dwarfed

This baby kangaroo is dwarfed by the larger mother kangaroo.

2 presence

Wildlife photographers have to be careful that their presence doesn't scare away animals.

3 procedure

The veterinarian explained the procedure and said the cat would be fine.

4 outfitted

This woman is outfitted, or equipped, with a glove to protect her from the owl's talons.

Go Digital

▶ Study each Context Card.

▶ Use a dictionary or a glossary to clarify the part of speech of each Vocabulary word.

5 **transferred**

This baby alligator will be transferred, or moved, to another area when it grows larger.

6 **calculate**

To calculate a cheetah's speed, measure the time it takes to cover a certain distance.

7 **snug**

It is important for an animal's collar to be snug, but not so tight that it is uncomfortable.

8 **perch**

Eagles and many other birds roost high on a perch to see prey or to avoid predators.

9 **enthusiastic**

This dog is quite enthusiastic about chasing and catching flying discs.

10 **beaming**

This girl is beaming over the news that her family is going to adopt the puppy.

Read and Comprehend

Go Digital

☑ TARGET SKILL

Cause and Effect As you read "Quest for the Tree Kangaroo," look for causes and their effects. A **cause** is an event that makes something else happen. An **effect** is something that happens because of an earlier event. Use text evidence and a graphic organizer like this one to help you identify the cause-and-effect relationships in the selection.

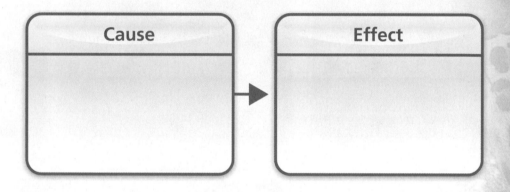

Cause	Effect

☑ TARGET STRATEGY

Question As you read "Quest for the Tree Kangaroo," pause frequently to ask yourself what events lead to others and what events are caused by earlier ones. Asking and answering **questions** as you read can help you identify cause-and-effect relationships.

Wild Animals

Wild animals are those that have not been domesticated, or tamed, by humans. They include the squirrels and pigeons you see every day and the exotic animals that live in faraway jungles and deep ocean waters. Many wild animals are endangered—their numbers are so low that they might disappear completely. Climate change, loss of habitat, and overhunting all contribute to the decline in animal populations.

The Matschie's tree kangaroo is an endangered species. It lives in the rain forests of Papua New Guinea. Because tree kangaroos spend most of their time in trees, scientists must work hard to locate and study them. When you read "Quest for the Tree Kangaroo," you will go along on one of these scientific adventures.

ANCHOR TEXT

QUEST FOR THE TREE KANGAROO
AN EXPEDITION TO THE CLOUD FOREST OF NEW GUINEA
text by SY MONTGOMERY
photographs by NIC BISHOP

 TARGET SKILL

Cause and Effect Determine which events lead to others. Trace the relationships between causes and effects.

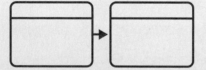

 GENRE

Informational text gives facts and examples about a topic. As you read, look for:
▶ text structure, or the way ideas and information are organized
▶ facts and details about a specific topic

 COMMON CORE **RI.5.3** explain the relationships between individuals/events/ideas/concepts in a text; **RI.5.10** read and comprehend informational texts; **L.5.6** acquire and use general academic and domain-specific words and phrases

 Go Digital

MEET THE AUTHOR

Sy Montgomery

Award-winning author Sy Montgomery travels the world to study animals. Sometimes she faces the unexpected. "Once, in Borneo, an orangutan ate my interview tapes," she says, describing one of many memorable incidents. Her adventures can require her "to hike for days and swim for miles." She calls her trip to the cloud forest of New Guinea her most physically difficult one so far.

MEET THE PHOTOGRAPHER

Nic Bishop

Nic Bishop is a nature photographer and author of many books. Some of his animal photographs are taken in a studio, while others are taken in far-off places, in animals' natural habitats. After traveling a great distance for a project, there is a lot of pressure to capture great photographs. "I simply cannot afford to be tired, or get ill, since there is never going to be a chance to repeat anything," he says.

QUEST FOR THE TREE KANGAROO

by Sy Montgomery
photographs by Nic Bishop

ESSENTIAL QUESTION

Why is it important to research and protect endangered animals?

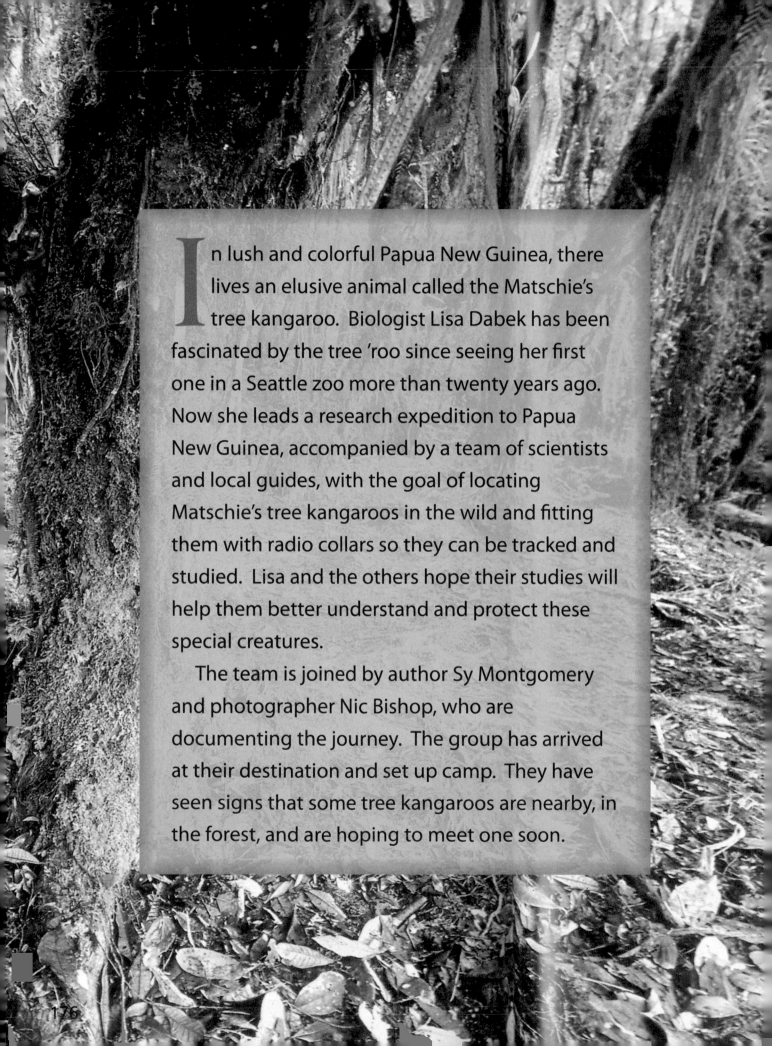

In lush and colorful Papua New Guinea, there lives an elusive animal called the Matschie's tree kangaroo. Biologist Lisa Dabek has been fascinated by the tree 'roo since seeing her first one in a Seattle zoo more than twenty years ago. Now she leads a research expedition to Papua New Guinea, accompanied by a team of scientists and local guides, with the goal of locating Matschie's tree kangaroos in the wild and fitting them with radio collars so they can be tracked and studied. Lisa and the others hope their studies will help them better understand and protect these special creatures.

The team is joined by author Sy Montgomery and photographer Nic Bishop, who are documenting the journey. The group has arrived at their destination and set up camp. They have seen signs that some tree kangaroos are nearby, in the forest, and are hoping to meet one soon.

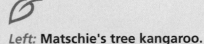

Left: **Matschie's tree kangaroo.**

Opposite page: **Cool winds have dwarfed some parts of the forest so it is only about twenty feet high.**

LISA IS WASHING HER CLOTHES IN THE RIVER WHEN WE GET THE NEWS: "TREE 'ROOS," CALLS HOLLY. "TWO OF them!"

One of the trackers has run back to camp to tell us. The two tree kangaroos are "klostu"[1] us—and still up a tree. While Holly and Christine ready the medical equipment, the rest of us race after the tracker to see.

We run past the tree kangaroo house, past the kunai,[2] down a trail—and then into the trackless bush. Will the tree kangaroos still be there when we get there?

It takes us nearly an hour to reach the site. We see the long golden tail hanging down from the branches of a Saurauia[3]—and then the animal to whom it belongs: a gorgeous red and gold tree kangaroo sitting eighty feet above us, looking down with ears pricked forward.

"I can't believe it!" Lisa says.

And then, in the tree right next to this tree kangaroo, we see another tail—leading to another tree kangaroo.

"Bigpela pikinini!" one of the trackers exclaims. "Pikinini" is Tok Pisin for child or baby. And "bigpela"? You guessed it: If this is her baby, it's a big one.

---

[1] klostu: "close to" in Tok Pisin—a popular language spoken in Papua New Guinea
[2] kunai: the area where Lisa and her team have set up camp, named for the kind of grass it has
[3] Saurauia: tree kangaroos love to eat the shoots of this flowering tree

ANALYZE THE TEXT

Cause and Effect When the tracker climbs a nearby tree, what effect does it have on the tree kangaroos?

Matschie's tree kangaroo is one of the world's rarest and most elusive mammals.

"This is the miracle of doing work here," Lisa says. "They are so elusive. And then you finally find them. The whole field season is riding on these moments."

The men had left camp that morning feeling lucky. "It was sunny and warm," Gabriel recalled. "A good day for the tree 'roos to come out and warm themselves." They changed their strategy: "For the first three days, we were traveling more than one kilometer each day to find tree 'roos. I had wanted our presence to drive them closer to camp. So we decided today to try closer—and it worked."

The men spread out. One tracker decided he would look for a plant that the tree kangaroos love to eat. It grows high on tree branches and is easy to spot. The underside is brown and the top green. He found one in a tree— but no tree kangaroo. He scanned the next tree over—the *Saurauia*—and there was the tail!

"Immediately," the tracker explained through Gabriel, "I barked like a dog because that would keep her up in the tree. Everyone else heard the barking and knew what happened. Everyone ran and admired the 'roo. We all stood looking for about two minutes. And then someone noticed there was another tail."

We photograph and videotape and watch the two tree kangaroos for ten minutes. Now to get the animals down …

The trackers have been thinking about this puzzle. Shortly after they spotted the animals, they began to cut sticks and brush to build a low fence they call an "im" around the tree. If the tree kangaroo leaps down and starts to hop away, the im will slow him down.

One of the trackers takes off his tall rubber boots. Barefoot, he begins to climb a smaller tree next to the *Saurauia*. Within two minutes, he's as high as the tree kangaroo.

"Joel, do you see where she is?" asks Lisa. Joel has the 'roo in his binoculars. "She's still there," he assures.

But the tree kangaroo isn't happy to see a human approaching. She climbs another 30 feet up to get away. If she jumps, it's a 110-foot drop.

Suddenly, she leaps, her forearms outstretched. She drops 30 feet. She grabs a smaller tree on the way down. And now she begins to back down the tree.

She's almost to the ground when one of the trackers grabs her by the tail and puts her in the burlap bag.

"Pikinini! Pikinini!" the men call. The other tree kangaroo is 65 feet up in a *Decaspermum* tree, and they don't want him to get away. The tree kangaroo lets go of the branch. Like an acrobat, he catches a vine with his front paws, turns himself around, and lands on the ground on his feet. One tracker holds the chest, another holds the back legs, and another man holds the front.

It's only now that we realize that the "baby" is a fully grown adult male. "Man na meri" the trackers say—this pair is no mother and baby, but a grown-up male and female on a tree kangaroo date. By 10:10 A.M., both tree kangaroos are in burlap bags, heading back to camp.

Twenty-five minutes later, we're all back in camp, where Holly and Christine have set up the exam table—a picnic table built from saplings lashed with vines. They've laid out medical supplies and sample vials, measuring tools and data sheets. Each tree kangaroo will be given medicine to make it sleep while the team puts on the radio collar and conducts a health exam.

We want to find out as much as we can. Because so little is known about tree kangaroos, every detail is important.

First, while the animals are in their burlap bags, they are weighed. The female weighs 6.4 kilograms (about 14 pounds) with the bag. The scientists will make sure to subtract the weight of the bag alone later. The male, with bag, weighs 8 kilograms.

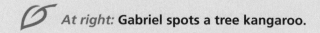

At right: **Gabriel spots a tree kangaroo.**

Joel notes the temperature and humidity, too: It's 56.2 degrees Fahrenheit, 81 percent humidity.

"Let's measure the male's neck, to make sure the radio collar will fit on him," says Lisa. "But let's do the female first."

"With the female, we'll have the same priorities," Holly tells the group. "We'll measure the neck, put on the radio collar, insert the ID chip, pluck fur for more testing, check the pouch—see if she has a baby."

We hope to find out as much as we can while the animal is asleep. But anesthesia can be dangerous. That's why we'll be carefully watching how often she breathes in and out and how fast her heart is beating during the procedure. We'll have to work fast. Everyone will help.

"Christine will call out pulse and respiration every five minutes," says Holly. "Is everybody ready?"

"Do you have the radio collar?" Lisa asks Gabriel.

Gabriel is holding a leather collar much like one a dog might wear. Instead of metal tags, though, it has a little box of waterproof plastic. This contains a transmitter powered by a square battery and outfitted with an internal antenna. Each radio collar also has a computer chip. Without knowing it, the tree kangaroos will be sending their position not only to the scientists tracking them on the ground, but also to satellites circling thousands of miles above Earth. At six A.M. and six P.M.—times the 'roos are likely to be in the trees and the weather is likely to be less cloudy—the satellites read the animals' exact position on the earth's surface. They download this information to the chips in the collars, and this data can be transferred to a computer when the collar automatically falls off, after five months. The whole thing weighs less than half a pound.

Above: **A Matschie's looks down from eighty feet in the canopy.**

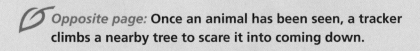
Opposite page: **Once an animal has been seen, a tracker climbs a nearby tree to scare it into coming down.**

ANALYZE THE TEXT

Domain-Specific Vocabulary
What science terminology does the author use on this page while describing the purpose of the radio collar being fitted on the tree kangaroo? How does it affect your understanding?

183

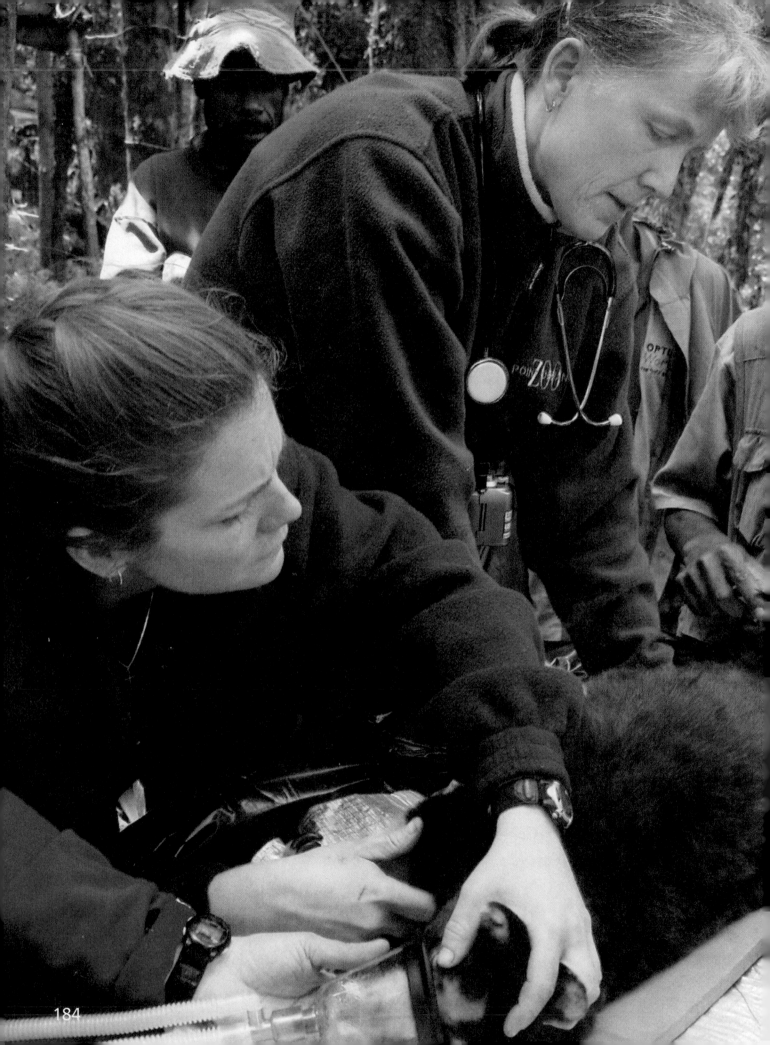

"Do you have the screwdriver to put the collar on?" asks Lisa.

"Yes, yes," says Gabriel, holding the squirming bag on his lap. "We're ready!"

But the tree kangaroo isn't. Gabriel talks to the animal in the bag. "Wait, wait, come here," he says gently. And then, to two trackers: "Hold 'im!" Soon a pink nose pokes out through a hole in the bag.

It's 10:55 A.M. and Holly places the mask on the nose. A paw comes out through the hole. But within forty-five seconds, the tree kangaroo relaxes. The anesthesia's working. She's asleep.

Out comes the kangaroo. "Thermometer?" Holly requests.

The kangaroo's body temperature is similar to a person's: 97.1 degrees.

"Respiration is thirty-two," says Christine. That means she's breathing thirty-two times a minute. That's healthy.

Holly leans forward to listen to the heart through her stethoscope. For five seconds, she counts the beats. She wants to calculate the beats per minute. "Heart rate is sixteen times twelve. You do the math," she tells Joel, who is recording everything on a data sheet.

Meanwhile, Gabriel is putting on the collar. "Make sure the collar is comfortable but snug," says Lisa. (Yesterday Christine discovered that Ombum[4] had taken his off and left it on the floor of his cage.)

---

[4] Ombum: a tree kangaroo that was examined earlier and is being treated for an injured leg

Opposite page: **Christine and Holly get to work.**

ANALYZE THE TEXT

Quotes and Description Why do you think the author includes quotes from the research team and detailed descriptions of their work?

Holly takes a hair sample for DNA analysis.

Everything is going like clockwork. Then Christine warns, "Respiration slowing …"

"That's it. Let's pull the mask off," says Lisa.

It's 11:37 A.M. "His ears are twitching. Let's get him back in the bag," says Holly.

It's all over in just ten minutes. "Great work," says Lisa.

Noon. We're at the tree kangaroo house.[5] The men have cut fern fronds and lined the two apartments inside with this soft, moist carpet. They've used ferns to screen the wall between the new pair and Ombum, so the animals won't upset each other. Ombum looks calm. Though his leg is no better, he is now taking banana leaves from Christine's hands.

We all sit quietly while one of the trackers opens the cage door. Tess climbs out of the bag and scurries up a perch. She regards us with interest, but no fear. Lisa has named the male Christopher—in honor of my pig, who grew to 750 pounds and lived to age fourteen. The kangaroo Christopher rushes out of his bag and climbs to the highest perch.

Joel and Gabriel want to make sure the collars are working, so they have brought their radio receivers along to check. Each animal has its own frequency, almost like a phone number. If Joel wants to tune in to Tess, he dials up channel 151.080. Christopher's channel is 150.050. Both collars work fine.

We're all delighted. One tracker is so enthusiastic, he wants to go out and hunt for more tree kangaroos this very afternoon. "But the hotel is full!" says Lisa. Since Christopher and Tess are healthy enough to return to the wild, they will be released tomorrow. For now, though, the cage has all the tree kangaroos it can hold.

We all shake hands, hug, and smile. Everyone is beaming with a mixture of excitement, exhaustion—and relief.

"The first collared male Matschie's tree kangaroo," says Gabriel. "History!"

---

[5] tree kangaroo house: a fourteen-foot by eight-foot enclosure the team has built using sticks, vines, and mosses to keep the kangaroos comfortable

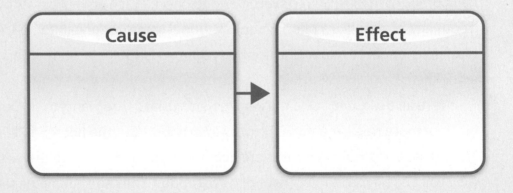

Dig Deeper

How to Analyze the Text

Use these pages to learn about Cause and Effect, Quotes and Description, and Domain-Specific Vocabulary. Then read "Quest for the Tree Kangaroo" again to apply what you learned.

Cause and Effect

In the informational text "Quest for the Tree Kangaroo," many of the events have **cause-and-effect** relationships. One event, called the cause, leads to a later event, called the effect. This effect can then become the cause for another effect, creating a chain of events that are related.

Look back at page 189 of "Quest for the Tree Kangaroo." After the male tree kangaroo has been under anesthesia for several minutes, his respiration begins to slow. What decision does Lisa make as a result? What effect does her decision have?

Cause	Effect

COMMON CORE

RI.5.3 explain the relationships between individuals/events/ideas/concepts in a text; **RI.5.4** determine the meaning of general academic and domain-specific words and phrases; **RI.5.10** read and comprehend informational texts; **RF.5.4a** read on-level text with purpose and understanding

Quotes and Description

To share information with readers in an engaging way, the author of "Quest for the Tree Kangaroo" includes **quotations**, or the exact words spoken by the team members. She also writes detailed **descriptions** of what the scientists see and do. Look back at pages 186–189. The conversation and the explanation of the scientists' actions help readers imagine they are right there as the tree kangaroos are examined.

Domain-Specific Vocabulary

Many subject areas have their own special set of vocabulary. These terms, known as **domain-specific words**, express precise ideas and concepts related to the subject. By using domain-specific terms in their writing, authors can communicate accurate information to their readers. For example, the scientists in this selection don't just give the tree kangaroos "some medicine"—they administer *anesthesia*, a medicine that makes the animals unconscious for a short time.

Habitat

Your Turn

RETURN TO THE ESSENTIAL QUESTION

 Turn and Talk Review the selection to prepare to discuss this question: *Why is it important to research and protect endangered animals?* With a partner, list reasons drawn from text evidence and your prior knowledge. Share them with the class.

 Classroom Conversation

Continue your discussion of "Quest for the Tree Kangaroo" by using text evidence to answer these questions:

1. How do the team members feel about the work they are doing? How do you know?

2. What are the challenges of studying the tree kangaroo?

3. Does the author do a good job of presenting information about tree kangaroos? Explain.

WHAT DOES IT MEAN?

Look It Up Many domain-specific words are used in this selection, including *tracker, humidity, anesthesia, respiration, stethoscope, transmitter, antenna, microscope,* and *frequency.* Use a print or digital dictionary to look up the definitions of these words or others that you find in the text. Then write a new sentence using each word. Share your sentences with a partner.

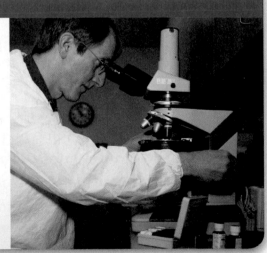

WRITE ABOUT READING

Response Think about all the effort that Lisa and her team put into studying the Matschie's tree kangaroo. What do they hope to learn? Why? Write a paragraph in which you explain how the information that Lisa and her team collect will help protect the species. Use specific facts and details from the text to develop your explanation.

Writing Tip

As you write your draft, use precise language and domain-specific vocabulary. Include transitions to show the connections between your ideas.

Go Digital

COMMON CORE **RI.5.3** explain the relationships between individuals/events/ideas/concepts in a text; **W.5.2d** use precise language and domain-specific vocabulary; **W.5.9b** apply grade 5 Reading standards to informational texts; **SL.5.1a** come to discussions prepared/explicitly draw on preparation and other information about the topic; **L.5.4c** consult reference materials to find pronunciation and determine or clarify meaning; **L.5.6** acquire and use general academic and domain-specific words and phrases

MYTH

✓ GENRE

A **myth** is a story that tells what a group of people believes about the world or an aspect of nature.

✓ TEXT FOCUS

Characteristics of Myths
Many myths feature animal characters that act like people. These characters often have one special trait, such as determination or wisdom. Myths also include a lesson or an explanation meant to help readers understand how something in nature has come to be.

RL.5.10 read and comprehend literature

Why Koala Has no Tail

by Vivian Fernandez
illustrated by Micha Archer

One day, in a long-ago time, Tree Kangaroo sat high above the ground, chewing worriedly on her bottom lip. It had been many days since the last rains. The grasses had dried, and the normally lush trees were bare except for a few scraggly leaves.

"Friend 'Roo," someone called from below. "Do you see water from where you sit?"

Tree Kangaroo looked down and saw Koala tugging anxiously on his long, bushy tail. "No water," Tree Kangaroo said, jumping down to stand next to Koala.

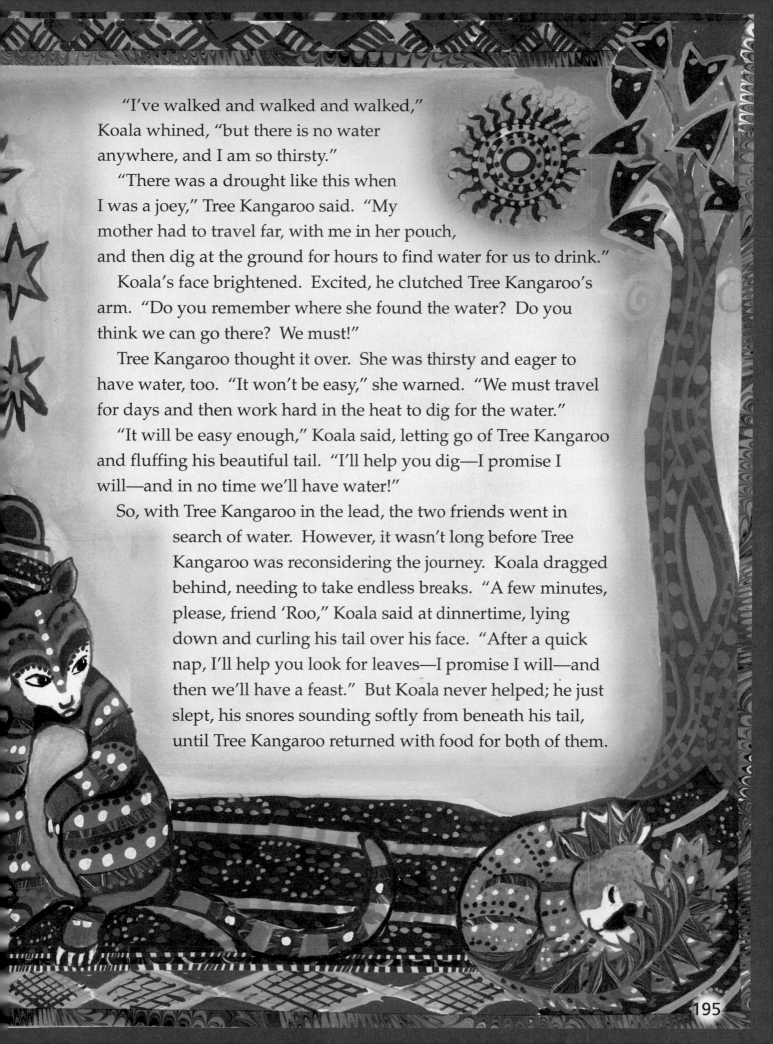

"I've walked and walked and walked," Koala whined, "but there is no water anywhere, and I am so thirsty."

"There was a drought like this when I was a joey," Tree Kangaroo said. "My mother had to travel far, with me in her pouch, and then dig at the ground for hours to find water for us to drink."

Koala's face brightened. Excited, he clutched Tree Kangaroo's arm. "Do you remember where she found the water? Do you think we can go there? We must!"

Tree Kangaroo thought it over. She was thirsty and eager to have water, too. "It won't be easy," she warned. "We must travel for days and then work hard in the heat to dig for the water."

"It will be easy enough," Koala said, letting go of Tree Kangaroo and fluffing his beautiful tail. "I'll help you dig—I promise I will—and in no time we'll have water!"

So, with Tree Kangaroo in the lead, the two friends went in search of water. However, it wasn't long before Tree Kangaroo was reconsidering the journey. Koala dragged behind, needing to take endless breaks. "A few minutes, please, friend 'Roo," Koala said at dinnertime, lying down and curling his tail over his face. "After a quick nap, I'll help you look for leaves—I promise I will—and then we'll have a feast." But Koala never helped; he just slept, his snores sounding softly from beneath his tail, until Tree Kangaroo returned with food for both of them.

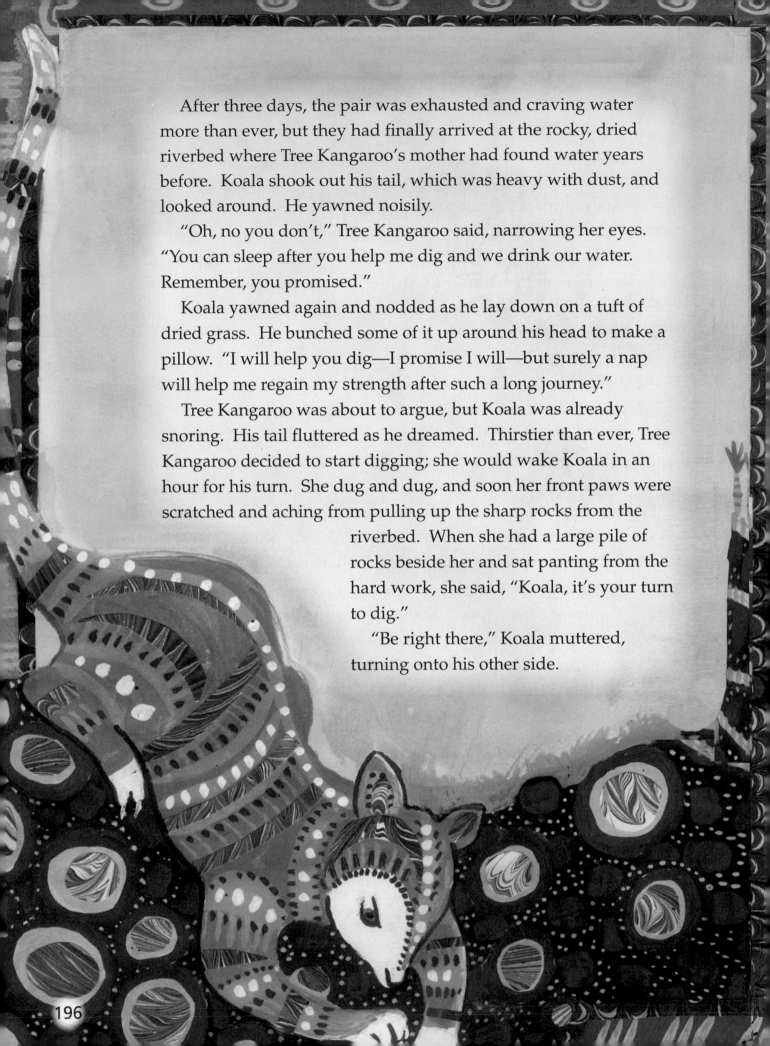

After three days, the pair was exhausted and craving water more than ever, but they had finally arrived at the rocky, dried riverbed where Tree Kangaroo's mother had found water years before. Koala shook out his tail, which was heavy with dust, and looked around. He yawned noisily.

"Oh, no you don't," Tree Kangaroo said, narrowing her eyes. "You can sleep after you help me dig and we drink our water. Remember, you promised."

Koala yawned again and nodded as he lay down on a tuft of dried grass. He bunched some of it up around his head to make a pillow. "I will help you dig—I promise I will—but surely a nap will help me regain my strength after such a long journey."

Tree Kangaroo was about to argue, but Koala was already snoring. His tail fluttered as he dreamed. Thirstier than ever, Tree Kangaroo decided to start digging; she would wake Koala in an hour for his turn. She dug and dug, and soon her front paws were scratched and aching from pulling up the sharp rocks from the riverbed. When she had a large pile of rocks beside her and sat panting from the hard work, she said, "Koala, it's your turn to dig."

"Be right there," Koala muttered, turning onto his other side.

Tree Kangaroo took another minute to catch her breath, using her paws to shield her eyes from the bright, hot sun. She was exasperated, but still thirsty, so she continued to dig. Koala slept on. Eventually, Tree Kangaroo began to see a shimmer of moisture on the rocks she was digging out, and her tender paws touched wet soil, and then—"Water!" she cried, overjoyed.

"Finally!" Koala said, instantly awake. He ran to where Tree Kangaroo was bent over the hole, tasting the delicious water at last. As he pushed Tree Kangaroo out of his way and took a long, greedy drink, his twitchy tail cut across the edge of one exceptionally sharp rock in Tree Kangaroo's pile. "My tail!" he cried when he saw it had been sliced clean off. Not even a small fluffy nub remained. Forgetting the water, he ran away, wailing, never to return to the area again.

Koala's laziness and greed had cost him his beautiful bushy tail, and since that day, all koalas have been born tailless as a reminder to work hard and to share.

Compare Texts

TEXT TO TEXT

Compare Genres Review "Quest for the Tree Kangaroo" and "Why Koala Has No Tail." With a partner, complete a T-Map, recording details from each selection that describe the tree kangaroo. Compare and contrast the details and images of the tree kangaroo that each selection conveys. Then discuss how the genre of each text—an informational text versus a myth— influences how the tree kangaroo is portrayed.

TEXT TO SELF

Write a Letter What do you find most interesting or admirable about the work that Lisa and her team are doing? Write a letter to a member of the expedition, sharing your feelings about the scientists' activities. Support your opinions with text evidence and quotes.

TEXT TO WORLD

Make a Poster With a partner, do further research on the tree kangaroo or another endangered animal. Use reliable print or electronic sources to find out more about the animal, why it is endangered, and what is being done to help protect it. Make an awareness poster, presenting the key points of your research. Share your poster with the class.

COMMON CORE **RI.5.1** quote accurately when explaining what the text says explicitly and when drawing inferences; **RI.5.7** draw on information from print and digital sources to locate answers or solve problems; **RI.5.9** integrate information from several texts on the same topic; **W.5.7** conduct short research projects that use several sources to build knowledge through investigation

Grammar

What Is a Verb? A **verb** is a word that can show action or state of being. Sometimes a verb is made up of more than one word—a main verb and a helping verb. **Verb tenses** can be used to convey various times, sequences, states, and conditions.

Verb Tenses Used to Convey Information
The trackers bark up the tree. The trackers barked up the tree. The trackers will bark up the tree. **Time** Three tenses of *bark* are used to show action occurring in the past *(barked),* present *(bark),* and future *(will bark).*
The trackers know that they made the right decision. **Sequence** Verb tense shows the order of events. The trackers know now that they made the right decision earlier.
The scientists will examine the tree kangaroo if the trackers catch it. **Condition** Verb tense shows that one action or state of being depends on a condition being met. The scientists will examine the animal in the future—but only if the trackers catch it in the present.
The trackers felt happy about their success. **State** Tenses of linking verbs indicate when the subject is in a particular state of being. The trackers were in a state of happiness in the past.

Try This! **Work with a partner. Identify helping verbs and main verbs in the sentences. Then tell whether each verb conveys time, sequence, state, or condition.**

1 After I read the tree kangaroo article, I will watch the video.

2 I will learn even more if I get that book from the library.

3 The book includes many illustrations and explanations.

4 I will be an expert on these fascinating animals.

You can make your writing strong by using verbs that convey details and information vividly and accurately.

Sentence with Vague Verb	Sentence with Exact Verb

The tree kangaroo went up into a tree.	The tree kangaroo scrambled up into a tree.

The scientist watched the tree branches.	The scientist peered into the tree branches.

 Connect Grammar to Writing

As you revise your procedural composition, replace vague verbs with exact verbs to show readers what you mean. Exact verbs will help clarify the actions and events you write about.

COMMON CORE W.5.2a introduce a topic, provide an observation and focus, group related information/include formatting, illustrations, and multimedia; W.5.2c link ideas within and across categories of information using words, phrases, and clauses; W.5.2d use precise language and domain-specific vocabulary; W.5.4 produce writing in which development and organization are appropriate to task, purpose, and audience

Informative Writing

✓ **Organization** In a **procedural composition**, you describe a process, or series of events or steps. You should begin by introducing the topic. Then explain each event in the order in which it happens or should happen. Using transition words such as *first*, *next*, *then*, and *finally* will make the order of events more clear to readers.

Barry wrote a procedural composition explaining how to plan a science fair project. Later, he reordered events and added transition words to link his ideas. Use the Writing Traits Checklist below as you revise your writing.

Writing Traits Checklist

✓ **Ideas**
Did I describe the steps in a process?

✓ **Organization**
Did I explain events in order and use transitions to link ideas?

✓ **Sentence Fluency**
Did I use verbs correctly?

✓ **Word Choice**
Did I use specific nouns and strong verbs?

✓ **Voice**
Did I express my ideas in a clear and interesting way?

✓ **Conventions**
Did I use correct spelling, grammar, and punctuation?

Revised Draft

The next steps have to do with planning your experiment and gathering supplies.

Include a hypothesis, or what you think you will discover. *Second,* Make a list of supplies that you will need. *First,* Write out a plan for how you will do your experiment. Finally, think about any special requirements.

How to Plan a Science Fair Project

by Barry Williams

Entering a science fair is a big job for most fifth graders. They have to prepare carefully for their experiments. What does it take to have a winning science fair project?

Think about your favorite science topic and write two or three experiments that relate to it. For example, maybe you'd like to study moonlight and whether it affects plants. Once you have written your experiments, choose the one you like best.

The next steps have to do with planning your experiment and gathering supplies. First, write out a plan for how you will do your experiment. Include a hypothesis, or what you think you will discover. Second, make a list of supplies that you will need. Finally, think about any special requirements. Will you need a special location or other students to help you? Put all of this information in your plan and get your teacher to approve it.

After your plan is approved, it is time to experiment. Work carefully and take many notes about what happens. Even after all your planning, there is a chance you will face challenges—but don't worry. One of these challenges could lead you to a great scientific discovery!

Reading as a Writer

Which steps did Barry reorder? What transitions did he use to clarify sequence? How can you clarify the process in your own composition for readers?

In my final paper, I reordered steps in the process and added transitions to make the sequence of events more clear. I also checked to see that I used verbs correctly.

☑ TARGET VOCABULARY

romp

strained

picturing

wheeled

shouldered

frantic

lunging

checking

stride

bounding

Vocabulary Reader

Context Cards

Black Bears

COMMON CORE

L.5.6 acquire and use general academic and domain-specific words and phrases

Vocabulary in Context

1 romp

For many kids in the 1800s, the trip West was a romp. For adults, it was a serious task.

2 strained

Gold-rush miners strained to sift gold from mounds of heavy soil.

3 picturing

In their imagination, many pioneers were picturing owning big cattle ranches.

4 wheeled

Teams of oxen wheeled the wagons around to form a circle for protection.

Go Digital

▶ Study each Context Card.

▶ Use a thesaurus to find a synonym for each Vocabulary word.

5 shouldered

Pioneers may have shouldered newborn animals to carry them, just like this farmer.

6 frantic

Frightened by the storm, this frenzied herd of buffalo began a frantic stampede.

7 lunging

These goats, like the ones on farms, enjoy lunging, or dashing, at each other.

8 checking

Stopping, or checking, the wandering ways of sheep is the job of these farm dogs.

9 stride

Pioneers who walked had to match their stride, or step, to the pace of the wagons.

10 bounding

This man is cheered by his happy dog bounding forward to greet him.

Read and Comprehend

☑ TARGET SKILL

Understanding Characters As you read "Old Yeller," note the ways in which the narrator, Travis, and his brother, Arliss, are similar and different. Look for text evidence to help you examine their **actions** and their **traits**. By comparing the two characters, you will learn more about who they are and why they behave as they do. Record your details in a graphic organizer like the one shown here.

Travis	Arliss

☑ TARGET STRATEGY

Visualize When you **visualize**, you use text details to form pictures in your mind. As you read "Old Yeller," use sights, sounds, and other details in the text to picture each scene. By visualizing what Travis experiences, you can better understand his actions.

Responsibility

You may have heard someone described as having "a sense of responsibility." This sense has nothing to do with hearing, smelling, tasting, touching, or seeing. Rather, it means that the person is dependable. He or she does what needs to be done, even when tasks are hard or unpleasant.

Travis, the narrator of "Old Yeller," has a strong sense of responsibility. While his father is away, he takes on all of the chores needed to keep the family farm going. As you read the story, you will see that he also feels responsible for keeping his brother safe.

ANCHOR TEXT

✓ TARGET SKILL

Understanding Characters

Use text details to compare Travis's actions and traits to those of his brother.

✓ GENRE

Historical fiction is a story set in the past. It contains characters, places, and events that actually existed or happened, or that could have existed or happened. As you read, look for:

▶ realistic characters
▶ some made-up events
▶ details that show the story took place in the past

 COMMON CORE **RL.5.3** compare and contrast characters, settings, or events, drawing on details; **RL.5.10** read and comprehend literature

Go Digital

MEET THE AUTHOR
Fred Gipson

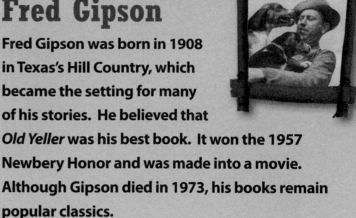

Fred Gipson was born in 1908 in Texas's Hill Country, which became the setting for many of his stories. He believed that *Old Yeller* was his best book. It won the 1957 Newbery Honor and was made into a movie. Although Gipson died in 1973, his books remain popular classics.

MEET THE ILLUSTRATOR
Marc Elliot

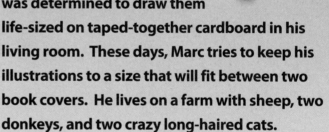

Like many kids, Marc Elliot loved to draw dinosaurs, only Marc was determined to draw them life-sized on taped-together cardboard in his living room. These days, Marc tries to keep his illustrations to a size that will fit between two book covers. He lives on a farm with sheep, two donkeys, and two crazy long-haired cats.

Old Yeller

by Fred Gipson
selection illustrated by Marc Elliot

ESSENTIAL QUESTION

How can dangerous
situations bring people
closer together?

It is the late 1860s. Travis lives with his family on the Texas frontier. When Papa leaves home to drive their cattle to market in Kansas, Travis must take over Papa's responsibilities. All goes well until a stray yellow dog shows up. Travis's younger brother, Little Arliss, loves the dog, but Travis thinks the mangy animal is nothing but a "meat-stealing rascal." Then one day something happens that changes Travis's feelings about the dog forever.

Swinging that chopping axe was sure hard work. The sweat poured off me. My back muscles ached. The axe got so heavy I could hardly swing it. My breath got harder and harder to breathe.

An hour before sundown, I was worn down to a nub. It seemed like I couldn't hit another lick. Papa could have lasted till past sundown, but I didn't see how I could. I shouldered my axe and started toward the cabin, trying to think up some excuse to tell Mama to keep her from knowing I was played clear out.

That's when I heard Little Arliss scream.

Well, Little Arliss was a screamer by nature. He'd scream when he was happy and scream when he was mad and a lot of times he'd scream just to hear himself make a noise. Generally, we paid no more mind to his screaming than we did to the gobble of a wild turkey.

But this time was different. The second I heard his screaming, I felt my heart flop clear over. This time I knew Little Arliss was in real trouble.

I tore out up the trail leading toward the cabin. A minute before, I'd been so tired out with my rail splitting that I couldn't have struck a trot. But now I raced through the tall trees in that creek bottom, covering ground like a scared wolf.

Little Arliss's second scream, when it came, was louder and shriller and more frantic-sounding than the first. Mixed with it was a whimpering crying sound that I knew didn't come from him. It was a sound I'd heard before and seemed like I ought to know what it was, but right then I couldn't place it.

Then, from way off to one side came a sound that I would have recognized anywhere. It was the coughing roar of a charging bear. I'd just heard it once in my life. That was the time Mama had shot and wounded a hog-killing bear and Papa had had to finish it off with a knife to keep it from getting her.

ANALYZE THE TEXT

Dialect Why does the author include less-formal language like *I felt my heart flop clear over, I tore out up the trail,* and *finish it off?* What does the character's dialect add to the story?

211

My heart went to pushing up into my throat, nearly choking off my wind. I strained for every lick of speed I could get out of my running legs. I didn't know what sort of fix Little Arliss had got himself into, but I knew that it had to do with a mad bear, which was enough.

The way the late sun slanted through the trees had the trail all cross-banded with streaks of bright light and dark shade. I ran through these bright and dark patches so fast that the changing light nearly blinded me. Then suddenly, I raced out into the open where I could see ahead. And what I saw sent a chill clear through to the marrow of my bones.

There was Little Arliss, down in that spring hole again. He was lying half in and half out of the water, holding on to the hind leg of a little black bear cub no bigger than a small coon. The bear cub was out on the bank, whimpering and crying and clawing the rocks with all three of his other feet, trying to pull away. But Little Arliss was holding on for all he was worth, scared now and screaming his head off. Too scared to let go.

How the bear cub ever came to prowl close enough for Little Arliss to grab him, I don't know. And why he didn't turn on him and bite loose, I couldn't figure out, either. Unless he was like Little Arliss, too scared to think.

But all of that didn't matter now. What mattered was the bear cub's mama. She'd heard the cries of her baby and was coming to save him. She was coming so fast that she had the brush popping and breaking as she crashed through and over it. I could see her black heavy figure piling off down the slant on the far side of Birdsong Creek. She was roaring mad and ready to kill.

And worst of all, I could see that I'd never get there in time!

Mama couldn't either. She'd heard Arliss, too, and here she came from the cabin, running down the slant toward the spring, screaming at Arliss, telling him to turn the bear cub loose. But Little Arliss wouldn't do it. All he'd do was hang with that hind leg and let out one shrill shriek after another as fast as he could suck in a breath.

Now the she bear was charging across the shallows in the creek. She was knocking sheets of water high in the bright sun, charging with her fur up and her long teeth bared, filling the canyon with that awful coughing roar. And no matter how fast Mama ran or how fast I ran, the she bear was going to get there first!

I think I nearly went blind then, picturing what was going to happen to Little Arliss. I know that I opened my mouth to scream and not any sound came out.

Then, just as the bear went lunging up the creek bank toward Little Arliss and her cub, a flash of yellow came streaking out of the brush.

It was that big yeller dog. He was roaring like a mad bull. He wasn't one-third as big and heavy as the she bear, but when he piled into her from one side, he rolled her clear off her feet. They went down in a wild, roaring tangle of twisting bodies and scrambling feet and slashing fangs.

As I raced past them, I saw the bear lunge up to stand on her hind feet like a man while she clawed at the body of the yeller dog hanging to her throat. I didn't wait to see more. Without ever checking my stride, I ran in and jerked Little Arliss loose from the cub. I grabbed him by the wrist and yanked him up out of that water and slung him toward Mama like he was a half-empty sack of corn. I screamed at Mama. "Grab him, Mama! Grab him and run!" Then I swung my chopping axe high and wheeled, aiming to cave in the she bear's head with the first lick.

ANALYZE THE TEXT

Author's Word Choice The author uses words such as *lunging, roaring, scrambling,* and *slashing* to provide sensory details. How do these words help you picture what is happening in the story?

But I never did strike. I didn't need to. Old Yeller hadn't let the bear get close enough. He couldn't handle her; she was too big and strong for that. She'd stand there on her hind feet, hunched over, and take a roaring swing at him with one of those big front claws. She'd slap him head over heels. She'd knock him so far that it didn't look like he could possibly get back there before she charged again, but he always did. He'd hit the ground rolling, yelling his head off with the pain of the blow; but somehow he'd always roll to his feet. And here he'd come again, ready to tie into her for another round.

I stood there with my axe raised, watching them for a long moment. Then from up toward the house, I heard Mama calling: "Come away from there, Travis. Hurry, son! Run!"

That spooked me. Up till then, I'd been ready to tie into that bear myself. Now, suddenly, I was scared out of my wits again. I ran toward the cabin.

But like it was, Old Yeller nearly beat me there. I didn't see it, of course; but Mama said that the minute Old Yeller saw we were all in the clear and out of danger, he threw the fight to that she bear and lit out for the house. The bear chased him for a little piece, but at the rate Old Yeller was leaving her behind, Mama said it looked like the bear was backing up.

But if the big yeller dog was scared or hurt in any way when he came dashing into the house, he didn't show it. He sure didn't show it like we all did. Little Arliss had hushed his screaming, but he was trembling all over and clinging to Mama like he'd never let her go. And Mama was sitting in the middle of the floor, holding him up close and crying like she'd never stop. And me, I was close to crying, myself.

Old Yeller, though, all he did was come bounding in to jump on us and lick us in the face and bark so loud that there, inside the cabin, the noise nearly made us deaf.

The way he acted, you might have thought that bear fight hadn't been anything more than a rowdy romp that we'd all taken part in for the fun of it.

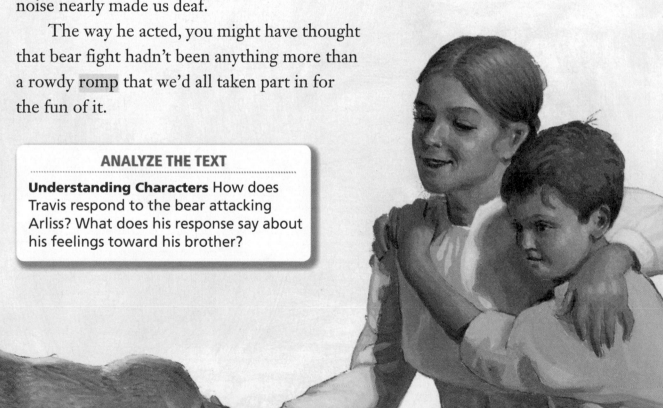

ANALYZE THE TEXT

Understanding Characters How does Travis respond to the bear attacking Arliss? What does his response say about his feelings toward his brother?

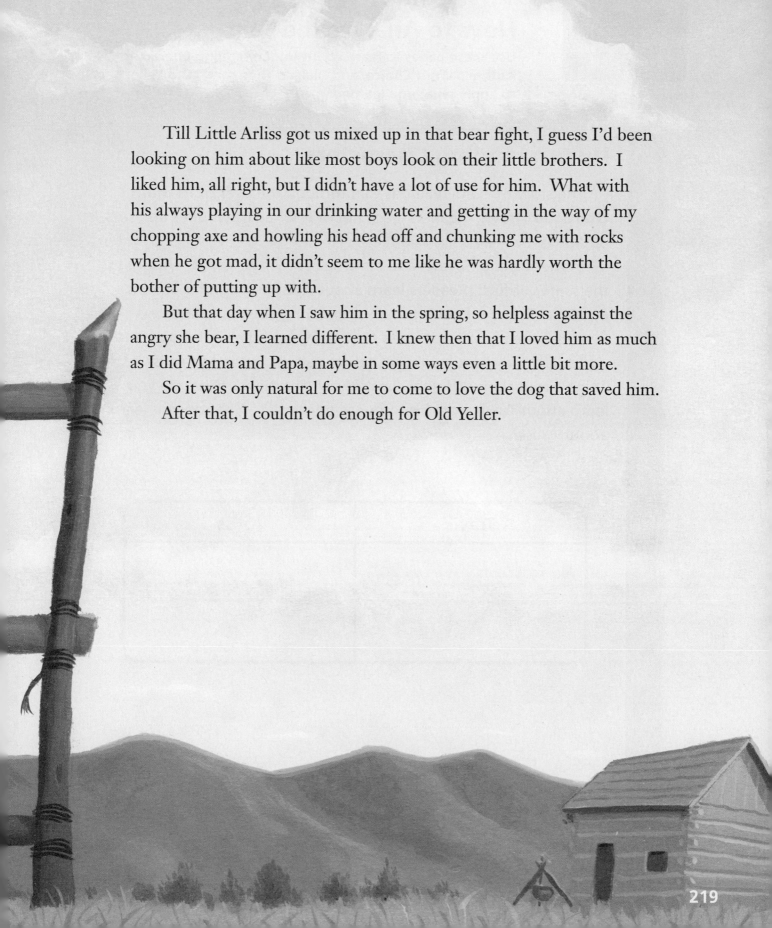

Till Little Arliss got us mixed up in that bear fight, I guess I'd been looking on him about like most boys look on their little brothers. I liked him, all right, but I didn't have a lot of use for him. What with his always playing in our drinking water and getting in the way of my chopping axe and howling his head off and chunking me with rocks when he got mad, it didn't seem to me like he was hardly worth the bother of putting up with.

But that day when I saw him in the spring, so helpless against the angry she bear, I learned different. I knew then that I loved him as much as I did Mama and Papa, maybe in some ways even a little bit more.

So it was only natural for me to come to love the dog that saved him.

After that, I couldn't do enough for Old Yeller.

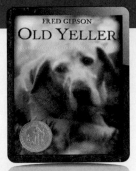

Dig Deeper

How to Analyze the Text

Use these pages to learn about Understanding Characters, Author's Word Choice, and Dialect. Then read "Old Yeller" again to apply what you learned.

Understanding Characters

The story of "Old Yeller" is told through the eyes of its **main character**, Travis. Readers learn not only what Travis does and says, but also what he thinks and feels.

In the selection, Travis and his little brother, Arliss, are caught in the same conflict. Readers learn about Arliss through his actions and what Travis tells about him. Comparing the two characters reveals more about each one's personality and their relationship.

Look closely for details that tell you about Travis and Arliss. Think about their different reactions to situations. What do you learn about Travis from his response to events? What do you learn about Arliss?

Travis	Arliss

RL.5.3 compare and contrast characters, settings, or events, drawing on details; **RL.5.10** read and comprehend literature; **RF.5.4a** read on-level text with purpose and understanding; **L.5.3b** compare and contrast varieties of English in stories, dramas, or poems

Author's Word Choice

Sensory language is language that helps readers see, hear, and experience what happens in a story. Recall the scene from "Old Yeller" in which Travis first realizes that a charging bear is after Little Arliss. The author uses words and phrases such as "popping," "breaking," and "awful coughing roar" to build the intensity of the moment and to make readers feel as if they are in the scene with Travis.

Dialect

Dialect, a variety of English associated with a certain place or group of people, adds realism to historical fiction such as "Old Yeller." On page 210, Travis uses expressions such as "worn down to a nub" and "I couldn't hit another lick" to describe how tired he is after chopping wood. These expressions fit his character and the story's setting. They also help establish Travis's voice as he begins to narrate the story.

Your Turn

RETURN TO THE ESSENTIAL QUESTION

 Turn and Talk Review the selection to prepare to discuss this question: *How can dangerous situations bring people closer together?* Take turns sharing your insights in a small group. Elaborate on each other's comments.

Classroom Conversation

Continue your discussion of "Old Yeller" by using text evidence to explain your answers to these questions:

1. How does the setting affect what happens in the story?

2. Is Travis a good choice for the narrator of this story? Explain.

3. What conclusions about life on the frontier can you draw from the story?

DISCUSS CHARACTER GROWTH

Partner Talk How do Travis's feelings toward his brother change during the story? With a partner, discuss how the incident with the bear affects Travis. Then evaluate whether his change in perspective is believable, based on your ideas about how real people react and feel in such situations. Share your observations with the class.

WRITE ABOUT READING

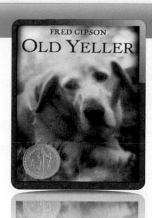

Response To determine the theme, or message, of a short story, think about how the main character responds to conflict. For example, how does Travis react when his brother is in danger? Write a paragraph explaining how Travis's actions reveal a general message about life or people. Support your ideas with quotations and other text evidence.

Writing Tip

Be sure to use quotation marks around phrases or sentences that you take directly from the text. Include only those details that support your main idea.

COMMON CORE   **RL.5.1** quote accurately when explaining what the text says explicitly and when drawing inferences; **RL.5.2** determine theme from details/summarize; **W.5.9a** apply grade 5 Reading standards to literature; **W.5.10** write routinely over extended time frames and shorter time frames; **SL.5.1a** come to discussions prepared/explicitly draw on preparation and other information about the topic; **SL.5.1c** pose and respond to questions, make comments that contribute to the discussion, and elaborate on others' remarks

PERSUASIVE TEXT

☑ GENRE

Persuasive text, such as this readers' theater, seeks to convince the reader to think or act in a certain way.

☑ TEXT FOCUS

Persuasive techniques, such as the authoritative tones used by the experts being interviewed in this selection, are used to sway readers' thinking or call readers to action.

RI.5.10 read and comprehend informational text

Readers' Theater

What Makes It Good?

by Cynthia Benjamin

Cast of Characters
Television Host
Animal Expert Kay Nyne
Historian Lester Year

Host: Welcome to *What Makes It Good?*, the movie review show that asks the experts if a movie is accurate enough to be good. Today we are reviewing the film version of *Old Yeller*, and we have two experts with us. One is historian Lester Year, who writes about life on the nineteenth-century Texas frontier. The other is animal expert Kay Nyne.

First up is our animal expert. What makes *Old Yeller* good?

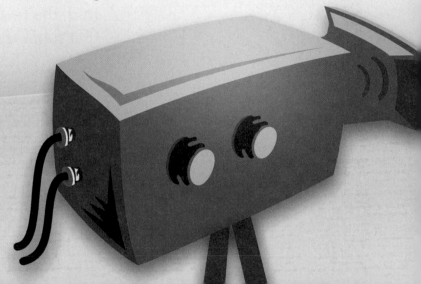

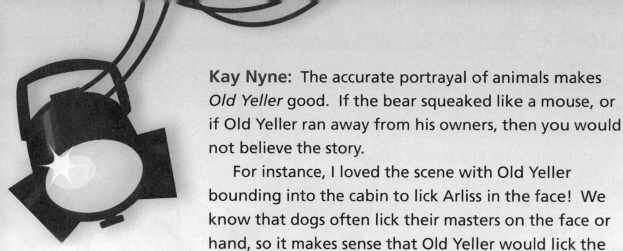

Kay Nyne: The accurate portrayal of animals makes *Old Yeller* good. If the bear squeaked like a mouse, or if Old Yeller ran away from his owners, then you would not believe the story.

For instance, I loved the scene with Old Yeller bounding into the cabin to lick Arliss in the face! We know that dogs often lick their masters on the face or hand, so it makes sense that Old Yeller would lick the young boy after saving him.

I also thought the way Old Yeller went lunging at the attacking bear in a frantic attempt to save Arliss was very realistic. Dogs are loyal animals. In fact, dogs and people have lived together for more than ten thousand years! Mother bears are fiercely protective of their cubs. I have no problem picturing a bear attacking if she thought her cub were in danger. It is details like these that make the movie believable and exciting.

225

Lester Year: Now wait a minute! That fight between Old Yeller and the bear was exciting, I admit. But what makes the movie truly great is its historical accuracy. If Travis had broken his stride, wheeled around and seen the bear, then dialed 9-1-1 on a cell phone, you would not believe it.

But he does not carry a cell phone. He has shouldered an ax. I hope you noticed the ax. It was an excellent example of an important 1860s tool. Living on the frontier was no romp on the playground, and pioneers depended on their tools for survival.

Ah, now that scene of Old Yeller licking Arliss after checking the bear's attack may be very accurate as far as dog behavior is concerned. But more important, the cabin looks very realistic, down to the notches holding the logs in place. If the cabin had wallpaper, you would have strained to believe the scene. That is why historical accuracy is more important.

Host: We are almost out of time. Let's summarize. *Old Yeller* is a good movie because it is . . .

Kay Nyne: Scientifically accurate.

Lester Year: Historically accurate.

Host: Well, they may never agree. Audience, I guess you have to decide for yourself what makes it good!

Compare Texts

TEXT TO TEXT

Analyze Viewpoint In "What Makes It Good?" Lester Year makes a clear argument about "Old Yeller" and provides evidence to support it. Identify Lester Year's viewpoint. Then make a list of all the ideas and text evidence from "Old Yeller" that supports his viewpoint. Include those that he mentions from the film, as well as those you find in the text. Use your list to write a sentence or two explaining how the ideas and text evidence work together to form a solid argument.

TEXT TO SELF

Write About an Animal Think about an experience you have had with an animal, or an experience you would like to have. Write a narrative paragraph about the experience. Include details that convey your thoughts and feelings. Draw a picture to accompany your paragraph, and provide a caption for your drawing.

Always view wildlife from far away.

TEXT TO WORLD

Compare Dialects The authors of "Old Yeller" and "Off and Running" (Lesson 3) use types of dialect to make their story characters realistic. With a partner, create a T-Map listing examples of dialect from each story. Compare and contrast the unique words and phrases found in each dialect. Discuss whether you think the dialect helps define the characters who use it, and why.

COMMON CORE **RI.5.8** explain how an author uses reasons and evidence to support points; **W.5.4** produce writing in which development and organization are appropriate to task, purpose, and audience; **W.5.10** write routinely over extended time frames and shorter time frames; **L.5.3b** compare and contrast varieties of English in stories, dramas, or poems

Grammar

What Is a Direct Object? A **direct object** is the word in the predicate that receives the action of the verb. It can be a noun or a pronoun, a word that takes the place of a noun. A **compound direct object** is made up of two or more words that receive the action of the same verb.

Verbs and Objects	What Receives the Action
action verb direct object The boy swung his axe.	*Axe* receives the action of the verb *swung*.
action verb compound direct object He chopped big logs and small branches.	*Logs* and *branches* receive the action of the verb *chopped*.

An **indirect object** usually tells to *whom* or to *what* the action of the verb is done. The indirect object comes between the verb and the direct object.

     action verb indirect object direct object
The boy gave his brother a treat.

Brother tells to whom the treat was given.

Try This! The action verb in each sentence is printed in bold type. Find the direct object. Then find the indirect object, if one is used.

1. Mom **wrote** Dad a letter.

2. She **described** the big fight.

3. Our dog **protected** my brother and me.

4. We **gave** our dog great praise.

You can improve the flow of your writing by combining sentences in which the direct objects receive the action of the same verb. First, identify the subject, verb, and direct object of each sentence. Then combine the sentences, using *and* or *or* to join the direct objects.

Separate Sentences

The brave dog fought a bear.

The brave dog fought a mountain lion.

Combined Sentence with Compound Direct Object

The brave dog fought a bear and a mountain lion.

 Connect Grammar to Writing

As you revise your compare-contrast essay this week, see where you can create compound direct objects to combine sentences. Combining sentences will help make your writing smoother.

W.5.2a introduce a topic, provide an observation and focus, group related information/include formatting, illustrations, and multimedia; **W.5.2b** develop the topic with facts, definitions, details, quotations, or other information and examples; **W.5.2e** provide a concluding statement or section; **W.5.5** develop and strengthen writing by planning, revising, editing, rewriting, or trying a new approach

Informative Writing

✔ **Word Choice** The author of "Old Yeller" uses vivid descriptions and action to tell a great story. You can analyze descriptions and events in a story to compare and contrast parts of it in your writing.

Stefania drafted a **compare-contrast essay** to explain how Old Yeller and the bear are alike and different. Later, she added quotations and precise details from the text to support her ideas.

Use the Writing Traits Checklist below as you revise your writing.

Writing Traits Checklist

✔ **Ideas**
Did I develop my topic with quotations and examples?

✔ **Organization**
Did I explain my comparisons and provide a conclusion?

✔ **Sentence Fluency**
Did I vary the structure of my sentences?

✔ **Word Choice**
Did I use precise words and details from the text?

✔ **Voice**
Is my writing clear and informative?

✔ **Conventions**
Did I use correct spelling and grammar?

Revised Draft

The most exciting scene in "Old Yeller" is when Old Yeller fights the mother bear in order to protect Arliss. The author describes both animals as ready to fight. The bear
"roaring mad and ready to kill."
is protecting her cub and ∧ Old Yeller is
and "roaring like a mad bull."
protecting Little Arliss ∧. When Old Yeller sees that Little Arliss is in danger, he ~~takes action~~.
∧
⟨runs at the bear and knocks her off her feet⟩

230

Old Yeller and the Bear

by Stefania Almeida

The most exciting scene in "Old Yeller" is when Old Yeller fights the mother bear in order to protect Arliss. The author describes both animals as ready to fight. The bear is protecting her cub and "roaring mad and ready to kill." Old Yeller is protecting Little Arliss and "roaring like a mad bull." When Old Yeller sees that Little Arliss is in danger, he runs at the bear and knocks her off her feet. The bear stands her ground, as well. She keeps fighting until the end when Old Yeller outruns her and goes back to the family's house.

The main difference between the two animals is their size. The bear is much bigger and stronger than Old Yeller. This size difference does not scare Old Yeller, though. He acts on his protective instincts and takes on an animal three times his size. The bear is brave, as well. She believes her cub is in danger and is willing to do anything to protect it. Once Old Yeller knows that Arliss and the rest of the family are out of danger, he stops fighting. Though the bear chases him for a bit, she eventually gives up, too, and probably returns home with her cub. Both animals do what is necessary to protect those they care about.

In my final paper, I used quotations and precise details from the text to support my ideas.

EVERGLADES FOREVER

National Parks of the West

☑ TARGET VOCABULARY

conserving
restore
regulate
vegetation
endangered
responsibility
attracted
adapted
unique
guardians

Vocabulary Reader

Context Cards

Mangrove Swamp

COMMON CORE

L.5.6 acquire and use general academic and domain-specific words and phrases

Vocabulary in Context

① conserving

Saving, or conserving, natural habitats is a main goal of our national park system.

② restore

Park workers restore harmed habitats by bringing them back to their original state.

③ regulate

Managers regulate, or control, access to an area. Fewer people cause less harm.

DUNES ARE FRAGILE KEEP OFF!

④ vegetation

Many animals survive by feeding on the vegetation, or plant life, in a habitat.

Go Digital

▶ Study each Context Card.

▶ Use a thesaurus to find an alternate word for each Vocabulary word.

5 endangered

Damaged habitats put **endangered** animals at risk of dying out.

6 responsibility

Humans have a duty, or **responsibility**, to preserve and protect wild habitats.

7 attracted

Birds are **attracted**, or drawn to, habitats that can hide their nests from predators.

8 adapted

Gills are specially **adapted** features that let fish breathe in the water.

9 unique

Many habitats support **unique** plants and wildlife that are not found elsewhere.

10 guardians

One day some of these students may become **guardians**, or caretakers, of wild habitats.

Read and Comprehend

 Go Digital

✓ TARGET SKILL

Author's Purpose Every author has a specific reason, or **purpose**, for writing. The author of "Everglades Forever" writes about the Everglades region. As you read the selection, think about whether the author's purpose is to entertain, to inform, to describe, or to persuade. Use the graphic organizer shown below to record facts and other details that help you determine the author's purpose.

Author's Purpose

Detail

Detail

✓ TARGET STRATEGY

Analyze/Evaluate As you read "Everglades Forever," **analyze** the facts and other text evidence the author presents to support her points. **Evaluate** this evidence by asking yourself questions such as *Does this fact really support the author's ideas? Do I feel convinced by her argument? Why or why not?*

 COMMON CORE

RI.5.3 explain the relationships between individuals/events/ideas/concepts in a text; **RI.5.8** explain how an author uses reasons and evidence to support points

234

Conservation

The term *conservation* refers to any activity that helps protect wildlife and natural resources, such as water and soil. Conservation includes what people can do every day, such as walking instead of driving, or turning down the thermostat. It also includes large projects conducted by experts, such as reintroducing a species of animal to a particular habitat.

In "Everglades Forever," the author goes along on a field trip in southern Florida to learn about conserving the Everglades. By sharing the students' discoveries, the author also shows readers how they can help and why their efforts are necessary.

ANCHOR TEXT

EVERGLADES FOREVER

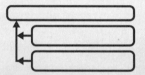

✅ TARGET SKILL

Author's Purpose Determine the author's purpose, and find details and information in the text that help her achieve it.

✅ GENRE

Narrative nonfiction tells about people, things, events, and places that are real. As you read, look for:

▶ factual information that tells a story
▶ features such as photographs and captions

 COMMON CORE **RI.5.3** explain the relationships between individuals/events/ideas/concepts in a text; **RI.5.8** explain how an author uses reasons and evidence to support points; **RI.5.10** read and comprehend informational texts

  Go Digital

MEET THE AUTHOR

Trish Marx

Trish Marx travels to the people and places she writes about to get firsthand information for her nonfiction books. For *Everglades Forever*, she spent time studying and going on field trips with Ms. Jacquelyn Stone's fifth-grade class at Avocado Elementary School in Homestead, Florida.

MEET THE PHOTOGRAPHER

Cindy Karp

Cindy Karp has worked with Trish Marx on several books for children. She is also a photojournalist whose pictures have appeared in national magazines and newspapers. Karp is a resident of Miami, Florida, and has spent many days exploring the Everglades.

EVERGLADES FOREVER

RESTORING AMERICA'S GREAT WETLAND

by Trish Marx • photographs by Cindy Karp

ESSENTIAL QUESTION

What reasons do people have for protecting the environment?

In Homestead, Florida, the students in Ms. Stone's fifth-grade class have been learning about the Everglades, a vast natural wetland located on the southern tip of Florida. Since 2000, the Comprehensive Everglades Restoration Plan has helped to preserve this wetland and its natural water system. Now all of Ms. Stone's students are visiting the Everglades to experience this amazing place and learn what they can do to preserve it. The map on the right shows where Everglades National Park is located in Florida and the areas Ms. Stone's class explored.

On the morning of the field trip, the bus traveled west from Avocado School. The students saw the landscape change from houses and shopping centers to a flat, grassy prairie that met the horizon miles away. Soon they arrived at the Royal Palm Visitor Center, part of Everglades National Park.

South Florida

Lake Okeechobee

Gulf of Mexico

Miami

Pinelands · Homestead

Anhinga Trail

Florida Bay

ATLANTIC OCEAN

Key West

0   25   50 Miles
0   25   50 Kilometers

Legend
- Everglades Agricultural Area
- Water Conservation Area
- Big Cypress National Preserve
- Everglades National Park
- ■ Visited by Ms. Stone's Class

Overlooking sawgrass on Anhinga Trail

Ms. Stone had arranged for the class to meet Ranger Jim at the visitor center. From there the ranger led them to the start of the Anhinga Trail, a boardwalk circling into a slough (sloo). It was the dry season, which lasts from December through April, so the water levels were low. But there is a deep part of the slough at the beginning of the trail that never dries up. Around the edge of this part, large waterbirds called Anhingas sunned their wings. Anhingas hold out their wings to thermoregulate (thur moh REHG yuh layt), or regulate their body temperature, by soaking up the sun's energy to keep their bodies warm. An Osprey, a fish-eating hawk, waited in a tree for a flash of fish in the water. In the distance an egret stood in the sawgrass, and a flock of endangered wood storks flew overhead.

Great Blue Heron feeding on fish

"Right now you'll see many animals close together around the deeper water areas," said Ranger Jim. Fish and smaller water animals had migrated to these deep water areas to search for food. Wading birds, alligators, Ospreys, and Cormorants (large diving birds with bright green eyes) followed to feed on the fish and smaller animals. Alligators also use their tails, snouts, and feet to dig deep holes, which fill with water. These holes are places for alligators to cool off while they wait for a meal of the small animals that are attracted to the water-filled holes. During the wet season, which lasts from May through November, water covers much of the land. Then the animals spread out because the water that carries their food is spread out.

The Everglades has wet and dry seasons, but it also has wetter and drier areas caused by how high the land is above the water level. Even a few inches of elevation can make a difference in how wet or dry the soil remains throughout the year. These differences in moisture help create unique habitats, each with its own special set of plants and animals.

Mangrove trees

One of the lowest Everglades habitats is the mangrove swamp, which is named for the mangrove trees that line the islands and bays leading into the ocean. Fresh rainwater flows toward these areas and mixes with the salty ocean water, making the water in mangrove swamps brackish. The mangrove trees have specially adapted roots and leaves so they can live in this salty, muddy water. The swamps also serve as nurseries for shrimp, bonefish, and other marine animals that need a protected place to grow before they head to the ocean. If the brackish water in mangrove swamps changes, these animals cannot survive. Since two goals of the Restoration Plan are to allow Everglades water to flow more naturally to the ocean and to regulate the amount of freshwater flowing during each season, animals of the mangrove swamps—including pelicans, sea turtles, and the endangered American crocodiles and manatees—will be helped to survive.

ANALYZE THE TEXT

Domain-Specific Vocabulary What domain-specific words does the author use on these two pages? How do these words help deepen your knowledge of the topic?

The class was too far from the ocean to see a mangrove swamp, but as they walked the Anhinga Trail, the students saw several of the Everglades habitats. The slough filled with slow-moving water stretched in the distance. A sawgrass prairie covered the shallow parts of the slough, and in the distance the rounded domes of hardwood hammocks rose above the surface of the water.

As the students came to the end of the Anhinga Trail, Ranger Jim pointed out a gumbo limbo tree. "It's also called a tourist tree," he said, "because the bark of the tree peels off, just like the skin of sunburned tourists." Then he directed the students back to the bus for a short ride to a pine forest called the Pinelands.

Ranger Jim took the class on a hike through the Pinelands, one of the driest habitats in the Everglades. The sunlight filtered through the trees. Everything was quieter than on the Anhinga Trail. The floor of the Pinelands is covered with cabbage palms, marlberry bushes, blue porter flowers, and other vegetation that help absorb sounds from the outside world.

"This is where you'll find solution holes," Ms. Stone told the students. They searched the forest for the large holes that have been carved out of the limestone by tannic acid, a chemical formed when rainwater mixes with the pine needles and other leaves in the forest. Small animals live, feed, and raise their young in the solution holes. The students also watched as a tiny yellow tree snail nestled under the bark of a tree, eating a growth on the tree called lichen. They saw a Red-Shouldered Hawk swirl in the sky, and they waited for a golden orb spider to catch its next meal in its web close to the ground.

Hiking through the Pinelands

242

"*Perhaps even in this last hour . . . the vast, magnificent, subtle and unique region of the Everglades may not be utterly lost.*"
Marjory Stoneman Douglas

As they walked through the Pinelands, the students talked with Ms. Stone and Ranger Jim about the circle of life—the Miccosukee (MIHK uh SOO kee) belief that all plant and animal and human life is connected. They had seen this today in the habitats they visited. The students also realized how terrible it would be if the habitats in this part of the Everglades were not protected from the effects of farming and development that were still putting the Everglades in danger. What would happen to all the unique plants and animals they had seen? Ranger Jim said they could help by conserving water, even when brushing their teeth or washing their faces, because most of the water used in southern Florida comes from the Everglades. With responsible water conservation, the Everglades Restoration Plan could, over the next thirty years, restore a healthy balance so all living things—plants, animals, and people—will be able to live side by side in the only *Pa-hay-okee*, "Grassy River," in the world.

It was the end of a long day for the class, but there was one more part of the Everglades to visit. Ms. Stone and Ranger Jim led the students into an open space hidden at the end of the hiking trail.

Flock of White Ibis

"This is a finger glade," Ms. Stone said. "It's a small part of the sawgrass prairie that does not stay wet all year." During the wet season, the finger glade would be filled with water and fish. But now the ground, which is higher than the larger sawgrass prairies, was dry and hard.

"For a few minutes you can walk as far as you like and enjoy the finger glade," said Ms. Stone.

The students fanned out. Some pretended they were birds, flying low overhead. Others studied the sawgrass, pretending to be explorers discovering the glade. Still others talked about how the hard ground on which they were walking would turn into a lake deep enough for fish to swim through during the wet season. And some just lay on their backs, looking at the sky and the ring of trees around the glade.

When the students came back, they sat in a circle close to Ms. Stone.

"Close your eyes," said Ms. Stone, "and listen."

"Do you hear cars?" she whispered.

"Do you hear sirens?"

"Do you hear people?"

"What do you hear?"

Silence.

"You are not going to find silence like this anyplace else in the world," Ms. Stone said quietly. "This glade is protected by a circle of trees and marshes and natural wildlife. It is far from the noise of the outside world. It's full of *silence.* Any time you are in a sawgrass prairie like this one, stop and listen to the silence."

ANALYZE THE TEXT

Explain Scientific Ideas Why do you think the author includes this description of the finger glade? What has it helped you understand about the sawgrass prairies of the Everglades? How does this area compare to the mangrove swamp and Pinelands habitats?

The sun was setting over the Everglades as the class walked back to the bus. Birds flew low over the sawgrass prairie. It was a peaceful time, a time for everything to settle down for the night. The students knew that for the near future the Everglades would look the same, and might even be almost the same. They also knew about the dangers facing the Everglades, and that it would not stay the same unless people watched over it and took care of it.

Restoring the Everglades will take a long time, and it may never be finished. But the students knew they could play a part as they grew older. They had learned that they too were a part of the Everglades, connected in the same circle of life with the tiniest insect and largest alligator. They knew that someday in the not-too-distant future, responsibility for the Everglades would pass on to them. They would become the guardians and protectors of the only Everglades in the world, helping this wild and wonderful place go on *forever*.

ANALYZE THE TEXT

Author's Purpose Why might the author have written about a class field trip to the Everglades? Why do you think she included so many vivid details about the wetlands?

Dig Deeper

How to Analyze the Text

Use these pages to learn about Author's Purpose, Explaining Scientific Ideas, and Domain-Specific Vocabulary. Then read "Everglades Forever" again to apply what you learned.

Author's Purpose

Authors of narrative nonfiction, such as "Everglades Forever," have a variety of reasons for writing. They may want to share information, describe an event or a person, or persuade readers to agree with their position on an issue. In their writing, they include details such as facts, examples, and descriptions that will help them fulfill their purpose.

In "Everglades Forever," the **author's purpose** is to persuade. She wants to convince readers that it is important to protect the Everglades. She presents her argument and main points in the form of a narrative about a school field trip. This structure allows her to give reasons and evidence in a way that interests readers.

Look through the selection. What are the facts, examples, and other pieces of text evidence that help convince you the Everglades should be preserved?

Author's Purpose

Detail

Detail

COMMON CORE **RI.5.3** explain the relationships between individuals/events/ideas/concepts in a text; **RI.5.4** determine the meaning of general academic and domain-specific words and phrases; **RI.5.8** explain how an author uses reasons and evidence to support points; **RI.5.10** read and comprehend informational texts; **RF.5.4a** read on-level text with purpose and understanding

 Go Digital

Explain Scientific Ideas

In "Everglades Forever," the author explains several important scientific ideas. For example, she talks about the migration of animals within the wetlands, their various habitats, and the need for water conservation. By thinking about the relationships between these different aspects of the same topic, readers can understand the author's argument more fully.

Domain-Specific Vocabulary

The author includes **domain-specific words** in her text. These are words directly related to the topic of Everglades conservation, such as *endangered*, *wetlands*, *habitat*, *thermoregulate*, and *slough*. Using domain-specific vocabulary allows textbook and informational text authors to explain things precisely and to show their knowledge of the subject. Domain-specific terms are often defined in the text. When they are not, readers can use context clues to figure out their meanings.

Your Turn

 Turn and Talk Review the selection to prepare to discuss this question: *What reasons do people have for protecting the environment?* Draw information from the text as well as your prior knowledge. Then share your ideas in a small-group discussion.

Save the Everglades

 Classroom Conversation

Continue your discussion of "Everglades Forever" by using text evidence to answer these questions:

1. What are some of the habitats found in the Everglades?

2. How does the selection help you understand the connections between humans, plants, animals, and natural resources?

3. What are some ways that you can help protect the environment?

ADD GRAPHIC FEATURES

Write Captions With a partner, use the Internet or print resources to find additional graphic features for the selection. Look for photographs of Everglades animals, maps of the wetlands, or charts about the area's resources. Write a brief caption for each. Explain how the graphic feature supports an important idea in the text.

WRITE ABOUT READING

Response The author of "Everglades Forever" believes it is important to preserve the Everglades. What reasons and evidence does the author include to support her point? Write a paragraph to explain whether you agree or disagree with the author's argument. Use facts, examples, and other text evidence to support your position.

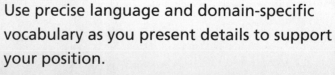

Writing Tip

Use precise language and domain-specific vocabulary as you present details to support your position.

COMMON CORE **RI.5.8** explain how an author uses reasons and evidence to support points; **W.5.2d** use precise language and domain-specific vocabulary; **W.5.9b** apply grade 5 Reading standards to informational texts; **W.5.10** write routinely over extended time frames and shorter time frames; **SL.5.1a** come to discussions prepared/explicitly draw on preparation and other information about the topic; **SL.5.1c** pose and respond to questions, make comments that contribute to the discussion, and elaborate on others' remarks

INFORMATIONAL TEXT

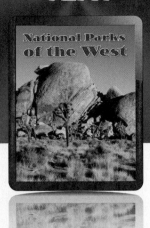

✓ GENRE

Informational text,
such as this website, gives facts and examples about a topic.

✓ TEXT FOCUS

Graphic Sources
Informational text may include a graph, which shows how different facts and numbers relate to each other and to the text.

COMMON CORE **RI.5.10** read and comprehend informational text

---

File Edit View Favorites

National Parks of the West

Big Bend National Park: Texas

Big Bend National Park is located along the Rio Grande, also called the Rio Bravo, the river that forms the boundary between Mexico and the United States. The park is open year-round. more

Wildlife and Vegetation

Big Bend is the home of more than 1,200 plant species, including 60 kinds of cactus, and more than 4,000 animal and insect species. This diversity is due to the park's many natural habitats, from the Chihuahuan Desert to the Chisos Mountains. more

search

Hiking in Big Bend National Park

Big Bend's 150 miles of trails have attracted hikers for years. Many choose the easy Window View Trail. Others prefer the challenge of a hike to the summit of 7,832-foot Mt. Emory. <u>more</u>

Hikers' Guidelines

Thousands of hikers visit Big Bend every year. National park rangers, guardians of the park, regulate the hiking. They ask hikers and backpackers to follow these tips:

- Your safety is your responsibility. Do not start your hike without the right supplies and equipment.
- Clean up after yourself.
- Do not climb within 50 feet of any Native American rock art.
- Do not harm or disturb nature. Conserving the environment is important!

A hiker in Big Bend National Park

Yellowstone National Park: Wyoming, Montana, and Idaho

Yellowstone National Park is the first and oldest national park in the United States. It was established in 1872. Yellowstone has at least 150 geysers. The most famous geyser is Old Faithful. This natural wonder shoots hot water as high as 200 feet in the air. <u>more</u>

A gray wolf running

Wildlife

Yellowstone has dozens of animal species. Today, wolves are among them, but in 1994, Yellowstone had no wolves. Humans had killed off the park's native gray wolves.

In the 1990s, scientists decided to restore this endangered wolf species to the park. In 1995 and 1996, scientists captured thirty-one gray wolves in Canada and brought them to Yellowstone. At first, the wolves lived in three large pens. In time, they were released into the wild.

The wolf restoration program is not unique. It was modeled after other similar programs. But it is one of the most successfully adapted programs of its kind. In 2006, 136 gray wolves lived in Yellowstone. They live in thirteen different areas of the park.

Analyze the graph below. In what year was the wolf population the highest? The lowest? How **m**any wolves were there in each of these years?

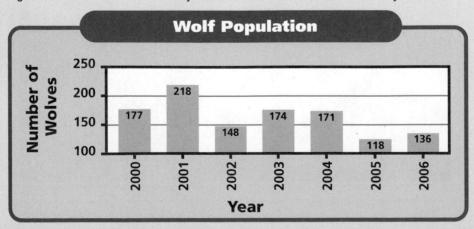

Wolf Population

Number of Wolves / Year

Year	2000	2001	2002	2003	2004	2005	2006
Number of Wolves	177	218	148	174	171	118	136

Compare Texts

Compare and Contrast Texts With a partner, review "Everglades Forever" and "Quest for the Tree Kangaroo" (Lesson 6). Take notes on what you learn about wildlife conservation and human interaction with nature. Consider how the text structure, or overall organization of each text, affects your understanding of the topic. Discuss and compare the two selections.

TEXT TO SELF

Write an Informal Letter Write a letter to your classmates to persuade them to plan a field trip to the Everglades. Use facts and details from "Everglades Forever" to make a strong case.

TEXT TO WORLD

Identify Viewpoint Review the website features on pages 254–256. What viewpoint is presented? Think about how that viewpoint affects your interest in national parks. Then search the Internet for a website about another wildlife preserve similar to Yellowstone. Discuss with classmates your thoughts about the website's information and its viewpoint.

Go Digital

COMMON CORE **RI.5.5** compare and contrast the overall structure in two or more texts; **RI.5.7** draw on information from print and digital sources to locate answers or solve problems; **W.5.4** produce writing in which development and organization are appropriate to task, purpose, and audience; **W.5.10** write routinely over extended time frames and shorter time frames

Grammar

What Is a Conjunction? A **conjunction** is a word that connects other words in a sentence. *And*, *but*, and *or* are **coordinating conjunctions**. They can connect two words, two groups of words, or two sentences. A sentence formed when a coordinating conjunction is used to connect two sentences is called a **compound sentence**. Words such as *if*, *because*, *although*, *after*, and *when* are **subordinating conjunctions**. A subordinating conjunction can connect a sentence and a dependent clause to form a **complex sentence**.

Coordinating Conjunction in a Compound Sentence
The egret stood in the sawgrass, and the osprey dived into the slough.

Subordinating Conjunction in a Complex Sentence
When the osprey dived, the egret flew away.

Try This! **Work with a partner. Identify each conjunction in the sentences below and tell whether it is coordinating or subordinating. Then explain the purpose of the conjunction in each sentence.**

1. Most plants cannot live in salty water, but mangrove trees thrive in it.

2. Where mangrove trees grow, shrimp and other marine animals can raise their young.

3. If the water in a swamp becomes too salty, some animals cannot survive there.

4. Fresh water is needed, and only rainfall can provide that.

A good writer avoids run-on sentences. One way to correct a run-on sentence is to add a comma and a coordinating conjunction to turn the run-on sentence into a compound sentence. Another way to correct a run-on sentence is to add a subordinating conjunction to turn it into a complex sentence.

Run-On Sentence

The hikers entered the Pinelands the world became very quiet.

Compound Sentence	Complex Sentence
The hikers entered the Pinelands, and the world became very quiet.	When the hikers entered the Pinelands, the world became very quiet.

 Connect Grammar to Writing

As you revise your cause-and-effect essay, look for run-on sentences. Correct a run-on sentence by dividing it into separate sentences or by using conjunctions to form a compound or complex sentence.

Informative Writing

✔️ **Ideas**   The author of "Everglades Forever: Restoring America's Great Wetland" uses specific facts and details to inform readers about the Everglades habitat. When you revise your **cause-and-effect essay**, make sure your supporting details are specific.

Colin drafted an essay on what would happen if alligators disappeared from the Everglades. Later, he made his supporting details more specific so that his key points would be easy to follow.

Writing Traits Checklist

✔️ **Ideas**
Did I support my ideas with specific details?

✔️ **Organization**
Did I group related information logically and make relationships between causes and effects clear?

✔️ **Sentence Fluency**
Did I use clauses effectively to link ideas?

✔️ **Word Choice**
Did I use precise words?

✔️ **Voice**
Is my writing clear and informative?

✔️ **Conventions**
Did I use correct spelling, grammar, and punctuation?

Revised Draft

Alligators help create the habitats of other living things in the Everglades ~~others~~. They dig deep holes, and the , which is part saltwater and part freshwater, holes fill with water. This brackish water that other animals depend on for food is home to young bonefish and shrimp.

Protecting the Everglades

by Colin Diep

What would happen if alligators left the Everglades? In an ecosystem, every creature plays an important part in keeping the others alive. No part of life can be taken away or harmed without affecting other animals and plants.

Alligators help create the habitats of other living things in the Everglades. They dig deep holes, and the holes fill with water. This brackish water, which is part saltwater and part freshwater, is home to young bonefish and shrimp that other animals depend on for food. Many plants and animals gather in these wet alligator holes and use them to survive the dry season.

If alligators were to disappear, the life that depends on alligator holes in the dry season would not survive. The birds that feed on those plants and animals would have to find food elsewhere, or they would not survive either. By protecting alligators, we can help protect all life in the Everglades.

Reading as a Writer

How do specific details make the causes and effects more clear? Where can you strengthen words and details in your cause-and-effect essay?

In my final paper, I made my supporting details more specific. I also made clear connections between my ideas.

STORM WARRIORS

Pea Island's **Forgotten Heroes**

critical

demolished

elite

commotion

bundle

annoyance

secured

squalling

clammy

realization

Vocabulary Reader

Context Cards

SAVED from the SEA

L.5.6 acquire and use general academic and domain-specific words and phrases

Vocabulary in Context

1 **critical**

Rescue workers can provide critical, or vital, aid when a hurricane strikes.

2 **demolished**

These people returned to search the ruins of their home after a tornado demolished it.

3 **elite**

Medals for bravery are given to an elite group of the best and most skilled lifeguards.

4 **commotion**

Rescue dogs are trained to stay calm in spite of chaos and commotion.

Go Digital

▶ Study each Context Card.

▶ Break each Vocabulary word into syllables. Use your glossary to check your answers.

5 bundle

Rescuers bundle, or wrap, injured skiers in blankets for warmth or to prevent shock.

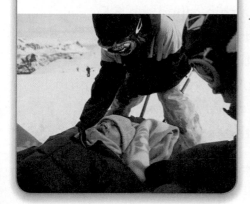

6 annoyance

During a fire, people who get too close can distract firefighters and cause them annoyance.

7 secured

In mountain rescues, one person is secured to another by safety fasteners.

8 squalling

The squalling of a child can lead rescuers to the frightened, crying victim.

9 clammy

The protective clothing worn by firefighters can make them feel clammy and damp.

10 realization

The realization, or understanding, that rescuers save lives makes families proud.

Read and Comprehend

 Go Digital

☑ TARGET SKILL

Conclusions and Generalizations Using text evidence to figure out something in a story that isn't directly stated by the author is called drawing a **conclusion.** A **generalization**—a broad statement that is true most of the time—is a type of conclusion. As you read "Storm Warriors," notice the details the author provides about a rescue crew and the people on a ship called the *E.S. Newman.* Their actions and words can help you draw conclusions and make generalizations about the characters. Use a graphic organizer like this one to record a conclusion, as well as the details you used to draw your conclusion. Details may include quotes from the text.

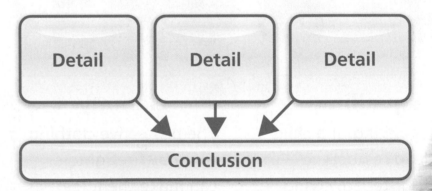

| Detail | Detail | Detail |

Conclusion

☑ TARGET STRATEGY

Infer/Predict As you read "Storm Warriors," make **inferences** based on details and characters' actions, and try to **predict** how the story will end.

RL.1.1 quote accurately when explaining what the text says explicitly and when drawing inferences

Courage

Nearly everyone has an opinion on the topic of courage. Most people consider courage to be a positive character trait. But what does it mean to be courageous?

There are many different kinds of people and many unique situations that might require courage. So, it makes sense that there are many different ways to be courageous. In "Storm Warriors," you learn what one boy thinks about courage as he assists in rescuing people after a shipwreck. Reading this selection will help you expand your definition of courage.

ANCHOR TEXT

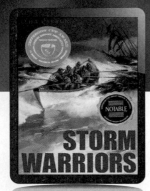

STORM WARRIORS

☑ TARGET SKILL

Conclusions and Generalizations Use details to explain ideas that aren't stated by the author.

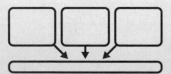

☑ GENRE

Historical fiction is a story in which characters and events are set in a real period of history. As you read, look for:

▶ a setting that is a real time and place in the past
▶ realistic characters and events
▶ some made-up events and details

COMMON CORE RL.5.6 describe how a narrator's or speaker's point of view influences how events are described; **RL.5.10** read and comprehend literature

  Go Digital

MEET THE AUTHOR
Elisa Carbone

To research *Storm Warriors*, Elisa Carbone went to North Carolina's Outer Banks to experience a storm for herself. She says, "I would go out onto the beach for as long as I could stand it, feeling the force of the wind, taking in all of the sensations. Then I'd . . . write it all down."

MEET THE ILLUSTRATOR
James Ransome

There were no art classes offered in James Ransome's school when he was a boy, so he studied books on how to draw. Then in high school and college, he had the chance to study painting, drawing, and film. Now he is the award-winning illustrator of over twenty-five books for children.

STORM WARRIORS

by Elisa Carbone
selection illustrated by James Ransome

It's 1896 on Pea Island, part of North Carolina's Outer Banks. Nathan dreams of becoming a fearless surfman with Pea Island's elite African American lifesaving crew. However, his father, a fisherman, doesn't want Nathan to risk his life rescuing people from shipwrecks. Nevertheless, Nathan studies medical books and learns critical lifesaving skills. Then a hurricane hits the Outer Banks. The E.S. Newman runs aground in the storm. This is Nathan's chance to help the surfmen. As the storm rages, he begins to realize that knowledge is as important as bravery.

I stumbled forward and caught my balance on the side of the beach cart. I faced the sea and the wind. There was the sunken ship, hardly thirty yards from us. She was a mass of dark hull and white torn sails against the foaming sea, rocking on her side, her cabin and much of her starboard already demolished by the heavy surf. As I stood with my mouth open, panting, the wind blew my cheeks floppy and dried my tongue.

A cheer went up from the sailors aboard the ship. They'd spotted us and had high hopes that they would soon be rescued. I expected to hear the command "Action," to begin the breeches-buoy rescue, but heard nothing. It took me a moment to realize what Keeper Etheridge must already have figured out: our equipment was useless. There was no way to dig a hole for the sand anchor under these rolling waves, nowhere to set up the Lyle gun.

That's when I heard Mr. Meekins's voice above the din of wind and surf. "Those waves won't stop me from swimming through them—they're all blown over, hardly taller than a man," he said.

Swim? Swim out into that raging sea?

I stood rigid and watched as Mr. Etheridge pulled a large-sized shot line out of the beach cart and helped Mr. Meekins tie it around his waist. Mr. Pugh was tied in as well, and the heaving stick, attached to its own line, was secured to Mr. Meekins's body. The wind shoved at me and buffeted my ears. It was unthinkable, what these men were doing. Violence swirled around us—a deadly, churning mix of wind and sea. And these two surfmen were walking *into* it.

"Man the ropes," shouted Mr. Etheridge. "One of them goes down, we'll haul them both back in."

Mr. Meekins and Mr. Pugh were dark forms against the white foam, plodding into the surf. Powerful waves smacked them in the chest. They ducked their heads down and pushed forward.

I watched with a sick feeling in my stomach as the realization crept over me: I would never be able to do what these men were doing. The words of their motto ran through my head: "You have to go out, but you don't have to come back." In that moment I knew, with not a shred of doubt, that I did not have the courage to risk my life that way. The dream, and all the months of hoping, blew away as quickly as the foam off the waves. William and Floyd and Daddy were right. I would never be a surfman.

There was no time for me to wallow in my loss. The men were paying out the ropes, and I was a fisherman—here to help. I took hold of one of the ropes. I turned my face sideways to the wind, but still it made my eyes blurry with tears. Blindly, I let the rope out, hand over hand, then squinted out toward the ship. A ladder had been lowered, and the sailors leaned over the side, waiting. Mr. Meekins and Mr. Pugh were almost there.

I heard another cheer from the men on the ship. When I peered out, Mr. Meekins was swinging the heaving stick and line. He let it fly and it landed on deck. The sailors would tie the line to the ship so that the rope could help steady the surfmen as they made their way from ship to shore and back again.

Soon we were hauling rope back in. The surfmen would be carrying one of the sailors between them now. I squinted into the spray. Where was the rescued sailor? Mr. Meekins and Mr. Pugh were on their way back, but without a third man between them. Mr. Meekins was carrying something a little larger than a Lyle gun.

ANALYZE THE TEXT

Conclusions and Generalizations
The narrator says that the men on the ship cheered. Why do you think they did this?

What in the world could be more important to save off that ship than the lives of the men on board? I shook my head and hauled rope. The surfmen were half walking, half swimming, pushing forward, the waves smacking against their backs and seeming to want to spit them out of the sea.

As the surfmen drew closer, I heard what sounded like the squalling of an alley cat. Mr. Meekins handed over his bundle and shouted, "Get it into dry blankets before it goes blue!" The bundle was passed from man to man, until it was handed to me and I found myself looking into the terrified eyes of a screaming child.

Daddy put his arm around my shoulders. "The driving cart," he shouted over the din of the waves and wind. In the driving cart, which was nothing more than an open wagon, dry blankets were packed under oilskins.

We crouched next to the cart, and it gave us some protection from the storm. The child clung to my neck. He was drenched and shivering miserably. I tried to loosen his grip so I could get his wet clothes off, but he just clung tighter. He was crying more softly now. "Mamma?" he whimpered.

I gave Daddy a pleading look. What if his mother had already been washed overboard and drowned? Daddy stood, cupped his hands around his eyes, and looked in the direction of the ship. "They're carrying a woman back now," he said.

"Your mamma is coming," I told the child. He looked to be about three or four years old, with pale white skin and a shock of thick brown hair. "Let's get you warm before she gets here."

We had the boy wrapped in a dry blanket by the time his mother came running to him, cried, "Thomas!" and clutched him to her own wet clothing with such passion that she probably got him half drenched again.

The lady, who told us her name was Mrs. Gardiner, said she'd be warm enough in her wet dress under blankets and oilskins. No sooner had we settled her with Thomas than we heard the cry "Ho, this man is injured!"

ANALYZE THE TEXT

Point of View How would the description of the story's events change if it were told from Mr. Meekins's third-person limited point of view?

273

I ran to see. A young sailor had just been delivered by the surfmen. Blood dripped from his head and stained his life preserver. His lips were a sickly blue. He took two steps, then collapsed face first into the shallow water. Mr. Bowser dragged him up by his armpits and pulled him toward the driving cart.

"George, take over my place with the ropes," he shouted to Daddy. "Nathan, come help me."

The sailor looked hardly older than me, with dirty blond hair that had a bloody gash the size of a pole bean running through it.

"Treat the bleeding first, then the hypothermia," I said as I recalled the words from the medical books and they comforted me with their matter-of-factness.

Mr. Bowser grunted as we lifted the sailor into the driving cart. "You did study well, Nathan," he said.

Mr. Bowser sent me for the medicine chest, then I held a compress against the man's head wound while Mr. Bowser began to remove his wet clothes. That's when Mr. Bowser seemed to notice Mrs. Gardiner for the first time.

"Ma'am, we're going to have to . . ." He cleared his throat. "This boy's hypothermic, so his wet clothes have to . . ."

Mrs. Gardiner rolled her eyes in annoyance. "Oh, for heaven's sake!" she exclaimed. She immediately went to work to pull off the man's boots, help Mr. Bowser get the rest of his clothes off, and bundle him in a dry blanket.

"Are there any other injured on board?" Mr. Bowser asked as he wrapped a bandage around the man's head.

"No, only Arthur," she said. "He took quite a fall when the ship ran aground."

Arthur groaned and his eyes fluttered open. "I'm cold," he complained.

Suddenly there was a commotion at the ropes. "Heave!" Mr. Etheridge shouted. "Haul them all in!"

"They've lost their footing!" I cried.

Mr. Bowser grasped me by the arms. "Take over here. I'm sure you know what to do." Then he ran to help with the ropes.

My hands felt clammy and shaky, but once again the words from the books came back to steady me: "Rub the legs and arms with linseed oil until warmth returns . . ." I rummaged in the medicine chest, found the linseed oil, and poured some into my palm.

"This will warm you, sir," I said loudly enough to be heard over the wind.

Arthur nodded his bandaged head and watched nervously as I rubbed the oil into his feet and calves, then his hands and arms. He gave Mrs. Gardiner a quizzical look. "Ain't he young to be a doctor?" he asked her.

She patted his shoulder and smoothed the hair off his forehead. "He seems to know what to do, dear," she said.

"I am warming up," he said.

I lifted the lantern to look at Arthur's face and saw that his lips were no longer blue.

ANALYZE THE TEXT

Characterization At first, Nathan was worried that he would not be helpful to the rescue effort. What evidence does the author give to show that Nathan is helpful after all?

Just then a tall white man appeared, dressed in a captain's coat, his long hair flying in the wind. He reached up into the driving cart and pulled Mrs. Gardiner to him, pressing his cheek against hers. He must have asked about Thomas, because she pointed to him, bundled and sleeping in the cart. "They've saved the whole crew!" he cried. He looked around at me and Arthur, and at the other rescued sailors and the surfmen who were now gathering around the driving cart in preparation for the long trip back through the storm to the station.

"My good men," he said, his voice shaking, "we owe you our lives."

Dig Deeper

How to Analyze the Text

Use these pages to learn about Conclusions and Generalizations, Point of View, and Characterization. Then read "Storm Warriors" again to apply what you learned.

Conclusions and Generalizations

Characters' actions and words can help you draw conclusions and make generalizations about a text in order to better understand it. A **conclusion** is a judgment reached by thinking about text details. A **generalization** is a broad statement that is true most of the time.

Authors do not always directly state information for readers to use in drawing conclusions or making generalizations. You can understand what is not directly stated in a story by using dialogue, details, and events to make **inferences.** As you read the selection again, use the text to draw conclusions and make generalizations about the characters' experiences. Remember to use quotations and evidence from the text to support your thoughts.

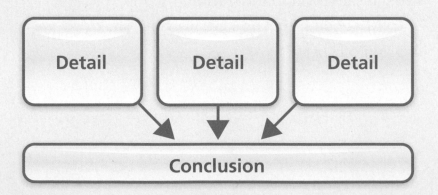

RL.5.1 quote accurately when explaining what the text says explicitly and when drawing inferences; **RL.5.6** describe how a narrator's or speaker's point of view influences how events are described; ; **RF.5.4a** read on-level text with purpose and understanding

Point of View

When an author writes in the **first-person point of view,** one character tells the story as he or she experiences it. Words such as *I, we, me,* and *mine* are used in first-person point of view. A **third-person limited point of view** means that a narrator tells what one character observes, feels, and knows. A third-person narrator is outside the story and uses words such as *he, she, him, his,* and *her* to discuss the characters.

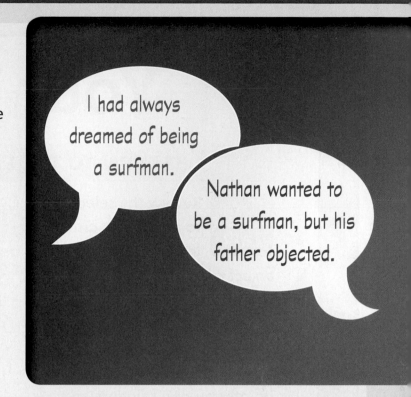

I had always dreamed of being a surfman.

Nathan wanted to be a surfman, but his father objected.

Characterization

An author describes a character's actions, words, and thoughts to help define the character's traits and personality. This technique is called **characterization.** In a story written from the first-person point of view, the narrator is a character in the story. The narrator's way of speaking, as well as thoughts about events and other characters in the story, helps characterize him or her.

Your Turn

RETURN TO THE ESSENTIAL QUESTION

Review the selection to prepare to discuss this question: *How can an act of courage reveal a person's true nature?* As you discuss, take turns reviewing and explaining each other's key ideas. Ask questions to clarify points you don't understand.

Classroom Conversation

Continue your discussion of "Storm Warriors" by using text evidence to explain your answers to these questions:

1. What reasons does Nathan have for admiring the surfmen? Are his reasons valid? Why or why not?

2. What does Nathan learn about the nature of courage?

3. How might Nathan's life change because of what he learns about himself during the story?

WHO IS THIS CHARACTER?

Discuss Nathan Review the story to find evidence of Nathan's character traits. Look for examples of his intelligence, courage, kindness, and resourcefulness. Record the page numbers of the examples or passages you find. Then share your information with a partner. Work together to identify the best text evidence for each trait.

WRITE ABOUT READING

Response "Storm Warriors" is written from the main character's—Nathan's—point of view. How does his point of view affect descriptions in the story? Think about what would be different if one of the surfmen or sailors told the story. Write a paragraph explaining how Nathan's point of view shapes the story and affects how you see events and other story characters. Use quotes and evidence from the text to support your ideas.

Writing Tip

Use conjunctions to combine sentences and help your readers understand the relationships between your ideas.

COMMON CORE **RL.5.6** describe how a narrator's or speaker's point of view influences how events are described; **W.5.9a** apply grade 5 Reading standards to literature; **W.5.10** write routinely over extended time frames and shorter time frames; **SL.5.1a** come to discussions prepared/explicitly draw on preparation and other information about the topic; **SL.5.1c** pose and respond to questions, make comments that contribute to the discussion, and elaborate on others' remarks

Pea Island's
Forgotten
Heroes

☑ GENRE

Informational text, such as this magazine article, gives facts and examples about a topic.

☑ TEXT FOCUS

Primary sources are original photographs, documents, or quotes from the topic's time period. The author of this selection includes photographs of Pea Island, the surfmen, and the surfmen's rescue equipment to support the text.

RI.5.10 read and comprehend informational texts

Go Digital

Pea Island's Forgotten Heroes

by Cecelia Munzenmaier

The photograph at the museum in Beaufort, North Carolina, was small. Still, it caught Katie Burkhart's eye. Seven men in uniform stood in front of U.S. Life-Saving Service Station #17. A caption explained that these were the Pea Island surfmen. Led by Chief Richard Etheridge, they saved nine people from the *E.S. Newman* in 1896.

Fourteen-year-old Burkhart wanted to know more. She looked up information about the surfmen for an eighth-grade history project. Then she wrote a paper titled, "Forgotten Legacy: African-American Storm Warriors." It won a National Award of Merit from the American Association of State and Local Historians.

It also helped bring attention to some forgotten heroes.

Finding a Lost Story

Burkhart learned that Etheridge and his surfmen were an elite group. They were known for their skill and bravery. They were also the only African American group whose job was to save lives.

Then she came to a realization. Their bravery had never been officially recognized. "I immediately felt I had to do something about it," she says.

The eighth-grader wrote to Senator Jesse Helms and President Bill Clinton. She asked why the crew had not been given a medal. She learned that Coast Guard Officer Steve Rochon and graduate students David Zoby and David Wright were also trying to correct this wrong.

"Again and again, the crew went back through the raging sea."

The Pea Island surfmen in about 1890

Reclaiming a Legacy

The researchers found Chief Etheridge's own account of what happened. He described the commotion of the hurricane that demolished the ship. "The storm was raging fearfully, the storm tide was sweeping across the beach, and the team was often brought to a standstill by the sweeping current," he wrote in the station log. Lending any help seemed impossible, yet they had to try.

Secured by a rope, two team members swam to the sinking ship. They brought back a crewman. Then a fresh team heard the squalling of the captain's baby and saved him. For six hours, they ignored their own needs. They were too busy to feel annoyance. Missed meals and clammy clothes were not important. As they saved people, they would bundle them into warm blankets at the station.

The research was critical in winning recognition for the team. One hundred years to the day after the rescue of the *E.S. Newman*, the Pea Island crew was awarded a Gold Lifesaving Medal. Katie Burkhart and several descendants of the surfmen listened with pride to the speech that described how "again and again, the Pea Island Station crew went back through the raging sea, literally carrying all nine persons from certain death to the safety of the shore."

Pea Island, 1917

Beach rescue equipment

Compare Texts

Compare Texts About Heroes Talk with a partner about how heroes are portrayed in "Storm Warriors" and "Pea Island's Forgotten Heroes." After you have discussed your ideas, make a list describing the characteristics of heroes. For each characteristic, quote one detail or example from either text to support your generalizations about heroes.

TEXT TO SELF

Design a Medal The Pea Island crew members were awarded a Gold Lifesaving Medal for their heroism. Design a medal for a modern-day hero whom you admire. Include an image and a message to go on the medal. Write a short speech explaining why the person deserves the medal, and present your information to a partner.

TEXT TO WORLD

Research Hurricanes The Pea Island rescuers had to fight a hurricane in order to rescue the passengers and crew of the *E.S. Newman*. Work with a partner to brainstorm research questions about hurricanes or another kind of natural disaster you would like to learn more about. Then choose one of the questions and conduct research in print and digital sources to answer it.

COMMON CORE **RI.5.1** quote accurately when explaining what a text says explicitly and when drawing inferences; **RI.5.7** draw on information from print and digital sources to locate answers or solve problems; **RI.5.9** integrate information from several texts on the same topic; **W.5.7** conduct short research projects that use several sources to build knowledge through investigation

Grammar

What Is a Complex Sentence? A **complex sentence** is made up of two clauses joined by a **subordinating conjunction,** such as *because.* The part of the sentence that contains the subordinating conjunction tells about the other part, and cannot stand on its own.

What Is a Correlative Conjunction? Correlative conjunctions work in pairs. Some examples are *both / and* and *neither / nor.* Correlative conjunctions can be used to join parallel words or phrases—for example, two nouns, two verbs, or two adjectives.

Complex Sentences and Correlative Conjunctions

can stand on its own	cannot stand on its own

The crew members were in danger because their ship had been wrecked.

cannot stand on its own	can stand on its own

Although the waves were big, two surfmen swam to the ship.

noun   noun

Both courage and knowledge are important in an emergency situation.

Try This! **Copy each sentence onto a sheet of paper. Circle the subordinating conjunctions. Underline the correlative conjunctions and the words or phrases they join.**

1. The surfmen could neither dig a hole for the sand anchor nor set up the Lyle gun.

2. After the men rescued the child, Nathan took care of him.

3. The child warmed up once he was wrapped in a dry blanket.

4. Both Nathan and Mrs. Gardiner wanted to help the injured sailor.

Good writers establish clear relationships between ideas. Combining shorter sentences to form a complex sentence can show how ideas are linked or which idea is more important. Use a comma after the first part of a complex sentence if that part begins with a subordinating conjunction. Correlative conjunctions can also be used to combine related sentences.

Separate Sentences

The snow was dangerously deep.

The governor declared an emergency.

Subordinating Conjunction

Since the snow was dangerously deep, the governor declared an emergency.

Correlative Conjunctions

Neither the town nor the governor was prepared for the dangerously deep snow.

 Connect Grammar to Writing

As you revise your research report next week, look for sentences with related ideas. Try using subordinating or correlative conjunctions to combine these related sentences.

COMMON CORE

W.5.5 develop and strengthen writing by planning, revising, editing, rewriting, or trying a new approach; **W.5.7** conduct short research projects that use several sources to build knowledge through investigation; **W.5.8** recall information from experiences or gather information from print and digital sources/summarize and paraphrase information and provide a list of sources

Informative Writing

Reading-Writing Workshop: Prewrite

✔ **Ideas** To plan a **research report,** find reliable print and digital sources to answer your questions about your topic. Record facts and their sources on notecards. Then organize your notes into an outline, with details to support each main idea. Each main topic in your outline will become a paragraph in your report. Josie researched the sinking of the *Andrea Doria*. For her outline, she grouped her notes into four main topics.

Writing Process Checklist

▶ **Prewrite**

☑ Did I choose a topic that will interest my audience and me?

☑ Did I ask questions to focus my research?

☑ Did I gather facts from a variety of good sources?

☑ Did I organize facts into an outline with main topics and subtopics?

Draft

Revise

Edit

Publish and Share

Exploring a Topic

What happened to the <u>Andrea Doria</u>?
— captain did not slow ship's speed in the fog
— <u>Stockholm's</u> bow cut into the hull.
Ballard, Robert, and Rick Archbold. <u>Ghost Liners: Exploring the World's Greatest Lost Ships</u>. Boston, MA: Little, Brown and Company, 1998.

How were the passengers rescued?
— <u>Stockholm</u> rescued hundreds of passengers and crew from the <u>Andrea Doria</u>
— lifeboats were used <u>The Andrea Doria The Greatest Rescue of All Time</u>. 11 June 1998. ThinkQuest. 4 Feb. 2012. <http://library.thinkquest.org>

Outline

I. The accident

    A. July 25, 1956, off the coast of Massachusetts

    B. The *Andrea Doria* and the *Stockholm* hit each other.

II. Details of the crash

    A. Foggy night

    B. Both ships using radar to navigate

    C. The *Stockholm*'s bow hit the *Andrea Doria*'s side.

III. Help arrives

    A. Several ships came to the rescue.

    B. The *Ile de France* rescued passengers.

    C. The *Stockholm* was damaged but not sinking. It helped in the rescue.

IV. A historic rescue

    A. The *Andrea Doria* took 11 hours to sink.

    B. All but 46 people were rescued.

Reading as a Writer

Is Josie's outline well organized? Why do you think so? What parts of your outline can you organize better or make more complete?

In my outline, I organized facts into main topics and subtopics. I listed subtopics in logical order to support my main ideas.

Cougars

"Purr-fection"

Vocabulary in Context

resemble
detecting
keen
vary
unobserved
mature
particular
available
ferocious
contentment

Vocabulary Reader

Context Cards

Big Cats

1 resemble

Some house cats resemble, or look like, cougars, but cougars are much bigger.

2 detecting

Excellent eyesight and a good sense of smell help lions in finding, or detecting, their prey.

3 keen

All cats have sharp, keen night vision. It is a great aid to them when hunting.

4 vary

The color of tiger stripes can vary from black and orange to black and white.

COMMON CORE **L.5.6** acquire and use general academic and domain-specific words and phrases

Go Digital

▶ Study each Context Card.

▶ Use a dictionary to determine the part of speech of each Vocabulary word.

5 unobserved

Hiding under the rug, this kitten is unobserved, or unseen, by its owner.

6 mature

As cougars mature from cubs to adults, their eyes change from blue to greenish-yellow.

7 particular

A house cat may prefer a particular, or certain, brand of food. It will eat only that kind.

8 available

Big cats can live only where plenty of food is available, or obtainable.

9 ferocious

The savage, ferocious roar of a tiger signals that the animal is angry.

10 contentment

Like wild cats, house cats purr with contentment when they are satisfied.

Read and Comprehend

 Go Digital

☑ TARGET SKILL

Main Ideas and Details As you read "Cougars," look for the **main ideas,** or most important points, that the author makes about cougars and their habitats. Each main idea is supported by **details,** such as facts, examples, and descriptions. You can use these main ideas and important details to **summarize** part or all of a text. To keep track of the main ideas in each part of the selection, use a graphic organizer like this one.

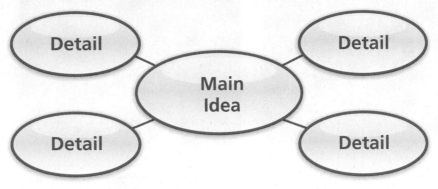

☑ TARGET STRATEGY

Monitor/Clarify As you read "Cougars," remember to **monitor,** or notice, how well you understand the text. If there is something you do not understand, pause to **clarify** it, or make it clear.

RI.5.2 determine two or more main ideas and explain how they are supported by details/summarize; **RI.5.3** explain the relationships between individuals/events/ideas/concepts in a text

Animal Behaviors

Have you ever seen a dog trample the ground in circles before it settles down to sleep? Have you noticed how squirrels drop nuts from trees to crack the shells? Behaviors like these teach us about animals' intelligence and adaptability. Observing the behaviors of wild animals helps us find ways to protect both the animals and their habitats.

In "Cougars," the author shares many details about the behavior of these wild cats. Although cougars are not easy to study, scientists have tried to learn as much as they can about them. In certain regions, cougars are an important part of the ecosystem and play a crucial role in the chain of life.

ANCHOR TEXT

Our WILD WORLD **Cougars**

 TARGET SKILL

Main Ideas and Details
Identify a topic's main ideas and the details that support them.

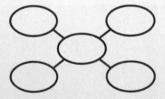

 GENRE

Informational text gives facts and details about a topic. As you read, look for:

▸ information that is clearly organized

▸ domain-specific vocabulary that aids understanding

▸ photographs and captions that enhance the text

COMMON CORE **RI.5.2** determine two or more main ideas and explain how they are supported by details/summarize; **RI.5.4** determine the meaning of general academic and domain-specific words and phrases; **RI.5.10** read and comprehend informational texts

 Go Digital

MEET THE AUTHOR

PATRICIA CORRIGAN

Patricia Corrigan began writing for her local newspaper while she was still in high school. Since then, she has been a writer for the *St. Louis Post-Dispatch* and has published numerous magazine articles, nonfiction books for adults, and nature books for children. She loves to travel and has taken trips to Argentina and Egypt.

COUGARS

BY PATRICIA CORRIGAN

ESSENTIAL QUESTION

What can a scientist learn by observing the behaviors of a particular animal?

Cougars are seldom seen and rarely heard. In fact, they often live their entire lives unobserved by humans!

But we do know that these members of the cat family live in eleven western U.S. states. They are found from the southernmost tip of Alaska down to where the California border meets Mexico and east all the way to the edge of Texas. Their cousins, Florida panthers, live in Florida. In Canada, cougars are found in British Columbia and parts of Alberta. Cougars also live throughout Mexico, Central America, and South America.

In different areas of the world, cougars have different names. They may be called mountain lions, wildcats, pumas, painters, fire cats, swamp lions, or catamounts. In Mexico, Spanish for cougar is *el león* (leh OHN), which means "the lion." And sometimes they are known by nicknames like "ghost of the wilderness" and "ghost walker."

Fortunately, cougars are able to live in many different habitats. Over time, they have adapted, or evolved, for living in places such as snow-capped mountains, jungles thick with vegetation, cool pine forests, grassy plains, and murky swamps. For instance, cougars that live in northern mountains tend to be larger and have a thicker coat of fur than cougars that live elsewhere. They learned to climb trees. And they also can swim if necessary, but usually prefer to stay dry—like their relative, the house cat!

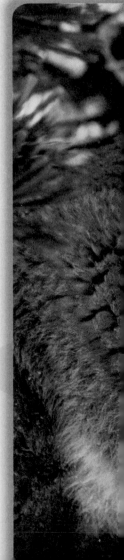

The average cougar measures from 3.3 to 5.3 feet long and stands about 2 feet high at the shoulder. Adult male cougars weigh up to 225 pounds, and adult females usually are slightly smaller. A cougar's tail may measure up to 32 inches, almost two-thirds the length of the animal's body.

ANALYZE THE TEXT

Main Ideas and Details What is the topic of this selection? How do you know? Choose a paragraph on one of these two pages. State its main idea and explain how it is supported by details.

Cougars don't hunt from trees, but a high branch makes a good lookout spot.

Cougars have good balance and can easily leap over fallen trees and onto rocks without slowing down.

The cougar is one species (SPEE sees), or kind, of wild cat. Cougars are medium-sized, along with bobcats and lynxes. Tigers, lions, and leopards all are larger and heavier.

Cougars are muscular and sleek, with little fat on their bodies. Fat usually serves as excellent insulation and keeps an animal's body warm. But because cougars have little of this kind of insulation, they have another natural defense against the cold: their fur coats keep them warm.

The layer of hair closest to the skin, called the underfur, is woolly and short. The top layer is made up of longer hairs, called guard hairs. These hairs are hollow and trap the air to keep cold temperatures from reaching the animal's skin.

Unlike humans, cougars have no sweat glands, so the cougars that live in warm climates cool themselves the same way dogs do, by panting to release heat from their bodies.

ANALYZE THE TEXT

Domain-Specific Vocabulary The author defines several domain-specific words on pages 298–299. How does the author's use of these words help strengthen the text? Does she seem more or less credible as a science writer? Why?

Cougars' coats are usually tawny, or orange-brown. They also may be gray, sandy brown, reddish-brown, and tan. All adult cougars have black markings on the sides of the muzzle, or snout, where the whiskers are. Some people say this area looks as if the cougar has a "mustache." If cougars were less secretive, scientists might be able to tell individual animals apart by the dark patterns on the muzzles, but few of the animals are ever seen.

The chin is white, as is the area right under the pinkish-brown nose. The tips of their tails also are black. The underside of most cougars is light, sometimes nearly white. At first glance, adult cougars resemble female lions.

Their coloring helps them blend in with their surroundings. It is good camouflage (KAM uh flahj) and helps them hide from their prey (PRAY), or the animals they hunt for food.

Cougars have good eyesight. In fact, vision is their best-developed sense. Researchers believe that they can see moving prey from long distances. The cougar's yellow eyes have large, round pupils that take in all available light. That helps the animal see at night almost as well as during the day.

A keen sense of hearing is important for cougars. They even can move their small, rounded ears to take in sounds coming from different directions. Cougars also have a strong sense of smell, which can really be useful when following prey. Still, their sense of smell is not as well developed as their senses of sight or hearing.

Like all of their cat relatives, cougars have whiskers. These sensitive hairs are also called vibrissae (vy BRIHS ee). They grow on either side of the animal's nose and mouth, above the eyes, and sometimes on the chin.

These whiskers vary in length, but most of the whiskers found on the muzzle are long enough to stretch past the side of the face and back to the edge of the ear. The cougar uses whiskers to gather information through touch. With its whiskers, a cougar can determine the height of the grass, the width of the space under a rock, and whether a bush would be easy or difficult to push through.

Cougars make a variety of sounds, or vocalizations. Their meow, which is a sign of contentment, is much louder than that of a pet cat. They also purr when they are contented. Cougars hiss first and then growl when they feel threatened. Unlike lions, cougars cannot roar.

Like all cats, cougars groom themselves. Grooming helps keep their coats clean. They use their rough tongues to remove any loose hair and to untangle any matted hair. Female cougars groom their babies constantly, and young siblings have been seen grooming one another.

Mothers pick up their kittens by the scruff of the neck to move them one at a time to a new den site.

When a cougar sees an enemy nearby, it may try to look ferocious and scare it away by showing its teeth and growling.

Cougars have very strong jaws. And they have three kinds of teeth, 24 in all. The carnassial (kar NASS ee uhl) teeth are located on both the top and bottom jaws. They are long and sharp, used for slicing or shearing. The canine (KAY nyn) teeth are thick and sharp, used for puncturing. The incisors (ihn SYZ ohrz) are small and straight, used for cutting and some chewing. But cougars don't chew their food very well. They mostly gulp down large chunks.

Most adult cougars are solitary, which means they live alone. They protect their territory from intruders, including other cougars. Each cougar needs a lot of space, an average of as much as 200 square miles for adult males and less than half that for adult females. They may walk as far as 30 miles in a day, searching for food or patrolling their territory.

Males and females look alike, but it is the female that cares for the young.

Newborn kittens have soft, fluffy-looking fur that is speckled with brown spots. This coloring helps camouflage them.

The spots disappear when the kittens are about eight months old. Kittens also have curly tails, which straighten out as they get older.

The kittens are born with blue eyes, which stay closed for about the first two weeks. Their eye color soon changes to yellow.

Kittens are totally dependent on their mother for food. They nurse for up to three months. Immediately after birth, and often in the next few weeks, the female licks the kittens to clean their fur. This helps them stay safe from enemies that might find the den site by detecting the scent of the newborn kittens.

If a female cougar thinks that her kittens are in danger in a particular spot, she often finds a new hiding place and moves them. A mother cougar will do whatever is necessary to keep the kittens away from dangerous predators, or enemies, such as wolves.

When the mother leaves to hunt for food, the kittens stay hidden and quiet at the den site. When the kittens are about two months old, their teeth have grown and they nurse less. Their mother begins to bring them food every two or three days. The mother makes no special effort to catch small prey for her small offspring. At first, the young kittens just want to play with the food, no matter what she brings. One of the first lessons the mother teaches her kittens is how to eat this new food.

By example, she shows them how to bite, how to tear meat off the bone, and how to chew. She also teaches the kittens that their rough tongues are good for cleaning the meat off bones. After about six months the kittens are good at eating this food, and they begin to explore away from the den site.

ANALYZE THE TEXT

Explain Scientific Ideas What ideas has the author shared about cougar kitten development on these two pages? How do these ideas relate to what you have learned about the lives of adult cougars?

This young cougar still has some of its baby spots. It is practicing stalking its prey.

The kittens stay with their mother for about eighteen months. During this time, she teaches them many things about surviving in their habitat. As the kittens mature, the mother cougar takes them hunting. They learn how to find and carefully follow prey. This is called stalking.

They also learn when to pounce, or jump out suddenly, to capture the prey. They are taught how to hide their kill and protect it from other animals. With a lot of practice, they learn to hunt for themselves.

Then, the young cougars go out on their own to find a territory and a mate. If they find a good habitat with plenty of prey animals and water in the area, cougars may live about eight to ten years.

Cougar eyesight may be
five times better than
human eyesight.

Dig Deeper

How to Analyze the Text

Use these pages to learn about Main Ideas and Details, Explaining Scientific Ideas, and Domain-Specific Vocabulary. Then read "Cougars" again to apply what you learned.

Main Ideas and Details

Informational texts, such as "Cougars," contain several main ideas and supporting details. A **main idea** is a major point brought out in the text or in a section of the text. Sometimes, a main idea is stated directly. If it is not stated directly, the reader must look at the information in that part of the text to infer, or guess, the main idea.

Supporting details are key facts, examples, descriptions, and other text evidence used to develop each main idea. For example, the main idea of the third paragraph on page 298 is that cougars have different layers of hair. The supporting details name and explain the purpose of each layer. As you revisit "Cougars," identify main ideas and details, and use them to summarize the text.

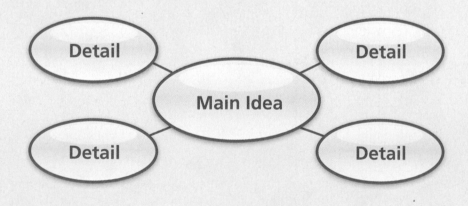

COMMON CORE

RI.5.2 determine two or more main ideas and explain how they are supported by details/summarize; **RI.5.3** explain the relationships between individuals/events/ideas/concepts in a text; **RI.5.4** determine the meaning of general academic and domain-specific words and phrases; **RF.5.4a** read on-level text with purpose and understanding

Explain Scientific Ideas

The purpose of most informational texts is to inform, or to share knowledge about a topic with readers. When that topic is related to science, the author carefully explains scientific ideas in ways that will help readers gain a solid understanding. For example, the author of "Cougars" uses clear, descriptive details to explain the ideas of cougar behavior and development.

Domain-Specific Vocabulary

Authors of informational texts often use **domain-specific words.** These are words from the content area that they are writing about— such as social studies, art, or science. Using domain-specific vocabulary enables authors to explain ideas precisely. It also shows the author's expertise or familiarity with the subject and lends credibility to his or her writing.

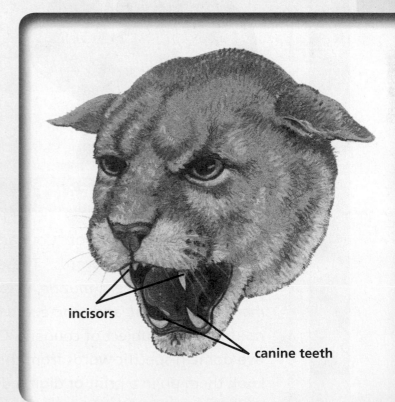

incisors

canine teeth

Your Turn

 Turn and Talk Review the selection to prepare to discuss this question: *What can a scientist learn by observing the behaviors of a particular animal?* As you discuss, take turns reviewing each other's key points.

 Classroom Conversation

Continue your discussion of "Cougars" by using text evidence to explain your answers to these questions:

1. How do you think the author feels about cougars? Why?

2. What did you learn about cougars in this selection that surprised you?

3. What qualities do scientists who observe animals need to have?

WHAT DOES IT MEAN?

Look It Up The author of "Cougars" uses many domain-specific words. These words, such as *prey*, *whiskers*, *muzzle*, *vocalizations*, *matted*, *carnassial*, and *canine*, are directly related to the subject of cougars. Choose five domain-specific words from the text. Look them up in a print or digital dictionary. Write a new sentence for each word. Then share your sentences with a partner.

WRITE ABOUT READING

Response The last section of the text is about mother cougars and their kittens. Would you agree that one of the main ideas of this section could be stated as "mother cougars know best"? Write a paragraph explaining your opinion about the main ideas of this section of text. Show how the details in the text support the main ideas. Use specific quotations to develop your paragraph.

Writing Tip

State your opinion at the beginning of your paragraph. Be sure to include a conclusion that restates this opinion and makes it memorable for readers.

Go Digital

COMMON CORE **RI.5.2** determine two or more main ideas and explain how they are supported by details/summarize; **RI.5.4** determine the meaning of general academic and domain-specific words and phrases; **W.5.9b** apply grade 5 Reading standards to informational texts; **W.5.10** write routinely over extended time frames and shorter time frames; **SL.5.1a** come to discussions prepared/explicitly draw on preparation and other information about the topic; **L.5.4c** consult reference materials, both print and digital, to find pronunciation and determine or clarify meaning; **L.5.6** acquire and use general academic and domain-specific words and phrases

POETRY

"Purr-fection"

✓ GENRE

Poetry uses the sounds and rhythms of words to suggest images and express feelings in a variety of forms.

✓ TEXT FOCUS

Alliteration Poets often use repeating consonant sounds at the beginnings of words. Doing so draws attention to vivid images that appeal to the senses.

RL.5.10 read and comprehend literature

COMMON CORE

 Go Digital

"Purr-fection"

Have you ever wondered how a cat uses its keen eyesight and hearing for detecting mice? Have you ever wished you could be a cat, napping in perfect contentment? From ferocious tigers to timid tabbies, cats have always fascinated people. The reasons may vary from person to person and culture to culture.

There are few animals that have inspired poets as much as cats. As you read the following poems, notice how the poets have tried to capture the particular way cats move, their mysterious nature, and their entertaining antics.

Tiger

by Valerie Worth

The tiger
Has swallowed
A black sun,

In his cold
Cage he
Carries it still:

Black flames
Flicker through
His fur,

Black rays roar
From the centers
Of his eyes.

A Tomcat Is

by J. Patrick Lewis

Nightwatchman of corners
Caretaker of naps
Leg-wrestler of pillows
Depresser of laps

A master at whining
And dining on mouse
Designer of shadows
That hide in the house

The bird-watching bandit
On needle-point claws
The chief of detectives
On marshmallow paws

A crafty yarn-spinner
A stringer high-strung
A handlebar mustache
A sandpaper tongue

The dude in the alley
The duke of the couch
Affectionate fellow
Occasional grouch

As male cats mature from kittens to tomcats, they take on different traits. The imagery in this poem describes all the different things a tomcat can resemble.

311

Disturbed, the cat
Lifts its belly
On to its back.

—Karai Senryū

Write Using Alliteration

Write a poem using alliteration. Use "Tiger" on page 310 as a model. Choose the subject of your poem and think of unusual details that are available to describe it. Create imagery that will reveal things that may go unobserved by most people. For each image, focus on a single repeating initial consonant sound. Alliteration can draw attention to unique imagery in a poem and make reading it exciting.

Compare Texts

Analyze Writers' Approaches The author of "Cougars" and the poets in "Purr-fection" write about the traits and behaviors of cats. Compare and contrast the representations of cats in "Cougars" and in one of the "Purr-fection" poems. Use evidence from both selections to support your points. Pay special attention to the writers' uses of sensory details, figurative language, and sound.

Respond to a Poem Rhyme is a technique used by many poets. Quietly read the poem "A Tomcat Is" to yourself a few times. What rhyming words do you hear, and where? How do the rhymes affect the way you read the poem? Do you think they enhance the poem's imagery? How might you use this technique when writing your own poems? Discuss these questions with a partner.

Compare and Contrast Texts Both "Quest for the Tree Kangaroo" (Lesson 6) and "Cougars" contain information about wild animals. How is the presentation of concepts, information, and other details in "Quest for the Tree Kangaroo" different from or similar to the presentation of these elements in "Cougars"? Support your answer with specific references to both texts. What did you learn about animals in the wild that you didn't know before?

RI.5.5 compare and contrast the overall structure in two or more texts; **RI.5.9** integrate information from several texts on the same topic

COMMON CORE

Grammar

Direct Quotations Direct quotations give a speaker's or an author's exact words. They can be used when writing story dialogue and when quoting from a text to support ideas in an essay or a research report. Capitalize the first word, and use a comma and quotation marks to set off a direct quotation from the other words in a sentence. At the end of a direct quotation, put a comma or other punctuation inside the quotation marks.

Interjections To show a speaker's strong emotion, or to make a character's voice more lively, include an **interjection** such as *Hey* or *Wow,* and punctuate it with a comma or an exclamation point.

Direct Quotations and Interjections
Ravindra said, "I can recognize cougar tracks." He was on a hike with his friends Paula and Bethany.
"Draw a sketch of a print," said Paula. She handed Ravindra her sketch pad and a pencil.
"Hey, I see a cougar print!" shouted Bethany.

Try This! **With a partner, talk about what you would capitalize and punctuate in these sentences. Then identify each interjection and explain its function in the sentence.**

1. Sam asked are you sure it's a cougar print

2. Belinda replied it looks just like the one in the book.

3. Wow we have to tell people about this exclaimed Andre.

4. I will take a photo of the print said Nell.

To let readers know which words are a speaker's exact words, make sure quotation marks, commas, and end punctuation are placed correctly. When you are writing dialogue, start a new paragraph each time the speaker changes, making sure to indent the first line. Any interjections can be set off with a comma or can stand alone with an exclamation point.

Incorrect	Correct
I saw a cougar, Tom said.	"I saw a cougar," Tom said.
"Where was it? asked Lin."	"Where was it?" asked Lin.
Pete said "you just saw a housecat"	Pete said, "You just saw a housecat."
Tom yelled", No It was a cougar"!	Tom yelled, "No! It was a cougar!"

 Connect Grammar to Writing

As you edit your research report, make sure you have written direct quotations and interjections correctly. Check for both capitalization and punctuation errors. Correct any errors you find.

W.5.2a introduce a topic, provide an observation and focus, group related information/include formatting, illustrations, and multimedia; **W.5.2b** develop the topic with facts, definitions, details, quotations, or other information and examples; **W.5.2c** link ideas within and across categories of information using words, phrases, and clauses; **W.5.2d** use precise language and domain-specific vocabulary

Informative Writing

Reading-Writing Workshop: Revise

✓ **Sentence Fluency**   In a **research report**, good writers are careful not to copy sentences or phrases from their sources. As you revise your report, use synonyms—different words with similar meanings—to help you rephrase quotes from your sources.

Josie drafted her report on the sinking of the *Andrea Doria*. Later, she rephrased sentences that she had accidentally copied. She made other revisions to improve her writing, as well.

Writing Process Checklist

Prewrite

Draft

▶ **Revise**

- ✓ Does my first paragraph introduce the main ideas in an interesting way?

- ✓ Did I write at least one paragraph for each main topic?

- ✓ Did I develop my topic with facts, details, and examples?

- ✓ Did I use transitions to link ideas?

- ✓ Did I use quotations, and domain-specific words and their definitions?

- ✓ Does my conclusion sum up my main ideas?

- ✓ Did I include an accurate list of sources?

Revised Draft

The night was foggy, and each ship was using its radar to navigate.

~~The Andrea Doria was surrounded by a fog~~

~~bank. When radar showed another ship (the~~
    The Andrea Doria's radar showed the

~~Stockholm) nearby, she continued her course.~~
Stockholm nearby, but the crew decided not to turn the ship.
Eventually, the ships got close enough to see

each other through the fog, and the captains

realized they were too close to avoid a crash.
    The bow, or front end, of the Stockholm
      "slammed into the
~~The Stockholm's bow ripped into the side of~~

Andrea Doria's side."
~~the Andrea Doria.~~

A Successful Rescue

by Josie Teicher

It was the night of July 25th, 1956. A terrible accident was about to happen. An Italian ship, the *Andrea Doria*, and a Swedish ship, the *Stockholm*, were headed straight for each other.

The night was foggy, and each ship was navigating by radar. The *Andrea Doria*'s radar showed the *Stockholm* nearby, but the crew decided not to turn the ship. Eventually, the ships got close enough to see each other through the fog, and the captains realized they were too close to avoid a crash. The bow, or front end, of the *Stockholm* "slammed into the *Andrea Doria*'s side."

The *Andrea Doria* put out an SOS, which is a radio call for help. The *Ile de France* arrived just three hours after the crash. It was able to rescue hundreds of *Andrea Doria* passengers. Even the *Stockholm* was able to rescue people because it was damaged but not sinking.

Partly because the *Andrea Doria* took so long to sink, all but forty-six of the 1,706 people on board were saved. This sea rescue was one of the most successful in history.

Reading as a Writer

In what other ways could Josie have reworded the sentences she copied? How can you reword any copied sentences in your report?

In my final paper, I included facts, definitions, details, and a quotation. I also made sure to avoid plagiarism by rephrasing sentences I had copied from sources during my research.

Read the article "The King of Ragtime." As you read, stop and use text evidence to answer each question.

The King of Ragtime

Scott Joplin was born in Texas in 1868. The Civil War had recently ended, and times were tough for many families. To support the Joplin family, Scott's father worked for the railroad, and his mother worked long hours cleaning other people's houses and doing their laundry. When Scott was young, his family moved to Texarkana, a city on the border of Texas and Arkansas.

Music was important in Scott Joplin's family. His father played the violin. His mother sang and played the banjo. All of the children played at least one instrument, and they all loved to sing.

As a child, Scott Joplin showed a gift for music. He became an excellent banjo player at a very young age. When Scott was seven years old, he saw a piano for the first time at a neighbor's house. The neighbor played some music, and Scott was fascinated by the sounds the piano made, especially when the neighbor played several notes together at the same time. After that, Scott spent as much time as he could learning to play the piano. Whenever his mother was cleaning a house that had a piano he could use, Scott went with her and practiced playing.

> **1** How does the information about Scott Joplin's ability to learn both the banjo and the piano at such a young age support the author's point about his showing a gift for music?

Although the Joplin family was poor, Scott's mother saved money to buy him a piano of his own. The instrument was old and broken. Many of the keys stuck and the pedals squeaked, but Scott thought it was the most wonderful present in the world. He often played for family and friends in Texarkana. Gradually, word spread about this talented young musician.

One day, a stranger knocked on the door of the Joplin house. The man introduced himself as Julius Weiss and explained that he was a music teacher. He said that he would like to meet the young musician he had heard so much about. Scott played for Julius Weiss, and Weiss offered to teach the boy for no charge. Weiss said that when he was a poor young boy in Germany, he had been given a scholarship to study music. He wanted to help Scott in the same way that he had been helped.

COMMON CORE **RI.5.3** explain the relationships between individuals/events/ideas/concepts in a text; **RI.5.4** determine the meaning of general academic and domain-specific words and phrases; **RI.5.6** analyze multiple accounts of the same event or topic; **RI.5.8** explain how an author uses reasons and evidence to support points

For several years, Weiss taught Scott about the musical scales and harmony used in the European style of music. Scott learned to play the music of famous European composers such as Mozart and Beethoven. As he learned, he tried to change the music to fit his own style. Weiss was angered by this and reprimanded Scott for trying to change the music. Weiss encouraged him to compose his own music instead. Weiss also told Scott stories that were the plots of famous European operas. Scott loved the stories. He asked why they were always written in other languages, such as German, French, and Italian. Weiss explained that very few operas had been written in English.

 2 Based on what you have read in this article, how would you describe the relationship between Scott Joplin and Julius Weiss?

When Scott was a young man in the late 1880s, he left home and began traveling around the Mississippi River Valley and the Midwest. He sang and played the piano for audiences, both by himself and with music groups. As he traveled, he listened to songs that African Americans sang as they worked. These simple melodies were known as "rags." Scott began to mix the stories and rhythms of these rags with the harmony and scales that Weiss had taught him. This style of music became known as "ragtime." A special feature of ragtime is its rhythm. Instead of having a steady beat like most music does, ragtime's beats fall in unexpected places.

For the rest of his life, Scott Joplin focused on writing music. Of the sixty pieces that he composed, forty-one were piano rags. His most famous rags were "Maple Leaf Rag" and "The Entertainer." Shortly before he died, he became determined to write an American opera. He ended up writing two operas, *A Guest of Honor* and *Treemonisha*, neither of which was successful during his lifetime.

Scott Joplin died in 1917 at the age of forty-eight. Like many famous composers, he did not receive recognition for his work until after his death and never knew that the world would long remember his music. His song "The Entertainer" and his opera *Treemonisha* both won important awards. In 1976, almost sixty years after his death, the famous Pulitzer committee gave Scott Joplin an award for his contribution to American music.

Read the article "Understanding Ragtime." As you read, stop and answer each question.

Understanding Ragtime

You probably have experienced clapping along to a song or marching to a musical beat. When you clap or march along with most songs, you do so in a steady rhythm that repeats over and over. For example, soldiers sometimes step to the beat of a marching song: *left-right, left-right, left-right*. When you clap to a tune, you clap on the accented beats. The beats follow a predictable pattern.

Ragtime, though, is a kind of music unlike any other. Instead of having a regular beat, ragtime melodies are syncopated. Accented beats occur in an unpredictable pattern. The syncopated melody is played along with a bass line of music that does have a regular beat. This combination produces a lively and interesting rhythm. When ragtime was first developed, some people described the syncopated rhythm as "ragged." That is how the music came to be called ragtime or rag.

 What does the word *syncopated* mean in reference to music?

By far the most important ragtime instrument is the piano. A ragtime pianist plays the syncopated melody with one hand while the other hand plays the bass pattern with a steady beat. Both hands play some harmony as well. It takes talent to play ragtime!

In the early years, rags were improvised. After a time, ragtime musicians began composing their own rags. Rag publishers began publishing prints of the compositions, called sheet music, which helped to increase ragtime's popularity in the American music scene. The sheet music also provided the primary source documents that help us trace the history of ragtime.

"Harlem Rag" by Tom Turpin was published in 1897, and "Maple Leaf Rag" by Scott Joplin was published shortly afterward, in 1899. Joplin, a leading composer and pianist, was eventually given the nickname "King of Ragtime."

 How do the articles "The King of Ragtime" and "Understanding Ragtime" each provide insight into the creation of ragtime music?

Unit 3

Vocabulary in Context

✓ TARGET VOCABULARY

embark

surveyed

conduct

cramped

bracing

pressing

distracted

representatives

viewpoint

shattered

Vocabulary Reader

Context Cards

L.5.4c consult reference materials, both print and digital, to find pronunciation and determine or clarify meaning

322

---

1 embark

In the 1770s, it took courage to **embark**, or set sail, on an ocean voyage.

2 surveyed

These soldiers **surveyed** the harbor, scanning for signs of the enemy navy.

3 conduct

The captain made sure that all jobs were done. He was responsible for the ship's **conduct**.

4 cramped

In storms, travelers were thrown about in their **cramped**, crowded quarters.

Go Digital

▶ Study each Context Card.

▶ Use a dictionary or a glossary to verify the meanings of the Vocabulary words.

5 **bracing**

These sailors got used to bracing, or securing, themselves when storms struck.

6 **pressing**

Sailing vessels served a pressing need when they delivered urgently needed trade goods.

7 **distracted**

The sunset distracted this sailor. She stopped working to look at the clouds.

8 **representatives**

Ben Franklin and other representatives of the U.S. sailed to France on diplomatic missions.

9 **viewpoint**

From the viewpoint of the British, their navy was best. U.S. sailors had another opinion.

10 **shattered**

Divers still find the shattered remains of vessels that broke up and sank long ago.

Read and Comprehend

✓ TARGET SKILL

Cause and Effect Many texts are made up of a series of **causes** and **effects** that create the story's overall structure. As you read "Dangerous Crossing," look for one or more events that make something else happen. Record these causes and their effects in a graphic organizer like this one.

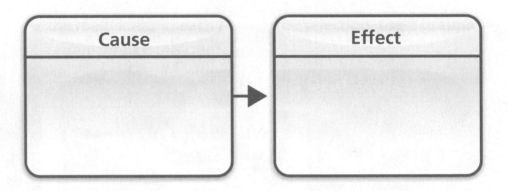

Cause		Effect
	→	

✓ TARGET STRATEGY

Visualize Use text evidence to **visualize**, or create a mental picture of, each event as it happens. Visualizing will help you to understand how events in the text are related.

Early American Government

After winning the Revolutionary War in 1783, the colonists had to form their new government. They had to write a constitution that gave individual states the right amount of power—neither too much nor too little. They also had to make sure the rights of citizens were protected.

John Adams played an important role in creating the Constitution. It established a strong central government while ensuring states' rights and protecting individual citizens. He then served as the first vice president and the second president of the new nation. However, as you will learn from "Dangerous Crossing," his work began long before the Revolutionary War ended. Without his efforts, the war might have had a different outcome.

ANCHOR TEXT

The Revolutionary Voyage of John Quincy Adams

Dangerous Crossing

Stephen Krensky · Illustrated by Greg Harlin

 TARGET SKILL

Cause and Effect Tell how events are related and how one event causes another.

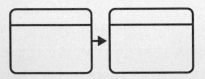

 GENRE

Historical fiction is a fictional story set in the past. It contains characters, places, and events that actually existed or happened, or that could have existed or happened. As you read, look for:

- ▶ a setting that was a real time and place in the past
- ▶ actual historical figures
- ▶ details that show the story took place in the past

COMMON CORE **RL.5.5** explain how chapters, scenes, or stanzas fit together to provide the overall structure; **RL.5.7** analyze how visual and multimedia elements contribute to the meaning, tone, or beauty of a text; **RL.5.10** read and comprehend literature

  Go Digital

MEET THE AUTHOR
Stephen Krensky

Stephen Krensky writes fiction, nonfiction, picture books, and novels. He writes different kinds of books because "I just happen to have a lot of different-sized ideas," he says. "Being able to try so many different kinds of books has helped me stay enthusiastic about every book I write."

MEET THE ILLUSTRATOR
Greg Harlin

Greg Harlin uses watercolors to create believable historical and scientific paintings. His art has appeared in many magazines, including *National Geographic* and *Kids Discover*. He lives with his daughter and two cats, one black and one white.

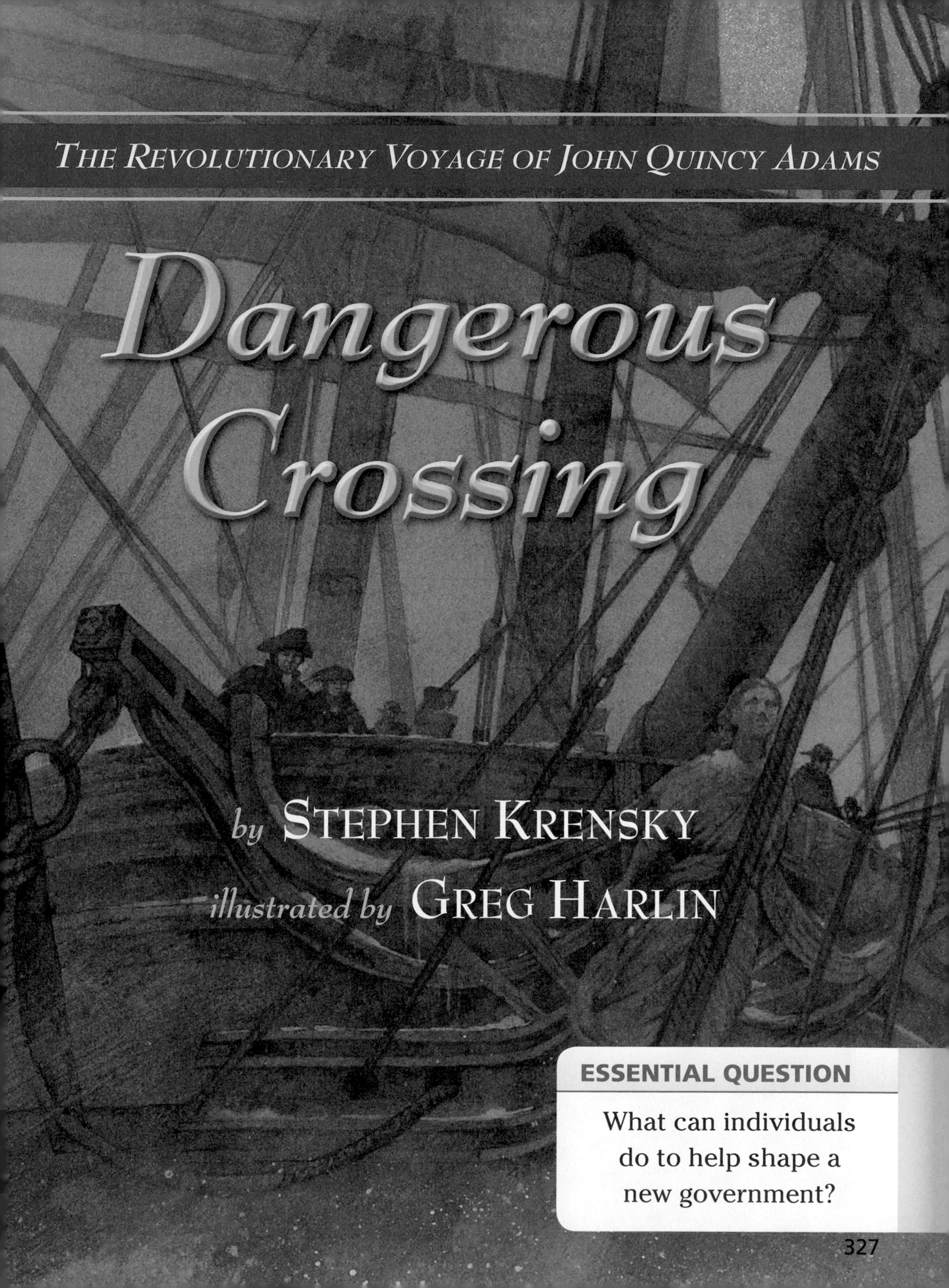

THE REVOLUTIONARY VOYAGE OF JOHN QUINCY ADAMS

Dangerous Crossing

by STEPHEN KRENSKY

illustrated by GREG HARLIN

ESSENTIAL QUESTION

What can individuals do to help shape a new government?

Young Johnny Adams could hardly believe his good fortune. On a cold February day in 1778, he stood at the ocean's edge, a few miles from home. The wind blew fiercely around him, and the blustering snow stung his cheeks like nettles.

But Johnny didn't mind. Ten years old, he had never been farther than a day's ride from home. Yet here he was, about to sail to France with his father. What did stinging cheeks matter compared to that? He could still hear the words that an elderly cousin had declared in warning.

"Mr. Adams, you are going to embark under very threatening signs. The heavens frown, the clouds roll, the hollow winds howl, the waves of the sea roar upon the beach." Johnny could not have been more pleased.

Soon the barge arrived to fetch them to the ship waiting offshore. Although they were leaving Massachusetts in a hurry and in secret, they were not going unprepared. Their baggage included two fat sheep, two hogs, one barrel of apples, five bushels of corn, some chocolate, sugar, eggs, paper, quills, ink, a double mattress, a comforter, and a pillow.

There was room for it all, and soon father and son were settled in some dry hay, bobbing up and down like corks in a bottle.

It was dangerous to cross the ocean in mid-winter, but time was pressing. The war with England, now almost three years old, was not going well. The rebel army had barely limped into their winter quarters. Many colonial soldiers lacked muskets and powder. They were also short of clothes, blankets, and shoes.

The new Americans desperately needed the support of other countries—especially France, England's greatest rival. Other representatives were in Paris already, but their progress was uncertain. It was hoped that the calm and thoughtful John Adams could do more. Captain Samuel Tucker welcomed Johnny and his father aboard just before dusk.

Captain Tucker's new twenty-four gun frigate (FRIHG uht), the *Boston*, had a deck more than a hundred feet long. Three towering masts stood guard overhead, clothed in endless furls of sail.

Down below, the view was less grand. The passageways were cramped, and everywhere was a terrible smell—of sea and sailors mingled together. Johnny and his father found their tiny cabin clean, at least, and with their blankets and pillows, it felt a little like home.

Once the *Boston* put out to sea, Johnny noticed a change. The waves looked bigger. They felt bigger, too. A strange feeling swept over him. His head was spinning, and his stomach as well. He soon took to his bed, glad that his groans were lost amid the creaking masts and the howling wind.

Though John Adams also felt ill, he distracted himself by writing in his diary. *"Seasickness,"* he wrote, *"seems to be the Effect of Agitation. . . . The smoke of Seacoal, the Smell of stagnant putrid Water, the odour of the Ship where the Sailors sleep, or any other offensive Odor"* would not trigger it alone.

No doubt this was good to know, but it did not make Johnny feel any better. The next day, a calmer sea improved everyone's mood. Johnny and his father returned to the deck, glad for a breath of fresh air.

"A ship on the weather quarter!" shouted the lookout.

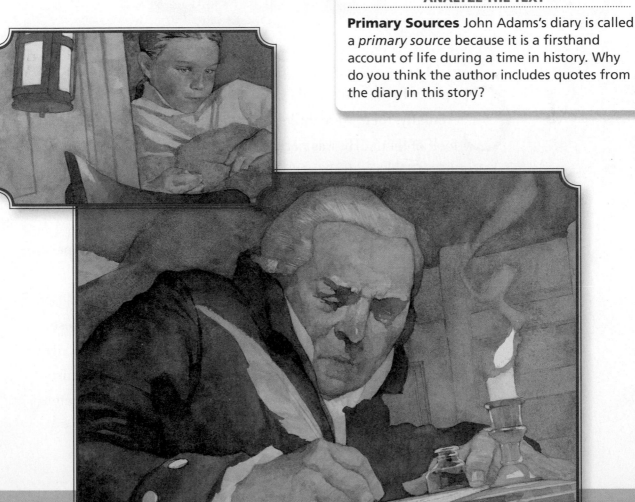

ANALYZE THE TEXT

Primary Sources John Adams's diary is called a *primary source* because it is a firsthand account of life during a time in history. Why do you think the author includes quotes from the diary in this story?

Captain Tucker turned his glass upon the distant speck.
Actually, there were three ships, and British frigates by the look of them. He was not pleased with the three-to-one odds.

But his officers protested. "We will not run from an enemy before we see him," they said. "We will not fly from danger before we know we are in it."

Besides, they were thinking, what if these were merchant ships loaded with valuable goods?

Bowing to their enthusiasm, the captain ordered the *Boston* closer.

It was soon clear, though, that his fears were well founded. These were frigates, indeed. And from their viewpoint, the odds were just right.

All three now gave chase. Two quickly fell behind, but the third kept pace. For two more days, it followed them. The sailors on watch said the frigate was closing the gap, but Johnny could not tell. His eyes were not as sharp as theirs.

"Our Powder and balls were placed by the Guns," his father noted in his diary, *"and every thing ready to begin the Action."*

Almost three years earlier, Johnny and his mother had stood on high ground, watching the Battle of Bunker Hill eight miles away. But that had been almost make-believe, little more than flashes of light and distant cries.

Here, he would be right in the thick of things. Cannons would fire and swords flash. One of the ships would be boarded. The two crews would grapple with knives and pistols and anything else that came to hand.

An officer interrupted Johnny's thoughts. He and his father should take shelter below. As if the frigate wasn't trouble enough, a storm was coming.

ANALYZE THE TEXT

Visual Elements Review the illustrations on pages 327–333. In what ways do these illustrations add meaning to the story and communicate the tone?

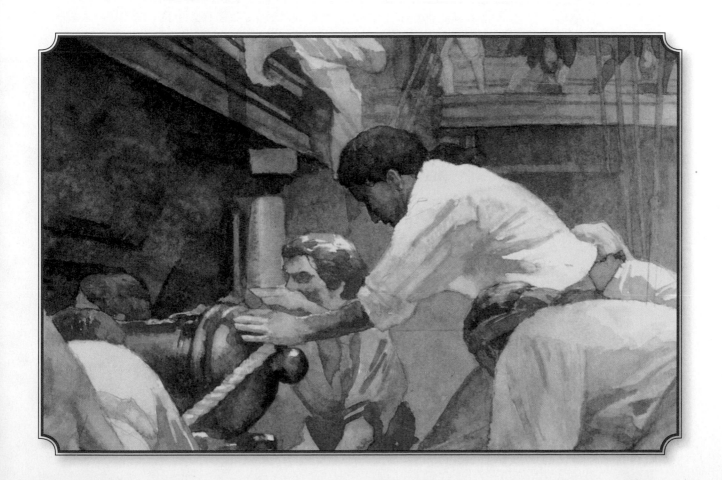

They went straight to their cabin. Soon the ship began to pitch, rocking violently back and forth. They could not sit or stand without being knocked about. "It was with the utmost difficulty," John Adams remembered, "that my little son and I could hold ourselves in bed with both our hands, and bracing ourselves against the boards, planks, and timbers with our feet."

Suddenly, there was a flash of light. *C-R-R-AAACK!* The ship shuddered from the blow. Johnny and his father shared a worried glance. Was that cannon fire? Had the British frigate overtaken them? Would the firing continue until they surrendered? Or would the *Boston* fight until it sank beneath the waves?

In truth, there were no cannons at work. "The ship has been struck by lightning!" an officer told them. The main mast was shattered, and four crew members were hurt.

For three more days and nights, the storm continued. Chests and casks were tossed about like straw, and no one could stay dry or walk steadily on deck. "The Wind blowing against the current . . . produced a tumbling Sea," Adams observed. "Vast mountains of water breaking on the ship threatened to bury us all at once in the deep."

Through it all, Johnny was proud that his father stayed calm. He was a practical man, and there was nothing to gain by making a fuss.

Finally, the skies cleared. But the pale sunlight fell on a broken ship. Sails were ripped, masts splintered. Even worse, the *Boston* had been blown hundreds of miles off course. As the captain surveyed the damage, he had only one bit of good news.

At least the British frigate was gone.

As the sailors began making repairs, Johnny took some French lessons from the ship's doctor and learned the names of the sails. "I am most satisfied with myself," Johnny had once told his father, "when I have applied part of my time to some useful employment."

ANALYZE THE TEXT

Cause and Effect What caused Johnny to think the crack he heard was cannon fire? What really caused the crack?

One day a sailor pulled up a Portuguese man-of-war in a bucket. Johnny looked on in wonder. Was this truly a fish from the sea? *"Careful,"* the sailor warned him. One touch of its twisted cords would sting like a hundred bees.

Johnny's father and the captain often spoke together of their mission and the conduct of the ship. Even from a distance, Johnny recognized his father's impatience. He spoke of a ship at sea "as a kind of prison." He was especially tired of the view. "We see nothing but Sky, Clouds, and Sea," he noted. "And then Seas, Clouds, and Sky."

After four weeks at sea, the *Boston* spotted another ship—a British merchantman loaded with precious goods. This was a prize worth catching. The passengers were ordered below as the *Boston* let out its sails.

But while Johnny and the rest stayed put, John Adams returned to the deck. He heard a loud boom—and then a cannonball shot over his head. The other ship had fired on them! Captain Tucker ordered the *Boston* brought about so that the merchantman could see the strength of her guns. Would the enemy captain, Adams wondered, choose to sink or surrender?

The surrender came quickly. The crew of the merchantman were taken prisoner, and their ship remanned with some of the *Boston*'s sailors. But even in victory, Captain Tucker was angry at Johnny's father for risking his life by returning to the deck.

"My dear sir, how came you here?" he asked. Had Adams forgotten his mission? Wasn't his safe arrival in France of the greatest importance to the Revolution?

John Adams stood his ground. "I ought to do my fair share of fighting," he explained simply. Johnny was not surprised. Until now, his father had been defending his country with ideas and words. But he would not shrink from any conflict if the cause was just.

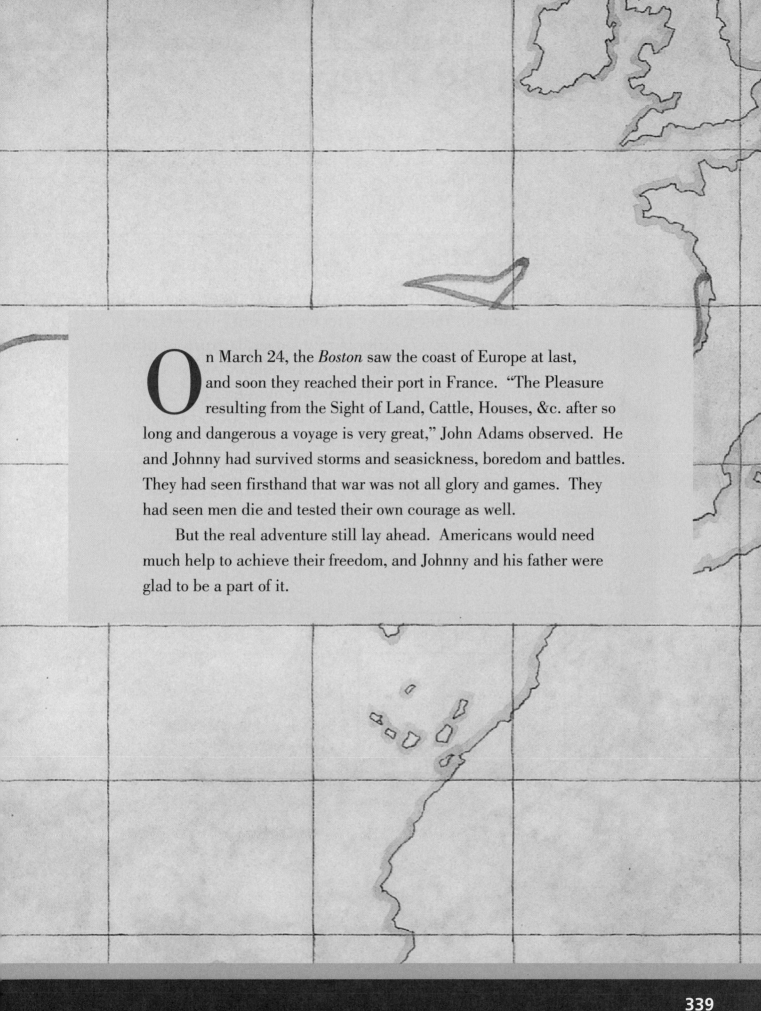

On March 24, the *Boston* saw the coast of Europe at last, and soon they reached their port in France. "The Pleasure resulting from the Sight of Land, Cattle, Houses, &c. after so long and dangerous a voyage is very great," John Adams observed. He and Johnny had survived storms and seasickness, boredom and battles. They had seen firsthand that war was not all glory and games. They had seen men die and tested their own courage as well.

But the real adventure still lay ahead. Americans would need much help to achieve their freedom, and Johnny and his father were glad to be a part of it.

Dig Deeper

How to Analyze the Text

Use these pages to learn about Cause and Effect, Visual Elements, and Primary Sources. Then read "Dangerous Crossing" again to apply what you learned.

Cause and Effect

In the historical fiction story "Dangerous Crossing," some of the events are **causes**. They lead to later events, which are **effects**. These causes and effects contribute to the overall structure of the story. Several causes may contribute to a single effect, or a single cause may have many effects. To identify cause-and-effect relationships, look for signal words and phrases such as *because, as a result of, due to*, and *consequently*. When there are no signal words, use other text evidence to infer connections between events.

Look back at page 329. In this part of the story, the events that cause John Adams to go to France are explained. What leads to his trip? What do the colonists hope will be the result, or effect, of his visit to France?

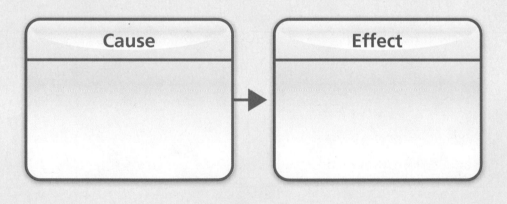

Cause	Effect

COMMON CORE **RL.5.5** explain how chapters, scenes, or stanzas fit together to provide the overall structure; **RL.5.7** analyze how visual and multimedia elements contribute to the meaning, tone, or beauty of a text; **RL.5.10** read and comprehend literature

340

Visual Elements

Illustrations are **visual elements** that add meaning to the text of a story. They present readers with concrete images of the characters, settings, and events. Some reinforce important ideas, while others communicate **tone**, or a particular attitude toward the subject. On page 333, for example, the illustration of the sailors working hard to prepare for battle suggests a tone of respect for their courage and skill.

Primary Sources

A **primary source** is an original photograph, quotation, interview, or other piece of information. "Dangerous Crossing" includes direct quotations from John Adams's diary. By using the quotations, the author makes his interpretation of this historical event believable. Readers know that the story is based on research and facts. As you reread the selection, consider what reading Adams's own thoughts and observations adds to your appreciation of the story.

Your Turn

Turn and Talk Review the selection to prepare to discuss this question: *What can individuals do to help shape a new government?* As you discuss your ideas in a small group, pause to ask questions or add to each other's comments.

Classroom Conversation

Continue your discussion of "Dangerous Crossing" by using text evidence to answer these questions:

1. What does John Adams's behavior reveal about his character?

2. Why is John Adams willing to undertake a dangerous sea voyage to travel to France?

3. What new insights about the Revolutionary War did you gain from reading this story?

ANALYZE CHARACTER

Roundtable Discussion What kind of man do you think Johnny will be when he grows up? Will he be similar to or different from his father? Identify details from the text that foreshadow what Johnny will become. Then discuss your conclusions in a small group, citing direct quotations and other text evidence as support.

WRITE ABOUT READING

Response Think about the cause-and-effect relationships that you identified in the story. Write a paragraph explaining which causes and effects help you see how setting, historical context, and character affect the action of the story. Use direct quotations and other specific details from the text to support your ideas.

Writing Tip

Choose the best organization for your paragraph. Unify it with a strong topic sentence at the beginning and a restatement of the main idea at the end.

COMMON CORE **RL.5.1** quote accurately when explaining what the text says explicitly and when drawing inferences; **RL.5.3** compare and contrast characters, settings, or events, drawing on details; **W.5.4** produce writing in which development and organization are appropriate to task, purpose, and audience; **W.5.9.a** apply grade 5 Reading standards to literature; **W.5.10** write routinely over extended time frames and shorter time frames; **SL.5.1a** come to discussions prepared/explicitly draw on preparation and other information about the topic; **SL.5.1c** pose and respond to questions, make comments that contribute to the discussion, and elaborate on others' remarks

✓ GENRE

Informational text provides facts and details about a certain time period, topic, person, or historical event.

✓ TEXT FOCUS

Political Documents
Informational texts about American history may contain images of, or facts about, important political documents such as the Constitution or the Bill of Rights.

COMMON CORE RI.5.10 read and comprehend informational texts

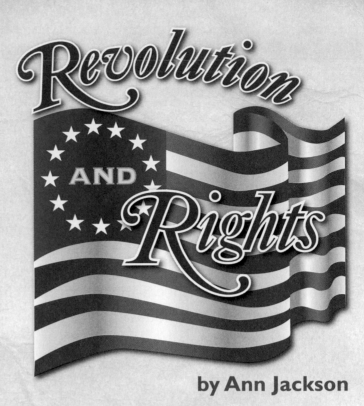

Revolution AND Rights

by Ann Jackson

Before the American Revolution

In 1754, Great Britain and France went to war over territory that is now the upper Ohio River valley of North America. Both countries claimed the area belonged to them. French and British forces—which included colonists and Iroquois—fought each other for many years. The war finally ended in 1763, with France giving up its land east of the Mississippi River to Britain.

Go Digital

Along with Great Britain's victory came problems. A main one was figuring out how to cover the expense of the war that had been fought against the French. To help pay for it, the British government passed a tax law called the Stamp Act in 1765. This tax charged colonists a fee for special stamps on newspapers, pamphlets, legal documents, cards, and other official papers. In 1767, new taxes on other goods were passed so that Britain could collect more money from the colonists.

The colonists were angry. They did not help to elect the British government; they felt they had no representation and no say in their fate. They thought it was unfair for the British government to make laws for them. Many colonists protested the taxes and refused to buy British goods. In 1773, a group of colonists showed their displeasure by throwing hundreds of chests of tea from a British ship into the Boston Harbor. This event became known as the Boston Tea Party.

A New Nation

From September to October of 1774, colonial leaders met in Philadelphia, Pennsylvania, in a gathering they called the First Continental Congress. The leaders—which included John Adams, George Washington, and Patrick Henry—discussed how to deal with the British government. Not everyone wanted to risk breaking away from Great Britain. However, Adams and some of the other leaders believed strongly that independence was the only option.

On April 19, 1775, 700 British soldiers marched into Lexington, Massachusetts. They found a group of Minutemen and other armed colonists. A shot was fired during the standoff, and after a brief battle, several colonists lay dead or injured. It was the beginning of the American Revolution.

Leaders met again for the Second Continental Congress in May 1775. They decided to form the Continental Army. John Adams nominated George Washington to lead the army during the rest of the war.

Nearly a year later, in the spring of 1776, the Congress decided the colonies should become free and independent states. Thomas Jefferson, a leader from Virginia, wrote a document explaining why the colonies should be free from Great Britain. That document was the Declaration of Independence. It would be several years before American independence became official. In September of 1783, American and British leaders signed an agreement called the Treaty of Paris. This peace treaty ended the war. It also established the United States of America as a free and independent nation.

A New Government

The young nation of the United States needed a new national government. The first attempt by members of the Continental Congress was to draft a document called the Articles of Confederation. However, leaders were afraid of creating another powerful government that could take away people's rights and set laws people did not want. As a result, the Articles were weak. A new plan for the government was needed.

In May of 1787, leaders met again in Philadelphia in what is known today as the Constitutional Convention. On September 17, 1787, leaders signed the United States Constitution. However, it could not become official law until at least nine of the thirteen states ratified, or approved, it.

The Constitution stated that the people ruled the government. It formed three separate branches—executive, legislative, and judicial—with different powers that balance one another. However, it included few individual rights. After the treatment of the British government, some leaders, called Anti-Federalists, worried that the Constitution did not protect individual rights enough. Federalists, those in favor of the Constitution, worried they wouldn't have the votes needed to ratify the new law. Federalists agreed to add changes called amendments to the Constitution that would protect individual rights. Doing so changed the minds of enough Anti-Federalists that, in 1788, the Constitution was ratified.

Events Before and After the American Revolution

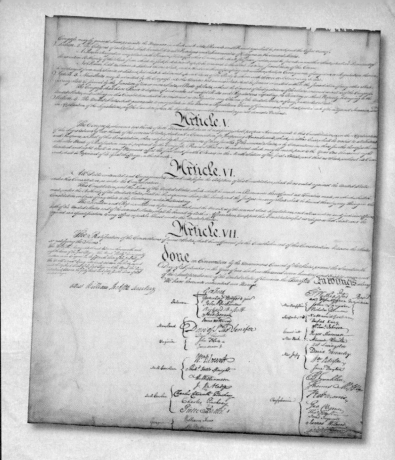

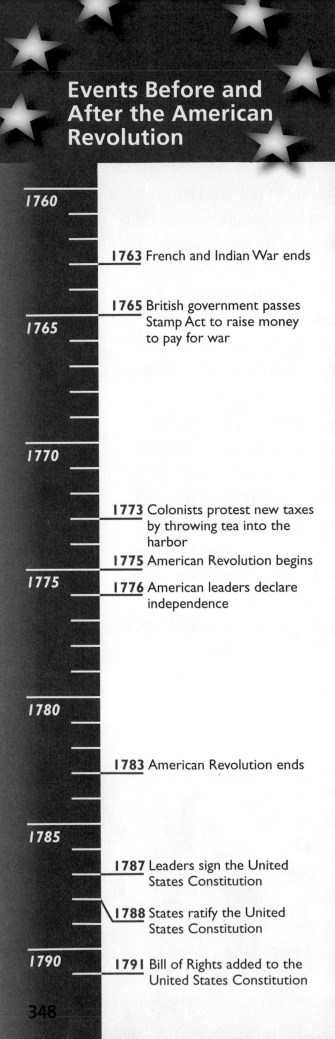

1760	
1763	French and Indian War ends
1765	British government passes Stamp Act to raise money to pay for war
1770	
1773	Colonists protest new taxes by throwing tea into the harbor
1775	American Revolution begins
1776	American leaders declare independence
1780	
1783	American Revolution ends
1785	
1787	Leaders sign the United States Constitution
1788	States ratify the United States Constitution
1790	
1791	Bill of Rights added to the United States Constitution

The first ten amendments added to the Constitution in 1791 became known as the Bill of Rights. These rights are freedoms guaranteed to the people of the United States. They include the freedoms of religion, speech, and the press; the right to own and bear arms; and protection from unfair searches. They also give power to the states or the people in cases where the federal government does not have power.

Additional amendments have been made since the original Constitution and Bill of Rights were created. Adding an amendment is a big decision. It requires a lot of discussion and thought, and it must be approved by a majority of states during a national vote. The purpose of these individual rights is to make our country stronger and better for the people who call it home.

Compare Texts

Analyze Texts About Early American Politics With a partner, discuss these questions about "Dangerous Crossing" and "Revolution and Rights." Then record your answers and share them with the class. *How does the information about John Adams in "Revolution and Rights" add to your understanding of his character and political skills? What do both selections help you understand about why the U.S. government and the Bill of Rights were created?*

TEXT TO SELF

Write a Review Imagine you are a writer for a literary magazine. Write a brief review of "Dangerous Crossing." Use details about the story's conflicts and exciting events to persuade your audience to read the story. Explain how the Revolutionary War setting adds drama, affects the characters, and shapes the story's theme.

TEXT TO WORLD

Make Connections Using the two selections in Lesson 11, work with a partner to create a timeline of the important events from 1778 (the date of John Adams's trip to France) to 1791, when the Bill of Rights was added to the Constitution.

Forming a New
GOVERNMENT

1778

Go
Digital

COMMON
CORE

RL.5.2 determine theme from details/summarize; **RI.5.3** explain the relationships between individuals/events/ideas/concepts in a text; **RI.5.9** integrate information from several texts on the same topic; **W.5.10** write routinely over extended time frames and shorter time frames; **SL.5.1a** come to discussion prepared/explicitly draw on preparation and other information about the topic

Grammar

Kinds of Pronouns A **pronoun** is a word that takes the place of a noun. A **subject pronoun** takes the place of a noun used as the subject of a sentence. An **object pronoun** takes the place of a noun used after an action verb or after a word such as *to, for, with, in,* or *out.*

Subject Pronouns		Object Pronouns	
I	we	me	us
you	you	you	you
she, he, it	they	her, him, it	them

The **antecedent** of a pronoun is the noun or nouns that the pronoun replaces. A pronoun must agree with its antecedent in number and gender.

antecedent

subject pronoun

Johnny was at the ocean. Soon he would sail to France.

Try This! Work with a partner. Find the pronouns in these sentences. Tell whether they are subject pronouns or object pronouns. Then name their antecedents.

1. Three boats approached. They were British frigates.

2. One boat gave chase. The sailors watched it carefully.

3. Johnny remembered a battle. He and his mother had seen it.

4. Johnny's mother was at home. Johnny would not see her for a long time.

5. Johnny's father would speak with French leaders. He represented the American colonies.

To avoid repeating the same noun too often in your writing, you can replace that noun with a pronoun. Do this with care! It is easy to repeat the same pronoun too many times, too. Be certain that your reader knows to which noun a pronoun refers. Remember that the pronoun must agree with its antecedent in number and gender.

Noun Repetition	Improved with Pronouns
Travelers in the eighteenth century had to go by ship across an ocean full of danger. Travelers suffered many hardships. Travelers had no contact with those at home. Travelers had no fresh food. Travelers on today's ocean liners, though, cruise in luxury.	Travelers in the eighteenth century had to go by ship across an ocean full of danger. They suffered many hardships. They had no contact with those at home, and no fresh food. Travelers on today's ocean liners, though, cruise in luxury.

 ## Connect Grammar to Writing

As you revise your opinion essay, look for nouns that are used too many times. Replace an overused noun with a pronoun. Make sure that it is clear to which noun the pronoun refers.

W.5.1a introduce a topic, state an opinion, and create an organizational structure; **W.5.1b** provide logically ordered reasons supported by facts and details; **W.5.1c** link opinion and reasons using words, phrases, and clauses; **W.5.1d** provide a strong concluding statement or section; **W.5.4** produce writing in which development and organization are appropriate to task, purpose, and audience

Opinion Writing

✓ **Voice**   In an **opinion essay**, you present your position on a topic. To make your writing strong and convincing, include reasons that explain and support your feelings about the topic. As you write, think about your audience, or who will be reading your essay.

Sonya wrote an opinion essay explaining why she thinks team sports build leadership skills. Later, she revised her draft by adding precise verbs and vivid adjectives to make her voice stronger and her opinion more clear. She also added questions to engage her audience.

Use the Writing Traits Checklist below as you revise your writing.

Writing Traits Checklist

✓ **Ideas**
Did I state my opinion and provide a strong conclusion?

✓ **Organization**
Did I group reasons and support logically?

✓ **Sentence Fluency**
Did I use transitions and clauses to link ideas?

✓ **Word Choice**
Did I use words that engage the audience?

✓ **Voice**
   Does my writing sound natural?

✓ **Conventions**
Did I use correct spelling, grammar, and punctuation?

Revised Draft

daydream
Do you ~~dream~~ about one day being
a great leader like John Adams was
~~President~~? Do you wonder how you
          the   skills you would need
can develop leadership? ~~One way to~~
                        └An excellent
start is by playing a team sport.
Why?
~~There are several reasons for this.~~

352

Why Kids Should Play a Team Sport

by Sonya Sanchez

Do you daydream about one day being a great leader like John Adams was? Do you wonder how you can develop the leadership skills you would need? An excellent way to start is by playing a team sport. Why? It is the perfect way to learn about leadership, collaboration, and the rewards that can come from hard work.

First, you'll discover your own strengths and how best to use them. You will also discover how to identify your weaknesses and ask for help from others. That is important knowledge for any leader to have. Second, you'll learn to play by the rules. Government leaders are experts at playing by the rules. They have to follow all the laws and procedures that apply to their work. Finally, when you play on a team, you'll learn how to help others and rely on them for help in return.

It takes a whole basketball team to win a game. Likewise, it takes cooperation and teamwork to run a government successfully. If you are a fifth grader with your eye on the White House, choose a sport you like and join a team now.

Reading as a Writer

Which words did Sonya add to make her voice stronger and her opinion more clear? What words could you add or delete to make your own voice stronger?

In my final paper, I added words to make my voice stronger and my opinion more convincing. I also used pronouns correctly and engaged my audience with questions.

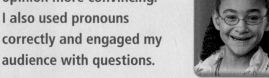

Vocabulary in Context

Can't You Make Them Behave, King George? by Jean Fritz, pictures by Tomie de Paola

Tea Time!

rebellious
objected
benefit
repeal
contrary
midst
temporary
advantages
previously
prohibit

Vocabulary Reader

REDCOATS in America

Context Cards

354

1 rebellious

In April 1775, who fired first at Lexington: a rebellious patriot or a loyal British soldier?

2 objected

Colonists objected to the Stamp Act of 1765, protesting that its taxes were unfair.

3 benefit

Sam Adams argued that it would be a help, or benefit, to be independent.

4 repeal

In 1766, Parliament voted to repeal the hated Stamp Act. The act was withdrawn.

Go Digital

▶ Study each Context Card.

▶ Use the glossary to determine the correct pronunciation of each Vocabulary word.

5 contrary

Willful, contrary patriots refused to obey British laws. Troops were sent to enforce the laws.

6 midst

In the Boston Massacre of 1770, five colonists died in the midst, or middle, of a riot.

7 temporary

For the Boston Tea Party, patriots wore temporary disguises, then removed them.

8 advantages

More soldiers and guns were the British army's advantages, or superior qualities.

9 previously

Many men, previously peaceful farmers, became patriot soldiers during the Revolution.

10 prohibit

The Declaration of Independence sought to prohibit, or forbid, political tyranny.

Read and Comprehend

☑ TARGET SKILL

Fact and Opinion As you read "Can't You Make Them Behave, King George?," look for both **facts** and **opinions**. To determine which is which, ask yourself whether the information can be proved true or false. If so, it is a fact. If not, it is an opinion—someone's belief or feeling. Authors may use reasons and text evidence to support opinions. Record the facts and opinions from the text in a graphic organizer like the one shown below.

Facts	Opinions

☑ TARGET STRATEGY

Question To improve your comprehension, pause now and then to ask yourself **questions** about the people and events in the selection. Questioning helps you figure out how people and events are related and what you need to reread to clarify. Look for text evidence to help you answer your questions as you read.

 RI.5.3 explain the relationships between individuals/events/ideas/concepts in a text; **RI.5.8** explain how an author uses reasons and evidence to support points

356

PREVIEW THE TOPIC

Independence

As a result of the Revolutionary War, fought from 1775 to 1781, the thirteen American colonies gained their independence from Britain and established their own government. These facts are in all of our history books, and it's hard to imagine that things could have gone any differently. However, the colonists' decision to fight for their freedom was not simple or obvious at the time.

As you read "Can't You Make Them Behave, King George?," you will learn that many factors led to the outbreak of the Revolutionary War. You will also learn how radical the idea of independence was— especially for the king, who stood to lose a big slice of his empire.

ANCHOR TEXT

Can't You Make Them Behave, King George?
by Jean Fritz
pictures by Tomie dePaola

 TARGET SKILL

Fact and Opinion Determine which statements in the text can be proved true or false and which express someone's feelings or beliefs.

 GENRE

Narrative nonfiction tells about people, places, and events that are real. As you read, look for:

▶ events in time order
▶ factual information that tells a story

 COMMON CORE — **RI.5.8** explain how an author uses reasons and evidence to support points; **RI.5.10** read and comprehend informational texts; **L.5.5a** interpret figurative language in context

 Go Digital

MEET THE AUTHOR

Jean Fritz

Jean Fritz says it takes lots of research to learn about the subjects of her nonfiction books. She loves finding quirky details and funny facts about real people. She never makes up the things people say in her books. All the dialogue she uses comes from accounts in real letters, journals, and diaries.

MEET THE ILLUSTRATOR

Tomie dePaola

Tomie dePaola has been drawing ever since he can remember. When he was young, his parents let him work in a special space in the attic. Now he has his own studio where he paints and illustrates popular children's books such as *26 Fairmount Avenue*. He receives over 100,000 fan letters per year!

CAN'T YOU MAKE THEM BEHAVE, KING GEORGE?

by Jean Fritz

illustrated by Tomie dePaola

ESSENTIAL QUESTION

How can people's differences of opinion lead to a revolution?

Before the American Revolution, most people who had come from England to settle in North America were English subjects loyal to King George the Third. However, some of these colonists did not like that the king made them pay money called taxes to the English government. They did not like that they had no say in the decisions made by the English government. This was the beginning of a disagreement that led to the American Revolution.

When George came to the throne, the government was costing a great deal. England had been fighting a long and expensive war, and when it was over, the question was how to pay bills. Finally, a government official suggested that one way to raise money was to tax Americans.

"What a good idea!" King George said. After all, the French and Indian part of the war had been fought on American soil for the benefit of Americans, so why shouldn't they help pay for it? The fact that Americans had also spent money and lost men in the war didn't seem important. Nor did the fact that Americans had always managed their own money up to now. They were English subjects, weren't they? Didn't English subjects have to obey the English government? So in 1765 a stamp tax was laid on certain printed items in America.

King George was amazed that Americans objected. He was flabbergasted that they claimed he had no *right* to tax them. Just because they had no say in the matter. Just because they had no representatives in the English government. What was more, Americans refused to pay. If they agreed to one tax, they said, what would come next? A window tax? A tax on fireplaces?

Now King George believed that above all a king should be firm, but the government had the vote, and in the end it voted to repeal the tax. Still, King George was pleased about one thing: The government stood firm on England's *right* to tax the colonies. And in 1767 the government tried again. This time the tax was on lead, tea, paint, and a number of items England sold to America. Part of the money from this tax was to be used to support an English army to keep order in America; part was to pay governors and judges previously under the control of the colonies. Who could object to that? King George asked.

Americans also contended that if they had been asked (instead of being forced) to raise money for England, they would have done so as they had done on previous occasions.

In King George's day the king was a "constitutional monarch." He had lost the enormous powers that a king had once had and had to abide by the vote of the government. On the other hand, unlike present kings, he took an active and leading role in the government.

The Americans did. They hated the whole business so much, especially the English soldiers stationed in their midst, that even when the other taxes were repealed and only the tea tax remained, they would not put up with it. When tea arrived in Boston, they dumped it into Boston Harbor.

When he heard this news, King George felt more like a father than he ever had in his life. A father with a family of very, very disobedient children. And of course, he must punish them. So he closed the port of Boston and took away the right of Massachusetts to govern itself.

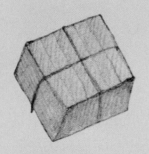

Many Americans disapproved of the Boston Tea Party. They were willing to pay for the lost tea, but when instead the king punished them so severely, they became more united against him.

Firm, firm, firm. From now on he would be firm. After the Battle of Lexington and the Battle of Bunker Hill, King George said he felt strong as a lion. People would soon see, he said, that Americans would back down, meek as lambs.

Instead, on July 4, 1776, Americans declared their independence. Naturally King George was annoyed. But he wasn't worried. How could children, however rebellious, succeed against a firm father? How could a few colonies hold out against a powerful empire? He'd just send a few more regiments over and then watch the Americans come around! It never occurred to George the Third that he might not be right. "I wish nothing but good," he once said, "therefore everyone who does not agree with me is a traitor or a scoundrel."

For a while King George had every reason to feel confident. The English troops captured New York, and when George heard this, he said one more battle and it would be over. When he was told that his troops had marched into Philadelphia, he ran into the queen's room. "I have beat them!" he shouted. "Beat all the Americans!"

But he hadn't beaten them. The fighting went on, and meanwhile, George the Third had to go about the business of being a king. He put his seal on official papers, gave out medals and titles, memorized the name of every ship in the navy, tasted the food sent to the troops, checked on who was spending what, and for hours on end he listened to people talk.

> **ANALYZE THE TEXT**
>
> **Similes** Similes are comparisons that use the word *like* or *as*. On this page, a simile can be found in the common saying "strong as a lion." Identify another simile on this page and explain what comparison is being made.

Indeed, being a king, especially a good king, was often boring. He couldn't even drop a glove without half the palace, it seemed, stooping to pick it up and arguing about who should have the honor of returning it. "Never mind the honor," the king once said. "Never mind, never mind. Just give me my glove. What? what? what? Yes, you all picked it up, yes, yes, yes, all, all, all—you all picked it up." (King George had a habit of talking rapidly and repeating himself so that his talk often sounded like a gobble.)

But as king, he did have a few advantages. He was, for instance, the most prayed-for man in the empire. Naturally it was pleasant to think of the heavy traffic of prayers ascending on his behalf every Sunday morning. From every country church and every city cathedral in every corner of the kingdom. (But not in America. There the preachers gave up praying for him when the Punishment started.) The king was also the most toasted man. No party (except in America) began without all the people present raising their glasses and wishing the king a long life. (The king wished it, too.) And he had the biggest birthday celebration. Each year on June 4 all his subjects (except in America, of course) celebrated his birthday with parades and banquets and speeches and gunfire and fireworks.

All those prayers and toasts and fireworks were not to be sneezed at. Still, there were times when George wanted to forget about being a king. Fortunately he had hobbies to turn to. For one thing, he made metal buttons (he loved turning a lathe). He wrote articles on farming and signed himself "Ralph Richardson," which was the name of one of his shepherds. He played backgammon with the officers of the royal household, and he collected ship models, coins, clocks, and watches. (He had a four-sided clock that even showed the tides.) He played the flute and harpsichord, hunted, and studied the stars in his private observatory. And for the queen's special amusement, he maintained a zoo, which consisted of one elephant and one zebra.

But always in the end he had to go back to being a king. Back to the problem of America. This was the way he thought of America. A problem. King George did not really think of the Revolutionary War as a *war* until the fall of 1777, when 5,000 English soldiers surrendered to the Americans at Saratoga.

ANALYZE THE TEXT

Fact and Opinion Is the first sentence on page 364 a fact or the author's opinion? What reasons does the author include to support this statement?

In 1788 when the king was 50 years old, he became violently ill of a disease that has since been diagnosed as porphyria. One of the symptoms of the disease is that one's mind is affected, but in those days people thought that the king had simply gone mad. He recovered from his first attack but in later years suffered again. For the last 10 years of his life he was a wretched-looking figure dressed in a purple bathrobe with wild white hair and a wild beard. He died in 1820 at the age of 82.

How could such a thing happen? the king asked. Hadn't he been told, even by an ex-governor of Massachusetts, that Americans would give up? That only a small number of Americans were really against him? And how could he, a peace-loving king, find himself in an honest-to-goodness war with his own colonies? He tried to console himself. He was a good king, he said. Good kings deserve to win. So this must be a temporary setback. All he had to do was to show the world that he wasn't the least bit worried. So that night after hearing about the defeat, King George went to a court party and spent the evening telling stupid jokes and laughing so uproariously that his Prime Minister, Lord North, had to take him aside and try to quiet him down.

The war dragged on. France, impressed with the victory at Saratoga, joined the war on America's side. There were people in England now who wanted to stop fighting, but not George. No, no, no. Never, never. No independence. No peace without honor. If one group of English colonies got away, what would happen to the others? What would be left of the empire?

But no matter how he showed himself in public, privately George was depressed. The world was not staying settled, everything in place, the way he liked it. Not only was America acting up, but there were difficulties in England as well. Riots even. And George's own family was misbehaving. Two of his brothers were involved in scandals, and George's son, the Prince of Wales, was so contrary he deliberately arrived for meals as much as an hour late although he *knew* that the king wanted everyone to be *exactly* on time.

ANALYZE THE TEXT

Tone The author uses a humorous tone to describe King George's thoughts and actions. Why do you think she does this?

On November 25, 1781, the news reached London that the English army under General Cornwallis had surrendered at Yorktown to General Washington. When Lord North heard this, he threw up his arms. "It's all over!" he said.

But the king said nothing was over. They still had ships, hadn't they? (He named them.) They still had officers. (He had learned their names, too.) They still had troops. They still had guns and gunpowder.

King George set his lips firmly and wrote a letter to the Secretary of State for America. This defeat, he said, should not make the smallest difference in their plans. Still, King George was so upset that when he dated the letter, he forgot to record the hour and the minute of the writing.

Two days later the king addressed the government. "I prohibit you from thinking of peace," he thundered.

But the government did think of peace, and eventually the government voted for it.

So now what? King George couldn't fight the war all by himself. He couldn't chop off the heads of all those who had voted for peace. Kings didn't do that anymore. He could, of course, abdicate—quit the king business altogether. For a time he thought seriously of this. He even drafted an announcement of his abdication, but then he put it away in his desk. He was so *used* to being a king. So when the time came for him to sign the peace proclamation, he signed. As soon as he had finished, he jumped on his horse and took a hard gallop away from the palace. When the time came to announce in public the separation of the two countries and the independence of America, he swallowed hard and announced. Afterward he asked a friend if he had spoken loudly enough.

As long as he lived, King George had nightmares about the loss of the American colonies. It certainly hadn't been his fault, he said. He hadn't done anything wrong. *He* had just wanted to teach Americans a lesson.

Dig Deeper

How to Analyze the Text

Use these pages to learn about Fact and Opinion, Tone, and Similes. Then read "Can't You Make Them Behave, King George?" again to apply what you learned.

Fact and Opinion

After reading "Can't You Make Them Behave, King George?," you know a few more facts about the American Revolution. **Facts** are statements that can be proved true or false. The statement "Britain lost the American colonies during the reign of King George III" is a fact. It can be looked up in a reference source.

The selection also told you about the opinions of some of the people involved in the revolution. **Opinions** are statements that express thoughts, feelings, or beliefs. They often include adjectives or judgment words. The statement "King George III was the worst ruler in British history" cannot be proved true or false. Therefore, it is an opinion. Look for reasons and text evidence that support the author's opinion. Do you agree with it?

When reading narrative nonfiction, you must distinguish between facts and opinions. Use a graphic organizer like this one to record examples of each from the text.

Facts	Opinions

RI.5.8 explain how an author uses reasons and evidence to support points; **RI.5.10** read and comprehend informational texts; **L.5.5a** interpret figurative language in context

Tone

Tone is the writer's attitude toward his or her subject. This selection has a humorous tone. The author views some of the king's thoughts and actions as absurd. She chooses words and details that convey her attitude. On page 365, for example, she writes that when King George felt tired of being king, he turned to hobbies such as making metal buttons. This detail shows him as less than serious about his responsibilities.

Similes

Common sayings such as "He runs like the wind" and "She is as stubborn as a mule" are **similes**. They compare two unlike things using the word *like* or *as*. Similes create vivid pictures in readers' minds. On page 363, for example, King George says that he feels "strong as a lion." Readers imagine a powerful lion and immediately understand what the king means.

Your Turn

RETURN TO THE ESSENTIAL QUESTION

Turn and Talk Review the selection to prepare to discuss this question: *How can people's differences of opinion lead to a revolution?* In a small group, take turns expressing your ideas, asking questions to clarify any confusing points.

 Classroom Conversation

Continue your discussion of "Can't You Make Them Behave, King George?" by using text evidence to explain your answers to these questions:

1. What is the purpose of the gold sidebar information in the text?

2. What impression of King George do you get from this selection?

3. How might history have been different if King George had been a different kind of monarch?

DISCUSS MAIN IDEAS

Outline It Author Jean Fritz develops several main ideas in the selection. With a partner, identify the main ideas in each part of the text. Record them in an outline. Remember that the main idea is what a paragraph or a section of text is mostly about. Discuss the details that support each idea. Then state the overall main idea of the selection.

> Outline of Main Ideas
> 1. The British government angered colonists by imposing a stamp tax.
> 2.

WRITE ABOUT READING

Response The author of "Can't You Make Them Behave, King George?" includes many of the king's opinions as well as facts related to the American Revolution. Write a paragraph to explain why you think King George's thoughts and feelings are important to understanding the topic. How did the king's opinions influence events in America? Use evidence from the text, including quotations, to support your ideas.

Writing Tip

Before you write your paragraph, identify the reasons that you will include and the details that support each one. Present them in a logical order.

COMMON CORE **RI.5.1** quote accurately when explaining what the text says explicitly and when drawing inferences; **RI.5.2** determine two or more main ideas and explain how they are supported by details/summarize; **W.5.1b** provide logically ordered reasons supported by facts and details; **W.5.9b** apply grade 5 Reading standards to informational texts; **SL.5.1a** come to discussions prepared/explicitly draw on preparation and other information about the topic; **SL.5.1c** pose and respond to questions, make comments that contribute to the discussion, and elaborate on others' remarks

NARRATIVE NONFICTION

COMMON CORE **RI.5.6** analyze multiple accounts of the same event or topic; **RI.5.10** read and understand informational text

Tea Time!

by Lawrence Tolbert

Why Toss Tea?

On November 29, 1773, a handbill, or flyer, was posted all over Boston. It stated,

> *Friends! Brethren! Countrymen! That worst of Plagues, the detested tea, shipped for this port by the East India Company, is now arrived in the harbor. . . .*

The flyer called for the colonists of Massachusetts to unite and protest the importing of this tea. Weeks later, on the evening of December 16, 1773, the water in Boston Harbor became one giant pot of tea as the revolt against King George and the British government took place. In just a few hours, colonists tossed thousands of pounds of tea overboard. This famous event would later become known as the Boston Tea Party.

The Boston Tea Party took place on December 16, 1773.

Send It Back!

So, just what led to this wasteful tossing of perfectly good tea?

Taxes! That's what led to this famous event in history. In 1767 the British government passed laws giving its country the right to tax American colonies. The colonies protested that, with no one to represent them in England, they had no say in how they were being governed, what items were to be taxed, and how the tax money would be spent. In the end, the British government dropped all the taxes, except for the one on tea—the beloved drink of British people and American colonists alike.

Drinking tea was a custom that had traveled to the new land with the American colonists. Even before the Boston Tea Party, the stiff taxes placed on tea by the British government led many colonists to boycott tea altogether.

However, King George III was certain that the colonists could not hold to their boycotts and tea replacements for long. He continued to send ships filled with tea, and he expected the colonists to pay the required taxes.

When three ships filled with tea arrived in Boston around early December 1773, the colonists had finally had enough and refused to pay the tax. They called for the tea to be sent back. Town meetings were called to "devise measures for getting rid of this annoyance," according to Samuel Cooper, a Boston Tea Party participant.

Despite repeated requests, Governor Hutchinson of the Massachusetts Bay Colony refused to send the tea back to England. Instead, he insisted that the tea be unloaded and the taxes paid by midnight, December 16. If not, he would force the unloading of the tea with the use of warships and cannons. To prove his point, he ordered two ships to stand guard at the entrance to Boston Harbor. No ships could leave the harbor without his permission.

Town meetings were called to decide what should be done with the tea being held onboard three ships in the harbor.

Many of the more outspoken Bostonians felt that the governor's refusal to send the tea back to England left them few options.

On December 16, 1773, Samuel Adams, a leader known for organizing protests against the British government, announced to those at a special town meeting, "This meeting can do no more to save the country." Were his words a signal that the time had come for action?

A group of men at the meeting hollered and whooped a war cry. Groups of men marched down to Griffin's Wharf in disguise. Hundreds of onlookers followed to watch events unfold.

Samuel Adams encouraged his fellow colonists to protest the tax on tea.

377

That Fateful Night

Joshua Wyeth, age 16, was one of many to march upon the wharf. He described his experience to a journalist many years later. Here is a paraphrase of what he said:

> I had but a few hours warning of what was intended to be done. To prevent discovery we agreed to wear ragged clothes . . . , dressing to resemble Indians. Our most intimate friends among the spectators had not the least knowledge of us.
>
> At the appointed time, we met in an old building at the head of the wharf, and fell in one after another, as if by accident, so as not to excite suspicion . . . .
>
> We boarded the ship moored by the wharf, and our leader ordered the captain and crew to open the hatchways, and hand us the hoisting tackle and rope, assuring them that no harm was intended them. . . . Some of our number then jumped into the hold, and passed the chests to the tackle. As they were hauled on deck others knocked them open with axes, and others raised them to the railing and discharged their contents overboard. All who were not needed on this ship went on board the others, where the same ceremonies were repeated.
>
> We were merry, in an undertone, at the idea of making so large a cup of tea for the fishes, but [we used] no more words than were absolutely necessary. . . . I never worked harder in my life.

Accounts vary as to just how many colonists took part in the "ceremonies."

378

Quietly and swiftly, the chests of tea were dumped into the harbor.

George Hewes, a Boston shoemaker, also joined in. Over fifty years after the event, Hewes recalled that night:

It was now evening, and I immediately dressed myself in the costume of an Indian, equipped with a small hatchet, . . . and a club. . . . [A]fter having painted my face and hands with coal dust in the shop of a blacksmith, I repaired to Griffin's wharf, where the ships lay that contained the tea.

When I first appeared in the street after being thus disguised, I fell in with many who were dressed, equipped and painted as I was, and who fell in with me, and marched in order to the place of our destination.

When we arrived at the wharf, there were three of our number who assumed an authority to direct our operations, to which we readily submitted. They divided us into three parties, for the purpose of boarding the three ships which contained the tea at the same time. The name of him who commanded the division to which I was assigned was Leonard Pitt. The names of the other commanders I never knew.

Once aboard the ships, the colonists demanded that the ships' captains hand over the keys to the hatches, or compartments, where the tea was stored. The chests of tea were hauled on deck and split open with tomahawks. The contents were then dumped overboard. Tea leaves scattered across the water. As Hewes recalls,

In about three hours from the time we went on board, we had thus broken and thrown overboard every tea chest to be found in the ship, while those in the other ships were disposing of the tea in the same way at the same time. We were surrounded by British armed ships, but no attempt was made to resist us.

The following day, tea leaves could still be seen floating in the harbor. Colonists in rowboats beat the tea with their paddles until they were certain the tea would be of no use for drinking.

Caught in the Act

Several accounts describe how a few citizens quietly attempted to save some tea for their own use. With hopes that no one was looking, they filled their coat pockets with the precious leaves. However, their deeds were soon discovered and their pockets emptied of the tea. With a few swift kicks as punishment, these citizens were sent on their way!

King George III ruled Britain during the time of the Boston Tea Party.

Standing Up to the King

Despite the pounds of tea destroyed on the evening of December 16, 1773, the disguised colonists did no other damage to the ships or the people aboard them. Overall, it was a peaceful protest meant to send a strong message to King George and the British government.

Here is how Hewes recalled the conclusion to the event:

We then quietly retired to our several places of residence, without having any conversation with each other, or taking any measures to discover who were our associates; nor do I recollect of our having had the knowledge of the name of a single individual concerned in that affair, except that of Leonard Pitt. . . . There appeared to be an understanding that each individual should volunteer his services, keep his own secret, and risk the consequences for himself.

The days and nights that followed this event were more quiet in Boston. If for only a short time, the colonists had spoken out against British rule. Eventually, King George ordered punishment for his disobedient subjects, leading the colonies one step closer to revolution!

For many days after the historic protest, the streets of Boston were quiet and orderly.

Compare Texts

Analyze Multiple Accounts In a small group, discuss the following questions about the texts in Lesson 12, and support your ideas with text evidence from both selections. *From whose perspective does each author describe the events of the Boston Tea Party? How does each account affect readers' understanding of the events? What do you learn from reading both texts together?*

Write a Letter Imagine that King George III has asked you how he should deal with the disobedient colonists. Write a letter in which you advise him on how to calm the colonists and keep the colonies under British rule.

Research Taxes Just as the colonists did, Americans today pay taxes. Tax money has a special purpose. Use the Internet or print reference sources to research both a national and a state tax. Find out which people or government agencies are responsible for collecting the taxes and for what the collected taxes are used. Share your information with a partner.

COMMON CORE **RI.5.6** analyze multiple accounts of the same event or topic; **RI.5.7** draw on information from print and digital sources to locate answers or solve problems; **W.5.4** produce writing in which development and organization are appropriate to task, purpose, and audience; **W.5.10** write routinely over extended time frames and shorter time frames

Grammar

What Are the Simple Verb Tenses? A verb in the **present tense** tells what is happening now or what is happening over and over. A verb in the **past tense** tells what happened in the past. Many verbs in the past tense end with -*ed*. A verb in the **future tense** tells what will happen in the future. Verbs in the future tense use the helping verb *will*.

Sentence	Tense of Verb
Americans value freedom.	present tense
Long ago, England ruled America.	past tense
We will celebrate our independence and freedom on July 4.	future tense

Try This! **Copy these sentences onto another sheet of paper. Circle the verb in each sentence. Label it as present tense, past tense, or future tense.**

1 England needed money after the French and Indian War.

2 King George III agreed to new taxes for American colonists.

3 Even today's kings and queens expect obedience.

4 Still, most people dislike unfair taxes.

5 Years from now, Americans will remember the colonists' protests with pride.

Your readers will be confused if you shift the verb tense within a sequence of events you are writing about. Tell readers whether events are happening, have already happened, or will happen in the future by choosing the correct tense and using it consistently.

Shifting Tenses

When my family **visited** Boston last summer, we **see** Paul Revere's house.

We **toured** the house, and then we **will tour** the USS *Constitution*, an early American battleship.

We **have** a great time!

Consistent Tense

When my family **visited** Boston last summer, we **saw** Paul Revere's house. We **toured** the house, and then we **toured** the USS *Constitution*, an early American battleship. We **had** a great time!

 Connect Grammar to Writing

As you edit your problem-solution composition, look for inappropriate shifts in verb tenses and correct them. Using consistent verb tenses will make your writing easier to understand.

W.5.1a introduce a topic, state an opinion, and create an organizational structure; **W.5.1b** provide logically ordered reasons supported by facts and details; **W.5.1c** link opinion and reasons using words, phrases, and clauses; **W.5.1d** provide a concluding statement or section; **W.5.5** develop and strengthen writing by planning, revising, editing, rewriting, or trying a new approach

Opinion Writing

✔️ **Organization** When you write a **problem-solution composition**, you describe a problem and how you think it should be solved. Discuss the problem first. Then propose your solution. You should take a strong position and give reasons you think your solution will work. Include facts and examples to support your proposal.

Noah wrote a problem-solution composition about what his community should do to make the local park safer. Later, he added transition words to connect his ideas more clearly. He also moved a sentence in paragraph 1 that was confusing.

Use the Writing Traits Checklist below as you revise your writing.

Writing Traits Checklist

✔️ **Ideas**
Did I clearly explain the problem and its solution?

✔️ **Organization**
Did I put my reasons and support in a logical order?

✔️ **Sentence Fluency**
Did I use transitions to link my ideas?

✔️ **Word Choice**
Did I choose words that make the problem and solution clear?

✔️ **Voice**
Did I present a convincing argument?

✔️ **Conventions**
Did I use correct spelling, grammar, and punctuation?

Revised Draft

My family used to enjoy Greenville
Park. ~~I~~ However, we don't go there anymore. The

playground equipment is no longer safe.
Move to ¶ 2
(We need the park to be a nice place

for us to visit again.) Many swings are

rusted, and the jungle gyms are broken.
Also,
The children's sandbox is full of leaves

and broken toys.

Save Greenville Park!

by Noah Friedman

My family used to enjoy Greenville Park. However, we don't go there anymore. The playground equipment is no longer safe. Many swings are rusted, and the jungle gyms are broken. Also, the children's sandbox is full of leaves and broken toys. There is no place for people to bring their dogs for exercise and fresh air.

We need the park to be a nice place for us to visit again. I realize that park renovations can be costly. I also realize that it isn't possible to tax the community in order to raise money to pay for the park. I propose a fundraiser and volunteer effort instead, in which my neighbors and I fulfill our civic duty by taking care of our community.

There are many improvements that we could make with a little extra money and time. First, we could paint the swings and fix or replace broken equipment. We also could clean up litter and install new trash bins. Finally, we could add a fence to make a separate area where dogs could exercise away from the play areas. Greenville Park is located at the center of three neighborhoods. Hundreds of people would benefit from these park improvements!

Reading as a Writer

What transitions did Noah add to make the organization of his points clearer? What transition words could you use to connect points in your problem-solution composition?

In my final paper, I added transition words to make my points easy to follow. I also used past, present, and future verb tenses correctly.

Vocabulary in Context

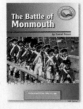

TARGET VOCABULARY

revolution
strategy
foes
legendary
formal
gushed
plunged
magnificent
retreat
shimmering

Vocabulary Reader

Context Cards

COMMON CORE **L.5.6** acquire and use general academic and domain-specific words and phrases

1 revolution

The goal of the American patriots in their revolution was to overthrow British rule.

2 strategy

General George Washington thought up a strategy, or plan, for the colonial army.

3 foes

Patriots sometimes fired on their British foes, or enemies, from behind rocks and trees.

4 legendary

This boy is pretending to be Paul Revere on his legendary, or famous, midnight ride.

Go Digital

▶ Study each Context Card.

▶ Use the context of the sentences to clarify the meaning of each Vocabulary word.

5 formal

Crispus Attucks was shot without formal, or proper, warning at the Boston Massacre.

6 gushed

As water gushed into his damaged ship, John Paul Jones vowed to keep fighting.

7 plunged

Molly Pitcher was a patriot hero even before she plunged a ramrod into a cannon.

8 magnificent

"Give me liberty or give me death," were grand, magnificent words of patriot Patrick Henry.

9 retreat

Patriot troops trained by General Steuben forced Hessians to retreat, or pull out, from battle.

10 shimmering

The signal for Paul Revere to ride was two shimmering, flickering lantern lights.

Read and Comprehend

Go Digital

☑ TARGET SKILL

Conclusions and Generalizations As you read "They Called Her Molly Pitcher," notice the details the author provides about the people on the battlefield. The descriptions of their appearance and actions can help you draw conclusions and make generalizations about participants in the American Revolution. Use a graphic organizer such as the one below to record a conclusion about the actions of Molly Hays. Then quote the text evidence that you used to draw your conclusion.

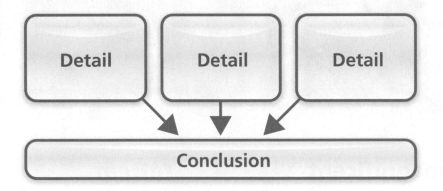

| Detail | Detail | Detail |

Conclusion

☑ TARGET STRATEGY

Analyze/Evaluate Use your graphic organizer to **analyze** details in "They Called Her Molly Pitcher." Ask yourself questions about the author's points, and **evaluate** how well those points are supported with reasons and evidence.

COMMON CORE

RI.5.1 quote accurately when explaining what the text says explicitly and when drawing inferences; **RI.5.8** explain how an author uses reasons and evidence to support points

PREVIEW THE TOPIC

Life on the Battlefield

During the American Revolution, many men joined the army. Some of their wives and children went with them and lived in army camps. Life on the battlefield was difficult. Women and children suffered from the same conditions as the soldiers whom they tried to help.

In "They Called Her Molly Pitcher," you'll learn about one woman who traveled with her husband and assisted the soldiers during a battle. Her actions helped save lives. Reading this selection will expand your understanding of what people experienced on the battlefield during the American Revolution.

ANCHOR TEXT

 TARGET SKILL

Conclusions and Generalizations Use details to explain ideas that aren't directly stated or that are generally true.

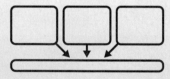

 GENRE

Narrative nonfiction tells about real people, things, events, and places. As you read, look for:

▶ factual information that tells a story
▶ illustrations that help convey ideas from the text
▶ events in time order

COMMON CORE **RI.5.1** quote accurately when explaining what the text says explicitly and when drawing inferences; **RI.5.4** determine the meaning of general academic and domain-specific words and phrases; **RI.5.10** read and comprehend informational texts

MEET THE AUTHOR

Anne Rockwell

Anne Rockwell always wanted to create art, but an injury made it difficult for her to draw, so she developed her writing talent. She tries very hard to write exciting nonfiction with "color." Her American biographies include *Only Passing Through: The Story of Sojourner Truth* and *Big George*, about George Washington.

MEET THE ILLUSTRATOR

Cynthia von Buhler

In addition to being a children's book illustrator, Cynthia von Buhler is an award-winning fine artist, performer, and musician. She lives with her many pets in a castle on Long Island in New York. She has also written and illustrated her own picture book, *The Cat Who Wouldn't Come Inside*.

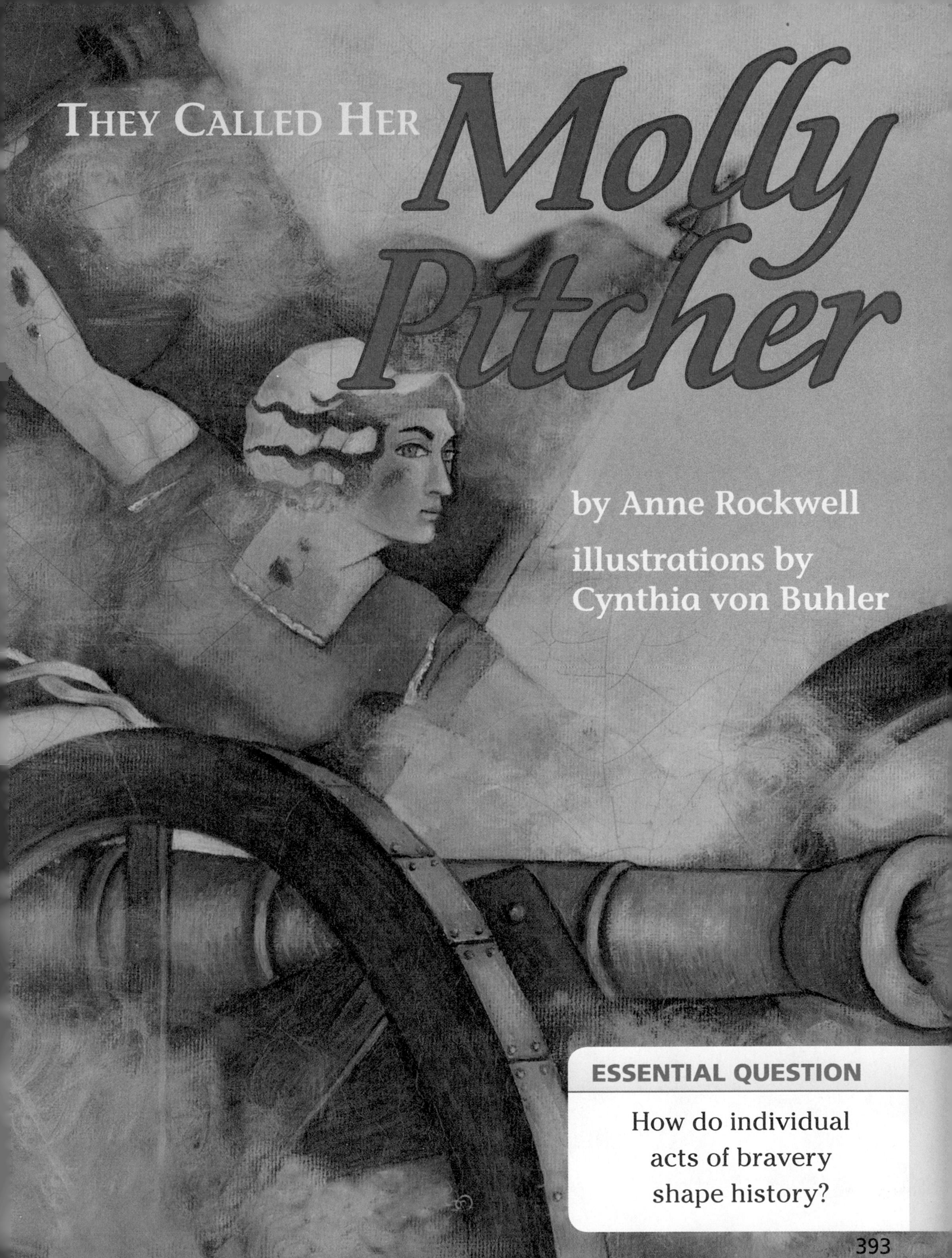

THEY CALLED HER Molly Pitcher

by Anne Rockwell

illustrations by Cynthia von Buhler

ESSENTIAL QUESTION

How do individual acts of bravery shape history?

In 1777 a barber named William Hays closed up shop and joined George Washington's Continental Army in the revolution against England. He went to Valley Forge, Pennsylvania, where a Prussian general named Baron von Steuben was training the Patriot troops in the formal rules of battle that armies used in those days. Like many women of the time, Hays's wife, Mary, nicknamed Molly, went with him. Some people think that she is the legendary heroine Molly Pitcher.

General George Washington was commander in chief of the Continental Army. He and other officers, plus a bedraggled army of about 12,000 men and boys, were camped at Valley Forge just before Christmas of 1777. Snow lay deep on the ground, and Washington's troops had run out of everything they needed to keep on fighting. Washington begged the Second Continental Congress for food and supplies, but none came.

It was so cold that soldiers had to stand on their hats in the snow to keep their feet from freezing. Their shoes had holes in them from tramping over miles of rough and stony ground. They had no blankets or warm clothes. They didn't have enough to eat. Their camp was a filthy mess. Many of them were very sick. Every day, more and more soldiers deserted. Others died.

Molly and other women who'd followed husbands, sons, fathers, and brothers to Valley Forge did whatever they could to help. They cooked and cleaned, washed and mended clothes, and nursed the sick. But no matter what they did, more soldiers died each day.

Things began to look up when the Second Continental Congress finally sent supplies. General Washington began planning to go to battle again.

At the end of June, a scout brought news. A large number of British soldiers, led by Sir Henry Clinton, were gathered at Monmouth (MAHN muhth) Courthouse, near the New Jersey shore. The fight everyone had been preparing for was coming very soon.

Washington ordered General Charles Lee to lead an advance guard of 5,000 soldiers to attack the British. He'd send in a rear guard of more men soon after the fighting was under way.

William Hays was among Lee's advance guard marching to battle. As she always had, Molly followed.

ANALYZE THE TEXT

Conclusions and Generalizations
Based on text evidence, what can you conclude about what life was like for Washington's soldiers?

Winter at Valley Forge had been bitter cold, but June of 1778 in New Jersey was hotter than anyone could remember.

It was just after sunrise when American soldiers fired on the British near Monmouth Courthouse. Molly could see that the day was going to be a scorcher. Heat and humidity were already shimmering up from the ground. She decided what her job would be that day.

She'd spotted a green and mossy place where a spring gushed up. She ran and filled her pitcher with cold water. She raced back to the battlefield, dodging cannon and musket fire, carrying her pitcher full of water for any American soldier who needed a drink.

The Americans knew all about such hot and humid summer days. They knew they had to keep cool any way they could. They ignored what Baron von Steuben had taught them about looking neat and military at all times. They stripped off coats, belts, wigs, hats, boots, shoes, and stockings and tossed them onto the grass.

Smoke, noise, and the smell of gunpowder filled the air. Molly paid no attention. All morning, she ran back and forth from battlefield to spring, spring to battlefield, bringing water to men who'd collapsed in the heat. Over and over she heard the urgent cry of

"Molly – Pitcher!"

Still more British soldiers, under orders from Lord Cornwallis, marched toward Monmouth Courthouse. The men formed a line of scarlet like a winding river of blood. They were a magnificent and terrifying sight. But their fine uniforms weren't what they should have been wearing in the sun that blazed down on them.

Each man wore a tall black fur hat; a scarlet coat of thick, warm wool; a wide and shining black belt that held a sharp sword; a white waistcoat; and matching woolen pants with knee-high, brightly polished black boots. Each marched with his eyes straight ahead, a musket on his shoulder, a knapsack full of heavy lead balls of ammunition on his back. They moved to the stirring music of war. Drums were beating, fifes were playing, trumpets were sounding.

The soldiers started dropping as the sun rose higher. These Englishmen had never felt such heat in their home across the sea. It was almost a hundred degrees in New Jersey that day. Men grew faint and dizzy, and fell to the ground. But their companions went on marching. They never stopped or broke step, even when one man or more collapsed. Fifty-six British soldiers died of heat stroke that day.

That didn't stop them, though. All morning, more and more scarlet coats marched onto the field. Many American soldiers panicked at the sight of so many. General Lee couldn't maintain order. His soldiers forgot all about fighting in the disciplined ways Baron von Steuben had taught them. Instead, they ran in terror this way and that, hiding in ditches, up in apple trees, beneath hedges.

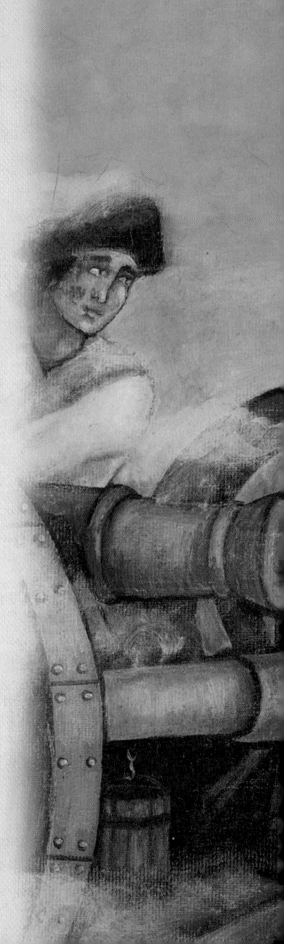

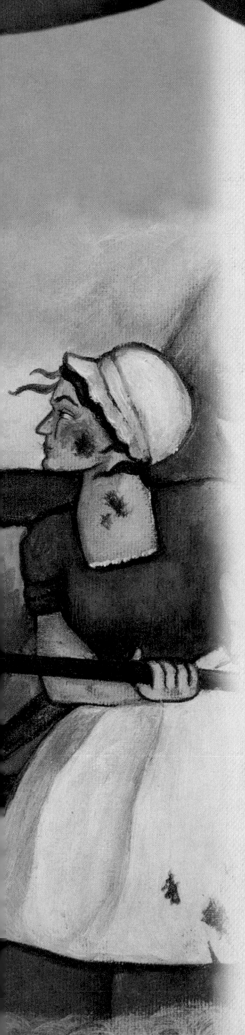

General Lee was sure there'd be a massacre of his troops before morning turned to noon. He gave the orders to retreat.

Molly saw that some of the men, including William, disobeyed the order and kept on fighting. The sun was growing hotter. As long as any member of the Continental Army needed water to drink, Molly Hays wasn't going anywhere.

On one of her trips to the spring, she stumbled over the body of an American soldier. She assumed he was dead until she heard him moan.

The British were advancing quickly, guns aimed straight at their foes. Molly knew she could run to safety, but the wounded man couldn't walk, let alone run. He lay directly in the line of fire and would surely be killed if he stayed there.

He was a good-sized fellow, but Molly wasted no time wondering how she'd do what she had to. She picked the man up, slung him over her shoulder, and ran to a clump of bushes away from the gunfire. She laid him down there on the grass in the shade.

She ran back toward the spring and passed the cannon William was firing just in time to see a ball from a British musket hit him. William fell to the ground. She examined her husband's wound and saw that he wouldn't die from it, but he couldn't fire his cannon.

Someone had to.

Molly grabbed the long ramrod, plunged it into the barrel of the cannon, and fired it off. She kept on firing.

ANALYZE THE TEXT

Domain-Specific Vocabulary On page 398, the author uses domain-specific words such as *waistcoat*, *musket*, *knapsack*, *lead*, and *ammunition*. What clues can help you determine the meanings of these words?

A ball fired low from a British musket came whizzing straight toward Molly. She quickly spread her legs wide. The musket ball passed between them. It never touched her, but her skirt and petticoat were ripped and became a good deal shorter than they had been.

She muttered that it could have been worse and went back to work firing the cannon.

Soon General Washington galloped onto the field riding Nelson, his fine horse who never shied at the noise of guns or cannons, no matter how close they were. Washington carried the flag of commander in chief—thirteen stars in a circle on a field of blue silk. The flag fluttered and flew above the smoke of battle. It wasn't as bright as the scarlet coats the British soldiers wore, but to everyone who'd stayed on to fight, it was a cheering and glorious sight.

For the rest of that hot and steamy day, the Continental Army fought the way Baron von Steuben had taught it to. George Washington saw to that.

As he galloped over the battlefield, shouting orders and spurring his men on, he was amazed to catch a glimpse of a woman. She was blurred by the smoke that surrounded her. Her face was smudged with gunpowder and sweat. But George Washington saw her take a deep breath, then run and shove the long ramrod into the big gun with as much force as possible. The cannon boomed. The explosion shook the ground, but the woman paid no attention—she just got ready to fire the cannon again.

When the sun set, the fighting stopped. Neither side could go on in darkness. Exhausted British and American soldiers put down their guns and tended to their dead and wounded. Late that night, they sat down to eat and rest, to prepare themselves for another day of fighting.

That same night, General Washington asked some of his officers about the woman he'd seen firing a cannon. He listened to what they said about how she'd carried water through the gunfire to the soldiers all that morning.

Washington ordered that the woman be brought before him. He told her she'd been as brave in battle as any man he'd ever heard of. He decided she'd earned the rank of sergeant in the Continental Army.

As she listened to what the tall, strong general said, Molly Hays had never felt so proud in her life.

No man who heard General Washington speak to her that night doubted that Molly had earned her rank. As the news spread through the troops, no soldier sneered at the thought of a woman being a sergeant in *his* army, even though no one present had ever heard of such a thing.

That night, Sergeant Molly Hays lay down on the grass at the edge of the field beside William and the rest of the soldiers of the Continental Army. Long after the stars filled the sky, General George Washington spread his cape over the grass, tied Nelson to a tree, and lay down with his weary soldiers.

As he lay gazing up at the stars, planning his strategy for the next day's battle, fires danced on the hill across the field where the British were camped. The voices of many men carried through the night. Sentries marched back and forth, keeping their endless watch. It was very late before everything was quiet except for the chorus of frogs singing in the nearby swamp.

ANALYZE THE TEXT

Text Structure The author uses a sequence-of-events text structure to tell the story of Molly Pitcher. How does this text structure help you understand the relationships between events in her life?

Molly and the other American soldiers rose before the sun. They'd had some sleep and were ready to fight again. Many believed they could win.

But they didn't fight the British that day. No scarlet-coated soldiers marched onto the field. They'd gone away.

Sir Henry Clinton and Lord Cornwallis had ordered a retreat. They didn't want their men to fight that wily old fox again this morning. They were afraid they'd lose. Washington's Continental Army didn't fight like farmers, as the British leaders had been sure they would. They fought like soldiers. And one of those soldiers was a woman.

Dig Deeper

How to Analyze the Text

Use these pages to learn about Conclusions and Generalizations, Domain-Specific Vocabulary, and Text Structure. Then read "They Called Her Molly Pitcher" again to apply what you learned.

Conclusions and Generalizations

Examining the facts and details in a text can help you draw **conclusions** and make **generalizations.** Doing so will help you figure out things the author does not state directly. A conclusion is a judgment based on text details. A generalization is a broad statement supported by text details that is true most of the time.

When you draw conclusions or make generalizations, you need to support your ideas with information. Some of this information can be from your own knowledge. Quotations and text evidence can also provide strong support for your ideas. You can use a graphic organizer like the one below to gather support from "They Called Her Molly Pitcher" for your conclusions or generalizations.

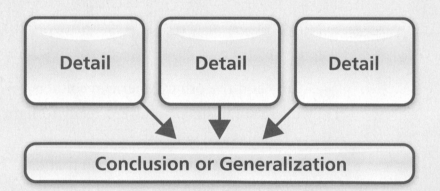

| Detail | Detail | Detail |

Conclusion or Generalization

COMMON CORE **RI.5.1** quote accurately when explaining what the text says explicitly and when drawing inferences; **RI.5.3** explain the relationships between individuals/events/ideas/concepts in a text; **RI.5.4** determine the meaning of general academic and domain-specific words and phrases; **RI.5.10** read and comprehend informational texts; **RF.5.4a** read on-level text with purpose and understanding; **L.5.6** acquire and use general academic and domain-specific words and phrases

Domain-Specific Vocabulary

Authors choose words carefully in order to make their writing clear and interesting. **Domain-specific words**, such as historical terms, add realism to a selection and show the author's knowledge of the topic. In "They Called Her Molly Pitcher," terms related to battlefield equipment, uniforms, and procedures—along with context clues and pictures—can help you understand and visualize the historical setting of the story.

Text Structure

All texts have a beginning, a middle, and an ending. Many texts also have other organizational **structures** that can show how events or ideas are related. For example, "They Called Her Molly Pitcher" is written in a sequence-of-events structure. Time-order words such as *first, next,* and *last* are clues that a text has a sequence-of-events text structure.

Your Turn

 Turn and Talk Review the selection with a partner to prepare to discuss this question: *How do individual acts of bravery shape history?* As you discuss, take turns reviewing and explaining each other's key ideas.

Classroom Conversation

Continue your discussion of "They Called Her Molly Pitcher" by using text evidence to answer these questions:

1. What might have changed about the battle if Molly Hays hadn't participated?

2. Has this selection changed your thoughts about women's roles during the Revolution? Explain.

3. Which is more important—a soldier's rank or a soldier's actions?

WASHINGTON'S DECISION

Discuss It Besides showing appreciation, what message did General George Washington convey to the soldiers when he gave the rank of sergeant to Molly Hays? Do you think he made a good decision? Discuss these questions in a small group. Use quotations from the text and what you already know about the Revolutionary War to support your ideas.

WRITE ABOUT READING

Response Molly Pitcher went with her husband when he joined Baron von Steuben at Valley Forge. Think about the contributions that she made to the American Revolution by helping the soldiers. Write two paragraphs describing Molly Pitcher's actions and how they showed her bravery and helped shape history. Include quotations and other text evidence to support your statements.

Writing Tip

Consider using similes to make your writing more interesting and to convey your ideas in a fresh way. Remember that a simile is a comparison that uses the word *like* or *as*. Before you finalize your writing, check that your similes compare two unlike things.

COMMON CORE **RI.5.1** quote accurately when explaining what the text says explicitly and when drawing inferences; **RI.5.2** determine two or more main ideas and explain how they are supported by details/summarize; **RI.5.3** explain the relationships between individuals/events/ideas/concepts in a text; **W.5.9b** apply grade 5 Reading standards to informational texts; **W.5.10** write routinely over extended time frames and shorter time frames

PLAY

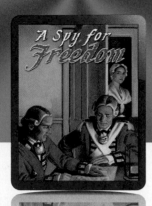

A Spy for
Freedom

by Ann Weil

Cast of Characters
Ann Darragh (Narrator)
Lydia Darragh
General Howe
Redcoat Officer #1
Redcoat Officer #2
Thomas Craig

Go Digital

(The dining room of the Darragh house in Philadelphia, 1777.)

Ann Darragh (Narrator): This story is about my mother, Lydia Darragh, a legendary hero of the American Revolution. She was a housewife living in Philadelphia in 1777. She was also a Patriot spy.

(Lydia sits at a table, folding napkins. There is a knock at the door. A Redcoat officer enters.)

Redcoat Officer #1: Mrs. Darragh?

Lydia Darragh: Yes?

Redcoat Officer #1: This is a formal notice on behalf of the magnificent King George the Third of England. The British army is taking your house to use for our meetings.

Lydia Darragh: But I have young children and nowhere to go!

Ann Darragh (Narrator): Those words gushed from my mother's mouth. Her eyes were shimmering with tears. Later, General Howe let her stay in the house, as long as she let the British use one room. It was a mistake for him but lucky for the Patriots.

(Lydia sneaks in and hides in the linen closet. British officers enter and sit at a table.)

General Howe: We will attack the Americans at Whitemarsh in two days. That should end this rebellion.

Redcoat Officer #1 and Redcoat Officer #2: *(together)* Yes, sir. *(The British leave.)*

Lydia Darragh: *(stepping out of the closet)* General Washington must hear of this!

(Lydia quickly writes a note. She leaves after she has plunged it into her pocket.)

Ann Darragh (Narrator): My mother left the city to warn the American troops. On her way, she ran into my brother's friend, Thomas Craig, who was a militia soldier.

(A street in Philadelphia. Lydia enters from the left, walking quickly. Thomas is walking slowly, unaware that Lydia is approaching.)

Lydia Darragh: Thomas! Thomas Craig! Is that you?

Thomas Craig: Hello, Mrs. Darragh! How is your family?

(Lydia quickly hands Thomas the piece of paper. As Thomas reads, his eyes get wider and wider.)

Thomas Craig: Thank you for this news, Mrs. Darragh! I must warn General Washington of the British strategy.

(He runs offstage.)

Ann Darragh (Narrator): Because of my mother's information, the Americans had time to prepare. They were able to make the British forces retreat at the Battle of Whitemarsh.

(British officers meeting in Darragh's house. Lydia listens from the linen closet.)

Redcoat Officer #1: *(angry, confused)* Our foes knew we were coming, but how?

Redcoat Officer #2: *(looks around the room, shrugs)* The walls must have ears.

Ann Darragh (Narrator): The walls did not have ears, but one Patriot housewife did. Her quick action helped to bring the Americans to victory.

Compare Texts

Compare Character Actions With a small group, discuss the different ways in which Molly Pitcher and Lydia Darragh demonstrated bravery and patriotism. In your group, ask and answer questions about the actions of these women. Support your thoughts with quotations and text evidence from the selections.

Write a Poem Think about the bravery displayed in this lesson's selections. Remember a time when you, someone you know, or someone you have read about did something brave. How did the act of bravery impact others? Write a poem about the event and your ideas about bravery. Use the sound and rhythm of your words to help you decide where to break lines.

Research American Patriots Lydia Darragh was a Patriot spy during the American Revolution. Research another Patriot spy, such as Nathan Hale or James Armistead Lafayette. Use print and online resources to find out how that person's actions affected the war's outcome. Then share what you learned with a partner.

COMMON CORE **RI.5.1** quote accurately when explaining what the text says explicitly and when drawing inferences; **RI.5.7** draw on information from print and digital sources to locate answers or solve problems; **W.5.10** write routinely over extended time frames and shorter time frames; **SL.5.1a** come to discussions prepared/explicitly draw on preparation and other information about the topic; **SL.5.1c** pose and respond to questions, make comments that contribute to the discussion, and elaborate on others' remarks

COMMON CORE **L.5.1c** use verb tense to convey times, sequences, states, and conditions; **L.5.2e** spell grade-appropriate words, consulting references as needed

Grammar

What Is a Regular Verb? What Is an Irregular Verb? A **regular verb** adds -*ed* to its present form to show action that happened in the past. A regular verb also adds -*ed* when it is used with the helping verb *has*, *have*, or *had*. An **irregular verb** does not add -*ed* in these situations. It changes in other ways. You should memorize the spellings of irregular verbs.

Regular and Irregular Verbs	
Regular Verbs	The Continental Army camped at Valley Forge. General Washington had asked for supplies. His request had been ignored by the congress.
Irregular Verbs	The soldiers wore thin, ragged clothes. They had eaten almost all of the food. Soldiers' toes had been frozen by the frigid weather.

 **Work with a partner. Identify each underlined verb as a regular verb or an irregular verb.**

1. Molly Pitcher <u>nursed</u> the sick at Valley Forge.

2. She <u>brought</u> the troops water during a battle.

3. One American soldier had been <u>wounded</u> by a musket ball.

4. Molly Pitcher <u>won</u> fame for her work with that soldier's cannon.

When you write, use vivid verbs to communicate action precisely. Vivid verbs keep your writing interesting and make it easier for readers to picture what happens.

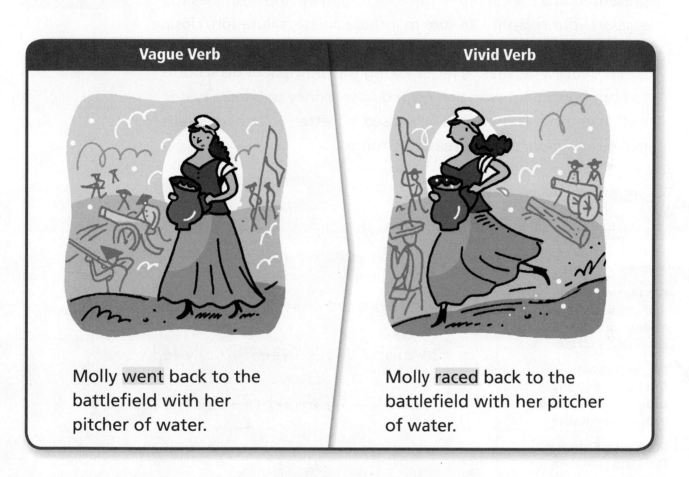

Vague Verb	Vivid Verb
Molly went back to the battlefield with her pitcher of water.	Molly raced back to the battlefield with her pitcher of water.

 Connect Grammar to Writing

As you revise your persuasive letter, look for vague verbs that you can replace with vivid verbs. Use vivid verbs to create clear pictures in your writing. Make sure you are using the correct forms of both regular and irregular verbs.

W.5.1a introduce a topic, state an opinion, and create an organizational structure; **W.5.1b** provide logically ordered reasons supported by facts and details; **W.5.1d** provide a concluding statement or section; **W.5.5** develop and strengthen writing by planning, revising, editing, rewriting, or trying a new approach

Opinion Writing

✓ **Ideas** When you write a **persuasive letter,** state your topic and opinion clearly. Your first paragraph should explain what you want the reader to think or do. Support your opinion with reasons presented in a logical order. Give facts, details, and examples to support your reasons. Be sure to include a date, salutation, closing, and signature.

Ed wrote a persuasive letter asking the principal of his school to honor a student who had helped raise money to build a water well in another country. As he revised his letter, Ed added details to make the support for his reasons stronger.

Writing Traits Checklist

✓ **Ideas**
Did I introduce my topic and state my opinion clearly, and provide a concluding statement?

✓ **Organization**
Did I give logically ordered reasons and support them well?

✓ **Sentence Fluency**
Did I use complete sentences?

✓ **Word Choice**
Did I carefully choose words that were strong and convincing?

✓ **Voice**
Did I express my interest in the subject?

✓ **Conventions**
Did I use correct spelling, grammar, and punctuation?

Revised Draft

to recognize students at Oak Ridge School
Each year we have an awards night.∧

This year, we should present a special

award to Molly Green. Molly led our

school in the effort to raise money to build

a well in another country. She organized a

, and more than 200 kids participated
walk-a-thon.∧

225 May Drive

Hilltop, TX 78443

January 15, 20XX

Dear Mr. Ramirez,

Each year we have an awards night to recognize students at Oak Ridge School. This year, we should present a special award to Molly Green. Molly led our school in the effort to raise money to build a well in another country. She organized a walk-a-thon, and more than 200 kids participated. We raised over $2,000! Thanks to Molly's caring and hard work, an entire village now has clean drinking water.

Through Molly's leadership, students at Oak Ridge saw that kids can make a difference. My classmates and I are already talking about other projects we can take on to help people. Molly Green is a hero and deserves to be recognized.

Sincerely,

Ed Fung

Reading as a Writer

Which details did Ed add to make his argument stronger? What details could you use to support your own argument?

In my final paper, I added details to support my reasons. I also used regular and irregular verbs correctly.

☑ TARGET VOCABULARY

provisions
dexterity
aspects
apprentice
influential
contributions
persuade
authorities
bondage
tentative

Vocabulary Reader

Context Cards

L.5.6 acquire and use general academic and domain-specific words and phrases

416

1 provisions

Colonial dockworkers unloaded needed goods, or provisions, from newly arrived ships in port.

2 dexterity

With dexterity, or skilled hands, this silversmith makes beautiful bowls.

3 aspects

Making frames and weaving fibers are aspects, or parts, of basketmaking.

4 apprentice

An apprentice to a blacksmith was trained to make horseshoes and nails.

Go Digital

▶ Study each Context Card.

▶ Use a thesaurus to determine a synonym for each Vocabulary word.

5 influential

Printers made books and newspapers that were influential in events before the Revolution.

6 contributions

Harvesting crops was one of many important contributions that kids made to the family farm.

7 persuade

A sign hanging above the door was used to persuade customers to enter the shoe shop.

8 authorities

Judges were the highest authorities, or officials, who could settle legal disputes.

9 bondage

Enslaved people, who were held in bondage, were often servants in the homes of the rich.

10 tentative

These merchants are shaking hands over a tentative deal. A contract will make it permanent.

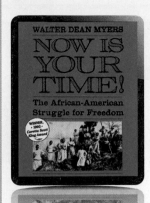

Read and Comprehend

Go Digital

☑ **TARGET SKILL**

Sequence of Events The events in "James Forten" are described in chronological order, or time order. As you read the selection, notice how this **sequence of events** is signaled by the use of dates, references to James's age, and words such as *after*, *soon*, and *later*. Use a graphic organizer like this one to help you track events as they occur in the text.

```
┌─────────────────────────────┐
│          Event 1            │
└─────────────────────────────┘
              │
              ▼
┌─────────────────────────────┐
│          Event 2            │
└─────────────────────────────┘
              │
              ▼
┌─────────────────────────────┐
│          Event 3            │
└─────────────────────────────┘
```

☑ **TARGET STRATEGY**

Summarize As you read "James Forten," pause now and then to **summarize,** or retell the main ideas of the text in your own words. Summarizing can help you understand and remember what you read.

RI.5.2 determine two or more main ideas and explain how they are supported by details/summarize; **RI.5.3** explain the relationships between individuals/events/ideas/concepts in a text

418

African American History

At the start of the Revolutionary War, about twenty percent of American colonists were of African ancestry. Many were enslaved; fewer were free. Enslaved people sometimes worked on plantations growing cotton or tobacco. In cities, they worked in homes as domestic servants. Free African Americans pursued trades or, if they were educated, entered into business.

In "James Forten," you will read about the courage of a free African American who fought for his country in the Revolutionary War. Later, as a successful businessman, he worked to secure basic freedoms for all Americans.

ANCHOR TEXT

WALTER DEAN MYERS
NOW IS YOUR TIME!
The African-American Struggle for Freedom

WINNER 1992 Coretta Scott King Award

✓ TARGET SKILL

Sequence of Events Identify the order of events used by the author.

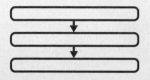

✓ GENRE

Biography tells about a person's life but is written by another person. As you read, look for:

▶ events in time order
▶ information about what the person accomplished and why he or she is important

COMMON CORE **RI.5.1** quote accurately when explaining what the text says explicitly and when drawing inferences; **RI.5.2** determine two or more main ideas and explain how they are supported by details/summarize; **RI.5.3** explain the relationships between individuals/events/concepts in a text; **RI.5.10** read and comprehend informational texts

Go Digital

420

MEET THE AUTHOR
Walter Dean Myers

Walter Dean Myers begins each new piece of writing with an outline because, he says, it "forces me to do the thinking." Then he tries to write ten pages a day until he finishes his first draft. After that he revises. Myers has written over eighty books for young people and has won numerous awards, including the Coretta Scott King Award and the Newbery Honor.

MEET THE ILLUSTRATOR
Steven Noble

Steven Noble uses a variety of techniques to create his realistically detailed illustrations. These include scratchboard, woodcut, pen and ink, and engraving. He lives in California.

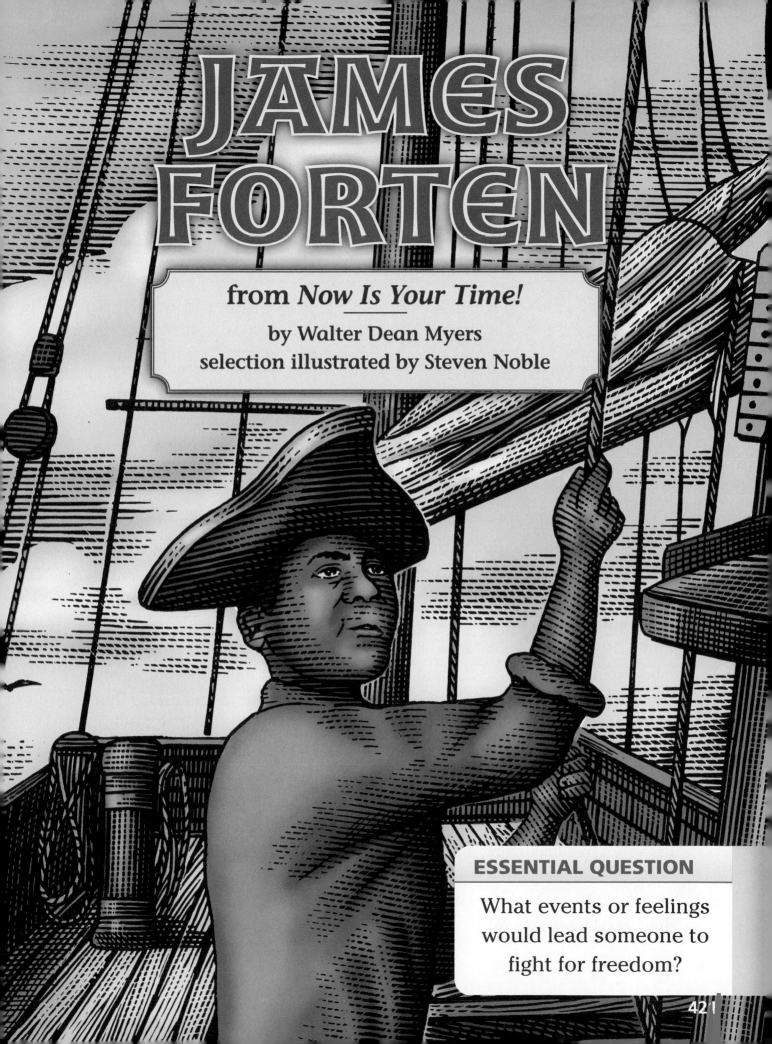

JAMES FORTEN

from *Now Is Your Time!*

by Walter Dean Myers

selection illustrated by Steven Noble

ESSENTIAL QUESTION

What events or feelings would lead someone to fight for freedom?

*James Forten was born in Philadelphia in 1766
and grew up during the American Revolution.
He overcame great obstacles to become one of the
most important African Americans of his time.*

Thomas Forten, a free African, was employed by Robert Bridges, a sailmaker in Philadelphia. Sail making was a profitable but difficult job. Sewing the coarse cloth was brutal on the hands. The heavy thread had to be waxed and handled with dexterity. A person trying to break the thread with his hands could see it cut through his flesh like a knife. But Forten appreciated his job. It paid reasonably well and the work was steady.

Forten helped in all aspects of sail making and assisted in installing the sails on the ships the firm serviced. With the income from his work he had purchased his wife's freedom. Now, on this early Tuesday morning, a new baby was due. The baby, born later that day, was James Forten.

Young James Forten's early life was not that different from that of other poor children living in Philadelphia. He played marbles and blindman's bluff, and he raced in the streets. When he was old enough, he would go down to the docks to see the ships.

Sometimes James went to the shop where his father worked and did odd jobs. Bridges liked him and let him work as much as he could, but he also encouraged Thomas Forten to make sure that his son learned to read and write.

The Fortens sent their son to the small school that had been created for African children by a Quaker, Anthony Benezet. He believed that the only way the Africans would ever take a meaningful place in the colonies would be through education.

Thomas Forten was working on a ship when he fell to his death. James Forten was only seven at the time. His mother was devastated, but still insisted that her son continue school. He did so for two more years, after which he took a job working in a small store.

What James wanted to do was to go to sea. He was fourteen in 1781 when his mother finally relented and gave her permission. America was fighting for its freedom, and James Forten would be fighting, too.

He knew about the difficulties between the British and the American colonists. He had seen first British soldiers and then American soldiers marching through the streets of Philadelphia. Among the American soldiers were men of color.

A black child in Philadelphia in the 1700's had to be careful. There were stories of free Africans being kidnapped and sold into slavery. He had seen the captives on the ships. They looked like him: the same dark skin, the same wide nose; but there was a sadness about them that both touched his heart and frightened him. He had seen Africans in chains being marched through the streets, on their way to the South. He never forgot the sight of his people in bondage, or accepted it as natural that black people should be slaves.

But the black soldiers Forten saw were something special. Marching with muskets on their shoulders, they seemed taller and blacker than any men he had ever seen. And there were African sailors, too. He knew some of these men. They had been fishermen and haulers before the conflict with Great Britain; now they worked on privateers and navy ships.

ANALYZE THE TEXT

Explain Historical Events Why are the black soldiers James sees marching on the American side special? What was happening during this time period in history that made their positions in the military unusual?

Sometimes he heard talk about naval battles, and he tried to imagine what they must have been like.

In the summer of 1781, James Forten signed onto the privateer *Royal Louis*, commanded by Stephen Decatur, Sr. The colonies had few ships of their own to fight against the powerful British navy and issued "letters of marque" to private parties. These allowed the ships, under the flag of the United States, to attack British ships and to profit from the sale of any vessel captured.

The *Royal Louis* sailed out of Philadelphia in August and was quickly engaged by the British vessel *Active*, a heavy armed brig sent from England to protect its trade ships.

The *Royal Louis*'s guns were loaded with gunpowder that was tamped down by an assistant gunner. Then the cannonball was put into the barrel and pushed against the powder. Then the powder would be ignited. The powder had to be kept belowdecks in case of a hit by an enemy ship.

Philadelphia harbor as it appeared around the time the *Royal Louis* defeated the *Active*.

Forten's job was to carry the gunpowder from below to the guns. Up and down the stairs he raced with the powder as shots from the British ship whistled overhead. There were large holes in the sails and men screaming as they were hit with grapeshot that splintered the sides of the ship. The smell of gunpowder filled the air as Captain Decatur turned his ship to keep his broadside guns trained on the *Active*. Sailors all about Forten were falling, some dying even as others cried for more powder.

Again he went belowdecks, knowing that if a shot ripped through to the powder kegs, or if any of the burning planks fell down into the hold, he would be killed instantly in the explosion. Up he came again with as much powder as he could carry.

After what must have seemed forever with the two ships tacking about each other like angry cats, the *Active* lowered its flag. It had surrendered!

Decatur brought his ship into Philadelphia, its guns still trained on the limping *Active*.

The crowd on the dock cheered wildly as they recognized the American flag on the *Royal Louis*. On board the victorious ship James Forten had mixed feelings as he saw so many of his comrades wounded, some mortally.

The *Royal Louis* turned its prisoners over to military authorities. On the twenty-seventh of September, the *Active* was sold; the proceeds were split among the owners of the *Royal Louis* and the crew.

The sailors with the worst wounds were sent off to be cared for. The others, their own wounds treated, were soon about the business of repairing the ship. Forten must have been excited. Once the fear of the battle had subsided and the wounded were taken off, it was easy to think about the dangerous encounter in terms of adventure. And they had won.

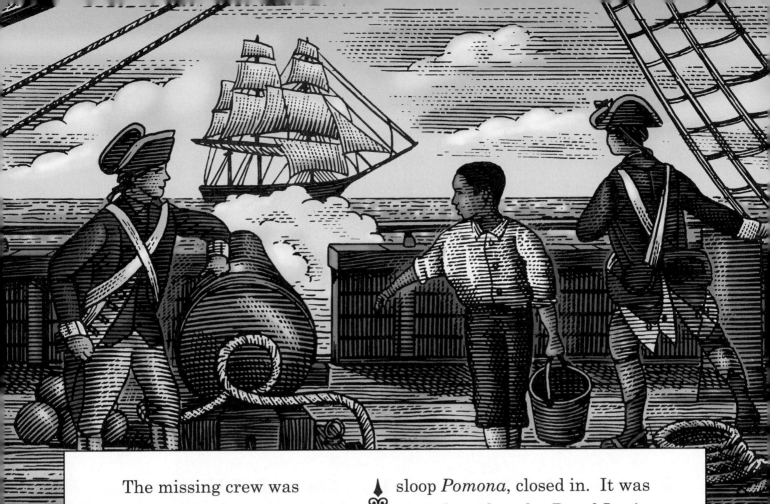

The missing crew was replaced. The ship was checked carefully by its captain and found to be in fine fighting condition. The crew carried more ammunition aboard, more powder, and fresh provisions. Once more they sailed for open waters.

On the sixteenth of October, 1781, they sighted a ship, recognized it as British, and made for it instantly. As they neared, a second ship was spotted, and then a third. Decatur turned to escape the trap, but it was already too late. The three British ships, the *Amphyon*, the *Nymph*, and the sloop *Pomona*, closed in. It was soon clear that the *Royal Louis* had two choices: to surrender or to be sunk.

The *Royal Louis* lowered its flag. It had surrendered, and its crew were now prisoners. Forten was terrified. He had heard the stories of the British sending captured Africans to the West Indies to be sold into slavery. He knew the *Pomona* had sailed back and forth from the colonies to the island of Barbados, where many Africans already languished in bondage. It was a time for dread.

The notorious British prison ship, *Jersey*, which was docked off Long Island, New York.

James was taken aboard the *Amphyon* with others from his crew. On board the British ship Captain Beasley inspected the prisoners. There were several boys among the American crew, and he separated them from the older men.

Captain Beasley's son looked over the boys who had been captured. Many of them were younger than he was. Although still prisoners, the boys were given more freedom than the men, and Beasley's son saw the Americans playing marbles. He joined in the game, and it was during this playing that he befriended Forten.

The result of this tentative friendship was that Captain Beasley did not, as he might have done, send Forten to a ship bound for the West Indies and slavery. Instead he was treated as a regular prisoner of war and sent to the prison ship the *Jersey*.

Dark and forbidding, the *Jersey* was a sixty-gunner anchored off Long Island, in New York. It had been too old to use in the war and had been refitted first as a hospital ship and then as a ship for prisoners. The portholes had been sealed and twenty-inch squares carved into her sides. Across these squares iron bars were placed.

The captain of the *Jersey* greeted the prisoners with a sneer. All were searched under the watchful eyes of British marines. The wounded were unattended, the sick ignored. The pitiful cries of other prisoners came from belowdecks. A few pale, sickly prisoners, covered with sores, were huddled around a water cask. Then came the cry that some would hear for months, others for years.

"Down, Rebels, down!"

They were rebels against the king, to be despised, perhaps to be hanged. Traitors, they were being called, not soldiers of America. James was pushed into a line on deck. The line shuffled toward the water cask, where each man could fill a canteen with a pint of water. Then they were pushed roughly belowdecks.

The hold of the ship was dark. What little light there was came from the small squares along the hull. The air was dank. Some of the prisoners were moaning. Others manned pumps to remove the water from the bottom of the boat.

Sleep was hard coming, and James wasn't sure if he wouldn't still be sold into slavery. Beasley's son had liked him, he remembered, and the boy had offered to persuade his father to take James to England. It would have been better than the hold of the *Jersey*.

In the morning the first thing the crew did was to check to see how many prisoners had died during the night. Many of the prisoners were sick with yellow fever. For these death would be just a matter of time.

Forten later claimed that the game of marbles with Beasley's son had saved him from a life of slavery in the West Indies. But on November first, two weeks after the capture of the *Royal Louis*, the news reached New York that Brigadier General Charles Cornwallis had surrendered to George Washington. Washington had strongly protested the British practice of sending prisoners to the West Indies. It was probably the news of his victory, more than the game of marbles, that saved the young sailor.

> ### ANALYZE THE TEXT
>
> **Sequence of Events** How did James Forten come to be on the ship with Captain Beasley's son?

An unknown artist probably painted this watercolor portrait of Forten during his lifetime.

James Forten was not a hero. He did not single-handedly defeat the British, or sink a ship. But he fought, like so many other Africans, for the freedom of America, and he fought well. He was only one of thousands of Africans who helped to create the country known as the United States of America.

In Philadelphia, after the war, James Forten became an apprentice to the man his father had worked for, Robert Bridges. Like his father, James was a hard worker. Eventually he would run the business for Robert Bridges, and by 1798 he owned it. At its height the business employed forty workers, both black and white. Forten became one of the wealthiest men in Philadelphia. He married and raised a family, passing on to them the values of hard work he had learned from his father. Forten made several major contributions to the sail-making business, among them a method of handling the huge sails in a shop, which allowed sails to be repaired much faster and saved precious time for ship owners. In the coming years he would use his great wealth to support both antislavery groups and the right of women to vote — at a time when over 90 percent of all Africans in America were still in a state of enslavement.

James Forten became one of the most influential of the African abolitionists. He spent much of his life pleading for the freedom of his people in the country his people had helped to create.

ANALYZE THE TEXT

Main Ideas and Details What are the main ideas of this text? How do you know? What seems to be the text's overall main idea?

Dig Deeper

How to Analyze the Text

Use these pages to learn about Sequence of Events, Explaining Historical Events, and Main Ideas and Details. Then read "James Forten" again to apply what you learned.

Sequence of Events

Authors of biographies such as "James Forten" often organize their writing by **sequence of events** to tell the story of a person's life. Sequence of events refers to the order in which the events take place. This pattern of organization, or **text structure**, helps readers understand what happened in the person's life and when.

Authors may include dates or tell the person's age to show the time order of events and how events are related. For example, the author says that James Forten "was only seven" when his father died. Words and phrases such as *after* and *then* also indicate time order.

Use a graphic organizer like the one below to keep track of events as they happen in the text.

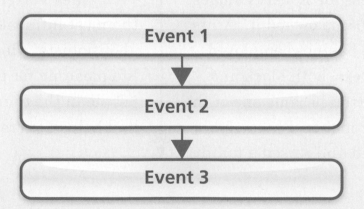

Event 1

↓

Event 2

↓

Event 3

RI.5.1 quote accurately when explaining what the text says explicitly and when drawing inferences; **RI.5.2** determine two or more main ideas and explain how they are supported by details/summarize; **RI.5.3** explain the relationships between individuals/events/ concepts in a text; **RI.5.10** read and comprehend informational texts

Explain Historical Events

James Forten lived during an exciting period of history. To fully tell his story, the author must include details of the **historical events** that affected him. Look back at page 429. Here readers learn about the surrender of Brigadier General Charles Cornwallis to George Washington. This event is important because it ended the war. It also saved James from being sold into slavery.

Main Ideas and Details

The **main idea** of each part of a biography contributes to the overall point the author wants to make about the subject. The author's choice of **details** helps support each main idea. For example, on page 426, the description of the battle between the two ships supports the main idea that James Forten was brave and dutiful. Even though he was in great danger, he continued to do his job of supplying gunpowder.

Your Turn

Turn and Talk Review the selection to prepare to discuss this question: *What events or feelings would lead someone to fight for freedom?* As you discuss your ideas with a partner, note your key points. Present a summary of your discussion to the class.

Classroom Conversation

Continue your discussion of "James Forten" by using text evidence to explain your answers to these questions:

1 How did James Forten's parents influence his life?

2 How would you summarize Forten's war experiences?

3 What makes James Forten a good subject for a biography?

ANALYZE AUTHOR'S PURPOSE

Roundtable Discussion Authors of biographies carefully choose details that will help readers "see" the person they are writing about. In a small group, reread the last page of "James Forten." Why do you think the author included this information about James Forten's life after the war? As a group, explain how these details affect your view of Forten.

WRITE ABOUT READING

Response James Forten went from working in a small store to dodging gunfire on an American vessel battling a British ship. What events led him down this path? Write a paragraph in which you explain how Forten came to serve his country during the Revolutionary War. Support your explanation with quotes and specific evidence from the text.

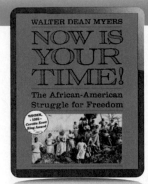

Writing Tip

Before you begin to write, jot down the events that you want to include in your paragraph. Make sure they are in sequential order.

COMMON CORE **RI.5.1** quote accurately when explaining what the text says explicitly and when drawing inferences; **RI.5.3** explain the relationships between individuals/events/ideas/concepts in a text; **W.5.9b** apply grade 5 Reading standards to informational texts; **SL.5.1a** come to discussions prepared/explicitly draw on preparation and other information about the topic; **SL.5.1d** review key ideas expressed and draw conclusions in light of information from the discussions

INFORMATIONAL TEXT

Modern Minute Man

☑ GENRE

Informational text, such as this magazine article, gives factual information about a topic or an event.

☑ TEXT FOCUS

Primary sources, such as the interview featured here, give additional information about the topic and its time period.

RI.5.10 read and comprehend informational texts

Modern Minute ∽ Man ∽

by Marcus Duren

Every year on April 19, Charles Price of Lexington, Massachusetts, is one of seventy-seven modern-day Lexington Minute Men who gather to reenact the events that took place at the Battle of Lexington in 1775. The first shot of the Revolutionary War was fired in this influential battle.

Modern Lexington Minute Men take the same oath as the original ones. Each plays a real person from history. Price plays Prince Estabrook, the only African American who fought in the battle. We asked him about different aspects of the reenactment.

How did you find information about Prince Estabrook?

It was quite difficult. For the most part, records weren't kept for slaves. There are some old documents, but some of them are in very poor condition.

How did it happen that Prince Estabrook was a militiaman?

I can only think of two reasons. One, it very well may be that his master sent him out in his place. The other reason is that maybe he felt if he fought he'd get his freedom.

The reenactment is so realistic! How do you make sure no one gets hurt?

We stress safety, safety, safety! We have many practices beforehand.

Charles Price as Prince Estabrook

It takes practice and dexterity to reenact a battle scene. Everything from the uniforms to the provisions is historically correct.

437

Are there kids in the reenactment?
We have kids come out to take care of the wounded soldiers. My daughter did it for about ten years.

What else should students know about the Lexington Minute Men?
These people risked everything to be out there. If they lost or were captured, they could have been hanged as traitors. I don't think people today realize how much of a chance they were taking. Every one of those people was a hero.

Freemen, Slaves, Soldiers

People of African descent made contributions to the Revolutionary War for different reasons. A freeman could often make better wages as a soldier than he could as a farmer or an apprentice. It was also common for slaves to serve in place of their owners, who chose not to fight.

Both the British and patriot armies badly needed soldiers. Authorities on both sides sometimes tried to persuade slaves to enlist by offering them freedom from bondage at the war's end. However, slaves knew that this tentative offer could be reversed if the side for which they fought lost.

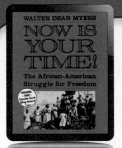

Compare Texts

Discuss Biographies Both "James Forten" and "They Called Her Molly Pitcher" (Lesson 13) tell about the lives of real people. With a partner, compare and contrast the two selections. Discuss these elements of each: kinds of details each author includes, pictures each author presents of his or her subject, ways in which the structure of each text is organized. Share your comparison with another pair.

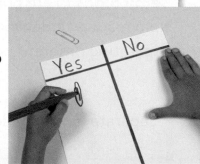

Describe a Contribution James Forten and Prince Estabrook were ordinary people who made important contributions to history. Think of an ordinary person you know who is making a difference in the lives of others. Write a short composition about his or her contribution. Include details and examples to make your points clear.

Learn About Reenactments "Modern Minute Man" describes a military reenactment that takes place each year in Lexington, Massachusetts. Work with a small group to research a historical reenactment in your region or state. Make a poster advertising the event. Then present your poster to another group. Discuss what you learned, and ask questions about information given in each presentation.

COMMON CORE **RI.5.5** compare and contrast the overall structure in two or more texts; **W.5.7** conduct short research projects that use several sources to build knowledge through investigation; **SL.5.1a** come to discussions prepared/explicitly draw on preparation and other information about the topic; **SL.5.1c** pose and respond to questions, make comments that contribute to the discussion, and elaborate on others' remarks

L.5.2a use punctuation to separate items in a series; **L.5.2b** use a comma to separate an introductory element from the rest of a sentence; **L.5.2c** use a comma to set off the words *yes* and *no* and to indicate direct address

Grammar

What Are Commas and Semicolons? Both **commas** (,) and **semicolons** (;) are punctuation marks used within sentences. They help readers understand the meaning of a sentence by clearly separating different parts.

Comma Usage	Example
Separate items in a series, or list	The African soldiers had courage, pride, and dignity.
Set off introductory words and phrases	By 1781, the war was almost over.
Set off the words *yes* and *no*	No, we won't have time to visit the war museum today.
Indicate a name used in direct address	Maria, can you imagine being on a ship in the middle of a battle?
Set off a tag question at the end of a sentence	That was an important battle, wasn't it?
Semicolon Usage	**Example**
Separate items in a series that contain commas	Battles occurred in Lexington, MA; Fort Ticonderoga, NY; and Trenton, NJ.

 **Rewrite each sentence on another sheet of paper, using the correct punctuation.**

1 Reading biographies is a good way to learn about history don't you think?

2 Yes the ship was resupplied with fresh water fruit and cornmeal.

3 Well we saw reenactments on May 17, 2011 June 4, 2011 August 5, 2011 and September 9, 2011.

4 "Get more gunpowder James and hurry!"

Omitting or misplacing commas and semicolons can confuse your readers. When you proofread your writing, make sure the different parts of your sentences are separated with the correct punctuation marks. Also make sure that you have not inserted commas or semicolons where they do not belong.

Incorrect Punctuation	Correct Punctuation

Yes our captain, steered the ship safely through high winds strong currents sharp rocks and other obstacles.	Yes, our captain steered the ship safely through high winds, strong currents, sharp rocks, and other obstacles.

 Connect Grammar to Writing

As you revise your persuasive essay next week, look closely for places where you need to insert commas or semicolons. Correct any errors you find. Using commas and semicolons properly will help make your writing clear and easy to follow.

Opinion Writing

Reading-Writing Workshop: Prewrite

✓ **Organization** Good writers organize their ideas before writing a **persuasive essay.** A graphic organizer can help you identify and organize your opinion and the reasons and details that support it.

For his persuasive essay, Derek chose to write about James Forten. He did some research and took notes about his sources. Then he used an idea-support map to organize his reasons and the supporting details. Later, he revised the map to state his ideas more clearly and to arrange them in a logical order.

Use the Writing Process Checklist below as you prewrite.

Writing Process Checklist

▶ **Prewrite**

✓ Did I state a clear opinion?

✓ Did I list reasons to support my opinion?

✓ Did I include facts, details, and examples to support my points?

✓ Did I organize my ideas in a clear and logical way?

Draft

Revise

Edit

Publish and Share

Exploring a Topic

James Forten During the Revolutionary War

—powder boy on ship

—carried gunpowder to cannons

—captured by the British

Myers, Walter Dean. _Now Is Your Time!_ New York, NY: HarperCollins Publishers, 1992. pp. 57—62

James Forten After the War

—leader in Philadelphia

—got 2,500 African Americans to fight the British (War of 1812)

—part of abolition movement

—antislavery newspaper

Ball, Maggie. _The Life and Times of James Forten._ Denver, CO: Sled Dog Press, 2007. pp. 35—37

442

Idea-Support Map

Opinion: James Forten should be recognized for his role in our nation's history.

Reason: James Forten worked on a war ship during the Revolutionary War.

Detail: He carried gunpowder to be put in the cannons.

Detail: He spent several months on a British prison ship.

Reason: James Forten was an important leader in Philadelphia after the war.

Detail: He got 2,500 African Americans to fight against the British in the War of 1812.

Detail: As part of the abolition movement, he gave money to an antislavery newspaper.

Reading as a Writer

How can Derek's idea-support map help him develop well-organized paragraphs? How could an idea-support map help you draft your persuasive essay?

I took notes about James Forten and used them to create an idea-support map. I listed reasons to support my opinion. Then I added details to support my reasons. This helped me organize my ideas.

Vocabulary in Context

TARGET VOCABULARY

rural

tedious

lacked

personally

organize

mocking

efficient

summons

mimic

peal

COMMON CORE **L.5.6** acquire and use general academic and domain-specific words and phrases

1 rural

Many colonial children lived with their families in rural areas, on farms in the countryside.

2 tedious

These children are bored by the tedious, dreary chore of collecting firewood.

3 lacked

Colonial soldiers who lacked shoes at Valley Forge wrapped their feet in cloth.

4 personally

In wealthy homes, family members were often personally attended by servants.

▶ Study each Context Card.

▶ Use a dictionary to clarify the part of speech of each Vocabulary Word.

5 organize

Only after their chores were done could colonial children set up, or organize, games.

6 mocking

Troublesome students had to wear a dunce cap mocking their misbehavior.

7 efficient

Girls learned to be efficient when they sewed. They didn't waste scarce thread.

8 summons

This painting of a girl summons, or calls up, thoughts of childhood in colonial America.

9 mimic

Colonial girls created mimic, or make-believe, situations to act out with their dolls.

10 peal

On Washington's birthday in 1846, a ring, or peal, of the Liberty Bell made it crack.

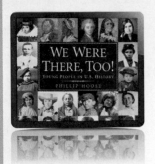

Read and Comprehend

☑ TARGET SKILL

Compare and Contrast The selection "We Were There, Too!" allows readers to compare and contrast the experiences of two young people involved in the American Revolution. As you read, look for text evidence that helps you think about how the situations, motives, and traits of the two subjects are alike and different. Use a graphic organizer like this one to record similarities and differences between the two patriots.

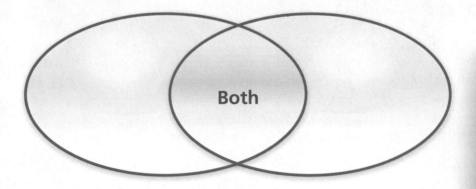

Both

☑ TARGET STRATEGY

Monitor/Clarify As you read the selection, pause frequently to **monitor** how well you understand what you are reading. Reread sections of the text or ask questions to help you **clarify,** or figure out, any details that don't make sense.

Patriotism

Patriotism is love for one's country. During the Revolutionary War, many colonists showed their patriotism by fighting for their new nation's freedom from British rule. At first, there was no regular American army, so colonists organized militias—armed forces made up of ordinary people rather than professional soldiers. Some of the key early battles of the Revolutionary War were fought by militia troops.

"We Were There, Too!" describes how two American teens showed their patriotism, one by enlisting in the army and the other by traveling across the countryside to call members of the militia to battle.

Lesson 15

ANCHOR TEXT

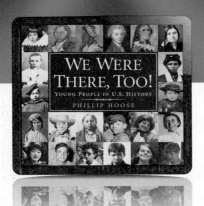

WE WERE THERE, TOO!
YOUNG PEOPLE IN U.S. HISTORY
PHILLIP HOOSE

 **TARGET SKILL**

Compare and Contrast
Examine how the author describes two subjects as alike or different.

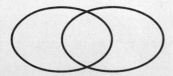

 GENRE

Biography is an account of a person's life told by someone else. As you read, look for:

▶ information about why the person is important
▶ events from the person's life in time order
▶ a third-person point of view

COMMON CORE

RI.5.3 explain the relationships between individuals/events/ideas/concepts in a text; **RI.5.10** read and comprehend informational texts

Go Digital

MEET THE AUTHOR

Phillip Hoose

The idea for *We Were There, Too!* came to Phillip Hoose while he was interviewing a young social activist named Sarah Rosen for his book *It's Our World, Too!* She said, "We're not taught about younger people who have made a difference. Studying history almost makes you feel like you're not a real person." Hoose decided to change that by writing about our nation's history through the stories of more than seventy amazing young people.

We Were There, Too!

by Phillip Hoose

"The smell of war began to be pretty strong."

Joseph Plumb Martin:

"And Now I Was a Soldier"

Milford, Connecticut, 1775

Joseph Plumb Martin was a tall, strong, hardworking boy who grew up on his grandparents' farm in Connecticut. Though he never went to school, he managed to write one of the best diaries of the Revolutionary War.

Joseph Martin forced the metal plow deep down into the soil while his grandfather walked alongside, guiding the horse that pulled it. It was a fresh April morning, a perfect planting day. Suddenly the silence was broken by the sound of bells and gunshots in Milford. Joseph dropped the plow and dashed into town, his grandfather following behind as fast as he could.

A crowd was gathered in front of the tavern, where an express rider from New Haven shouted news of three days before: There had been a bloody battle in Concord, Massachusetts. Many were dead. Soldiers were needed now. A silver dollar was the reward for anyone who would enlist in the American army and march off to New York to join General Washington.

Joseph was only fourteen, a year too young to enlist. Until that day, his thoughts about soldiering had always been clear: "I felt myself to be a real coward. What—venture my carcass where bullets fly! That will never do for me. Stay at home out of harm's way, thought I."

But now friends his age and even younger were scrawling their names and grabbing up those dollars while adults cheered. Joseph was torn. He hated to stay home while his friends marched off to glory, and the thought of a whole silver dollar made "the seeds of courage begin to sprout," but he needed more time to get used to the idea. Two months later, he was ready. On June 25, 1776, Joseph slipped away from his grandparents' house and hiked into town, his mind made up to enlist for six months, the shortest term possible. When a group of boys he knew saw him coming, they began to taunt him:

"'Come, if you will enlist, I will,' says one.

"'You have long been talking about it,' says another.

"'Come, now is the time.'

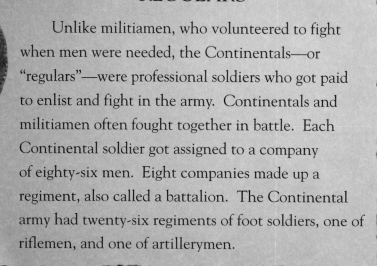

REGULARS

Unlike militiamen, who volunteered to fight when men were needed, the Continentals—or "regulars"—were professional soldiers who got paid to enlist and fight in the army. Continentals and militiamen often fought together in battle. Each Continental soldier got assigned to a company of eighty-six men. Eight companies made up a regiment, also called a battalion. The Continental army had twenty-six regiments of foot soldiers, one of riflemen, and one of artillerymen.

"Thinks I to myself, I will not be laughed into it or out of it. I will act my own pleasure after all. . . . So seating myself at the table, enlisting orders were immediately presented to me. I took up the pen, loaded it with the fatal charge, made several mimic imitations of writing my name, but took especial care not to touch the paper with the pen until an unlucky [friend] who was leaning over my shoulder gave my hand a strike which caused the pen to make a woeful scratch on the paper. 'O, he has enlisted,' said he. . . . Well, thought I, I may as well go through with the business now as not. So I wrote my name fairly upon the indentures. And now I was a soldier, in name at least."

His grandparents were unhappy, but they "fit him out" with clothing, a musket, and powder. His grandmother gave him cheese and cake and stuffed it into his knapsack. He sailed to New York City to join a Connecticut company. For more than a month all they did was march in parades and practice battle drills. Joseph's biggest problem was getting used to the food—salt pork or boiled beef, hard bread, and turnips or boiled potatoes.

ANALYZE THE TEXT

Text Structure To tell Joseph Plumb Martin's story, the author uses a sequence-of-events text structure. How does this text structure help you better understand Joseph's choices and actions?

A young man **summons** his courage and signs the enlistment roster that will make him a soldier in the Continental army.

But even as they practiced, hundreds of British warships were arriving at nearby Staten Island, unloading 32,000 redcoated soldiers. Late in August, Joseph's company was ordered to Long Island to stop British forces from taking New York City. Just before they marched off, Joseph climbed onto the roof of a house and squinted in the direction of the battlefield: "I distinctly saw the smoke of the field artillery, but the distance and the unfavorableness of the wind prevented my hearing their report, at least but faintly. The horrors of battle then presented themselves to my mind in all their hideousness. I must come to it now, thought I."

They took a ferry across the East River to Brooklyn and marched toward a field, the shots growing louder and louder with each step until they boomed like thunder. "We now began to meet the wounded men, another sight I was unacquainted with, some with broken arms, some with broken heads. The sight of these a little daunted me, and made me think of home."

And then all at once he was fighting, too. "Our officers . . . pressed forward towards a creek, where a large party of Americans and British were engaged. By the time we arrived, the enemy had driven our men into the creek . . . where such as could swim got across. Those that could not swim, and could not procure anything to buoy them up, sunk."

On the opposite bank of Gowanus Creek he could make out a long row of British soldiers—professional warriors from what was then the best army in the world. They stood straight and tall in red jackets as they fired on command at the retreating Americans. The creek was filling up with American bodies. Joseph's company shot back furiously, trying to provide cover for those still thrashing through the water.

Then they marched on to a part of Manhattan called Kip's Bay and readied themselves for another battle. One night they camped so close to a British warship that Joseph could overhear soldiers on board mocking the Americans. Early on a Sunday morning, Joseph slipped into an unlocked warehouse for a rare moment of privacy and peace. He was seated on a stool, reading some papers he'd discovered, when "all of a sudden there came such a peal of thunder from the British shipping that I thought my head would go with the sound. I made a frog's leap and lay as still as I possibly could and began to consider which part of my carcass would go first." They were soon dashing for their lives, leaping over the bodies of their friends. As Joseph put it, "fear and disorder seemed to take full possession of all and everything that day."

RECRUITING FOR THE CONTINENTAL ARMY

After the wave of enthusiasm that gripped Joseph Plumb Martin and his friends in 1775, recruiting for the army got harder each year. Part of the problem was that the Continental soldiers faced the well-equipped British forces in ragged uniforms that they had to provide for themselves. Often they fought with muskets that lacked bayonets. Food was scarce and soldiers were not always paid on time, if at all. Not that it mattered much—privates got only about seven dollars a month. Some soldiers deserted, but many more remained out of a desire for independence and a respect for General George Washington.

Joseph was still alive when October came and cool weather set in, and life got even more uncomfortable: "To have to lie, as I did almost every night on the cold and often wet ground without a blanket and with nothing but thin summer clothing was tedious . . . In the morning, the ground [often was] as white as snow with hoar frost. Or perhaps it would rain all night like a flood. All that could be done in that case was to lie down, take our musket in our arms and packe the lock between our thighs and 'weather it out'."

When Joseph was discharged from the Continental army on Christmas Day, 1776, he felt older than fifteen. A battle-tested patriot, he was proud that he had stood his ground against the British. He set off for home, fifty-two miles away, with four shillings of discharge pay in his pocket and enough stories to get him through the winter and more. He farmed for a year, got bored, and reenlisted. When the war ended six years later, he was still a soldier. And he was also a free citizen of a new nation.

WHAT HAPPENED TO JOSEPH PLUMB MARTIN?

He moved to Maine in 1794 and began to farm. He married and became the father of five children. He loved to write, tell stories, and draw pictures of birds. When he was seventy, his Revolutionary War account was published. He died in Maine at the age of ninety.

ANALYZE THE TEXT

Text and Graphic Features On pages 450–456, the author uses text and graphic features such as quotes, headings, feature boxes, images, and captions. What do these features help you understand about Joseph and the Revolution?

"The British are burning Danbury! Muster at Ludington's!"

Sybil Ludington:

Outdistancing Paul Revere

Fredericksburg, New York, April 26, 1777

Nearly everyone has heard of the midnight ride of Paul Revere. That's mainly because Henry Wadsworth Longfellow wrote a poem about it soon after it happened. But far fewer people know that two years later a sixteen-year-old girl rode much farther over rougher roads. Alone and unarmed, Sybil Ludington raced through the night for freedom.

Just after dark on the rainy evening of April 26, 1777, Colonel Henry Ludington, commander of a regiment of militiamen near the New York–Connecticut border, heard a rap at his door. Outside stood a saluting messenger, rain streaming from his cape. His words came fast. British soldiers had just torched the warehouse in Danbury, Connecticut. Food and guns belonging to the Continental army were being destroyed. Soldiers were burning homes, too. Could Colonel Ludington round up his men right away?

SYBIL RODE FARTHER

On April 18, 1775, Paul Revere raced from Boston to Lexington to warn American rebel leaders, "The British are coming!" He rode fourteen miles on good roads for some two hours, while Sybil Ludington rode all night—nearly forty miles over cart tracks and rutted fields in the blackness of rural farm country.

457

It was easier said than done. Colonel Ludington's militiamen were farmers and woodsmen whose homes were scattered throughout the countryside. Someone would have to go get them while the colonel stayed behind to organize them once they arrived. But who? Who besides he himself knew where they all lived and could cover so many miles on horseback in the dead of night? Deep in thought, he heard his daughter Sybil's voice. She was saying that she wanted to go.

For Sybil Ludington it was an unexpected chance to help the war effort. As the oldest of eight children, her days were filled with chores and responsibilities. Still, each week when her father's men drilled in their pasture, she paused from her work to watch them. She wished she could fight. People kept saying she was doing her part for liberty at home, but she wanted to do more. Suddenly, with this emergency on a rainy night, she had a chance.

The route of Sybil Ludington's night ride through the New York countryside

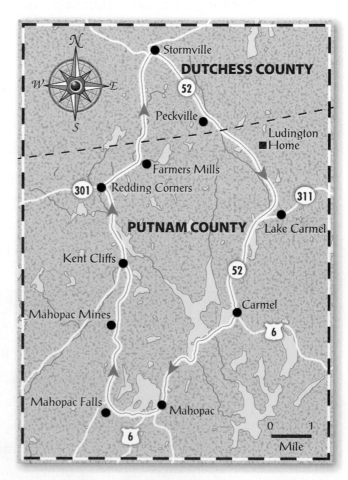

458

Her father looked at her. How could he let her take such a risk? The whole countryside was full of armed men. There were skinners and cowboys who stole cattle for the British, soldiers from both sides, and deserters trying to get back home under cover of darkness. But Sybil was right: She knew every soldier in her father's unit and she was a fine rider. Rebecca, her next oldest sister, could mind the children. Most of them were already asleep anyway.

Colonel Ludington walked with Sybil out to the barn and held a lantern while she threw a saddle over her yearling colt, Star. Together father and daughter went over the names of his men and where they lived. Then the colonel watched Sybil disappear into the darkness.

It was raining hard. Sybil put away thoughts of who might appear in the roadway and concentrated on the road map in her head. With no time to lose, she had to reach all the men, taking the most efficient route possible. She picked up a long stick to bang on doors. That way she wouldn't have to waste time dismounting and getting back on Star. One by one, hearing the rap of the stick, the sleepy farmers cracked their doors open, some poking muskets out into the darkness. Sybil said the same thing to all: "The British are burning Danbury! Muster at Ludington's!" Once she knew they understood, she galloped off, refusing all offers of rest and refreshment.

This bronze statue of Sybil Ludington riding Star is in Carmel, New York.

In 1975, the U.S. Postal Service issued a Sybil Ludington stamp to mark the American Bicentennial.

It took her till dawn to get back home. She was soaked and sore, but as she rode up to her farm she could hear the sounds of drums and bugles. Many of her father's men were already there, getting ready to march. Soon her father's militia set off to join five hundred other Colonial soldiers. They missed the British at Danbury but finally fought and defeated them at Ridgefield, Connecticut, a few weeks later.

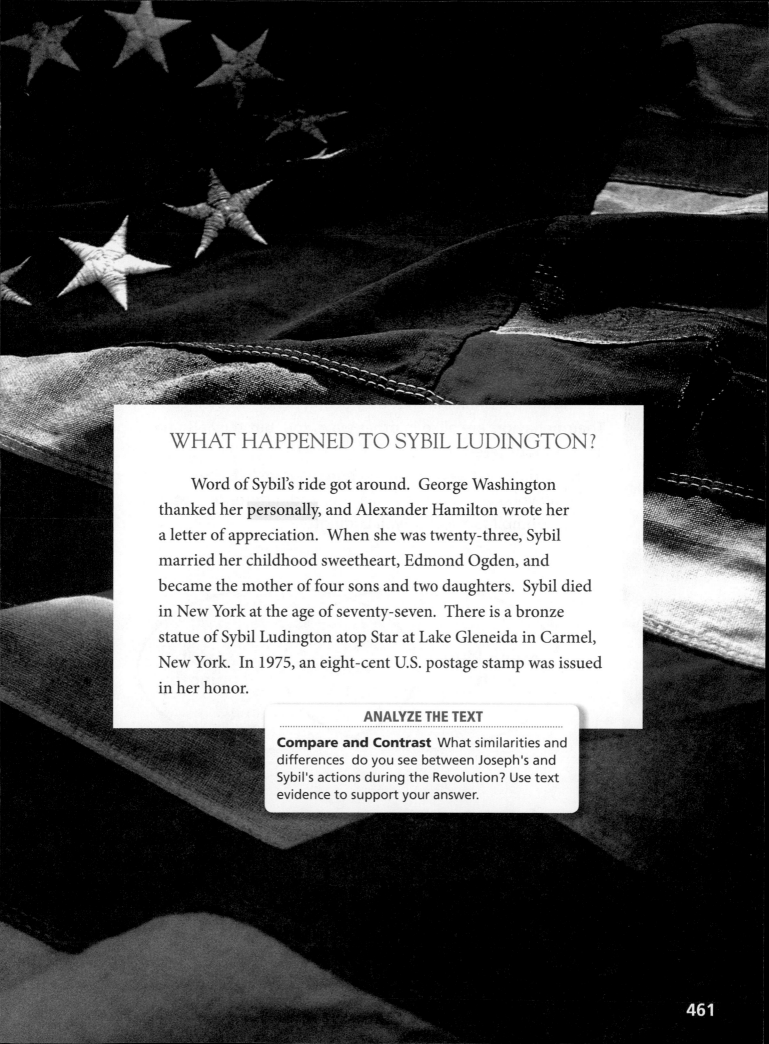

WHAT HAPPENED TO SYBIL LUDINGTON?

Word of Sybil's ride got around. George Washington thanked her personally, and Alexander Hamilton wrote her a letter of appreciation. When she was twenty-three, Sybil married her childhood sweetheart, Edmond Ogden, and became the mother of four sons and two daughters. Sybil died in New York at the age of seventy-seven. There is a bronze statue of Sybil Ludington atop Star at Lake Gleneida in Carmel, New York. In 1975, an eight-cent U.S. postage stamp was issued in her honor.

ANALYZE THE TEXT

Compare and Contrast What similarities and differences do you see between Joseph's and Sybil's actions during the Revolution? Use text evidence to support your answer.

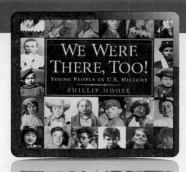

Dig Deeper

How to Analyze the Text

Use these pages to learn about Comparing and Contrasting, Text and Graphic Features, and Text Structure. Then read "We Were There, Too!" again to apply what you learned.

Compare and Contrast

When you **compare and contrast** the actions of two or more historical figures, you learn more about each one's character. The things they do and the choices they make show who they are inside.

In "We Were There, Too!" Joseph Plumb Martin and Sybil Ludington are similar in that they act on behalf of their country. Their behaviors are alike in other ways, too, but they also have some important differences.

Recording text evidence in a Venn diagram like the one below will help you keep track of similarities and differences between Joseph Plumb Martin and Sybil Ludington.

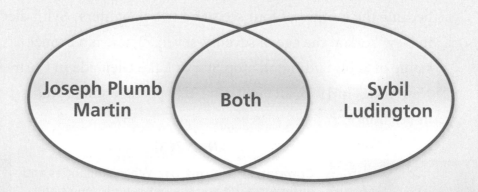

Joseph Plumb Martin — Both — Sybil Ludington

RI.5.3 explain the relationships between individuals/events/ideas/concepts in a text; **RI.5.10** read and comprehend informational texts; **RF.5.4a** read on-level text wth purpose and understanding

Go Digital

Text and Graphic Features

Text and graphic features include captions, images, maps, headings, and text boxes. Several of these elements are used throughout "We Were There, Too!" to give readers additional information or to help them visualize an important concept. For example, on page 451, the term *regulars* is explained in a separate text box. This feature provides helpful information for readers without interrupting the biography.

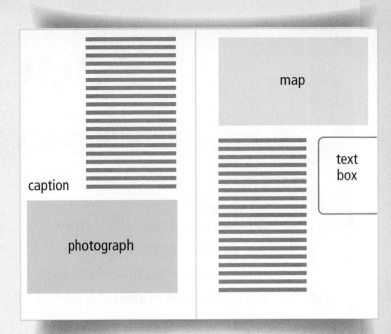

Text Structure

The way the information in a text is organized is its structure. In biographies, authors often use a sequence-of-events **text structure.** They tell about the person's life in chronological, or time, order. Signal words and phrases such as *for more than a month, just before, first, next,* and *then*—as well as dates—inform the reader that a sequence-of-events text structure is being used. They also help readers understand the text by showing the relationships between events.

Your Turn

RETURN TO THE ESSENTIAL QUESTION

Turn and Talk Review the selection to prepare to discuss this question: *How are patriotism and courage related?* Share your ideas with a partner and elaborate on each other's insights.

Classroom Conversation

Continue your discussion of "We Were There, Too!" by using text evidence to answer these questions:

1. Why does the author include details that show Joseph Plumb Martin's reluctance to enlist?

2. What do Sybil Ludington's actions reveal about her character?

3. How would you define *courage* after reading this selection?

YOUNG HEROES

Make a Speech Why is it important to know about young people who have changed history for the better? With a partner, compose a speech that you might give to an audience of writers. Explain why they should write more about young heroes in history. Use quotations and evidence from "James Forten" (Lesson 14) and "We Were There, Too!" to support your opinions and reasons.

WRITE ABOUT READING

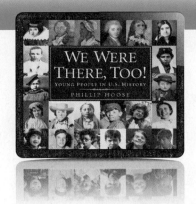

Response Consider the impressions you have of Joseph Plumb Martin and Sybil Ludington after reading their biographies. How are they similar and different? Which person do you admire more? Why? Write a paragraph in which you compare and contrast these historical figures and their accomplishments. Provide text evidence and quotations to support your ideas.

Writing Tip

State your opinion at the beginning of your response. Then make sure you support your reasons with specific details and quotations from the text.

COMMON CORE **RI.5.3** explain the relationships between individuals/events/ideas/concepts in a text; **W.5.1a** introduce a topic, state an opinion, and create an organizational structure; **W.5.1b** provide logically ordered reasons supported by facts and details; **W.5.9b** apply grade 5 Reading standards to informational texts; **SL.5.1c** pose and respond to questions, make comments that contribute to the discussion, and elaborate on others' remarks

POETRY

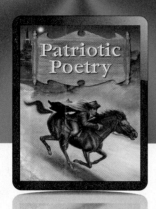

Patriotic Poetry

Patriotic Poetry

On April 18, 1775, the sight of lights in a church steeple summons Paul Revere to ride from Charlestown to Lexington, warning people that the British are coming. Other patriots, such as Sybil Ludington, make similar rides at other times, but Revere becomes a huge legend. One reason is the following poem, part of which is shown here.

The Midnight Ride of Paul Revere
by Henry Wadsworth Longfellow

Listen, my children, and you shall hear
Of the midnight ride of Paul Revere,
On the eighteenth of April, in Seventy-five;
Hardly a man is now alive
Who remembers that famous day and year.

He said to his friend, "If the British march
By land or sea from the town to-night,
Hang a lantern aloft in the belfry arch
Of the North Church tower, as a signal light,—
One if by land, and two if by sea;
And I on the opposite shore will be,
Ready to ride and spread the alarm
Through every Middlesex village and farm,
For the country folk to be up and to arm."

Go Digital

[Therefore], his friend, through alley and
    street
Wanders and watches with eager ears,
Till in the silence around him he hears
The muster of men at the barrack door,
The sound of arms, and the tramp of
    feet,
And the measured tread of the
    grenadiers,
Marching down to their boats on the
    shore. . . .

Meanwhile, impatient to mount and ride,
Booted and spurred, with a heavy stride
On the opposite shore walked Paul
    Revere. . . .

Now he patted his horse's side,
Now he gazed on the landscape far and
    near,
Then, impetuous, stamped the earth,
And turned and tightened his saddle girth;
But mostly he watched with eager search
The belfry tower of the Old North
    Church,
As it rose above the graves on the hill,
Lonely and spectral and somber and still.
And lo! as he looks, on the belfry's height
A glimmer, and then a gleam of light!
He springs to the saddle, the bridle he
    turns,
But lingers and gazes, till full on his sight
A second lamp in the belfry burns!

Most of colonial America lacked
good roads, especially in rural areas.
Travel was often slow and tedious.
A fast horse was the most efficient
way to travel. The peal of a horse's
hooves was as common then as the
roar of a car engine is today.

A hurry of hoofs in a village street,
A shape in the moonlight, a bulk in the
   dark,
And beneath, from the pebbles, in
   passing, a spark
Struck out by a steed flying fearless and
   fleet;
That was all! And yet, through the
   gloom and the light,
The fate of a nation was riding that
   night;
And the spark struck out by that steed, in
   his flight,
Kindled the land into flame with its
   heat. . . .

So through the night rode Paul Revere;
And so through the night went his cry of
   alarm
To every Middlesex village and farm,—
A cry of defiance, and not of fear,
A voice in the darkness, a knock at the
   door,
And a word that shall echo forevermore!
For, borne on the night-wind of the Past,
Through all our history, to the last,
In the hour of darkness and peril and
   need,
The people will waken and listen to hear
The hurrying hoof-beats of that steed,
And the midnight-message of Paul
   Revere.

Write a Patriotic Poem

Patriotism is the love that one personally feels for one's country. Write a patriotic poem with a rhyme scheme. First, brainstorm a list of ideas to organize your thoughts. You may create a mimic of Longfellow's style by beginning your poem with "Listen, and you shall hear. . . ." Then follow with your own story. Use rhyme to establish rhythm in your poem or to make parts of it more memorable for readers. Try to use figurative language in your writing, and include vocabulary words such as *mocking*.

Compare Texts

Compare Texts About Patriotism "We Were There, Too!" "James Forten," and "They Called Her Molly Pitcher" are about individuals making a difference during the American Revolution. With a partner, compare and contrast the text structures and main ideas of these selections. Then review the events in each selection. What does seeing events unfold in the same ways the people featured in the texts did help you understand about their experiences?

TEXT TO SELF

Express Your Views Think about how the heroes Joseph Plumb Martin, Sybil Ludington, and Paul Revere are portrayed in the selections in this lesson. Imagine that you are a newspaper journalist. Use examples from "We Were There, Too!" and "Patriotic Poetry" to write an article about patriotism. Include appropriate language and details as support.

TEXT TO WORLD

Learn About Places As you read "Patriotic Poetry" again, write down the names of unfamiliar places that are mentioned. Research these places to help you clarify the action in the poem. Then use a map of the United States to find each location.

COMMON CORE **RI.5.3** explain the relationships between individuals/events/ideas/concepts in a text; **RI.5.5** compare and contrast the overall structure in two or more texts; **RI.5.9** integrate information from several texts on the same topic; **W.5.10** write routinely over extended time frames and shorter time frames

Grammar

What Are Transitions? **Transitions** connect sentences and ideas. Some **transition words and phrases,** such as *first, then,* and *finally,* indicate time order or sequence-of-events structure and may be used in narrative writing. Others appear frequently in expository or persuasive writing. These transitions include *although, on the other hand, however,* and *nevertheless.* They may show comparison or contrast, cause and effect, or other relationships between ideas.

Transition Words and Phrases

Use transitions such as these to narrate events.
As soon as Sybil heard the news, she knew what she had to do. First, she told her father her plan. After he agreed, she saddled her horse. Then she set off on her mission. Hours later, she returned home. Her work was done. Finally, she could rest.

Use transitions such as these to explain or persuade.
It made sense for Sybil to be the one to alert the militia. Unlike some of the other volunteers, she knew where all the soldiers lived. She was also a good rider. In addition, she was eager to help her country. Moreover, she was responsible and smart.

Try This! **Work with a partner. Identify the transitions in the sentences. Explain whether each shows time order, cause and effect, or comparison and contrast. Then use the transitions in new sentences.**

❶ At first, Joseph Plumb Martin avoided enlisting.

❷ However, he later changed his mind.

❸ Because of his diary, we know more about his experiences.

❹ In addition, we have a better understanding of the Revolution.

Transitions show readers how your ideas are related. They also help your writing flow more smoothly. When you proofread your work, make sure you have used the correct type of transition and that you have placed transitions where you need them.

Unclear	Clear
Joseph Plumb Martin was more brave than Sybil Ludington. He was in constant danger. He had to serve for at least six months. He had to endure harsh living conditions. Sybil could return home. Her deed was done.	In my opinion, Joseph Plumb Martin was more brave than Sybil Ludington. As a soldier, he was in constant danger. He also had to serve for at least six months, not just one night. Furthermore, he had to endure harsh living conditions. In contrast, Sybil could return home after her task was done.

 Connect Grammar to Writing

As you edit your persuasive essay this week, look for sentences with related ideas. Insert transitions where you can to make the relationships between these ideas more clear.

COMMON CORE **W.5.1a** introduce a topic, state an opinion, and create an organizational structure; **W.5.1b** provide logically ordered reasons supported by facts and details; **W.5.1c** link opinion and reasons using words, phrases, and clauses; **W.5.1d** provide a concluding statement or section; **W.5.5** develop and strengthen writing by planning, revising, editing, rewriting, or trying a new approach

Opinion Writing

Reading-Writing Workshop: **Revise**

✓ Word Choice   In a **persuasive essay,** you state a clear opinion, or position, about what you want your audience to think or do. Include strong reasons to support your opinion, and support those reasons with facts and examples. To avoid plagiarizing, write the facts in your own words.

Derek wrote a first draft of his persuasive essay about James Forten, using his idea-support map. Then he revised his draft by replacing weak or vague words with strong, specific words to make his ideas more convincing and clear.

Use the Writing Process Checklist below as you revise your writing.

 Writing Process Checklist

Prewrite

Draft

▶ **Revise**

✓ **Did I introduce my topic and opinion clearly?**

✓ **Did I support my opinion with logically ordered reasons, facts, and details?**

✓ **Did I use transitions to link my opinion and reasons?**

✓ **Did I provide a strong conclusion?**

Edit

Publish and Share

Revised Draft

Every student studying the American

Revision will ~~teach~~ learn about John Adams,

George Washington, and Thomas Jefferson.

The name James Forten ~~can~~ may be less ~~known~~, familiar

but he, too, played an important ~~part~~ role in the

~~forming~~ founding of our nation.

James Forten was a free African whose

parents had also been free. During his youth,

James ~~was~~ worked as a powder boy on a Revolutionary

War ship.

472

Why We Should Remember James Forten

by Derek Johnson

Every student studying the American Revolution will learn about John Adams, George Washington, and Thomas Jefferson. The name James Forten may be less familiar, but he, too, played an important role in the founding of our nation.

James Forten was a free African whose parents had also been free. During his youth, James worked as a powder boy on a Revolutionary War ship. His job was to haul gunpowder from belowdecks so that it could be loaded into the cannons. It was a very dangerous job, and he did it well.

When Forten's ship was captured, he spent several months on a British prison ship. James did not become a war hero, but he served his country like thousands of other men and women. Without people like him, the war would not have been won.

After the Revolutionary War, James Forten continued to make valuable contributions to the country as a successful businessman, activist, and leader. He worked hard to support the idea of freedom for all Americans. Today's history students deserve to learn about him.

Reading as a Writer

Which words did Derek use to make his writing strong? What words could you replace in your own writing to make it sound more confident?

In my final paper, I replaced weak and vague words with stronger, more specific words. I also used transitions to link my opinion to my reasons and support.

Read the passage "Davy Crockett Gets a Pet." As you read, stop and use text evidence to answer each question.

Davy Crockett Gets a Pet

The legendary hero David "Davy" Crockett actually existed. Born in Tennessee in 1786, he grew up on the frontier, hunting and clearing land. Later, he went into politics and served in the United States Congress. Davy Crockett was famous for his bear-hunting skills and for his sense of humor. In 1815, Crockett became very ill while traveling and was reported to have died. It is said that he remarked on the reports of his death, "I know'd this was a whopper of a lie as soon as I heard it." After his death in 1836, stories about Crockett's life were embellished and wildly exaggerated, and became popular tall tales like this one.

Early Life

Long ago in Tennessee, a comet blazed across the sky. People watched in amazement as it smashed into the top of the tallest mountain and lit up the surrounding area like fireworks. When the smoke cleared, people were amazed to find a baby on that mountaintop! They took one look at this newborn baby, Davy Crockett, and realized that he was extraordinary.

Davy's remarkable differences from other children quickly became apparent. He shot up in height like a sapling. He consumed huge amounts of bear meat and drank gallons of buffalo milk. As a result, Davy already weighed more than 200 pounds by the time he was six years old! The broad-shouldered youngster was often seen carrying thunder in one hand and throwing lightning with the other. He boasted, "I can outrun, outfight, and outyell anyone!"

As Davy grew up, he seemed to possess both human and animal qualities. He ran as swiftly as a cheetah, swam as easily as a fish, and was as strong as an ox. He bragged about all the animals he had fought, including wildcats and bears.

---

1 What does the introductory paragraph help you infer about the details and descriptions in this passage?

COMMON CORE

RL.5.1 quote accurately when explaining what the text says explicitly and when drawing inferences; **RL.5.3** compare and contrast characters, settings, or events, drawing on details; **RL.5.5** explain how chapters, scenes, or stanzas fit together to provide the overall structure; **RL.5.6** describe how a narrator's or speaker's point of view influences how events are described

474

Big Trouble

Bragging can sometimes cause trouble, however, and that is exactly what happened to Davy. One day as he was walking home through a thick forest, dark clouds began rolling in and the sky grew as black as night. The wind gusted violently, and thunder rumbled ominously above. Davy had been walking for a long time with nothing to eat, and by this time he was famished. As torrents of rain began to fall, he knew that he had to find something to eat.

Davy saw two eyes shining from behind a group of trees. "Aha!" he exclaimed, "here's an opportunity for a meal!" To the animal hiding behind the trees he said, "My name is Davy Crockett, and I'm a hungry fellow. That's bad news for you because I intend to eat you!"

At that moment, lightning lit up the forest and Davy saw that the creature behind the tree was not small and meek as he had imagined. The animal he had threatened to eat was a huge, strong cougar! Davy quickly changed his tune. "Excuse me," he said, "I've apparently mistaken you for someone else."

 How does this section of the passage build on the previous one and establish Davy's conflict?

The cougar paid no attention to Davy's words. Instead, it crept slowly from behind the tree, growling and snarling and baring its teeth. Then it crouched low, preparing to pounce.

Davy decided to try a little humor, so he chuckled and said, "You want to sing, do you? How about we try a duet?" Still, the cougar kept inching toward him. Since humor did not appear to be working, Davy decided it was time to get serious. "I've fought my share of wildcats, and bears and other critters," he told the cougar. "I guess I can fight you, too."

The Battle

Davy began to mimic the cat, growling and snarling and baring his teeth until he looked and sounded as fierce as the cougar. The two circled around each other for a while until they both were a little dizzy. All the while, the cougar kept twitching its tail and its ears, and Davy did his best to imitate every move.

Suddenly, Davy crouched low and moved swiftly toward the cougar. He started to pounce, but the cougar was ready for him. Down they went together onto the wet ground, wrestling furiously and rolling around in the puddles. Wrestling a cougar is not an easy task, but neither is wrestling Davy Crockett! The ferocious fight went on and on, with Davy sometimes on top, and sometimes the cougar. It began to seem as if the battle would continue forever.

 In what ways are Davy Crockett and the cougar similar and different?

Finally, Davy got free, slipped quickly around behind the cougar, and picked it up by the tail. He swung the huge cat around and around in the air like a lasso until the cougar yowled in pain and frustration. "I'll stop swinging," Davy hollered, "if you promise to stop fighting and behave!"

He set the subdued cougar back on the ground without loosening his grasp on its tail. "You are coming home with me," Davy told the cougar sternly. "I'm going to teach you some manners!" So they headed home through the pouring rain, covered with mud and wet leaves. Davy did not relinquish his hold on that tail all the way back to his cabin.

A Happy Ending

After they had both cleaned themselves up, Davy told the cougar, "You'd better learn to make yourself useful around here." The cougar decided that might not be a bad idea. So Davy taught his new pet how to help with household chores and yard work. It could rake leaves with its huge claws even faster than Davy could with rakes in both hands! Its long tail came in handy for sweeping dust out from under the furniture.

As the weeks went by, Davy and the wildcat became the best of companions. They often went walking about the countryside together. On dark nights, the cat used its keen eyesight to lead Davy home. They would practice singing as they walked along. The cougar became such a good singer that it even joined a choir. People passing by Davy's cabin often reported hearing Davy and his beloved friend singing duets.

 What is the narrator's point of view, and how does it affect the way events in the passage are described?

Unit 4

☑ **TARGET VOCABULARY**

feature
record
assuming
mental
launch
thumbed
developed
incredibly
episodes
villains

Vocabulary Reader

Context Cards

COMMON CORE **L.5.6** acquire and use general academic and domain-specific words and phrases

Vocabulary in Context

1 feature
Storytellers often feature, or focus on, tales from their own cultural tradition.

2 record
One of these tiny volumes could claim the record as the world's smallest book.

3 assuming
Mimes can tell stories without words, assuming viewers follow their motions.

4 mental
Exact words help readers create mental pictures of a story's characters and setting.

 Go Digital

▶ Study each Context Card.

▶ Use a dictionary or a glossary to verify the meaning of each Vocabulary word.

5 launch

After the launch, or initial printing, of his book, this author signs a copy of it at a store.

6 thumbed

At the library, this student thumbed through books to find a story to read later.

7 developed

An artist developed, or planned, this character from pencil sketch to final color drawing.

8 incredibly

Roman heroes like Hercules are often incredibly, or unbelievably, strong.

9 episodes

A story told in several episodes, or parts, is sometimes called a series.

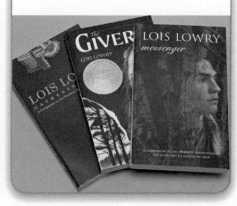

10 villains

In old movies most villains had evil grins, wore black clothes, and battled the heroes.

Read and Comprehend

☑ TARGET SKILL

Author's Purpose In "Lunch Money," details about the main character, the setting, and the plot help reveal the **author's purpose,** or reason for writing. As you read, record text quotes and details in a graphic organizer like the one below. Then use text evidence in the organizer to help you infer, or figure out, the author's purpose.

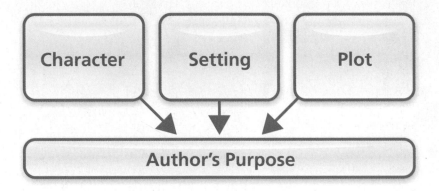

☑ TARGET STRATEGY

Monitor/Clarify As you read, **monitor** your understanding of the details in the text. Monitoring what you read for text evidence will help **clarify** the author's purpose and give you a better understanding of characters and events.

RL.5.1 quote accurately from a text when explaining what the text says explicitly as well as when drawing inferences

Visual Arts

If you've ever looked at a painting or seen a movie, then you are familiar with the visual arts—art forms that can be viewed. Comic books are another kind of visual art. They tell stories through vivid drawings, crisp dialogue, and exciting action.

Comic book characters include both heroes and villains. These characters often have extraordinary powers. In "Lunch Money," a boy named Greg has created his own series of comic books. The heroes of his books have adventures in several different settings. From the selection, you will learn how much work can go into creating just one edition of a comic book.

ANCHOR TEXT

☑ TARGET SKILL

Author's Purpose Use text details to figure out the author's viewpoint and purpose for writing.

☑ GENRE

Realistic fiction includes characters and events that are like people and events in real life. As you read, look for:

▶ a setting that is familiar to most readers
▶ a main character who overcomes a challenge
▶ characters' thoughts and actions that are believable

 RL.5.1 quote accurately when explaining the text and when drawing inferences; **RL.5.6** describe how point of view influences how events are described; **RL.5.7** analyze how visual elements contribute to the meaning, tone, or beauty of a text; **RL.5.10** read and comprehend literature.

MEET THE AUTHOR
Andrew Clements

Andrew Clements says, "I mostly write realistic fiction, novels that feel a lot like real life." Like his character Greg, Clements works hard at his writing. To avoid distractions, he writes in his backyard shed with no phone, no television, and no Internet!

MEET THE ILLUSTRATOR
Adam Gustavson

Adam Gustavson wanted to be a cowboy, but he was allergic to horses. Then he wanted to be a crocodile farmer, but there weren't any crocodiles in New Jersey where he lived. He finally settled on art. He has illustrated several books for young people.

LUNCH MONEY

by Andrew Clements

**selection illustrated by
Adam Gustavson**

ESSENTIAL QUESTION

In what ways can
illustrations enhance a
reader's experience?

Standing in the cafeteria line, Greg opened his red plastic pencil case. He counted once, and then he counted again, just to be sure. Then he grinned. There were thirteen left.

Sweet! That means I sold seventeen units.

That's what Greg called the comic books he'd been selling—units. And selling seventeen units before lunch was a new sales record.

Greg's comic books weren't the kind for sale at stores. Regular comic books were sort of tall. Also a little floppy. Not Greg's.

Greg's comic books were about the size of a credit card, and they could stand up on one end all by themselves. They were only sixteen pages long, and he could fit about fifty of them into his pencil case. These comic books were short and sturdy. And that's why they were called Chunky Comics.

Greg loved that name. He had chosen it himself. He got to pick the name because he was the author of all the Chunky Comics stories. He had drawn all the pictures too. And he was also the designer, the printer, and the binder. Plus he was the marketing manager, the advertising director, and the entire sales force. Chunky Comics was a one-kid operation, and that one kid was Greg Kenton.

Greg snapped the pencil case shut and grabbed a tray. He took a grilled cheese sandwich, a cup of carrot sticks, and then looked over the fruit cocktail bowls until he found one with three chunks of cherry. He got a chocolate milk from the cooler, and as he walked toward his seat, Greg did some mental math.

Monday, the first day Chunky Comics had gone on sale, he had sold twelve units; Tuesday, fifteen units; Wednesday, eighteen units; and today, Thursday, he had already sold seventeen units—before lunch. So that was . . . sixty-two units since Monday morning, and each little book sold for $.25. So the up-to-the-minute sales total for September 12 was . . . $15.50.

Greg knew why sales were increasing: word of mouth. Kids had been telling other kids about his comic book. The cover illustration was powerful, the inside pictures were strong, and the story was loaded with action. The title was *Creon: Return of the Hunter*, and it was volume 1, number 1, the very first of the Chunky Comics. So that made it a collector's item.

Greg sat down at his regular lunch table, next to Ted Kendall. Ted nodded and said, "Hi," but Greg didn't hear him. Greg picked up his sandwich and took a big bite. He chewed the warm bread and the soft cheese, but he didn't taste a thing. Greg was still thinking about sales.

Fifteen fifty in three and a half days—not so hot.

Greg had set a sales goal for the first week: twenty-five dollars— which meant that he had to sell one hundred units. It looked like he was going to fall short.

ANALYZE THE TEXT

Voice Authors can use word choice and point of view to show what a character is like. Explain how the author uses these techniques to make Greg's personality and voice come through.

The idea of making and selling comic books had hit Greg like a KRAK over the head from Superman himself. It made perfect sense. Candy and gum were against school rules, and tiny toys were boring—and also against the rules. But how could he go wrong selling little books? School was all about books and reading. True, reading a comic book wasn't exactly the same as reading a regular book, but still, there was a rack of comics right in the kids' section at the public library downtown, and some new graphic novels, too.

Comic books had been part of Greg's life forever, mostly because of his dad's collection. His dad's collection filled three shelves in the family room—and it was worth over ten thousand dollars. Once Greg had shown he knew how to take care of the comic books, he had been allowed to read and look at them all he wanted. Greg had even bought a few collectible comics of his own, mostly newer ones that weren't very expensive.

It was his love of comic books that had first gotten Greg interested in drawing. Comics had led Greg to books like *How to Draw Comic Book Villains*, *You Can Draw Superheroes*, *Make Your Own Comic-Book Art*, and *Draw the Monsters We Love to Hate*. Back in third grade Greg had used his own money to buy india ink, dip pens, brushes, and paper at the art supply store. And drawing new comic-book characters was one of his favorite things to do—when he wasn't earning money.

That whole summer before sixth grade Greg had worked toward the launch of Chunky Comics. From the start he had felt pretty sure he could come up with a story idea, and he knew he would be able to do the drawings.

But first he'd had to deal with a lot of *hows*: How does a whole comic book get put together? How big should each be? How was he going to print them? How much would it cost him to make each one? And finally, how much money should he charge for his finished comic books—assuming he could actually make some?

But one by one, Greg had found the answers. An encyclopedia article about printing books had helped a lot. It showed how pages of a book start as one large sheet of paper that gets folded in half several times. Each time the sheet is folded, the number of pages is doubled. So Greg took a piece of regular letter-size paper, and folded it in half three times the way it showed in the encyclopedia. That one piece of paper turned into a chunky little sixteen-page book—Chunky Comics. It was so simple.

But not really. Greg figured out that making little comic books was a ten-step process.

1. Write a story that can be told on twelve to fourteen mini-comic book pages.

2. Sketch, draw, ink, and then letter all sixteen minipages—which include the front and back covers.

3. Paste eight of the minipage drawings into their correct positions on a piece of paper to make "master copy one"—a sheet that can be copied again and again.

4. Paste up the other eight minipages to make "master copy two."

5. Using a copier, print the images from "master copy one" onto one side of a "press sheet"—a piece of regular letter-size paper.

6. Print "master copy two" onto the flip side of the press sheet— making eight page images on the front, and eight on the back.

7. Carefully fold the press sheet with the sixteen copied minipages on it.

8. Put in two staples along the crease at the very center of the little book—between pages 8 and 9.

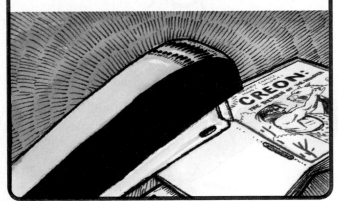

9. Trim the three unstapled edges— and that makes one finished mini-comic book.

10. Repeat.

And each of the ten steps had to be done perfectly, or no one would ever want to spend money on his little comics.

After all the *hows* had been settled, then came the writing. But Greg hadn't written just one story. He had developed a master publishing plan. Volume 1 was going to be about Creon, an incredibly intelligent Stone Age hero who helped his tribe deal with ancient dangers, like prehistoric beasts and Cro-Magnon marauders. Greg figured there could be seven or eight issues about Creon.

Chunky Comics volume 2 would feature the future, where a superhero named Eeon tried to protect a small colony of humans living in a world of melting ice caps and mutant life-forms that were part human, part toxic sludge, and part recycled trucks and airplanes. Again, there would be seven or eight issues featuring Eeon.

> ### ANALYZE THE TEXT
>
> **Visual Elements** What do you notice about this story's illustrations? What do they help you understand about the story and the main character?

Then Chunky Comics volume 3 would feature Leon, a fairly normal modern-age technodude who suddenly finds himself energized when his digital atomic watch overheats and burns its circuits into the nerves on his wrist. Leon learns that the watch can be set for the future or the past. The six or seven time-travel adventures of volume 3 would follow Leon to the past, where he would team up with Creon, and then to the future, where he would offer his services to the amazing Eeon. And eventually, all three characters would have some final episodes together: Creon, Leon, and Eeon—past, present, and future.

Once the master plan was set, writing the first Creon story, *Return of the Hunter*, had been pretty easy for Greg. But the drawing was more difficult than he'd thought it would be. It had taken a long time to get each small page looking just the way he wanted. It wasn't like doodling or sketching. These pictures had to be good— good enough to sell.

When both covers and the fourteen inside pages had been drawn and inked and pasted in place to make the two master copies, Greg tackled his first printing.

The copier he used was his dad's, and it was actually part of the printer that was hooked up to the computer in the family room. It was an ink-jet printer, plus a scanner, plus a copier—one of those "all-in-one" machines. It made copies in either black and white or color.

Greg had stuffed about forty ruined sheets of paper into the recycling bin before he had figured out how to get all sixteen page images copied correctly onto the front and back of one sheet of paper.

But finally, he had folded his first perfectly printed sheet, stapled it twice, and trimmed the top, front, and bottom edges. And then, one hot night in the middle of July, Greg stood there in his family room and thumbed through the very first volume of Chunky Comics. It had been a proud moment.

ANALYZE THE TEXT

Author's Purpose Why do you think the author uses such detail to explain how the comic books are made? What do these details reveal about the main character?

Dig Deeper

How to Analyze the Text

Use these pages to learn about Author's Purpose, Voice, and Visual Elements. Then read "Lunch Money" again to apply what you learned.

Author's Purpose

Authors of fiction have different purposes, or reasons, for writing. They may want to share a theme, create realistic characters and plots, or simply entertain their readers. To achieve their purpose, they develop the appropriate characters, events, settings, and other elements in their writing. By looking closely at the details in a work of fiction, you can understand the **author's purpose.**

To determine the author's purpose in "Lunch Money," examine the author's description of the main character, the setting, and the plot events. What overall impression do these elements create? What is revealed through the details and story elements about the author's reason for writing the story?

A graphic organizer like the one below can help you use details and elements in the story to determine the author's purpose.

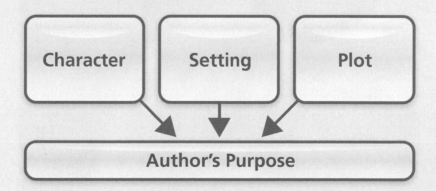

 RL.5.6 describe how a narrator's or speaker's point of view influences how events are described; **RL.5.7** analyze how visual and multimedia elements contribute to the meaning, tone, or beauty of a text; **RL.5.10** read and comprehend literature

Voice

Although Greg does not tell the story "Lunch Money," the narrator reveals Greg's thoughts and feelings as if Greg himself is sharing them. To create a **voice** that is realistic, the author chooses the main character's words carefully. Greg uses informal language such as "come up with" and "deal," as well as short sentences. This realistic way of speaking brings out Greg's personality and makes his character convincing.

Visual Elements

Authors of realistic fiction may use **visual elements**, such as graphic art and illustrations. These elements can help readers "see" what is happening more clearly. They also set the tone or feeling of the story. Look back at pages 488–491. These pages include detailed drawings of the steps involved in putting together comic books, as well as illustrations of Greg's comic characters.

Your Turn

RETURN TO THE ESSENTIAL QUESTION

Review the selection to prepare to discuss this question: *In what ways can illustrations enhance a reader's experience?* As you discuss, refer to specific text evidence to support your ideas and to elaborate on the comments of others.

Classroom Conversation

Continue your discussion of "Lunch Money" by explaining your answers to these questions:

1. How would reading the story be different if there were no illustrations?

2. How would you describe Greg's character based on his actions in the story?

3. Would you like to read Greg's comic books? Why or why not?

TALK ABOUT THEME

Discuss the Story The theme of a story is the message or lesson about life that the author wants readers to know. Theme is conveyed through the characters' actions, feelings, and thoughts. With a partner, identify the theme of "Lunch Money." Use text evidence to discuss how Greg's responses to challenges convey the theme.

WRITE ABOUT READING

Response In "Lunch Money," Greg publishes and sells his own comic books. Do you think that his comic-book series will be a success? Think about Greg's qualities, the planning he does, and the way he approaches his sales. Then write a paragraph explaining how well you think he will do. Use text evidence such as quotations and details to support your view.

Business Plan

Step 1

Writing Tip

Use transitions to relate your ideas to each other. Words and phrases such as *because*, *specifically*, and *as a result* can help show how your reasons support your opinions.

COMMON CORE   **RL.5.1** quote accurately when explaining what the text says explicitly and when drawing inferences; **RL.5.2** determine theme from details/summarize; **W.5.1c** link opinion and reasons using words, phrases, and clauses; **W.5.9a** apply grade 5 Reading standards to literature; **W.5.10** write routinely over extended time frames and shorter time frames; **SL.5.1c** pose and respond to questions, make comments that contribute to the discussion, and elaborate on others' remarks

Zap! Pow!

A History of the Comics

by Linda Cave

Do you read the funnies in the paper? They have been popular for more than one hundred years. They tell stories with words and pictures, and new episodes appear each day. Assuming you read comics, you know they can be funny. Sometimes they feature adventures or political issues. Some comics are in books, too.

Development of Comics

1907: Daily comics

1896: *Yellow Kid*

1934: *Flash Gordon*

1900   **1920**

1933: First comic books

1897: Speech balloons; story panels

Early Days

In 1896 the comic *Yellow Kid* appeared in a Sunday paper. The kid wore a wide yellow suit. The words he "spoke" were written on the suit. People thumbed through the papers just to read the comic. Soon comics were in many Sunday papers. When one artist used a speech balloon to show a character speaking, other artists began to use the balloons. At about the same time, artists developed panels, or boxes, to show a series of events. Later, publishers put comics in their papers every day.

1941: *Calling All Girls,* first comic for girls

1939–1945: Comic books popular with WWII soldiers

1970s: Comic book collecting

1940   **1960**   **1980**

1938: First Superman

1954: Standards for comic books set by Comics Code Authority

1950s: First comics for grownups

Present: Motion pictures based on comic books

Comic Strips to Comic Books

In the early 1930s, someone collected newspaper comics into books to give away to people who bought certain products. These were the first comic books. Writers and artists saw that people wanted the books and would buy them. Soon original stories began to appear in comic book form.

The Golden Age of Comic Books

Many historians say the golden age of comic books began with the launch of Superman in 1938. He was the first character to have super powers. His comic books were incredibly popular. They set a new sales record, with over one million copies sold per issue. Noticing the new superhero's popularity, other comic book artists created Batman, The Flash, the Green Lantern, Captain America, and Wonder Woman. They all fought villains. Some used amazing tools or had super physical and mental powers.

The Comics Code and After

Some adults worried that comic books were bad for children. A comics code was established in 1954 to make sure comics were safe for kids to read. For many, this marked the end of a golden age. Today comic books are still popular, with new superheroes and villains appearing each year. Classic superheroes like Superman and Batman find new audiences through new comic book adventures and in movies. Using words and artwork together to tell a story is still a winning combination.

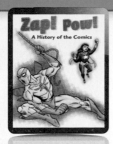

Compare Texts

Compare Characters Review the selection "Off and Running" (Lesson 3) with a partner. Using text evidence and a Venn diagram, work together to compare the character of Miata with Greg in "Lunch Money." Look at their goals, their character traits, and their work ethics. Present your Venn diagram in small groups. Summarize the important ways in which Miata and Greg are the same and different.

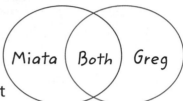

Write a Thank-You Letter You do not have to be a superhero to do incredible things. Write a thank-you letter to someone you know who has done something special or out of the ordinary. In your letter, explain why you think what that person did is special.

Expand a Timeline Work with a partner to add to the timeline in "Zap! Pow! A History of the Comics." Begin by studying the captions and illustrations on the timeline on pages 498–499. Use print and electronic sources to find additional information to include on the timeline. Add three other important events in the history of comics, and then review the revised timeline. How has the audience for comics changed over the years?

COMMON CORE **RL.5.1** quote accurately when explaining what the text says explicitly and when drawing inferences; **RL.5.9** compare and contrast stories in the same genre on their approaches to themes and topics; **W.5.7** conduct short research projects that use several sources to build knowledge through investigation; **W.5.10** write routinely over extended time frames and shorter time frames

Grammar

What Is an Adjective? An **adjective** is a word that gives information, such as *how many* and *what kind,* about a noun. An adjective that tells *what kind* is called a **descriptive adjective.** One special type of descriptive adjective tells the origin of the person, place, or thing being described. These adjectives are formed from names of places, so they are capitalized.

Descriptive Adjective	Suzette likes comics with dynamic artwork.
Descriptive Adjective Giving Origin	She especially likes the Japanese comics called manga.

Try This! Work with a partner. Find the descriptive adjectives in these sentences. Tell which identify the origin of a person, place, or thing.

1. Her favorite adventures take place in Asian cities.

2. Modern buildings make a great background for intense action.

3. Korean costumes from ancient times add appeal.

4. Phil has a comic with Chinese warriors in it!

5. A capable superhero knows karate, jiujitsu, and kickboxing.

When you write, use precise, descriptive adjectives to create clear images for your readers and to help make your writing more interesting.

Vague Adjective	Precise Adjectives
I photographed a big pyramid.	I photographed a massive Mexican pyramid.

 Connect Grammar to Writing

As you revise your friendly letter this week, look for opportunities to replace vague adjectives with descriptive adjectives. Using descriptive adjectives will help readers visualize what you are writing about.

Narrative Writing

☑ **Voice** In "Lunch Money," Greg's feelings are clear when he thinks, "Sweet! That means I sold seventeen units." A well-written **friendly letter** also shows your feelings and really sounds like you. Use informal words and phrases to let the real you shine through.

Nicole drafted a letter to her cousin telling him about something special she did. Later, she revised her letter to show her feelings. Use the Writing Traits Checklist below as you revise your writing.

Writing Traits Checklist

☑ **Ideas**
Do all of the details in my letter fit my purpose?

☑ **Organization**
Did I use the correct format for a friendly letter?

☑ **Sentence Fluency**
Did I vary my sentence types?

☑ **Word Choice**
Did I use informal words and expressions?

☑ **Voice**
Do my feelings and personality come through?

☑ **Conventions**
Did I use correct spelling, grammar, and punctuation?

Revised Draft

Dear Jerome,

~~I liked the~~ The comic book you made for me. It gave me a ~~good~~ super idea for my school project, too. I started reading about Colonial life. After ~~Then~~ I learned what the Pilgrims really ate, ~~Then~~ I made some drawings of their food. and ~~Then I~~ wrote funny captions for the drawings.

504

555 East Central Street

Rockford, IL 61102

March 25, 20XX

Dear Jerome,

The comic book you made for me was awesome! It gave me a super idea for my school project, too. I started reading about Colonial life. After I learned what the Pilgrims really ate, I made some drawings of their food and wrote funny captions for the drawings. Suddenly, I realized that I could turn my captions and drawings into a social studies project! I made a twelve-page comic book about cooking in Colonial times.

My project was a total success! My teacher wants her own copy of the book, and so does the principal. I'll make a copy for you, too. The next time we see each other, I might even cook you something delicious and give you a taste of life as a Pilgrim. I hope you're having as much fun at school as I am. Please write back and tell me all about it.

Your favorite cousin,

Nicole

Reading as a Writer

What words and expressions tell you how Nicole feels? Where can you show your feelings more clearly in your own letter?

In my final letter, I changed some words to show my feelings more clearly. I also replaced the overused adverb *then* and used precise adjectives.

Vocabulary in Context

TARGET VOCABULARY

impressed

collected

produced

destination

original

concentrate

suspense

admitted

compliment

rumor

Vocabulary Reader

Context Cards

1 impressed

This judge was impressed and awed by a young writer's remarkable talent.

2 collected

Chess players must remain calm and collected as they plot their next move.

3 produced

Amazing structures were produced, or created, at this sand castle contest.

4 destination

This marathoner's goal is to be the first to reach the finish line, his destination.

COMMON CORE

L.5.6 acquire and use general academic and domain-specific words and phrases

Go Digital

▶ Study each Context Card.

▶ Use a glossary to determine the pronunciation of each Vocabulary word.

5 original

Olympia, Greece, is the original, or first, place where Olympic Games were held.

6 concentrate

This tennis player has to concentrate on the ball in order to hit it back to her opponent.

7 suspense

These fans are in suspense, wondering who will win the big game.

8 admitted

This spelling bee contestant admitted, or confessed, how nervous he was.

9 compliment

A first-place trophy is a compliment praising the dog and its handler.

10 rumor

Sometimes a rumor, or unproved news, can spread about who won a contest.

Read and Comprehend

 Go Digital

☑ TARGET SKILL

Story Structure As you read "LAFFF," look for the elements that make up the story's structure, including the **setting**, the **characters**, and the **plot**. Think about the conflict or problem that the narrator faces. What events follow from this conflict? How is the conflict finally resolved? To trace how the story unfolds, use a graphic organizer like this one. Be sure to list story events in sequential order.

Setting	Characters
Plot	
Conflict: Events: Resolution:	

☑ TARGET STRATEGY

Infer/Predict As you read "LAFFF," use details and other text evidence to **infer**, or make logical guesses about, the characters' thoughts and feelings. Use these inferences and events in the story to help you **predict** what might happen next.

 COMMON CORE

RL.5.5 explain how chapters, scenes, or stanzas fit together to provide the overall structure

Creative Inventions

In the world of fiction, it is possible to invent anything. After all, only the writer's imagination limits what can be done with words! Sometimes writers come up with crazy inventions, such as computers or electric cars, that later become part of the everyday world. Time travel has not yet become a reality, but the idea of traveling between different time periods has fascinated many writers. In "LAFFF," you will see one author's vision of a time machine and how using it impacts the story's characters.

ANCHOR TEXT

☑ TARGET SKILL

Story Structure Examine details about characters, setting, and plot.

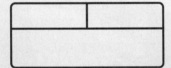

☑ GENRE

Science fiction is writing based on scientific ideas and often set in the future. As you read, look for:

▶ technology of the future
▶ unrealistic events
▶ characters that may or may not be like real people

 RL.5.5 explain how chapters, scenes, or stanzas fit together to provide the overall structure; **RL.5.6** describe how a narrator's or speaker's point of view influences how events are described; **RL.5.10** read and comprehend literature

MEET THE AUTHOR

Lensey Namioka

Lensey Namioka was only nine years old when she and her family moved to the United States from China, and although she adored spending time reading stories, she found learning the complexities of the English language difficult. Solving math problems came much more easily to her, so she majored in mathematics in college and became a math teacher. However, she never stopped reading, and eventually her love of stories led her to become a successful writer, too. Ms. Namioka has written books for children and for young adults, as well as several articles and popular short stories such as "LAFFF."

MEET THE ILLUSTRATOR

Hiromitsu Yokota

Hiromitsu Yokota has created illustrations for numerous books, magazines, and calendars. He likes to infuse his work with details and feelings from everyday life and experiences.

Mr. Yokota uses digital technology to create his illustrations because it allows him to manipulate color and light while producing pictures that appear to have been drawn by hand. He attended college in Tokyo and earned a degree in fine arts, and is a member of the Society of Illustrators.

LAFFF

from *Best Shorts*

by Lensey Namioka

selection illustrated by Hiromitsu Yokota

IMAGINE THE POSSIBILITIES

Did you know that science fiction writers have been thrilling audiences with stories about time travel for well over a century? One of the best-known novels about time travel is H.G. Wells's *The Time Machine*. This novel features a main character who builds an incredible time machine and uses it to explore and interact with periods and people far into the future—and it was written way back in 1888!

Readers throughout the world have had a long-standing love affair with science fiction because it stimulates their imaginations and weaves together elements of fantasy, science, adventure, mystery, and drama. Several popular science fiction authors have seen their work adapted into movies or television series that involve the creation of elaborate sets and futuristic inventions, and while translating a writer's vision of time travel to film or screen can be difficult and expensive, the payoff is that fans of the book get to see the future or past brought to life in whole new ways.

Despite the countless depictions of time travel in literature, film, and television, there is no evidence that it has ever happened or could happen; it is a testament to the talents of science fiction authors that they are able to write such believable stories about a future no one has yet experienced. Perhaps some of the inventions, environments, and ideas in those stories will be realized someday, though. Imagine that!

ESSENTIAL QUESTION

What role does imagination play in the invention process?

In movies, geniuses have frizzy white hair, right? They wear thick glasses and have names like Dr. Zweistein.

Peter Lu didn't have frizzy white hair. He had straight hair, as black as licorice. He didn't wear thick glasses, either, since his vision was normal.

Peter's family, like ours, had immigrated from China, but they had settled here first. When we moved into a house just two doors down from the Lus, they gave us some good advice on how to get along in America.

I went to the same school as Peter, and we walked to the school bus together every morning. Like many Chinese parents, mine made sure that I worked very hard in school.

In spite of all I could do, my grades were nothing compared to Peter's. He was at the top in all his classes. We walked to the school bus without talking because I was a little scared of him. Besides, he was always deep in thought.

Peter didn't have any friends. Most of the kids thought he was a nerd because they saw his head always buried in books. I didn't think he even tried to join the rest of us or cared what the others thought of him.

Then he surprised us all. As I went down the block trick-or-treating, dressed as a zucchini in my green sweats, I heard a strange, deep voice behind me say, "How do you do."

I yelped and turned around. Peter was wearing a long, black Chinese gown with slits in the sides. On his head he had a little round cap, and down each side of his mouth drooped a thin, long mustache.

"I am Dr. Lu Manchu, the mad scientist," he announced, putting his hands in his sleeves and bowing.

He smiled when he saw me staring at his costume. It was a scary smile, somehow.

Some of the other kids came up, and when they saw Peter, they were impressed. "Hey, neat!" said one boy.

I hadn't expected Peter to put on a costume and go trick-or-treating like a normal kid. So maybe he did want to join the others after all—at least some of the time. After that night he wasn't a nerd anymore. He was Dr. Lu Manchu. Even some of the teachers began to call him that.

When we became too old for trick-or-treating, Peter was still Dr. Lu Manchu. The rumor was that he was working on a fantastic machine in his parents' garage. But nobody had any idea what it was.

One evening, as I was coming home from a baby-sitting job, I cut across the Lus' backyard. Passing their garage, I saw through a little window that the light was on. My curiosity got the better of me, and I peeked in.

I saw a booth that looked like a shower stall. A stool stood in the middle of the stall, and hanging over the stool was something that looked like a great big shower head.

Suddenly a deep voice behind me said, "Good evening, Angela." Peter bowed and smiled his scary smile. He didn't have his costume on and he didn't have the long, droopy mustache. But he was Dr. Lu Manchu.

"What are you doing?" I squeaked.

Still in his strange, deep voice, Peter said, "What are *you* doing? After all, this is my garage."

"I was just cutting across your yard to get home. Your parents never complained before."

"I thought you were spying on me," said Peter. "I thought you wanted to know about my machine." He hissed when he said the word *machine*.

Honestly, he was beginning to frighten me. "What machine?" I demanded. "You mean this shower-stall thing?"

He drew himself up and narrowed his eyes, making them into thin slits. "This is my time machine!"

I goggled at him. "You mean . . . you mean . . . this machine can send you forward and backward in time?"

"Well, actually, I can only send things forward in time," admitted Peter, speaking in his normal voice again. "That's why I'm calling the machine LAFFF. It stands for Lu's Artifact For Fast Forward."

Of course Peter always won first prize at the annual statewide science fair. But that's a long way from making a time machine. Minus his mustache and long Chinese gown, he was just Peter Lu.

"I don't believe it!" I said. "I bet LAFFF is only good for a laugh."

"Okay, Angela. I'll show you!" hissed Peter.

He sat down on the stool and twisted a dial. I heard some *bleeps*, *cheeps*, and *gurgles*. Peter disappeared.

He must have done it with mirrors. I looked around the garage. I peeked under the tool bench. There was no sign of him.

"Okay, I give up," I told him. "It's a good trick, Peter. You can come out now."

Bleep, *cheep*, and *gurgle* went the machine, and there was Peter sitting on the stool. He held a red rose in his hand. "What do you think of that?"

I blinked. "So you produced a flower. Maybe you had it under the stool."

"Roses bloom in June, right?" he demanded.

That was true. And this was December.

"I sent myself forward in time to June when the flowers were blooming," said Peter. "And I picked the rose from our yard. Convinced, Angela?"

It was too hard to swallow. "You said you couldn't send things back in time," I objected. "So how did you bring the rose back?"

But even as I spoke I saw that his hands were empty. The rose was gone.

"That's one of the problems with the machine," said Peter. "When I send myself forward, I can't seem to stay there for long. I snap back to my own time after only a minute. Anything I bring with me snaps back to its own time, too. So my rose has gone back to this June."

ANALYZE THE TEXT
....

Literary Devices When authors use words, such as *buzz* or *clang*, that sound like the noises they describe, it is called **onomatopoeia**. Where has the author used onomatopoeia on this page, and what does it add to the story?

I was finally convinced, and I began to see possibilities. "Wow, just think: If I don't want to do the dishes, I can send myself forward to the time when the dishes are already done."

"That won't do you much good," said Peter. "You'd soon pop back to the time when the dishes were still dirty."

Too bad. "There must be something your machine is good for," I said. Then I had another idea. "Hey, you can bring me back a piece of fudge from the future, and I can eat it twice: once now, and again in the future."

"Yes, but the fudge wouldn't stay in your stomach," said Peter. "It would go back to the future."

"That's even better!" I said. "I can enjoy eating the fudge over and over again without getting fat!"

It was late, and I had to go home before my parents started to worry. Before I left, Peter said, "Look, Angela, there's still a lot of work to do on LAFFF. Please don't tell anybody about the machine until I've got it right."

A few days later I asked him how he was doing.

"I can stay in the future time a bit longer now," he said. "Once I got it up to four minutes."

"Is that enough time to bring me back some fudge from the future?" I asked.

"We don't keep many sweets around the house," he said. "But I'll see what I can do."

A few minutes later, he came back with a spring roll for me. "My mother was frying these in the kitchen, and I snatched one while she wasn't looking."

I bit into the hot, crunchy spring roll, but before I finished chewing, it disappeared. The taste of soy sauce, green onions, and bean sprouts stayed a little longer in my mouth, though.

It was fun to play around with LAFFF, but it wasn't really useful. I didn't know what a great help it would turn out to be.

Every year our school held a writing contest, and the winning story for each grade got printed in our school magazine. I wanted desperately to win. I worked awfully hard in school, but my parents still thought I could do better.

Winning the writing contest would show my parents that I was really good in something. I love writing stories, and I have lots of ideas. But when I actually write them down, my stories never turn out as good as I thought. I just can't seem to find the right words, because English isn't my first language.

I got an honorable mention last year, but it wasn't the same as winning and showing my parents my name, Angela Tang, printed in the school magazine.

The deadline for the contest was getting close, and I had a pile of stories written, but none of them looked like a winner.

Then, the day before the deadline, *boing*, a brilliant idea hit me.

I thought of Peter and his LAFFF machine.

I rushed over to the Lus' garage and, just as I had hoped, Peter was there, tinkering with his machine.

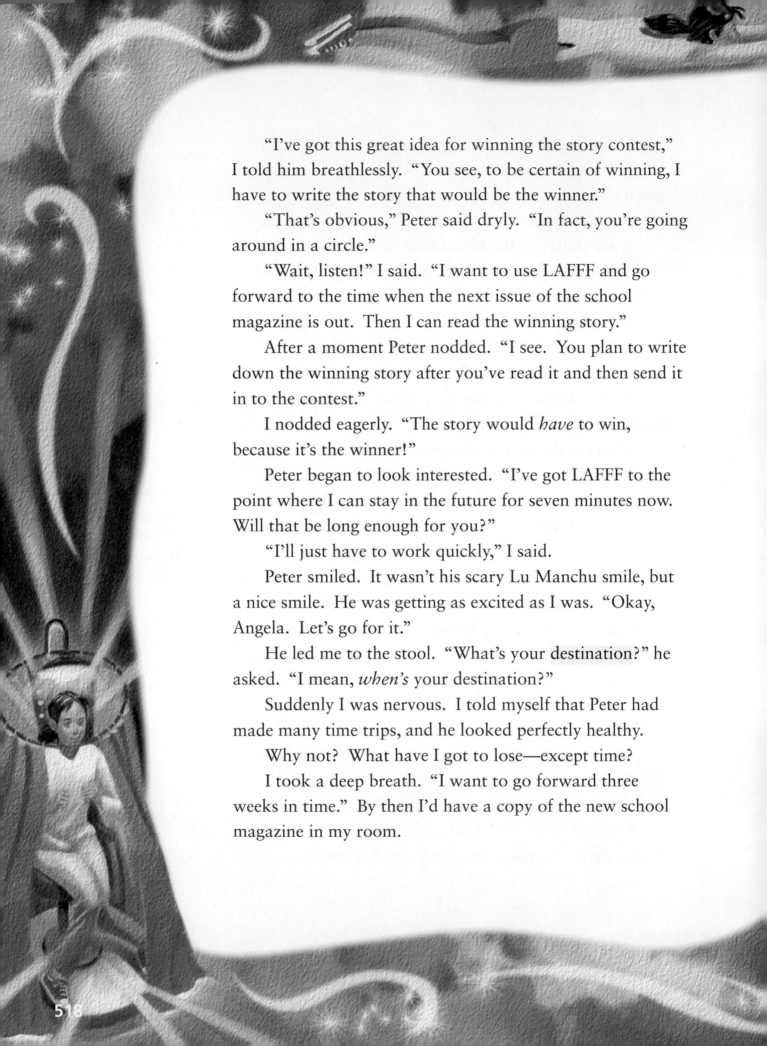

"I've got this great idea for winning the story contest," I told him breathlessly. "You see, to be certain of winning, I have to write the story that would be the winner."

"That's obvious," Peter said dryly. "In fact, you're going around in a circle."

"Wait, listen!" I said. "I want to use LAFFF and go forward to the time when the next issue of the school magazine is out. Then I can read the winning story."

After a moment Peter nodded. "I see. You plan to write down the winning story after you've read it and then send it in to the contest."

I nodded eagerly. "The story would *have* to win, because it's the winner!"

Peter began to look interested. "I've got LAFFF to the point where I can stay in the future for seven minutes now. Will that be long enough for you?"

"I'll just have to work quickly," I said.

Peter smiled. It wasn't his scary Lu Manchu smile, but a nice smile. He was getting as excited as I was. "Okay, Angela. Let's go for it."

He led me to the stool. "What's your destination?" he asked. "I mean, *when's* your destination?"

Suddenly I was nervous. I told myself that Peter had made many time trips, and he looked perfectly healthy.

Why not? What have I got to lose—except time?

I took a deep breath. "I want to go forward three weeks in time." By then I'd have a copy of the new school magazine in my room.

"Ready, Angela?" asked Peter.

"As ready as I'll ever be," I whispered.

Bleep, cheep, and *gurgle*. Suddenly Peter disappeared. What went wrong? Did Peter get sent by mistake, instead of me?

Then I realized what had happened. Three weeks later in time Peter might be somewhere else. No wonder I couldn't see him.

There was no time to be lost. Rushing out of Peter's garage, I ran over to our house and entered through the back door.

Mother was in the kitchen. When she saw me, she stared.

"Angela! I thought you were upstairs taking a shower!"

"Sorry!" I panted. "No time to talk!"

I dashed up to my room. Then I suddenly had a strange idea. What if I met *myself* in my room? Argh! It was a spooky thought.

There was nobody in my room. Where was I? I mean, where was the I of three weeks later?

Wait. Mother had just said she thought I was taking a shower. Down the hall, I could hear the water running in the bathroom. Okay. That meant I wouldn't run into me for a while.

ANALYZE THE TEXT

Point of View From what point of view does the author tell the story? How do you know? How does this point of view affect the way story events are described?

519

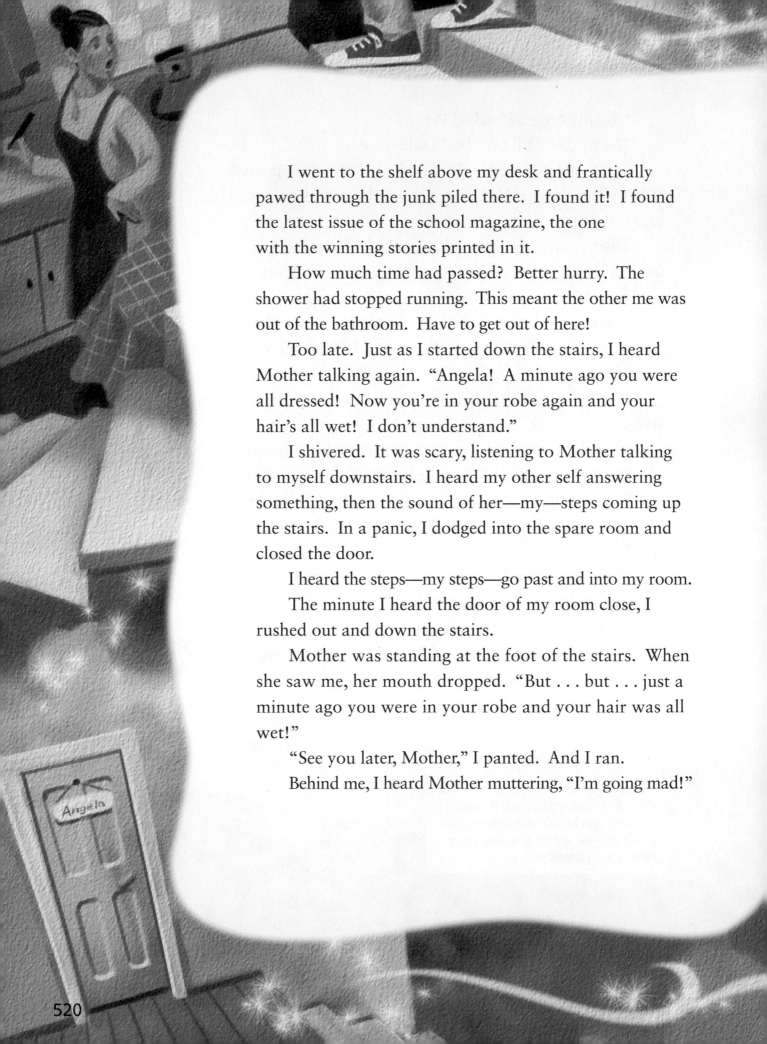

I went to the shelf above my desk and frantically pawed through the junk piled there. I found it! I found the latest issue of the school magazine, the one with the winning stories printed in it.

How much time had passed? Better hurry. The shower had stopped running. This meant the other me was out of the bathroom. Have to get out of here!

Too late. Just as I started down the stairs, I heard Mother talking again. "Angela! A minute ago you were all dressed! Now you're in your robe again and your hair's all wet! I don't understand."

I shivered. It was scary, listening to Mother talking to myself downstairs. I heard my other self answering something, then the sound of her—my—steps coming up the stairs. In a panic, I dodged into the spare room and closed the door.

I heard the steps—my steps—go past and into my room.

The minute I heard the door of my room close, I rushed out and down the stairs.

Mother was standing at the foot of the stairs. When she saw me, her mouth dropped. "But . . . but . . . just a minute ago you were in your robe and your hair was all wet!"

"See you later, Mother," I panted. And I ran.

Behind me, I heard Mother muttering, "I'm going mad!"

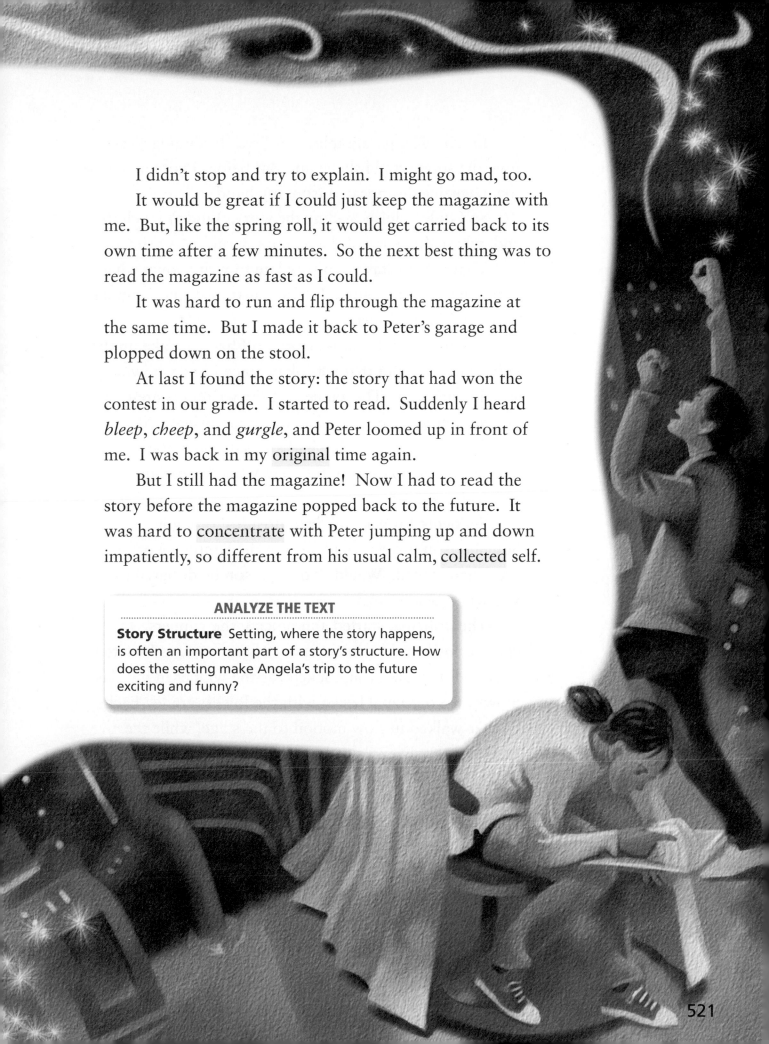

I didn't stop and try to explain. I might go mad, too.

It would be great if I could just keep the magazine with me. But, like the spring roll, it would get carried back to its own time after a few minutes. So the next best thing was to read the magazine as fast as I could.

It was hard to run and flip through the magazine at the same time. But I made it back to Peter's garage and plopped down on the stool.

At last I found the story: the story that had won the contest in our grade. I started to read. Suddenly I heard *bleep*, *cheep*, and *gurgle*, and Peter loomed up in front of me. I was back in my original time again.

But I still had the magazine! Now I had to read the story before the magazine popped back to the future. It was hard to concentrate with Peter jumping up and down impatiently, so different from his usual calm, collected self.

ANALYZE THE TEXT

Story Structure Setting, where the story happens, is often an important part of a story's structure. How does the setting make Angela's trip to the future exciting and funny?

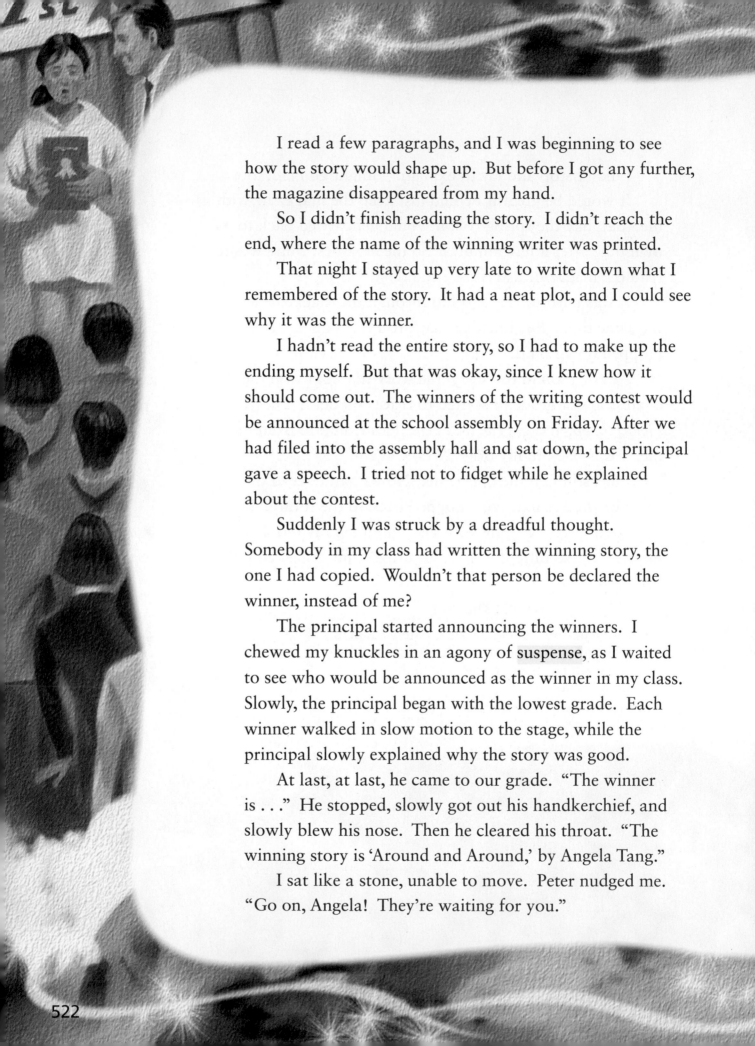

I read a few paragraphs, and I was beginning to see how the story would shape up. But before I got any further, the magazine disappeared from my hand.

So I didn't finish reading the story. I didn't reach the end, where the name of the winning writer was printed.

That night I stayed up very late to write down what I remembered of the story. It had a neat plot, and I could see why it was the winner.

I hadn't read the entire story, so I had to make up the ending myself. But that was okay, since I knew how it should come out. The winners of the writing contest would be announced at the school assembly on Friday. After we had filed into the assembly hall and sat down, the principal gave a speech. I tried not to fidget while he explained about the contest.

Suddenly I was struck by a dreadful thought. Somebody in my class had written the winning story, the one I had copied. Wouldn't that person be declared the winner, instead of me?

The principal started announcing the winners. I chewed my knuckles in an agony of suspense, as I waited to see who would be announced as the winner in my class. Slowly, the principal began with the lowest grade. Each winner walked in slow motion to the stage, while the principal slowly explained why the story was good.

At last, at last, he came to our grade. "The winner is . . ." He stopped, slowly got out his handkerchief, and slowly blew his nose. Then he cleared his throat. "The winning story is 'Around and Around,' by Angela Tang."

I sat like a stone, unable to move. Peter nudged me. "Go on, Angela! They're waiting for you."

I got up and walked up to the stage in a daze. The principal's voice seemed to be coming from far, far away as he told the audience that I had written a science fiction story about time travel.

The winners each got a notebook bound in imitation leather for writing more stories. Inside the cover of the notebook was a ballpoint pen. But the best prize was having my story in the school magazine with my name printed at the end.

Then why didn't I feel good about winning?

After assembly, the kids in our class crowded around to congratulate me. Peter formally shook my hand. "Good work, Angela," he said and winked at me. That didn't make me feel any better. I hadn't won the contest fairly. Instead of writing the story myself, I had copied it from the school magazine.

That meant someone in our class—one of the kids here—had actually written the story. Who was it?

My heart was knocking against my ribs as I stood there and waited for someone to complain that I had stolen his story.

Nobody did.

As we were riding the school bus home, Peter looked at me. "You don't seem very happy about winning the contest, Angela."

"No, I'm not," I mumbled. "I feel just awful."

"Tell you what," suggested Peter. "Come over to my house and we'll discuss it."

"What is there to discuss?" I asked glumly. "I won the contest because I cheated."

"Come on over, anyway. My mother bought a fresh package of humbow in Chinatown."

I couldn't turn down that invitation. Humbow, a roll stuffed with barbecued pork, is my favorite snack.

Peter's mother came into the kitchen while we were munching, and he told her about the contest.

Mrs. Lu looked pleased. "I'm very glad, Angela. You have a terrific imagination, and you deserve to win."

"I like Angela's stories," said Peter. "They're original."

It was the first compliment he had ever paid me, and I felt my face turning red.

After Mrs. Lu left us, Peter and I each had another humbow. But I was still miserable. "I wish I had never started this. I feel like such a jerk."

Peter looked at me, and I swear he was enjoying himself. "If you stole another student's story, why didn't that person complain?"

"I don't know!" I wailed.

"Think!" said Peter. "You're smart, Angela. Come on, figure it out."

Me, smart? I was so overcome to hear myself called smart by a genius like Peter that I just stared at him.

He had to repeat himself. "Figure it out, Angela!"

I tried to concentrate. Why was Peter looking so amused?

The light finally dawned. "Got it," I said slowly. "*I'm* the one who wrote the story."

"The winning story is your own, Angela, because that's the one that won."

My head began to go around and around. "But where did the original idea for the story come from?"

"What made the plot so good?" asked Peter. His voice sounded unsteady.

"Well, in my story, my character used a time machine to go forward in time . . ."

"Okay, whose idea was it to use a time machine?"

"It was mine," I said slowly. I remembered the moment when the idea had hit me with a *boing*.

"So you s-stole f-from yourself!" sputtered Peter. He started to roar with laughter. I had never seen him break down like that. At this rate, he might wind up being human.

When he could talk again, he asked me to read my story to him.

I began. "'In movies, geniuses have frizzy white hair, right? They wear thick glasses and have names like Dr. Zweistein . . . .'"

COUNT ON CREATIVITY!

The main character in Lensey Namioka's short story "LAFFF" goes to extreme measures to ensure that she takes home top honors in a writing competition and sees her story published in the school magazine. Winning the contest is a thrill, especially when she realizes she has learned a lesson much more valuable than a contest prize: the story was in her all along, and she needed only to believe in her own creative ability. This lesson is one that even the most celebrated professional authors have to continuously reinforce within themselves. Writing an imaginative story or a work of science fiction can feel particularly risky, and writers often question whether audiences will continue to find their scenes and settings interesting, or whether people will be eager to follow story characters on journeys that may seem extraordinary or at times even bizarre. Often the most challenging aspect of the writing process is coming to trust one's own instincts, talents, and ideas.

As you write your own plays and stories, remember that readers find it enjoyable to be transported into the world an author constructs in a story, even when (or, in some cases, especially when!) that world is utterly unlike their own. Although inventing a whole new world or new kind of character can be intimidating in the planning stages, have faith that others out there share your interests, and work to help readers visualize what you see in your mind. Vivid language and descriptions, relatable details, and fully formed characters and ideas—and a writer's confidence in his or her own original vision—can ensure that readers will find even the most far-fetched story irresistible.

Dig Deeper

How to Analyze the Text

Use these pages to learn about Story Structure, Literary Devices, and Point of View. Then read "LAFFF" again to apply what you learned.

Story Structure

Authors of science fiction such as "LAFFF" carefully organize the elements of their stories. A well-planned **story structure** means that the setting, characters, and plot fit together in a way that makes sense to readers and keeps their attention.

In "LAFFF," for example, the first part of the story gives readers important background information about the characters of Angela and Peter. Readers learn that Peter is a genius and that Angela wants to please her parents by succeeding in school. Knowing these details helps readers understand why the characters act as they do later in the story.

Use a graphic organizer like the one below to identify story elements and to analyze how they fit together to provide the overall structure.

Setting	Characters
Plot	
Conflict:	
Events:	
Resolution:	

 RL.5.5 explain how chapters, scenes, or stanzas fit together to provide the overall structure; **RL.5.6** describe how a narrator's or speaker's point of view influences how events are described; **RL.5.10** read and comprehend literature; **L.5.5a** interpret figurative language in context

Literary Devices

Writers use various kinds of literary devices, such as figurative language and sound, to convey meaning in a story. **Onomatopoeia** refers to words that sound like what they mean. *Crack*, *boom*, and *bang* are all examples of onomatopoeia. When you say them aloud, you hear the sounds they are describing. Authors of science fiction such as "LAFFF" use onomatopoeia to keep readers interested and to help them hear what the characters do.

Point of View

Point of view is the perspective from which a story is written. Because of the first-person point of view in "LAFFF," readers know only what Angela knows, thinks, and feels. She is not able to see how events will turn out before they actually happen. This creates suspense in the story. For example, Angela doesn't know if Peter's time machine really works. Neither do readers—they must keep reading to find out!

Your Turn

 Turn and Talk Review the selection to prepare to discuss this question: *What role does imagination play in the invention process?* As you discuss, ask questions to clarify others' ideas. With your partner or group, draw some conclusions from key points made during your discussion.

 Classroom Conversation

Continue your discussion of "LAFFF" by using text evidence to answer these questions:

1. How does Angela's imagination help set up the story's conflict?

2. What message about time travel do the events in the story send?

3. How does Angela change during the story?

The sky's the limit!

DISCUSS THE NARRATOR

Explore Point of View The point of view of "LAFFF" is first person. Angela is both the narrator and the main character. As a result, readers see events and other characters through her eyes. With a partner, discuss how seeing Peter from Angela's perspective affects your understanding of him. Share your observations with the class, supporting them with text evidence.

528

WRITE ABOUT READING

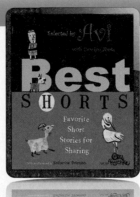

Response Think about the conflict, or problem, that Angela struggles with throughout "LAFFF." It is resolved after Angela wins first place in the writing contest—but is the solution to her problem logical and believable? Write a paragraph in which you discuss whether you are satisfied with the resolution of the story. Be sure to support your opinion with evidence from the text.

Writing Tip

Choose a logical order for your reasons, such as strongest to weakest. Support each reason with specific details from the text.

COMMON CORE **RL.5.2** determine theme from details/summarize; **RL.5.6** describe how a narrator's or speaker's point of view influences how events are described; **W.5.1b** provide logically ordered reasons supported by facts and details; **W.5.9.a** apply grade 5 Reading standards to literature; **SL.5.1a** come to discussions prepared/explicitly draw on preparation and other information about the topic; **SL.5.1c** pose and respond to questions, make comments that contribute to the discussion, and elaborate on others' remarks

From Dreams to Reality

Informational text, such as this magazine article, gives facts and examples about a topic.

Photographs and illustrations are used in both fiction and nonfiction selections to show events or important details or to support information.

COMMON CORE **RI.5.10** read and comprehend informational texts

From Dreams to Reality

Sci Fi Authors Predict the Future

Long ago, computers, fax machines, and satellites seemed impossible. There was not a hint or a rumor that they could ever be a part of our lives. Yet now we use them every day. They were first dreamed up not by engineers, but by science fiction writers. Jules Verne was a writer who could concentrate on amazing ideas. In 1863, he published an early science fiction book, *Five Weeks in a Balloon*. Since then, people have been impressed by how the genre can predict the future. Many predictions, like time travel, are not possible in the real world. But sometimes machines first dreamed up by writers *do* become real.

In this drawing from Verne's *From the Earth to the Moon,* a crowd watches in suspense as the space capsule is prepared to take off.

Go Digital

Manned Flight to the Moon

Verne was a master at predicting what lay ahead. In 1864, he wrote *From the Earth to the Moon.* The book tells about a flight to the moon. This was 105 years before the first manned mission to the moon reached its destination.

Verne's mission has a three-man team. That's the same number used in real moon landings. His space travelers are sent from Florida. NASA sends astronauts into space from there, too. The size of Verne's space capsule is also very close to that of the real Apollo spacecraft.

Not all the ideas that Verne produced are true. His space capsule is shot from a cannon. Today, rocket engines propel modern spacecraft.

A *Saturn V* rocket blasts off for the moon. On July 20, 1969, the world watched *Apollo 11* astronaut Neil Armstrong step onto the moon's surface. They heard him say in a collected voice, "That's one small step for a man, one giant leap for mankind."

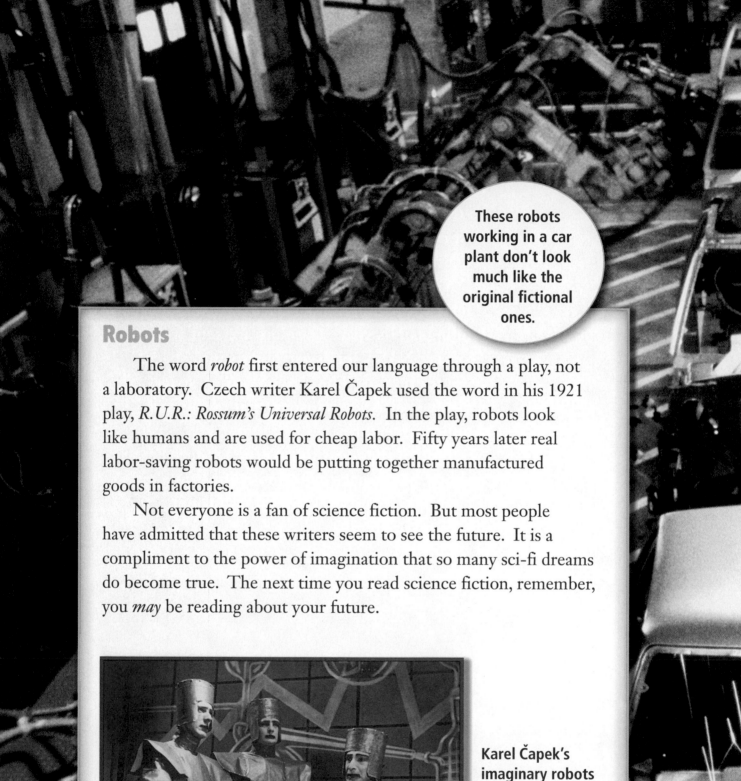

These robots working in a car plant don't look much like the original fictional ones.

Robots

The word *robot* first entered our language through a play, not a laboratory. Czech writer Karel Čapek used the word in his 1921 play, *R.U.R.: Rossum's Universal Robots*. In the play, robots look like humans and are used for cheap labor. Fifty years later real labor-saving robots would be putting together manufactured goods in factories.

Not everyone is a fan of science fiction. But most people have admitted that these writers seem to see the future. It is a compliment to the power of imagination that so many sci-fi dreams do become true. The next time you read science fiction, remember, you *may* be reading about your future.

Karel Čapek's imaginary robots looked like humans.

Compare Texts

Compare Story Characters With a partner, complete a Venn diagram that compares the characters of Angela and Peter. Be sure to consider their personalities, their strengths, and their interests. After you finish your comparison, discuss how Angela and Peter's interactions with each other change over the course of the story. Use text evidence, such as details and quotations, to support your ideas.

TEXT TO SELF

Describe a Talent In "LAFFF," Angela has a talent for writing. Think of something you are good at. Write a paragraph describing a time when you got to show off that talent to others. Describe how you felt as you displayed your talent.

TEXT TO WORLD

Research Technology With a partner, review the photographs, illustrations, and captions in "From Dreams to Reality." Use print sources and the Internet to find three additional facts about the moon landing or the development of robots. Create a timeline using all your information, and share it with another set of partners.

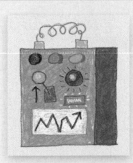

COMMON CORE **RL.5.1** quote accurately when explaining what the text says explicitly and when drawing inferences; **RL.5.3** compare and contrast characters, settings, or events, drawing on details; **W.5.7** conduct short research projects that use several sources to build knowledge through investigation; **W.5.8** recall information from experiences or gather information from print and digital sources/summarize and paraphrase information and provide a source list; **W.5.10** write routinely over extended time frames and shorter time frames

Grammar

What Is an Adverb? A word that describes a verb is an **adverb.**
Adverbs tell *how*, *when*, or *where* an action happens. Many adverbs
end with *-ly*.

How	The time machine buzzed loudly.
When	Soon its door opened.
Where	I took a deep breath and stepped inside.

An **adverb of frequency** tells *how often* something happens.
Adverbs of intensity often tell *how much* about a verb.

Adverb of Frequency: I sometimes feel cramped in small spaces.

Adverb of Intensity: When the time machine door closed,

I almost screamed!

Try This! **Identify the adverb that describes each underlined verb. Explain to a partner whether the adverb tells *how*, *when*, *where*, *how often*, or *how much*.**

❶ Karl <u>stared</u> intently at the blank screen.

❷ He usually <u>found</u> himself with no inspiration.

❸ He <u>closed</u> his eyes again and thought of story ideas.

❹ Karl imagined a future world in which time machines <u>worked</u>
everywhere.

❺ He typed the story at top speed and almost <u>sprained</u> his fingers.

To make your descriptions more vivid, try using precise adverbs. By doing so, you can make your writing more lively and create details that help readers visualize images clearly.

Less Precise Adverb	More Precise Adverb
The time traveler walked slowly down the corridor.	The time traveler walked stealthily down the corridor.

 Connect Grammar to Writing

As you revise your character description, look for opportunities to use precise adverbs. These adverbs will help readers visualize the details and actions you include in your writing.

W.5.3a orient the reader by establishing a situation and introducing a narrator or characters/organize an event sequence; **W.5.3b** use narrative techniques to develop experiences and events or show characters' responses; **W.5.3d** use concrete words and phrases and sensory details; **W.5.5** develop and strengthen writing by planning, revising, editing, rewriting, or trying a new approach

COMMON CORE

Narrative Writing

☑ **Word Choice** A good **character description** uses concrete words, sensory details, and dialogue to show what a character is like. You can almost see Angela's expression in "LAFFF" when she says, "I feel like such a jerk." When you write a descriptive paragraph, use words that will help your readers imagine your subject.

Theo drafted a description of his friend James. Later, he added details and changed some dialogue to bring his character to life.

Writing Traits Checklist

☑ **Ideas**
Do my details show what my character is like?

☑ **Organization**
Are my topic sentences and details in an order that makes sense?

☑ **Sentence Fluency**
Did I combine sentences for better flow?

☑ **Word Choice**
Did I use concrete words, sensory details, and dialogue?

☑ **Voice**
Do my words reveal my feelings or attitude about my character?

☑ **Conventions**
Did I use correct spelling, grammar, and punctuation?

Revised Draft

"Come with me!" shouted James
                        quickly
as he disappeared down the basement

stairs. ~~He was quick!~~ I followed him

and looked around. My red-haired,

freckle-faced neighbor was nowhere to
I'm in outer space, and it's awesome!
be seen. "~~I am in the box~~," he said.

in a loud whisper. The sound was coming

from a big box.

536

My Friend James

by Theo Pothoulakis

"Come with me!" shouted James as he quickly disappeared down the basement stairs. I followed him and looked around. My red-haired, freckle-faced neighbor was nowhere to be seen. "I'm in outer space, and it's awesome!" he said in a loud whisper. The sound was coming from a big box.

That was my introduction to James McGinnis and his fabulous imagination. His box could be a submarine, an intergalactic transporter, or a time machine. Later, when we were in third grade, James discovered the *Time Warp Trio* books, and we excitedly read the whole series together.

Last summer, James moved away. We keep in touch with letters and e-mails. Sometimes I send him drawings I have been working on, and he writes amazing science fiction stories to go with them. "What we need now is a distance-warp machine," he says. I agree!

Reading as a Writer

What details did Theo use to make his description of James vivid? How can you make your own description more vivid?

In my final paper, I made the dialogue sound more natural. I also used adverbs to create clear images for readers.

career
publication
background
household
insights
required
uneventful
edition
formula
destruction

Vocabulary Reader

Context Cards

COMMON CORE **L.5.6** acquire and use general academic and domain-specific words and phrases

Vocabulary in Context

1 career

The career, or chosen work, of a journalist involves carefully gathering the facts.

2 publication

A news publication might take the form of a newspaper, news magazine, or website.

3 background

Years of experience as reporters often give TV newscasters their needed background.

4 household

This boy delivers newspapers to nearly every household in his neighborhood.

Go Digital

▶ Study each Context Card.

▶ Break each Vocabulary word into syllables. Use a dictionary to verify your answers.

5 insights

During interviews, reporters hear the insights and opinions of other people.

6 required

TV cameras are often required, or needed, to record all the action at a sports event.

7 uneventful

This meteorologist predicts an uneventful week. The weather won't change much.

8 edition

A special edition, or version, of a newspaper might be published after a huge news event.

9 formula

Use this formula, or rule, in all news articles: tell *who*, *what*, *when*, *where*, *why*, and *how*.

10 destruction

Papers reported that the destruction caused by the hurricane left some people homeless.

Read and Comprehend

☑ TARGET SKILL

Fact and Opinion "The Dog Newspaper" contains both facts and opinions. **Facts** are statements that can be proven true or false. **Opinions** express someone's thoughts, feelings, or beliefs. They often begin with phrases such as *I think* or *It seems.* As you read the selection, use this graphic organizer to record quotes and details from the text that include important facts and opinions.

Facts	Opinions

☑ TARGET STRATEGY

Analyze/Evaluate As you read "The Dog Newspaper," **analyze**, or look closely at, the facts and opinions the author presents. **Evaluate**, or judge, how well the author uses reasons and evidence to support her opinions and key points.

COMMON CORE

RI.5.1 quote accurately when explaining what the text says explicitly and when drawing inferences from the text; **RI.5.8** explain how an author uses reasons and evidence to support points

Creative Writing

Have you ever expressed your ideas imaginatively in a poem, a short story, or even an e-mail? If so, then you have practiced creative writing. You can use creative writing to invent new stories or to describe real people, places, and events.

In "The Dog Newspaper," the author tells a true story about publishing a newspaper when she was a child. Her writing is lively and creative. However, her newspaper about dogs was not very creative, so it did not last long!

ANCHOR TEXT

Cinco páginas al día: A Writer's Journey
Peg Kehret

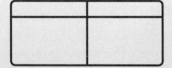
Fact and Opinion Determine which statements in the text can be proved true or false and which express someone's feelings or beliefs.

✓ **GENRE**

An **autobiography** is a person's account of his or her own life. As you read, look for:
▶ first-person point of view
▶ the author's personal thoughts and feelings
▶ information about the author's life

COMMON CORE **RI.5.1** quote accurately when explaining what the text says explicitly and when drawing inferences; **RI.5.2** determine two or more main ideas and explain how they are supported by details/summarize; **RI.5.10** read and comprehend informational texts

Go Digital

MEET THE AUTHOR
Peg Kehret

B.J. may have been the first animal to inspire Peg Kehret's writing, but he certainly was not the last. The author loves animals and lives with several adopted pets. She has written both fiction and nonfiction, including *Shelter Dogs: Amazing Stories of Adopted Strays*.

MEET THE ILLUSTRATOR
Tim Jessell

Tim Jessell calls his digital illustration style realistic "with a twist." He used to be a drummer for a rock band, but now he spends most of his time either with his three children or practicing the sport of falconry with his bird, Spike.

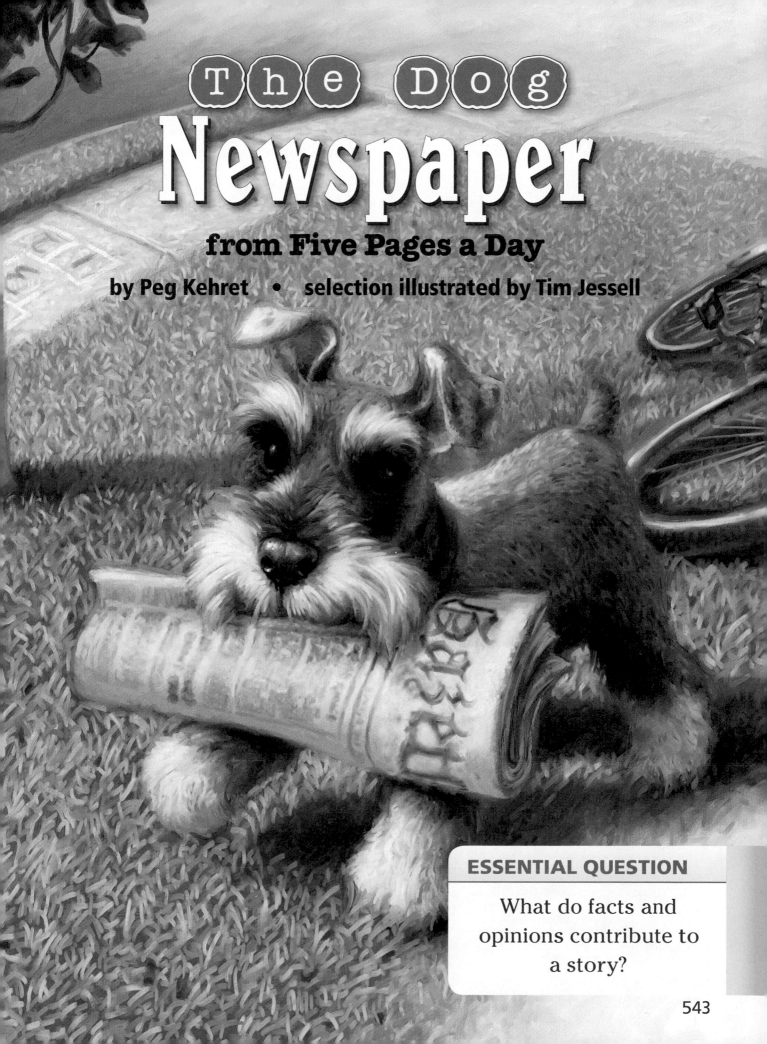

The Dog
Newspaper

from Five Pages a Day

by Peg Kehret • selection illustrated by Tim Jessell

ESSENTIAL QUESTION

What do facts and
opinions contribute to
a story?

I began my writing career at the age of ten when I wrote and sold the *Dog Newspaper*. This weekly publication, which cost five cents a copy, reported on the local dogs.

I interviewed every neighbor who had a dog. "What exciting thing has your dog done?" I asked.

People responded, "All Fluffy does is eat, sleep, and bark at the mailman." Or, "Max's only excitement is his daily walk on the leash." Such answers did not lead to important news stories.

I didn't give up. "If your dog could talk," I asked, "what do you think he would say?"

"Feed me," was the most common answer, followed by, "Let's play."

What could a writer do with such boring material? The solution sat at my feet, wagging his tail.

The first issue of the *Dog Newspaper* featured my dog, B.J., on the entire front page. Although his life at that time was as uneventful as the lives of the other neighborhood dogs, B.J. had a unique background.

Uncle Bill, my mother's younger brother, was a soldier in the U.S. Army during World War II. While in Germany, his unit went into a town that had recently been bombed. As they searched for survivors in a destroyed building, they came across a mother dog and her litter of puppies. The mother dog was dead. So were all the puppies except one.

The soldiers, who had seen far too much of death and destruction, carefully lifted that little brown dog from his littermates. One soldier tucked the puppy inside his jacket to keep him warm. The men fed him from their own food supplies, shared water from their canteens, and decided to keep him as the company mascot.

From then on, wherever Uncle Bill and his comrades went, the dog went, too. They named him B.J. because he was a Big Job to take care of, especially when they were fighting a war.

B.J. grew bigger and stronger as he traveled with the soldiers, tagging along on every mission and somehow surviving even when the men were too busy to pay attention to him.

As the soldiers fought to protect the free world, B.J. did his duty, too. He slept with them in foxholes; he trudged long miles across burned and barren land; he helped search rubble for signs of life. Most of all, he offered love and laughter to a group of lonely, weary men who were far from home.

When the war ended, the soldiers rejoiced. Soon they would be going home to their loved ones. But what about B.J.? They knew they could not leave him in Germany. The German people were faced with the task of rebuilding their cities and their lives; no one wanted to bother with a dog, especially a dog who belonged to the Americans.

The men decided to chip in enough money to fly B.J. back to the United States. Then they had a drawing to see who got to keep him. Each soldier wrote his name on a slip of paper and put the paper in a helmet. The winning name was drawn: Bill Showers! My uncle.

Uncle Bill lived with my family, so B.J. was flown from Germany to Minneapolis, where my parents picked him up at the airport and drove him to our home in Austin, Minnesota.

I was nine years old and delighted by the addition of this wire-haired schnauzer (at least, we thought he might be a schnauzer) to our household.

According to Uncle Bill, B.J. understood many commands in both English and German. Since none of us spoke German, we had no way to prove this claim.

B.J. quickly became my dog. Although B.J. was overjoyed when my uncle arrived home after his discharge, Uncle Bill did not stay in Austin long. He got married and headed to the University of Minnesota, where dogs were not allowed in student housing. B.J. stayed with my family.

I showered him with loving attention. I brushed him, tied ribbons on his collar, took him for walks, and read aloud to him. B.J. seemed especially fond of the Raggedy Ann and Andy stories, which were favorites of mine as well.

ANALYZE THE TEXT

Main Ideas and Details What main ideas has the author included so far? How are they supported by details? Explain how these details help you relate to the author's life.

B.J. had lived with us for a year when I launched the *Dog Newspaper*. He was a fascinating front-page subject, and the first edition of the *Dog Newspaper* sold twelve copies.

Even though my lead story required little research, this sixty cents was not easy money. All those interviews about the neighbor dogs took time. Also, I grew up before there were copy machines, so I couldn't just go to the local copy center and run off twelve copies of the paper. Using a pencil, I wrote every word twelve times. Then I delivered my newspapers and collected my pay.

B.J. and I became famous on our block. Neighbors were enthralled by the story, and I gobbled up congratulations on my writing the way B.J. ate his dinner. All of my customers agreed to purchase the next issue of the *Dog Newspaper*.

Giddy with success, I immediately began writing the second issue. The neighborhood dogs were still every bit as boring as they had been a week earlier, so I decided to repeat my winning formula and use B.J. as the main article again. Since I had already told the only unusual thing about my dog, this time I wrote a story called "B.J.'s Gingerbread House."

Our new washing machine had arrived in a large cardboard box. I kept the box to create a special house for B.J., who slept in the basement every night.

I spent hours decorating the box, copying a picture of a gingerbread house that was in one of my books. I colored curlicues; I blistered my hands cutting designs in the cardboard; I painted flowers on the sides. The gingerbread house was absolutely breathtaking.

At bedtime that night, I took B.J. down to the basement and put his blanket in the beautiful gingerbread house. I petted him and kissed him and told him I knew he would sleep well.

The next morning, I couldn't believe my eyes. B.J. had licked the glue from the cardboard, creating a sticky mess in his beard, and had chewed the house into dozens of pieces. He pranced toward me through the wreckage that littered the floor.

This story was quite a bit shorter than the story of B.J.'s rescue from a bombed-out house in Germany—and far less interesting. I filled the rest of issue number two of the *Dog Newspaper* with stirring reports such as "Rusty Knocks over Garbage Can" and "Cleo Chases Cat." After I delivered my papers, I eagerly waited for more compliments on my exciting journalism. None came. The next issue was even worse. Since B.J. still had done nothing newsworthy, I used the front page to describe what a beautiful and great dog he was. The other dogs, as always, got brief mention on the back page. Desperate to fill the space, I even wrote a story titled "Skippy Gets a Bath."

Issue number three was a publishing disaster. Few people read it, and the only person who purchased issue number four was my grandpa. Less than one month after its launch, the *Dog Newspaper* went out of business.

ANALYZE THE TEXT

Fact and Opinion Why is the author's statement above, "Less than one month after its launch, the *Dog Newspaper* went out of business," a fact? What are some other facts on this page?

I believed my writing career was over. My mistake, I thought then, was always putting my own dog on the front page. Now I realize that having dull material was an even bigger error. Would the *Dog Newspaper* have succeeded if I had featured Rusty or Fluffy or Cleo? Probably not, because Rusty, Fluffy, Cleo, and all the other neighborhood dogs hadn't done anything special.

If Fluffy had gotten lost and been returned home in a police car, or if Cleo had won a prize in a dog show, or if Rusty had given birth to puppies, then perhaps the neighbors would have wanted to read my articles.

Now I know that if I want people to read what I write, I must write something that they find interesting. I need exciting plots, unique information, and fresh insights.

ANALYZE THE TEXT

Narrative Pacing At what points in the story does the author speed up or slow down the narrative? What techniques does she use to do so?

When I wrote the *Dog Newspaper*, I was so caught up in the fun of creating a newspaper and getting paid for my work that I lost sight of my audience. What was in it for them? Except for the first issue, not much.

B.J. took one more plane ride, from Minneapolis to Fresno, California, where my parents moved shortly after I got married. He loved the California sunshine and spent his old age sleeping on the patio. He lived to be sixteen, a good long life for an orphaned puppy who entered the world during a wartime bombing.

No one bothered to save any issues of the *Dog Newspaper*. I can't imagine why.

Dig Deeper

How to Analyze the Text

Use these pages to learn about Fact and Opinion, Main Ideas and Details, and Narrative Pacing. Then read "The Dog Newspaper" again to apply what you learned.

Fact and Opinion

Authors of autobiographies use both facts and opinions to tell the stories of their lives. **Facts** are pieces of information that can be proved true or false. For example, the statement "That dog is a miniature schnauzer" is a fact. A veterinarian or a dog breeder could tell you whether the statement is accurate. **Opinions** are statements that tell thoughts, feelings, or beliefs. Someone might have the opinion that miniature schnauzers are great pets. Another person might say they are too fierce.

In "The Dog Newspaper," look for facts about the author's life and also about her dog B.J. Find reasons and evidence that support the author's opinions and key points. Record details and accurate quotes from the text as you identify facts and opinions.

Facts	Opinions

RI.5.1 quote accurately when explaining what the text says explicitly and when drawing inferences; **RI.5.2** determine two or more main ideas and explain how they are supported by details/summarize; **RI.5.8** explain how an author uses reasons and evidence to support points; **RI.5.10** read and comprehend informational texts

COMMON CORE

Main Ideas and Details

Shorter texts often focus on developing only one **main idea**. The main idea is what the text is mostly about. The **details** that the author includes support this central idea. In "The Dog Newspaper," the author conveys to readers an important idea about writing. She develops her main idea by describing her experiences and by sharing her thoughts and opinions.

Narrative Pacing

Although autobiographies are nonfiction, authors may use some of the same techniques that fiction writers do to keep their readers' attention. One technique is to vary the **pacing**, or the speed at which the narrative moves along. For example, an author may slow the narrative by adding description or pausing to share thoughts about an event. A **flashback** can keep the narrative moving by telling about earlier events in a brief and interesting way.

Your Turn

RETURN TO THE ESSENTIAL QUESTION

Turn and Talk Review the selection to prepare to discuss this question: *What do facts and opinions contribute to a story?* Take turns quoting examples of facts and opinions from the selection as text evidence to support your ideas.

Classroom Conversation

Continue your discussion of "The Dog Newspaper" by explaining your answers to these questions:

1. What details make the author's story interesting to readers?

2. How could the author have made her newspaper more interesting?

3. If the author were to write a dog newspaper today, what resources would she have that she lacked years ago?

ANALYZE AUTHOR'S PURPOSE

A Different Outlook At the end of the selection, the author reflects on her early writing efforts. She offers facts and opinions about her newspaper. With a partner, analyze her reasons for including this information. Discuss what these details reveal about the author's outlook and how it has changed since she created the newspaper. Use text evidence to support your thoughts.

WRITE ABOUT READING

Response The author of "The Dog Newspaper" believes that writers attract readers by writing about interesting topics. Do you agree? Does the author thoroughly support her view in the text? Write a paragraph to explain why you agree or disagree with her claim. Examine the author's reasons and evidence, and include your own supporting details from the text.

Writing Tip

State your opinion clearly at the beginning of the paragraph. Include a conclusion that summarizes or restates the main idea you want your readers to understand.

COMMON CORE **RI.5.1** quote accurately when explaining what the text says explicitly and when drawing inferences; **RI.5.8** explain how an author uses reasons and evidence to support points; **W.5.1a** introduce a topic, state an opinion, and create an organizational structure; **W.5.1d** provide a concluding statement or section; **W.5.9b** apply grade 5 Reading standards to informational text; **SL.5.1a** come to discussions prepared/explicitly draw on preparation and other information about the topic

555

POETRY

✓ GENRE

Poetry uses the sound and rhythm of words to suggest images and express feelings in a variety of forms.

✓ TEXT FOCUS

Form Poets may use different line shapes, line lengths, and groupings of lines called *stanzas* to create rhythm, to focus a reader's attention on certain images, or to reinforce meaning.

556

Poetry About Poetry

Poetry lovers agree that a really great poem can turn an uneventful afternoon into an exciting one for the reader. The poets on these pages write about their love of poetry or about poetry itself. Think about what you like most about poetry. Is it the rhythm of the language, the images it creates, or the way it makes you feel?

To Write Poetry/ Para escribir poesía

by Francisco X. Alarcón

To Write Poetry
we must
first touch
smell and taste
every word

Para escribir poesía
debemos
primero tocar
oler y saborear
cada palabra

Genius

by *Nikki Grimes*

"Sis! Wake up!" I whisper
in the middle of the night.

    Urgently, I shake her
    till she switches on the light.

The spiral notebook in my hand
provides her quick relief.

    It tells her there's no danger
    of a break-in by a thief.

"Okay," she says, then props herself
up vertically in bed.

    She nods for me to read my work.
    I cough, then forge ahead.

The last verse of my poem leaves
her silent as a mouse.

    I worry till she says, "We have
    a genius in the house."

How would you feel if you suddenly discovered your sister or brother was a poet? Nikki Grimes writes about this in her poem "Genius." In it, she uses insights from her own background.

Grimes had always wanted a career as a poet and writer. Her first poem was accepted for publication while she was in high school and was printed in an edition of a poetry journal. She was always close to members of her household, especially her sister. As you read "Genius," think about how Grimes shows the sisters' feelings for each other.

A Seeing Poem

by Robert Froman

A SEEING POEM HAPPENS WHEN WORDS TAKE A SHAPE THAT HELPS THEM TO TURN ON A LIGHT IN SOMEONE'S MIND

Write a Concrete Poem

Write your own concrete, or seeing, poem. There is no exact formula for writing one. The only element required is that the words you use create the shape of the object or action your poem describes. For instance, how could you create a concrete poem to show the destruction B.J. caused to Peg's gingerbread house in "The Dog Newspaper"?

Compare Texts

TEXT TO TEXT

Compare Narrator and Speakers The author of an autobiography narrates his or her own story. Poets use a speaker to communicate the message of a poem. With a partner, use text evidence to identify the theme or message about writing in "The Dog Newspaper" and in each of the three poems in "Poetry About Poetry." Then discuss how the narrator or speaker in each text communicates the theme. What techniques does each writer use to convey the message?

TEXT TO SELF

Write About Yourself Think about how the author of "The Dog Newspaper" tells the story of her creation of the first issue of her neighborhood paper. What language and devices does she use to help readers relate to her experience? Write a short paragraph about an interesting project you have worked on. Present your information in ways that will help readers relate to you and your experience.

TEXT TO WORLD

Research Rescue Dogs Revisit the flashback about B.J. on pages 545–546. Think about how B.J.'s rescue and experiences helped him survive his time in Germany. Then work with a group to find information, either in print or online, about rescue dogs. Discuss whether you think B.J. would have made a good rescue dog and why.

COMMON CORE **RL.5.2** determine theme from details/summarize; **W.5.7** conduct short research projects that use several sources to build knowledge through investigation; **W.5.10** write routinely over extended time frames and shorter time frames; **SL.5.1a** come to discussions prepared/explicitly draw on preparation and other information about the topic

Grammar

Prepositions and Prepositional Phrases **Prepositions** are words that show relationships between other words in a sentence. Some common prepositions are *above*, *after*, *at*, *during*, *for*, *through*, *in*, *of*, *to*, and *with*. Prepositions convey location, time, or direction. **Prepositional phrases** begin with a preposition and end with a noun or pronoun. They add meaning and details to sentences.

Prepositions and Prepositional Phrases	
Direction	A dog walker was moving toward the park.
Time	She had been walking three dogs for an hour.
Location	She stopped at the smallest dog's home.
Additional Details	A woman with red hair happily patted her dog.

Try This! Copy these sentences onto a sheet of paper. Circle each preposition. Then underline each prepositional phrase and explain whether its function is to convey location, time, or direction, or to provide details.

1. I am the dog walker for our family's dog.

2. We always walk to the southern part of town.

3. We visit the park on Seventh Street.

4. We play fetch the stick until five o'clock.

5. I write entries in my dog walker's diary.

In your writing, you can combine two short sentences by using a prepositional phrase. If two sentences tell about one subject, you can combine them by moving a prepositional phrase from one sentence to the other.

Short Sentences

Our dog Growler chased a cat.

Growler ran into Mr. Hernandez's garden.

Combined Sentence

Our dog Growler chased a cat into Mr. Hernandez's garden.

 ## Connect Grammar to Writing

As you revise your autobiography, look for short sentences that you can combine by moving a prepositional phrase from one sentence to the other. Using a variety of sentence lengths will make your writing more interesting to read.

COMMON CORE **W.5.3a** orient the reader by establishing a situation and introducing a narrator or characters/organize an event sequence; **W.5.3b** use narrative techniques to develop experiences and events or show characters' responses; **W.5.3d** use concrete words and phrases and sensory details; **W.5.3e** provide a conclusion

Narrative Writing

☑ **Voice** The author of "The Dog Newspaper" makes her feelings clear when she says she was "giddy with success." When you revise an autobiography, add words that express your own thoughts and feelings, and include details that help your readers picture the event in your life that you are writing about.

Amanda drafted an autobiography about a special summer in her life. Later, she revised it to express her feelings more clearly and to improve her sentence fluency.

Use the Writing Traits Checklist below as you revise your writing.

 Writing Traits Checklist

Ideas

☑ Did I establish a sequence of events and provide a strong conclusion?

Organization

☑ Will my beginning grab my readers' attention?

Sentence Fluency

☑ Did I combine sentences for better flow?

Word Choice

☑ Did I use concrete words and sensory details?

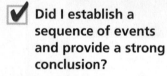

Does my narrative reveal my inner thoughts and feelings?

Conventions

☑ Did I use correct spelling, grammar, and punctuation?

Revised Draft

I ~~wanted~~ ^couldn't wait^ to show him to my best friend,

Ana. I called her and let her know that I

had a surprise, and we agreed to meet ^a^

~~There was a~~ ^at the^ neighborhood park. The real

surprise was that when I got ~~there~~ ^to the swingset^, I saw

her holding a new puppy, too. Both of our

families had adopted puppies!

Puppy Pals

by Amanda West

Two years ago, I experienced the best summer of my life. My family adopted a sweet little shelter puppy, and I fell instantly in love. We named him Max, after my grandpa, and he fit into our household instantly. I was in love from the first time I saw him!

I couldn't wait to show him to my best friend, Ana. I called her and let her know that I had a surprise, and we agreed to meet at the neighborhood park. The real surprise was that when I got to the swingset, I saw her holding a new puppy, too. Both of our families had adopted puppies!

One rainy day, when we were stuck indoors, I had a brilliant idea. I invited Ana and her puppy over for a puppy party. I put out little doggy toys and treats, but as soon as Ana arrived, the puppies started chasing each other around the house. A potted plant spilled out all over the rug. The pups grabbed a sock and played tug-of-war until it was ruined. The mess was a bit difficult to clean up, but the day was wonderful. Ana and I, and our puppies, were inseparable for that entire summer. Our dogs have become great friends, and they have allowed Ana and me to become even closer friends, as well.

Reading as a Writer

What thoughts or feelings does Amanda express in her autobiography? How can you make your thoughts and feelings clear in your writing?

In my final paper, I added words and details to show my voice and to paint a clear picture for readers. I also used prepositional phrases to combine sentences.

urge

minimum

effective

deteriorating

dependent

violations

granted

issue

ordinance

exception

Vocabulary Reader

Context Cards

COMMON CORE L.5.6 acquire and use general academic and domain-specific words and phrases

564

Vocabulary in Context

1 urge

Teachers can urge, or coax, students to get involved in helping their community.

2 minimum

The food collected by students exceeded the minimum, or least, amount needed.

3 effective

Picking up litter can be effective in keeping parks and beaches clean. It gets results.

4 deteriorating

Many deteriorating buildings will only get worse if volunteers don't help repair them.

Go Digital

▶ Study each Context Card.

▶ Use a thesaurus to find an alternate word for each Vocabulary word.

5 dependent

A literacy group may be **dependent** on volunteers. It needs them as reading tutors.

6 violations

If they pollute too much, companies can be fined for **violations** of clean air laws.

7 granted

The principal **granted**, or gave, these students and teacher permission to hold a car wash.

8 issue

Providing better care for senior citizens is an **issue**, or concern. You can help in many ways.

9 ordinance

An **ordinance**, or city law, can create volunteer community service groups.

10 exception

With the **exception** of rainy days, this class works in the school garden every day.

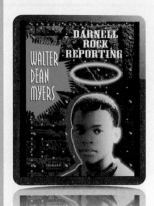

Read and Comprehend

☑ TARGET SKILL

Author's Purpose In "Darnell Rock Reporting," two characters present arguments about the best use for a piece of land near their school. As you read the story, use a graphic organizer like the one below to record details about how both arguments are presented and about how the story turns out. Then use this text evidence to identify the **author's purpose,** or reason for writing the story.

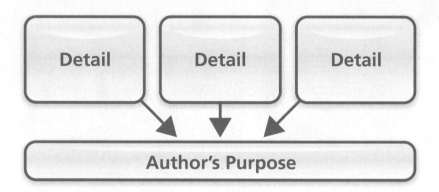

☑ TARGET STRATEGY

Summarize To help you understand the author's purpose, pause to **summarize** each part of the story, retelling the important ideas in your own words.

RL.5.2 determine theme from details/summarize

COMMON CORE

Have you ever looked around your school or community and noticed things that need improvement? In the story you are about to read, the main character does just that. He could simply wait for someone else to solve the problem. Instead, he decides to take responsibility himself.

In the real world, many people have the same reaction. That's why they get involved in community projects. Some projects are people-oriented, such as food or clothing drives. Others focus on making the community safer or more enjoyable. No matter what the project, the important thing is to get involved!

ANCHOR TEXT

✓ TARGET SKILL

Author's Purpose Examine details about the characters and their arguments to identify the author's purpose.

✓ GENRE

Realistic fiction has characters and events that are like people and events in real life. As you read, look for:

▶ realistic characters and events
▶ details that help the reader picture the setting
▶ challenges and problems that might happen in real life

COMMON CORE **RL.5.3** compare and contrast characters, settings, or events, drawing on details; **RL.5.10** read and comprehend literature; **L.5.3b** compare and contrast varieties of English in stories, dramas, or poems

568

MEET THE AUTHOR
Walter Dean Myers

Like Darnell Rock, Walter Dean Myers was nervous about speaking in public when he was young. But when his fifth-grade teacher invited students to read aloud their own writing, Myers found that he was able to relax. He began to write more and hasn't stopped since!

MEET THE ILLUSTRATOR
Jérôme Lagarrigue

Born in Paris, France, Jérôme Lagarrigue came to the United States to attend art school in the 1990s. In 2002, he won the Coretta Scott King–John Steptoe Award for best new talent for his illustration of the children's book *Freedom Summer*.

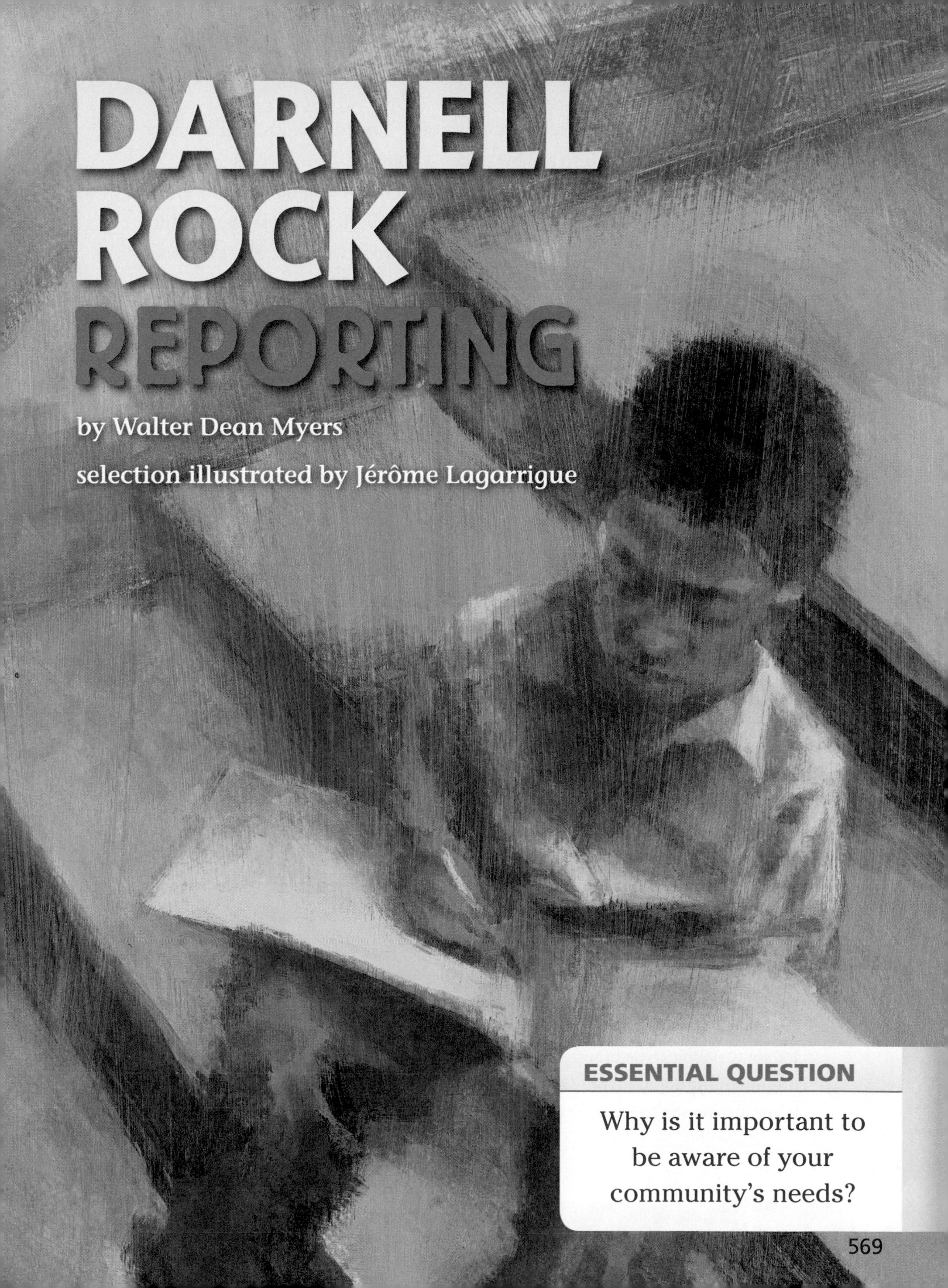

DARNELL ROCK REPORTING

by Walter Dean Myers

selection illustrated by Jérôme Lagarrigue

ESSENTIAL QUESTION

Why is it important to be aware of your community's needs?

Darnell Rock feels that his teachers only notice him, his friends, and his sister Tamika, when they get into trouble. Then a homeless man, Sweeby Jones, inspires Darnell to write an article in his school newspaper about turning a deteriorating basketball court into a garden to feed the homeless. Soon editor Peter Miller publishes Darnell's article in the town newspaper. Not everyone agrees with him, though, including student Linda Gold and teacher Miss Joyner. A city council meeting will decide what to do with the basketball court. Darnell is nervous about presenting his opinion, but his parents, and teachers like Mr. Baker and Miss Seldes, all support him. Before the meeting, everyone at school has read Darnell's article (pictured below) and an opposing article written by Linda that ran in the school newspaper (shown on page 571).

"Nobody wants to be homeless," Sweeby Jones said. He is a homeless man who lives in our city of Oakdale. It is for him and people like him that I think we should build a garden where the basketball courts were, near the school. That way the homeless people can help themselves by raising food.

"You see a man or woman that's hungry and you don't feed them, or help them feed themselves, then you got to say you don't mind people being hungry," Mr. Jones said. "And if you don't mind people being hungry, then there is something wrong with you."

This is what Mr. Sweeby Jones said when I spoke to him. I don't want to be the kind of person who says it's all right for some people to be hungry. I want to do something about it. But I think there is another reason to have the garden.

Things can happen to people that they don't plan. You can get sick, and not know why, or even homeless. But sometimes there are things you can do to change your life or make it good. If you don't do anything to make your life good, it will probably not be good.

"I was born poor and will probably be poor all my life," Mr. Sweeby Jones said.

I think maybe it is not how you were born that makes the most difference, but what you do with your life. The garden is a chance for some people to help their own lives.

Darnell Rock is a seventh-grader at South Oakdale Middle School. The school board has proposed that the site that Mr. Rock wants to make into a garden be used as a parking lot for teachers. The City Council will decide the issue tomorrow evening.

Teaching is a difficult profession. Teachers need as much support as they can possibly get. After all, we are dependent on them for our future. Education is the key to a good and secure future, and teachers help us to get that education. We must give them all the support we can. This is why I am supporting the idea of building a parking lot near the school.

There are some people in our school who think it is a good idea to build a garden so that the homeless can use it. Use it for what? Homeless people don't have experience farming and could not use the land anyway. This is just a bad idea that will help nobody and will hurt the teachers. The teachers give us good examples of how we should live and how we should conduct ourselves. The homeless people, even though it is no fault of theirs, don't give us good examples.

On Friday evening at 7:00 p.m., the City Council will meet to make a final decision. I urge them to support the teachers, support education, and support the students at South Oakdale.

"You see anybody from the school?" Larry looked over the large crowd at the Oakdale Court building.

"There goes Mr. Derby *and* Mr. Baker." Tamika pointed toward the front of the building.

Darnell felt a lump in the pit of his stomach. There were at least a hundred people at the City Council meeting.

Tamika led them through the crowd to where she had spotted Mr. Derby and South Oakdale's principal. The large, high-ceilinged room had rows of benches that faced the low platform for the City Council. Linda Gold was already sitting in the front row. Darnell saw that her parents were with her.

He had brought a copy of the *Journal* with him and saw that a few other people, grown-ups, also had copies of the paper.

The nine members of the City Council arrived, and the meeting was called to order. The city clerk said that there were five items on the agenda, and read them off. The first three items were about Building Code violations. Then came something about funding the city's library.

"The last item will be the use of the basketball courts as a parking lot at South Oakdale Middle School," the clerk said. "We have three speakers scheduled."

Linda turned and smiled at Darnell.

Darnell didn't know what Building Code violations were but watched as building owners showed diagrams explaining why there were violations. The first two weren't that interesting, but the third one was. A company had built a five-story building that was supposed to be a minimum of twenty feet from the curb, but it was only fifteen feet.

"You mean to tell me that your engineers only had fifteen-foot rulers?" one councilman asked.

"Well, er, we measured it right the first time"—the builder shifted from one foot to the other—"but then we made some changes in the design and somehow we sort of forgot about the er . . . you know . . . the other five feet."

To Darnell the builder sounded like a kid in his homeroom trying to make an excuse for not having his homework.

"Can you just slide the building back five or six feet?" the Councilman asked.

Everybody laughed and the builder actually smiled, but Darnell could tell he didn't think it was funny.

Somebody touched Darnell on his shoulder, and he turned and saw his parents.

"We have this ordinance for a reason," a woman on the Council was saying. "I don't think we should lightly dismiss this violation. An exception granted here is just going to encourage others to break the law."

"This is going to ruin me," the builder said. "I've been in Oakdale all of my life and I think I've made a contribution."

"Let's have a vote." The head of the Council spoke sharply.

"Let's have a vote to postpone a decision," the woman who had spoken before said. "We'll give Mr. Miller an opportunity to show his good faith."

"What do you want me to do?" the builder asked.

"That's up to you," the woman said.

"Next time you'd better get it right!" Tamika called out.

"She's right," the councilwoman said.

There was a vote, and the decision was postponed. The builder gave Tamika a dirty look as he pushed his papers into his briefcase.

The city library funding was next, and eight people, including Miss Seldes, spoke for the library, but the Council said it didn't have any more money. There was some booing, including some from Tamika and Larry. Darnell knew that if he didn't have to speak he would have enjoyed the meeting.

"The issue at South Oakdale is should the old basketball courts be used as a parking lot, or should they be used as a community garden?"

"Who's going to pay for paving the lot?" a councilman asked. "Does it have to be paved?"

"It's my understanding that it doesn't have to be paved," the head of the Council answered. "Am I right on that?"

"Yes, you are," Miss Joyner spoke up from the audience.

"We have two young people from the school to speak," the councilwoman said. "The first is a Miss Gold."

Linda went into the middle aisle, where there was a microphone. She began reading her article in the snootiest voice that Darnell had ever heard. He felt a knot in his stomach. He turned to look at his mother, and she was smiling. On the stage some of the councilmen were looking at some papers.

"I hope I don't mess up," he whispered to Tamika.

"You won't," Tamika said.

Linda finished reading her article and then turned toward Darnell.

"Although everybody would like to help the homeless," she said, "schools are supposed to be for kids, and for those who teach kids! Thank you."

There was applause for Linda, and Miss Joyner stood up and nodded toward her. Darnell felt his hands shaking.

Darnell's name was called, and he made the long trip to the microphone.

"When I first thought about having a garden instead of a parking lot, I thought it was just a good idea," Darnell said. "Then, when the *Journal* asked me to send them a copy of my interview with Mr. Jones, I was thinking that it was mainly a good idea to have a garden to help out the homeless people. But now I think it might be a good idea to have the garden to help out the kids—some of the kids—in the school.

"Sometimes, when people go through their life they don't do the things that can make them a good life. I don't know why they don't do the right thing, or maybe even if they know what the right thing is sometimes.

"But I see the same thing in my school, South Oakdale. Some of the kids always do okay, but some of us don't. Maybe their parents are telling them something, or maybe they know something special. But if you're a kid who isn't doing so good, people start off telling you what you should be doing, and you know it, but sometimes you still don't get it done and mess up some more. Then people start expecting you to mess up, and then *you* start expecting to mess up. Teachers get mad at you, or the principal, or your parents, and they act like you're messing up on purpose. Like you want to get bad marks and stuff like that. Then you don't want people getting on your case all the time so you don't do much because the less you do the less they're going to be on your case. Only that doesn't help anything, and everybody knows it, but that's the way it goes."

"You seem to be doing all right, young man," the head of the City Council said.

"I wasn't doing too hot before," Darnell said, taking a quick look over to where Mr. Baker sat. "But when I got on the paper and the *Journal* printed my article, then everybody started treating me different. People came up to me and started explaining their points of view instead of just telling me what to do. And you people are listening to me. The kids I hung out with, they called us the Corner Crew, are mostly good kids, but you wouldn't listen to them unless they got into trouble.

"In South Oakdale some kids have bad things happen to them—like they get sick—and I don't know why that happens, but all they can do is to go to the hospital. And some kids just get left out of the good things and can't find a way of getting back into them. People get mad at them the same way they get mad at the homeless people or people who beg on the street. Maybe the garden will be a way for the homeless people to get back into some good things, and maybe seeing the homeless people getting back into a better life will be a way for some of the kids to think about what's happening to them. Thank you."

ANALYZE THE TEXT

Characterization How are Linda's and Darnell's arguments different in tone and purpose? What do their actions and arguments reveal about each character?

577

There was some applause as Darnell turned to go back to his seat.

"Just a minute, young man," one of the councilmen called to him. "The girl said that these people don't know anything about raising a garden. Is that true?"

"It doesn't matter," someone said from the audience. "I'm from the college, and we can help with technical advice."

"I didn't ask you," the councilman said.

"I'm telling you anyway," the man said.

"I don't know how effective a community garden would be," the councilman said. "You can't feed people from a garden."

"You could sell what you grow," Darnell heard himself saying.

"I think bringing people who are . . . nonschool people into that close a contact with children might not be that good an idea," the councilman said. "Who's the last speaker?"

"A Mr. Jones," the clerk said. Sweeby came into the middle aisle, and a lot of people began to talk among themselves. There were a lot of things they were interested in, and most of them were not interested in the school parking lot.

"I just wanted to ask you why you don't want to listen to this boy," Sweeby asked.

"You have four minutes to speak," the councilman said. He seemed angry. "We don't have to answer your questions."

"You don't have to answer my questions," Sweeby said. "And you don't have to have the garden. You don't have to think about us—what did you call us?—nonschool people?

"But it's a shame you don't want to listen to this boy. I wish he had been my friend when I was his age. Maybe I would be sitting in one of your seats instead of being over here."

"Is there anything more?" the councilman asked.

"No, you can just forget about the whole thing now," Sweeby said. "Go on back to your papers."

"I think we can vote on this issue now," the councilman said. "I think Mr."—the councilman looked at the agenda to find Darnell's name—"Mr. Darnell Rock had some good points, but it's still a tough issue. Let's get on with the vote."

The vote went quickly. Three councilpeople decided not to vote, five voted against the garden, and only one voted for it.

Darnell took a deep breath and let it out slowly. Tamika patted him on his hand. When he looked at her she had tears in her eyes.

Darnell felt he had let Sweeby down. His father patted him on his back, and Miss Seldes came over.

"You did a good job," she said. "Really good."

"I lost," Darnell said.

"Sometimes you lose," Miss Seldes said. "But you still did a good job."

ANALYZE THE TEXT

Dialogue Compare and contrast the different tones and words that the meeting participants use. How do their different ways of speaking make the story more realistic?

Sweeby and some of his friends were waiting outside the Council meeting, and they shook hands with Darnell. Sweeby was telling him how the members of the Council didn't really care about people when Darnell saw Linda through the crowd. She waved and he waved back. She was smiling.

Larry's mother came over and asked his father for a lift home, and they were waiting for Larry when Peter Miller from the *Journal* came over.

"Hey, you want to write another article for the paper?" he said. "There's a guy who wants to donate a couple of lots for a garden in another location. My boss wants to run it as a human interest piece."

"Yeah, sure," Darnell said. "You want a long article or a short one?"

"I don't know. Call the paper tomorrow and ask for the city desk," the reporter said. "My editor will give you the word count."

"Okay!" Darnell said.

ANALYZE THE TEXT

Author's Purpose Why do you think the author focuses primarily on Darnell's argument in the story? What do you think the author wants readers to learn from Darnell's experience?

581

Dig Deeper

How to Analyze the Text

Use these pages to learn about Author's Purpose, Dialogue, and Characterization. Then read "Darnell Rock Reporting" again to apply what you learned.

Author's Purpose

The author of "Darnell Rock Reporting" has a **purpose,** or reason, for writing his story. He wants to convey to his readers a particular **theme,** or message about life. The author creates a contrast between two characters, Darnell and Linda, to reveal his message.

As you reread the story, note details about Darnell's relationship with the homeless man, his article in the newspaper, his speech before the city council, and his feelings. Also look for text evidence related to Linda's argument, her speech, and her character. Finally, note how the story ends. Why does the author focus more on Darnell's argument than on Linda's? How does this focus help you identify the theme and the author's purpose for writing?

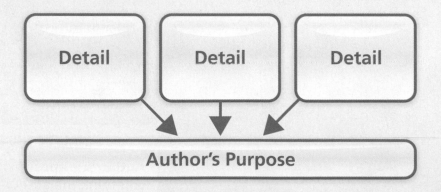

| Detail | Detail | Detail |

Author's Purpose

RL.5.2 determine theme from details/summarize; **RL.5.3** compare and contrast characters, settings, or events, drawing on details; **RL.5.10** read and comprehend literature; **L.5.3b** compare and contrast varieties of English in stories, dramas, or poems

Dialogue

Dialogue adds realism to a story and reflects characters' purposes and feelings. For instance, Sweeby Jones says to the council, "I just wanted to ask you why you don't want to listen to this boy." The councilman responds angrily, "You have four minutes to speak. We don't have to answer your questions." Sweeby's tone is respectful. The councilman's is scornful. The dialogue shows the characters' differences.

Characterization

Characterization includes all the ways in which an author shows readers what a character is like. Authors might describe a character's words, actions, and feelings, and show how other characters respond to him or her. For example, Miss Seldes congratulates Darnell on his speech. Her admiration reinforces readers' impression that Darnell is a person worthy of respect. This kind of text evidence can help you get to know story characters. Details about characters can also help you compare and contrast them.

Your Turn

 Turn and Talk Review the selection to prepare to discuss this question: *Why is it important to be aware of your community's needs?* Use text evidence and your prior knowledge to support your answer.

 Classroom Conversation

Continue your discussion of "Darnell Rock Reporting" by using text evidence to explain your answers to these questions:

1. What does Darnell think is needed for people to reach their potential and to succeed?

2. What do you think Darnell learns about himself from his experience at the city council meeting?

3. Is this story realistic? Explain.

POWERS OF PERSUASION

Partner Discussion Think about the speeches that Linda and Darnell give at the city council meeting. With a partner, discuss how the two students use persuasion to gain support for their arguments. Then evaluate which student is more convincing and why. Point out quotes from the text that support your position.

WRITE ABOUT READING

Response Do you agree with the city council's vote against the garden proposal? Do you think they made their decision based on the facts that Linda and Darnell presented, or for some other reason? Write a paragraph explaining your view on whether the council made the right decision in voting down the garden. Use quotes and details from the story as evidence to support your position.

Writing Tip

State your opinion at the beginning of your paragraph. Be sure to include strong reasons and text evidence to support it.

COMMON CORE **RL.5.1** quote accurately when explaining what the text says explicitly and when drawing inferences; **W.5.1a** introduce a topic, state an opinion, and create an organizational structure; **W.5.1b** provide logically ordered reasons supported by facts and details; **W.5.9a** apply grade 5 Reading standards to literature; **SL.5.1a** come to discussions prepared/explicitly draw on preparation and other information about the topic

PERSUASIVE TEXT

Volunteer!
by Derek Green

Persuasive text is meant to convince readers to think or act in a certain way. It includes an opinion or argument, as well as support such as examples and reasons.

Parts of an Argument
A strong argument contains a clearly stated opinion and logical reasons for why readers should agree with that opinion. The writer of an argument can also support his or her opinion with examples, quotes from experts, details, and facts.

Is there something in your community that you wish could be improved or changed?
Is there a person in your neighborhood who could use some help? If you're hoping for someone to come along and make a difference, that someone could be you! Volunteering your time is a great way to connect with others and make a difference in your community. And you'll feel good about doing something that helps people or improves the places around you.

Plant a garden!

COMMON CORE RI.5.8 explain how an author uses reasons and evidence to support points; RI.5.10 read and comprehend informational texts

 Go Digital

Join a beach clean-up!

This past summer, my friends and I started to notice how messy and neglected our neighborhood park had become. We wanted it to be different. We worked with our parents and teachers to organize a community restoration project. People came and volunteered their time to clean up the park grounds, fix the broken basketball hoop and swings, and paint the playground equipment. We had a great time making the park even better than it used to be, and now the whole neighborhood is able to share and enjoy it again.

Have a food drive!

FOOD DRIVE

FOOD
DRIVE
DONATE

Here are some more volunteer ideas:

Collect donations of pet food and give them to animal shelters.

Be a reading buddy to a younger student.

Help a neighbor take care of his lawn.

Gather new or gently used toys and deliver them to a children's hospital.

Help at a shelter!

Maybe cleaning up a park isn't quite what you have in mind, though. No problem! You can turn anything that matters to you into a volunteer project. Do you like playing chess, reading and studying, or spending time with your pet? There are places in your community that would love to have you volunteer to do the kinds of things you already enjoy. For example, you could volunteer at a senior center. Some seniors have families that live far away and can't visit often, and you could make their days better simply by talking or playing board games with them. If you're great at math or English, you could volunteer to be a homework helper at your school or community library. Animal shelters are always looking for volunteers to walk dogs, play with cats, or keep cages clean and food bowls filled. Most of these places will let kids volunteer if they have permission from their parents or guardians.

If you're more interested in community drives, some groups use volunteers to collect various items for people who need them. Homeless shelters often need blankets and toiletries—items such as soap, deodorant, and toothbrushes. Food banks need canned goods and other nonperishable items. Choose a cause and ask family members and friends for donations of these kinds of items. Touch base with the group first, to be sure of what they need and how to get it to them.

With so many volunteering opportunities available, there is something for everyone. Whether you want to clean up your neighborhood, help people in your community, or collect items for those in need, your time and effort will be appreciated— and that always feels good. Kids everywhere are making a difference by volunteering. You can, too!

Compare Texts

TEXT TO TEXT

Compare Arguments Both Darnell's newspaper article and the selection "Volunteer!" try to persuade readers to support community projects. With a partner, complete a two-column chart comparing the positions, reasons, and types of supporting details each author uses in his argument. Then discuss which you think offers more convincing evidence and why. Share your opinions with your classmates.

TEXT TO SELF

Write to Persuade Imagine that you are a reporter covering a cause that needs support in your community. Write a paragraph in which you describe the cause, what is needed from volunteers, and why it is important. Remember to include a call to action that will motivate readers to help!

TEXT TO WORLD

Discuss Media Techniques Work with a small group to think of a community or national issue that has been covered in various media. Make a list of where you have seen information about the issue, such as in newspaper articles, print ads, commercials, and documentaries. Then discuss how the different kinds of media present the issue. Consider how written text, sound effects, video, narration, and other techniques contribute to an overall message.

COMMON CORE **RI.5.8** explain how an author uses reasons and evidence to support points; **W.5.10** write routinely over extended time frames and shorter time frames; **SL.5.1a** come to discussions prepared/explicitly draw on preparation and other information about the topic

Grammar

More Kinds of Pronouns A **pronoun** is a word that takes the place of a noun. There are several kinds of pronouns. Words such as *someone* and *something* refer to a person or thing that is not identified. These pronouns are called **indefinite pronouns**. Pronouns that replace possessive nouns are called **possessive pronouns**. Words such as *who*, *what*, and *which* can be used to begin questions. These pronouns are called **interrogative pronouns**.

Pronouns	Examples
indefinite pronoun	Anyone can become a gardener here.
possessive pronoun	Mr. McGowan never had his own yard.
interrogative pronoun	What is that orange vegetable in the garden?

Try This! Copy each sentence below onto a sheet of paper. Underline each indefinite pronoun. Circle each possessive pronoun. Draw a box around each interrogative pronoun.

1. Who is the woman in the purple bonnet?

2. Everyone in the garden asks that woman for advice!

3. Her tomatoes are the biggest and reddest!

4. Which is Mr. Jackson's garden plot?

5. The plot with the sunflowers is his plot.

Possessive pronouns can help you avoid repeating proper nouns in your writing. When you use possessive pronouns, be sure that your readers will be able to understand to whom each possessive pronoun refers.

Excessive Use of Proper Noun

Carla will present Carla's proposal at the council meeting tonight. Carla's mother and aunt will attend the meeting, along with Carla's cousin. Carla has used their ideas in Carla's proposal.

Improved with Use of Possessive Pronoun

Carla will present her proposal at the council meeting tonight. Her mother and aunt will attend the meeting, and Carla's cousin will be there, too. Carla has used her mother's and aunt's ideas in her proposal.

 Connect Grammar to Writing

As you revise your personal narrative next week, make sure you have used possessive pronouns effectively. Check to see that readers will understand to whom each possessive pronoun refers.

COMMON CORE **W.5.4** produce writing in which development and organization are appropriate to task, purpose, and audience; **W.5.5** develop and strengthen writing by planning, revising, editing, rewriting, or trying a new approach; **W.5.8** recall information from experiences or gather information from print and digital sources/summarize and paraphrase information and provide a list of sources

Narrative Writing

Reading-Writing Workshop: Prewrite

✓ **Ideas** Good writers explore their ideas before they draft. You can collect your ideas for a **personal narrative** on an events chart. List the main events in the order they happened, and then add interesting details about each event.

Rama decided to write about his Warm Coat Project. First, he jotted down the notes below. Then he organized them in a chart.

Exploring a Topic

Topic:	My Warm Coat Project
What?	coat wouldn't fit in closet
Why?	too many coats
	other people need coats
How?	persuaded family members
	did research on Internet
Where?	took coats to an agency

Writing Process Checklist

▶ **Prewrite**

✔ Did I consider my audience and purpose?

✔ Did I choose a topic that I am eager to write about?

✔ Did I explore my topic to recall important events and interesting details from my experience?

✔ Did I list the events in the order in which they happened?

Draft

Revise

Edit

Publish and Share

Event: I tried to hang my coat in the closet.

Details: The closet was too full. Mom told me to clean up.

↓

Event: I saw how many coats we don't wear and got an idea to donate extras to people in need.

Details: I put the coats in piles. Mom wasn't happy about the mess.

↓

Event: I talked my family into giving coats to those who can't afford to buy them.

Details: My family loved my idea and agreed to donate coats.

↓

Event: I found an agency that gives away coats.

Details: We delivered our coats and learned more were needed.

↓

Event: I started a coat drive.

Details: Friends and relatives agreed to help out. Next year, I will get help from my whole school.

Reading as a Writer

How did Rama organize his events chart? Which parts of your chart can you organize more clearly?

In my events chart, I organized my ideas into main events and details. I added a new event and some details I remembered.

✓ TARGET VOCABULARY

piercing
descended
savage
quivered
delicacy
fitful
heave
diminishing
rhythmic
marveling

Vocabulary Reader   Context Cards

COMMON CORE   **L.5.4a** use context as a clue to the meaning of a word or phrase

Vocabulary in Context

1 piercing
The wind made a high, piercing sound as it whipped through the palms.

2 descended
The surfer descended on the face of the wave and turned sharply to continue riding.

3 savage
The savage snarl of a leopard is something no explorer wants to hear!

4 quivered
At the first sound of thunder, the wild horses quivered and bolted across the prairie.

Go Digital

▶ Study each Context Card.

▶ Use the context of each sentence to clarify the meaning of the Vocabulary word.

5 **delicacy**

Fruit would have been a delicacy for the crew, but none could be found on the island.

6 **fitful**

This boy had a fitful sleep after reading an adventure story last night. He is very tired.

7 **heave**

Divers often heave, or lift up, at least one large artifact as proof of their discovery.

8 **diminishing**

Overfishing is diminishing, or decreasing, the supply of fish.

9 **rhythmic**

The rhythmic sound of waves continuously beating the shore is relaxing.

10 **marveling**

For centuries, people have been marveling at the beauty of dramatic sunsets.

Read and Comprehend

✓ TARGET SKILL

Story Structure As you read "The Black Stallion," identify the setting and the main character. Then look for the **conflict** (the central problem faced by the main character), important plot events, and the **resolution** of the conflict. Use a graphic organizer like the one shown below to help you chart the overall structure of the story.

Setting	Character
Plot	
Conflict: Events: Resolution:	

✓ TARGET STRATEGY

Question As you read "The Black Stallion," ask yourself **questions** about the story structure. Where does the story take place? What is the main character's problem? What does he do to solve his problem? If you are unsure of the answers, reread the text to find the information.

Human-Animal Interaction

On any neighborhood street, you may see dogs walking with their owners and cats lounging in sunny windows. These animals and many others have a long history of interacting with humans. Thousands of years ago, people realized how animals could help them. Sheep, cows, and goats could supply them with wool and milk. Horses and oxen could pull carts and plows. Dogs could herd sheep. Cats could catch mice and other pests. In return, people could provide the animals with food, shelter, and protection.

"The Black Stallion" is a story about the interaction between a boy and a wild horse. Both the boy and the horse can benefit from the relationship, but first the boy must earn the horse's trust.

ANCHOR TEXT

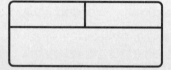

☑ TARGET SKILL

Story Structure Note details about the setting and characters. Trace important plot events.

☑ GENRE

Adventure stories include exciting action that takes place in unusual settings. As you read, look for:

- ▶ a mood of excitement or suspense
- ▶ an ongoing conflict or multiple conflicts
- ▶ characters who show strong personal qualities

RL.5.2 determine theme from details/ summarize; **RL.5.5** explain how chapters, scenes, or stanzas fit together to provide the overall structure; **RL.5.10** read and comprehend literature

MEET THE AUTHOR

Walter Farley

Walter Farley turned a childhood love of horses into his life's work. He began writing *The Black Stallion* when he was just 16 years old. The novel was published 10 years later while he was still in college. From there, Walter Farley went on to raise horses and write over 30 books during his lifetime. Many of those books are part of the popular *Black Stallion* series.

MEET THE ILLUSTRATOR

Robert Barret

In addition to being an incredibly talented painter, muralist, and illustrator, Robert Barret is also an award-winning college art professor. He has studied painting in Europe and exhibited his work in several museums and galleries.

The Black Stallion

by Walter Farley

illustrations by Robert Barret

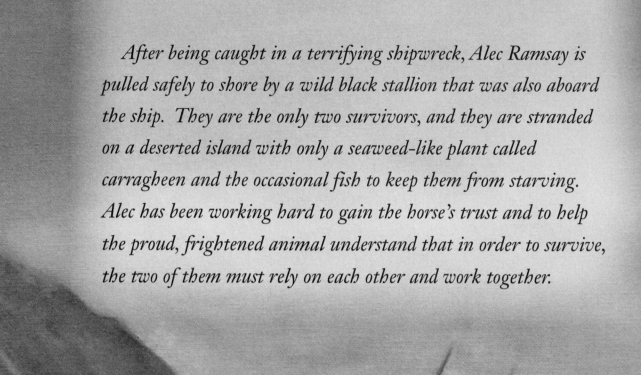

After being caught in a terrifying shipwreck, Alec Ramsay is pulled safely to shore by a wild black stallion that was also aboard the ship. They are the only two survivors, and they are stranded on a deserted island with only a seaweed-like plant called carragheen and the occasional fish to keep them from starving. Alec has been working hard to gain the horse's trust and to help the proud, frightened animal understand that in order to survive, the two of them must rely on each other and work together.

The next day Alec set out to obtain more of the carragheen. As he neared the rocks, he saw the stallion standing silently beside a huge boulder. Not a muscle twitched in his black body—it was as if an artist had painted the Black on white stone.

Alec climbed down into a small hollow and paused to look out over the rocks below. Suddenly he heard the stallion's scream, more piercing, more blood-curdling than he had ever heard it before. He looked up.

The Black was on his hind legs, his teeth bared. Then with a mighty leap, he shot away from the boulder toward Alec. Swiftly he came—faster with every magnificent stride. He was almost on top of him when he thundered to a halt and reared again. Alec jumped to the side, tripped on a stone and fell to the ground. High above him the Black's legs pawed the air, and then descended three yards in front of him! Again he went up and down—again and again he pounded. The ground on which Alec lay shook from the force of his hoofs. The stallion's eyes never left the ground in front of him.

Gradually his pounding lessened and then stopped. He raised his head high and his whistle shrilled through the air. He shook his head and slowly moved away, his nostrils trembling.

Alec regained his feet and cautiously made his way toward the torn earth, his brain flooded with confusion. There in front of him he saw the strewn parts of a long, yellowish-black body, and the venomous head of a snake, crushed and lifeless. He stood still—the suddenness of discovering life, other than the Black and himself on the island, astounding him! Sweat broke out on his forehead as he realized what a poisonous snake bite would have meant—suffering and perhaps death! Dazed, he looked at the stallion just a few feet away. Had the Black killed the snake to save him? Was the stallion beginning to understand that they needed each other to survive?

Slowly the boy walked toward the Black. The stallion's mane swept in the wind, his muscles twitched, his eyes moved restlessly, but he stood his ground as the boy approached. Alec wanted the horse to understand that he would not hurt him. Cautiously he reached a hand toward the stallion's head. The Black drew it back as far as he could without moving. Alec stepped closer and to the side of him. Gently he touched him for an instant. The stallion did not move. Again Alec attempted to touch the savage head. The Black reared and shook a little. Alec said soothingly, "Steady, Black fellow, I wouldn't hurt you." The stallion quivered, then reared again and broke. One hundred yards away he suddenly stopped and turned.

Alec gazed at him, standing there so still—his head raised high in the air. "We'll get out of this somehow Black—working together," he said determinedly.

ANALYZE THE TEXT

Story Structure What does the author do early in the story to help you understand the **conflict**, or problem, that Alec faces?

603

Alec walked back to the top of the rocks and again began his descent. He made his way carefully down to the water level. Cautiously he looked before he stepped—where there was one snake there might be more. Reaching the bottom, he once again filled his shirt full of the moss and made his way back. High above him he could see the Black looking out over the cliffs, his mane whipping in the wind. When he reached the top the stallion was still there. He followed a short distance behind as Alec went back to the spring.

Days passed and gradually the friendship between the boy and the Black grew. The stallion now came at his call and let Alec stroke him while he grazed. One night Alec sat within the warm glow of the fire and watched the stallion munching on the carragheen beside the pool. He wondered if the stallion was as tired of the carragheen as he. Alec had found that if he boiled it in the turtle shell it formed a gelatinous substance which tasted a little better than the raw moss. A fish was now a rare delicacy to him.

The flame's shadows reached out and cast eerie ghostlike patterns on the Black's body. Alec's face became grim as thoughts rushed through his brain. Should he try it tomorrow? Did he dare attempt to ride the Black? Should he wait a few more days? Go ahead— tomorrow. *Don't do it!* Go ahead—

The fire burned low, then smoldered. Yet Alec sat beside the fire, his eyes fixed on that blacker-than-night figure beside the spring.

The next morning he woke from a fitful slumber to find the sun high above. Hurriedly he ate some of the carragheen. Then he looked for the Black, but he was not in sight. Alec whistled, but no answer came. He walked toward the hill. The sun blazed down and the sweat ran from his body. If it would only rain! The last week had been like an oven on the island.

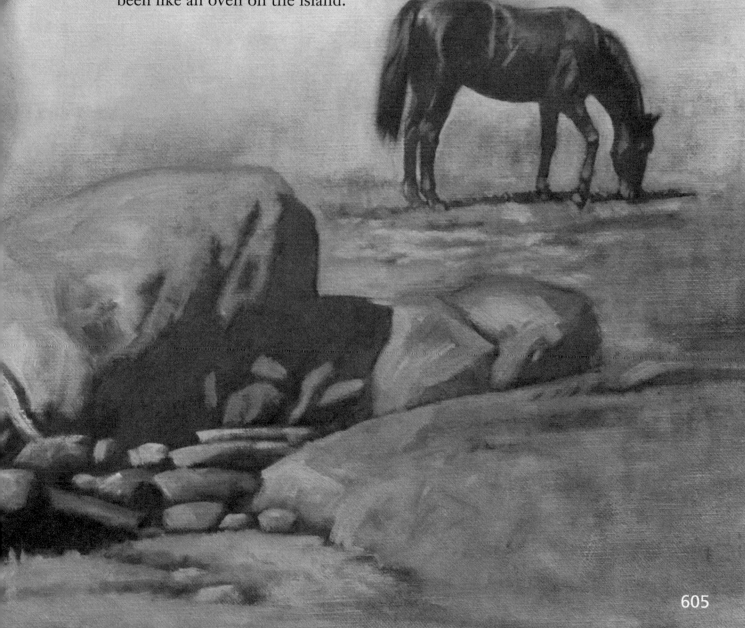

When he reached the top of the hill, he saw the Black at one end of the beach. Again he whistled, and this time there was an answering whistle as the stallion turned his head. Alec walked up the beach toward him.

The Black stood still as he approached. He went cautiously up to him and placed a hand on his neck. "Steady," he murmured, as the warm skin quivered slightly beneath his hand. The stallion showed neither fear nor hate of him; his large eyes were still turned toward the sea.

For a moment Alec stood with his hand on the Black's neck. Then he walked toward a sand dune a short distance away. The stallion followed. He stepped up the side of the dune, his left hand in the horse's thick mane. The Black's ears pricked forward, his eyes followed the boy nervously—some of the savageness returned to them, his muscles twitched. For a moment Alec was undecided what to do. Then his hands gripped the mane tighter and he threw himself on the Black's back. For a second the stallion stood motionless, then he snorted and plunged; the sand went flying as he doubled in the air. Alec felt the mighty muscles heave, then he was flung through the air, landing heavily on his back. Everything went dark.

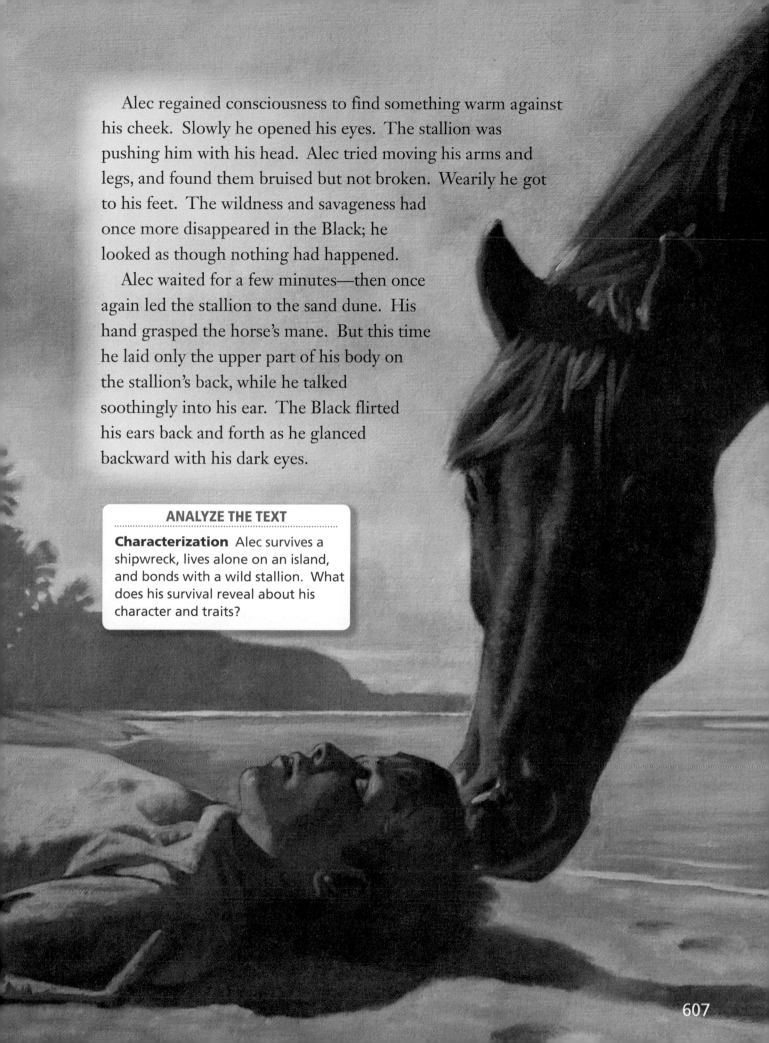

Alec regained consciousness to find something warm against his cheek. Slowly he opened his eyes. The stallion was pushing him with his head. Alec tried moving his arms and legs, and found them bruised but not broken. Wearily he got to his feet. The wildness and savageness had once more disappeared in the Black; he looked as though nothing had happened.

Alec waited for a few minutes—then once again led the stallion to the sand dune. His hand grasped the horse's mane. But this time he laid only the upper part of his body on the stallion's back, while he talked soothingly into his ear. The Black flirted his ears back and forth as he glanced backward with his dark eyes.

ANALYZE THE TEXT

Characterization Alec survives a shipwreck, lives alone on an island, and bonds with a wild stallion. What does his survival reveal about his character and traits?

"See, I'm not going to hurt you," Alec murmured, knowing it was he who might be hurt. After a few minutes, Alec cautiously slid onto his back. Once again, the stallion snorted and sent the boy flying through the air.

Alec picked himself up from the ground—slower this time. But when he had rested, he whistled for the Black again. The stallion moved toward him. Alec determinedly stepped on the sand dune and once again let the Black feel his weight. Gently he spoke into a large ear, "It's me. I'm not much to carry." He slid onto the stallion's back. One arm slipped around the Black's neck as he half-reared. Then like a shot from a gun, the Black broke down the beach. His action shifted, and his huge strides seemed to make him fly through the air.

Alec clung to the stallion's mane for his life. The wind screamed by and he couldn't see! Suddenly the Black swerved and headed up the sand dune; he reached the top and then down. The spring was a blur as they whipped by. To the rocks he raced, and then the stallion made a wide circle—his speed never diminishing. Down through a long ravine he rushed. Alec's blurred vision made out a black object in front of them, and as a flash he remembered the deep gully that was there. He felt the stallion gather himself; instinctively he leaned forward and held the Black firm and steady with his hands and knees. Then they were in the air, sailing over the black hole. Alec almost lost his balance when they landed but recovered himself in time to keep from falling off! Once again the stallion reached the beach, his hoofbeats regular and rhythmic on the white sand.

The jump had helped greatly in clearing Alec's mind. He leaned closer to the stallion's ear and kept repeating, "Easy, Black. Easy." The stallion seemed to glide over the sand and then his speed began to lessen. Alec kept talking to him. Slower and slower ran the Black. Gradually he came to a stop. The boy released his grip from the stallion's mane and his arms encircled the Black's neck. He was weak with exhaustion—in no condition for such a ride! Wearily he slipped to the ground. Never had he dreamed a horse could run so fast! The stallion looked at him, his head held high, his large body only slightly covered with sweat.

That night Alec lay wide awake, his body aching with pain, but his heart pounding with excitement. He had ridden the Black! He had conquered this wild, unbroken stallion with kindness. He felt sure that from that day on the Black was his—his alone! But for what— would they ever be rescued? Would he ever see his home again? Alec shook his head. He had promised himself he wouldn't think of that any more.

The next day he mounted the Black again. The horse half-reared but didn't fight him. Alec spoke softly in his ear, and the Black stood still. Then Alec touched him lightly on the side, and he walked—a long, loping stride. Far up the beach they went, then Alec tried to turn him by shifting his weight, and gently pushing the stallion's head. Gradually the horse turned. Alec took a firmer grip on his long mane and pressed his knees tighter against the large body. The stallion broke out of his walk into a fast canter. The wind blew his mane back into the boy's face. The stallion's stride was effortless, and Alec found it easy to ride. Halfway down the beach, he managed to bring him back again to a walk, then to a complete stop. Slowly he turned him to the right, then to the left, and then around in a circle.

Long but exciting hours passed as Alec tried to make the Black understand what he wanted him to do. The sun was going down rapidly when he walked the stallion to the end of the beach. The Black turned and stood still; a mile of smooth, white sand stretched before them.

Suddenly the stallion bolted, almost throwing Alec to the ground. He picked up speed with amazing swiftness. Faster and faster he went. Alec hung low over his neck, his breath coming in gasps. Down the beach the stallion thundered. Tears from the wind rolled down Alec's cheeks. Three-quarters of the way, he tried to check the Black's speed. He pulled back on the flowing mane. "Whoa, Black," he yelled, but his words were whipped away in the wind.

Swiftly the stallion neared the end of the beach, and Alec thought that his breathtaking ride of yesterday was to be repeated. He pulled back harder on the mane. Suddenly the Black's pace lessened. Alec flung one arm around the stallion's neck. The Black shifted into his fast trot, which gradually became slower and slower, until Alec had him under control. Overjoyed he turned him and rode him over the hill to the spring. Together they drank the cool, refreshing water.

ANALYZE THE TEXT

Theme How does Alec respond when faced with challenges? How do his actions and responses help you determine the story's theme?

With the days that followed, Alec's mastery over the Black grew greater and greater. He could do almost anything with him. The savage fury of the unbroken stallion disappeared when he saw the boy. Alec rode him around the island and raced him down the beach, marveling at the giant strides and the terrific speed. Without realizing it, Alec was improving his horsemanship until he had reached the point where he was almost a part of the Black as they tore along.

Dig Deeper

How to Analyze the Text

Use these pages to learn about Story Structure, Characterization, and Theme. Then read "The Black Stallion" again to apply what you learned.

Story Structure

The term **story structure** refers to the important parts of a story. These parts include the **setting**, **characters**, **conflict**, events, and **resolution**. The conflict, or problem, is usually introduced near the beginning of the story. The setting may play a major part in causing this conflict. The characters' efforts to resolve the conflict may lead to further challenges. The story becomes more and more exciting, until finally the conflict is resolved.

The setting, main character, and conflict of "The Black Stallion" are introduced in the note on page 600. The events that follow, woven into story scenes, fit together to provide the overall structure of the text.

Setting	Characters
Plot	
Conflict: **Events:** **Resolution:**	

COMMON CORE **RL.5.2** determine theme from details/summarize; **RL.5.5** explain how chapters, scenes, or stanzas fit together to provide the overall structure; **RL.5.10** read and comprehend literature

Characterization

The author of an adventure story reveals characters' qualities through what they do, say, and think. This process is called **characterization**. In "The Black Stallion," Alec is shipwrecked on a deserted island with only a wild horse for company. The way he responds to this challenge reveals his inner qualities. As you reread the story, think about Alec's actions and what they show about him.

Theme

The **theme** of a story is the message about life or human nature that the author shares with readers. This message is brought out through the characters' actions, especially in response to conflict. How a character changes or the way a character interacts with others may also suggest a theme. What theme or message do Alec's actions and experiences convey to you?

Your Turn

RETURN TO THE ESSENTIAL QUESTION

 Turn and Talk Review the selection to prepare to discuss this question: *What can a person learn by building a relationship with an animal?* In a small group, share your ideas, supporting them with text evidence and your own experiences.

 Classroom Conversation

Continue your discussion of "The Black Stallion" by using text evidence to answer these questions:

1 How does the author make the incident with the snake exciting and suspenseful for readers?

2 How does bonding with the horse help Alec survive on the island?

3 What do you think is the most important first step in building an animal's trust?

TALK ABOUT WORDS

List It What words and phrases help you "see" the black stallion in your mind? How does the author bring Alec's relationship with the horse to life? With a partner, list words and phrases that help you visualize the story's action and characters. Include powerful verbs and sensory language. Share your list with your classmates.

"he thundered to a halt and reared again"

WRITE ABOUT READING

Response In what ways does Alec's last ride on the stallion differ from his first attempt? What does this difference show about the relationship between the boy and the horse? Write a paragraph in which you explain how Alec's relationship with the stallion changes over the course of the selection. Support your explanation with details from each major interaction Alec has with the horse. Use direct quotations and other text evidence.

Writing Tip

State your main idea in the first sentence of your paragraph. Then connect your ideas by using transitional words, phrases, and clauses.

RL.5.1 quote accurately when explaining what the text says explicitly and when drawing inferences; **RL.5.3** compare and contrast characters, settings, or events, drawing on details; **W.5.9a** apply grade 5 Reading standards to literature; **SL.5.1a** come to discussions prepared/explicitly draw on preparation and other information about the topic; **SL.5.1c** pose and respond to questions, make comments that contribute to the discussion, and elaborate on others' remarks

COMMON CORE

GENRE

Informational text gives readers information about a person, topic, event, or idea. It may include text and graphic features such as headings, captions, and photographs.

TEXT FOCUS

Tone is a writer's attitude toward the topic he or she has written about. A text can have more than one tone. In this selection, the writer's tone is interested, respectful, and friendly. It highlights the special connection between humans and horses.

Horse Power

by Keelah Malcolm

People and horses have been companions for thousands of years. Before cars and trains, we used horses to do work and to travel from place to place. We still use horses to help round up cattle on ranches and to move about on large farms. Mounted police officers use horses to patrol crowded events such as concerts and fairs. We even use horses to compete in sporting events such as polo matches and horse races. More and more, however, people with special needs are using horses to make their lives better.

Guide Horses

You already know that dogs can be guides for blind people, but did you know that horses can be as well? In the United States, some people train miniature horses to act as guide animals. Why miniature horses instead of dogs? Horses live longer. Dogs live an average of twelve years, while miniature horses can live for twenty to thirty years. With an extended lifespan, horses are able to bond with and help their handlers for a much longer time than dogs. Guide horses also provide an alternative for people who are allergic to or afraid of dogs.

Caring for a guide horse can be hard work. A guide horse's handler needs to lift heavy bags of feed and bales of hay, and refill buckets—not bowls—of water. The handler also needs to clean up after the horse and keep it groomed. Even though a guide horse is small, it must have a large outdoor space where it can roam and exercise when it is not working. Learning to trust a guide horse takes time, too, and most handlers go through special training themselves in order to be matched to the right companion. For people who are willing and able to put in the effort, a guide horse can be a helper they will love and rely on for many years.

A guide horse helps this young woman to travel and to learn in the classroom.

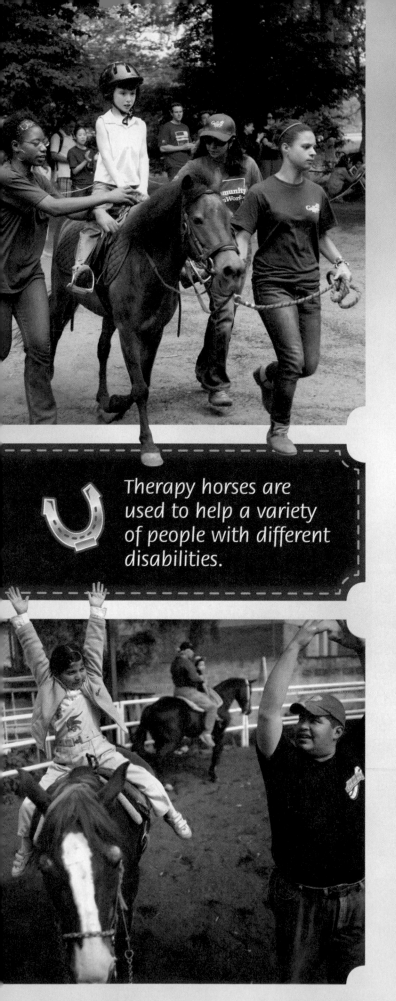

Therapy horses are used to help a variety of people with different disabilities.

Therapy Horses

Some standard-sized horses are trained to work in other ways with people who have special needs. These horses are called therapy horses, and they can help people both physically and emotionally. For example, people with physical disabilities often have weak muscle tone. Learning to ride a horse helps them strengthen their muscles so they can support themselves more easily. Riding also helps them improve their balance and coordination— all while having fun!

Some children with autism have trouble forming connections with the people around them. With therapy horses, they get a chance to form a connection with an animal. They learn to brush and care for the horse, which helps them learn about the needs of a living being. Some of these children don't communicate much, or at all, with family or friends. However, riding a horse is new and exciting. Sometimes, the experience is exciting enough that a child will begin to communicate with the horse by using gestures or calling the horse by name.

The relationship between people and horses is a special one. Horses are hard workers and can provide hours of pleasure as riding companions, but perhaps their most treasured quality is their ability to bond with people who need their help. Talk about horse power! There is no denying the healing benefits of spending time with these remarkable animals.

Compare Texts

TEXT TO TEXT

Compare Approaches to Theme Both Alec in "The Black Stallion" and Travis in "Old Yeller" (Lesson 7) have life-changing experiences with animals. What lessons can each character's experience teach about the potential for humans and animals to work together? With a partner, compare and contrast these lessons. Use evidence from both texts to support your ideas about their common theme.

TEXT TO SELF

Write a Story If you could befriend any wild animal, which would it be, and why? What would the experience be like? Write an imaginative story about your special relationship with the animal and how the two of you interact. Create an interesting plot with vivid details. Share your completed story with a small group.

TEXT TO WORLD

Research Wild Horses With a partner, find out more about the history of wild horses. Use print and electronic sources to find facts about the origin of wild horses, the different breeds, and the locations of various herds. Then write a paragraph summarizing what you find.

COMMON CORE **RL.5.2** determine theme from details/summarize; **RL.5.9** compare and contrast stories in the same genre on their approaches to themes and topics; **W.5.3b** use narrative techniques to develop experiences and events or show characters' responses; **W.5.7** conduct short research projects that use several sources to build knowledge through investigation

Grammar

What Are the Mechanics of Writing Titles? You have learned to capitalize proper nouns and important words in titles of various kinds. In handwritten work, you should **underline** titles of longer works, such as books, movies, and plays. In word-processed papers, these types of titles should be set in **italics**. Place titles of shorter works, such as stories, poems, and songs, inside quotation marks in both written and word-processed work.

Have you read <u>The Call of the Wild</u>, by Jack London?

Have you read *The Call of the Wild*, by Jack London?

Let's sing "Doggie in the Window."

You can also use underlining and italics for emphasis.

I <u>love</u> movies about friendships between humans and animals.

I *love* movies about friendships between humans and animals.

Try This! **Write each sentence on a sheet of paper. Capitalize proper nouns and important words in titles. Underline titles of longer works. Place titles of shorter works in quotation marks.**

1. The book Wild Horses has information about the early ancestors of horses.

2. Can you sing Mary Had a little lamb to us?

3. The movie The incredible Journey is a favorite of mine.

4. I've written a short story called Horse sense.

Your readers will have an easier time reading and understanding what you write if you check your work carefully to eliminate errors in the capitalization, punctuation, and mechanics of titles.

Incorrect	Correct
I love the scenes where Alec and the horse struggle to survive on the island. I even wrote a poem about them called Team survival. I can't wait to read "The Black Stallion Returns!"	I love the scenes where Alec and the horse struggle to survive on the island. I even wrote a poem about them called "Team Survival." I can't wait to read *The Black Stallion Returns!*

 Connect Grammar to Writing

As you edit your personal narrative, correct any errors you find in mechanics. Pay special attention to titles and proper nouns. Remember that you can also use italics and underlining for emphasis.

W.5.3a orient the reader by establishing a situation and introducing a narrator or characters/organize an event sequence; **W.5.3b** use narrative techniques to develop experiences and events or show characters' responses; **W.5.3c** use transitional words, phrases, and clauses to manage the sequence of events; **W.5.3d** use concrete words and phrases and sensory details; **W.5.3e** provide a conclusion

Narrative Writing

Reading-Writing Workshop: Revise

✔ **Voice** A good **personal narrative** tells about an important or interesting event in your life in ways that only you can express. As you draft, remember to use transitional words, phrases, and clauses to connect events and details. When you revise your narrative, add words and ideas that let the reader "hear" your own voice.

Rama used his events chart to draft a narrative about his Warm Coat Project. Later, he added a new opening to grab his readers' attention.

Writing Process Checklist

Prewrite

Draft

▶ **Revise**

☑ Did I begin with an attention-grabber?

☑ Did I include only important events and tell them in order?

☑ Did I use dialogue and sensory details?

☑ Do my feelings come through?

☑ Are my sentences smooth and varied?

☑ Does my conclusion show how the events worked out?

Edit

Publish and Share

Revised Draft

"What's this jacket doing on the floor?" demanded my mother.

"No room in the closet, that's what," I replied.

~~My mother~~ She told me to hang up ~~my~~ it anyway, of course. ~~coat.~~

~~Squeezing~~ my fat winter jacket into our overstuffed hall closet, I had a brainstorm.

"What's causing this closet to be crowded?" I thought. "There are only four of us Ramdevs."

(As I was trying to squeeze)

624

My Warm Coat Project

by Rama Ramdev

"What's this jacket doing on the floor?" demanded my mother.

"No room in the closet, that's what," I replied. She told me to hang it up anyway, of course.

As I was trying to squeeze my fat winter jacket into our overstuffed hall closet, I had a brainstorm. "What's causing this closet to be crowded?" I thought. "There are only four of us Ramdevs."

I started pulling everything out. Before long, I saw the problem. We all had at least one coat we didn't use anymore. When my mother came back and frowned at the mess I'd made, I quickly explained my idea. "We should give our extra coats away to people who need them."

The next day, with help from my mother and our local community center, I launched my Warm Coat Project. Now the Ramdevs have a neat closet, and other people are staying warm in their new coats. I can hardly wait for next winter, when I can get my entire school involved in a coat drive that will help members of our community who are in need!

Reading as a Writer

How does Rama's opening capture his readers' interest? Where could you add dialogue or interesting details in your story?

In my final paper, I added dialogue to grab readers' attention. I also used transitions to clarify the sequence of events.

Read the articles "Skateboarding Through the Decades" and "The Ollie and the Rock and Roll." As you read, stop and use text evidence to answer each question.

Skateboarding Through the Decades

Skateboarding has been around for more than fifty years. It all began in the 1950s. When the waves were flat and real ocean surfing wasn't an option, surfers who still wanted to have some fun decided they might be able to "surf the sidewalks." Someone came up with the idea of attaching roller skate wheels to the bottom of a wooden board, and the sport of skateboarding was born.

In the early 1960s, companies began manufacturing huge numbers of skateboards. More than 50 million of them were sold in just three years. Skateboarding competitions were organized. A famous music group even sang a number called "Sidewalk Surfing" while riding a skateboard across the stage. Then, in the late 1960s, the sport's popularity crashed, and it seemed that the fad was over.

The sport picked up again, however, after Frank Nasworthy developed urethane skateboard wheels in the early 1970s. Wheels made from this tough material gave a smooth and stable ride. Other improvements were made, too. Now skateboarders had better control and could do new tricks, such as the "ollie." In this trick, the skater kicks the tail of the board down while jumping, causing the board to pop into the air. During the 1970s, concrete skate parks sprang up.

 1 Why did skate parks spring up in the 1970s, after it had seemed that the fad was over?

Through the years, many skate parks were forced to close when insurance rates skyrocketed. With fewer skate parks, skaters in the 1980s took to the streets looking for places to skate. Any place that offered a ramp, a wall, or a set of steps would do. Some people constructed wooden skate ramps in their back yards or in empty lots.

In 1995, the sport gained greater attention when ESPN's Extreme Games televised skateboarding events. Skateboarding stars appeared in commercials, and skateboarding clothing became a fashion style. The sport had begun to make a comeback.

 COMMON CORE **RI.5.1** quote accurately when explaining what the text says explicitly and when drawing inferences; **RI.5.2** determine two or more main ideas and explain how they are supported by details/summarize; **RI.5.5** compare and contrast the overall structure in two or more texts; **RI.5.9** integrate information from several texts on the same subject

As the new century rolled around, so did the wheels of millions of skateboards. Many cities built new skate parks, and skateboarding camps were established in some places. There was even a new holiday created in 2004 to recognize skateboarding. Every year on June 21, skateboarders around the globe take part in Go Skateboarding Day. It will be exciting to see what new developments occur in the sport of skateboarding in the decades to come!

Extreme Sports Journal

 2   What two main ideas can you identify in this article? Explain how each main idea is supported by details.

The Ollie and the Rock and Roll

Experienced skateboarders do tricks that seem to defy gravity. There are many kinds of skateboarding tricks, and new ones are always being invented. Two of the most common tricks you may see skateboarders do are the ollie and the rock and roll.

The ollie was invented in 1978 by Alan Gelfand, whose nickname was Ollie. This trick has been a major influence on skateboarding ever since. The basic form of the ollie involves jumping in such a way that both skateboard and rider soar through the air. When you watch an ollie, you might think the skateboard is tied onto the skater's feet or held on by magnets, but of course that is not the case.

In doing a rock and roll, the skateboard doesn't fly through the air, as it does in an ollie. However, a rock and roll is equally impressive. The skater rides up a steep ramp, such as those found in skate parks. The front trucks, or steering devices, of the skateboard hang over the top edge of the ramp. Then the skater pivots on the back trucks to face in the opposite direction before riding back down the ramp.

Both tricks require a great deal of skill and a lot of practice. To master the ollie, a skater first needs to get the skateboard rolling. Then the skater crouches low and suddenly springs upward. The skater's back foot slaps the tail of the skateboard so that the tail hits the ground. The force created by striking the ground propels the board into the air.

To complete the ollie, the skater shifts his or her weight. Friction between shoe soles and the board is used to bring the board level in the air. It is amazing to see how high off the ground some skaters can get and how long they can stay up there. When the board lands, the skater's knees are bent to soften the impact.

Shifting one's weight plays an important role in doing a rock and roll, as well. As the skater approaches the top of the ramp, he or she leans forward to get the front trucks over the top edge of the ramp. By shifting his or her weight and moving the arms, the rider then rocks the board up. When the move is done correctly, the front trucks pop up. Then the skater pivots swiftly. When the front trucks hit the ramp again, it is important for the skater's weight to be toward the front of the board.

 3 What kind of text structure is used in this article? How does it differ from the text structure used in the previous article?

There are several variations on the rock and roll. Most depend on which way the skater turns, as well as other factors. The ollie is the basis for a great many other tricks. For inventing this enduring and versatile trick, Alan Gelfand was named to the skateboarding hall of fame in 2002.

 4 What have you learned about the topic of skateboarding from the information given in both articles?

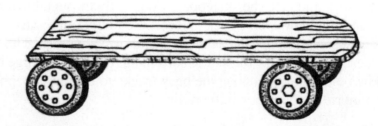

Unit 5

Vocabulary in Context

pace

undoubtedly

seep

evident

factor

vain

mirages

shuffled

salvation

stunted

Vocabulary
Reader

Context
Cards

1 pace

Pony Express riders rode at a fast pace in order to deliver mail as quickly as possible.

2 undoubtedly

Westbound travelers were undoubtedly glad to make it across the mountains alive.

3 seep

If a storm lasted awhile, rain could seep through protective clothes and hats.

4 evident

When it is evident, or obvious, that a wagon wheel is broken, it is repaired or replaced.

Go Digital

▶ Study each Context Card.

▶ Make up a new context sentence that uses two Vocabulary words.

5 factor

The weather was just one **factor**, or element, that determined the speed of a journey.

6 vain

These pioneers made a **vain**, or fruitless, attempt to cross the river. It was too deep.

7 mirages

Travelers could be fooled by **mirages**. It was a blow to learn these visions were false.

8 shuffled

The journey was tiring. Many walkers **shuffled** slowly along the trail after a few weeks.

9 salvation

A freshwater spring could be the **salvation** of thirsty travelers, saving their lives.

10 stunted

Only small, **stunted** trees can grow in the harsh desert conditions of the Southwest.

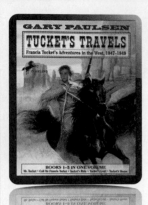

Read and Comprehend

☑ TARGET SKILL

Sequence of Events As you read "Tucket's Travels," look for words and phrases that help you determine the **sequence of events**. For example, words such as *first*, *last*, *until*, *before*, and *after* can signal the order in which events happened. Use a graphic organizer like this one to record events from the selection and to analyze how the scenes fit together to provide the overall structure.

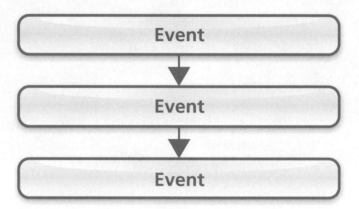

☑ TARGET STRATEGY

Visualize Use text details to help you **visualize** the action in the story. Creating mental pictures of what is happening makes the story more vivid and interesting.

Extreme Environments

Weather on the American plains can be severe. Thunderstorms, wind, hail, lightning, extreme heat and cold, and pounding rain are just some of the hazards that people traveling in the region encounter.

In "Tucket's Travels," set in the mid-1800s, you will read about a fifteen-year-old boy and two younger children who are traveling through the region. They are in danger because some men are hunting them, but a tremendous thunderstorm with hail and lightning changes their fate.

ANCHOR TEXT

✓ TARGET SKILL

Sequence of Events Identify the time order in which events take place.

✓ GENRE

Historical fiction is a story set in the past. It contains characters, places, and events that actually existed or happened, or that could have existed or happened. As you read, look for:

▶ a setting that was a real time and place in the past

▶ details that show the story took place in the past

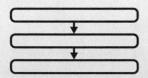 **RL.5.5** explain how chapters, scenes, or stanzas fit together to provide the overall structure; **RL.5.10** read and comprehend literature; **L.5.5a** interpret figurative language in context

Go Digital

MEET THE AUTHOR

Gary Paulsen

Gary Paulsen's characters often rely on wilderness survival skills to survive tough situations. Paulsen sometimes recreates a scene, such as digging for water, in real life so that he can write about it from a firsthand perspective. He has lived in many places, including the Alaskan wilderness and on a boat in California.

MEET THE ILLUSTRATOR

Bill Farnsworth

To create illustrations for a story, Bill Farnsworth travels to its location, takes photographs, and sketches. Then he's ready to paint. He says, "My goal is to give the viewer a sense of what the main character in the story is feeling, so you can imagine yourself actually there!"

TUCKET'S TRAVELS

by Gary Paulsen

selection illustrated by Bill Farnsworth

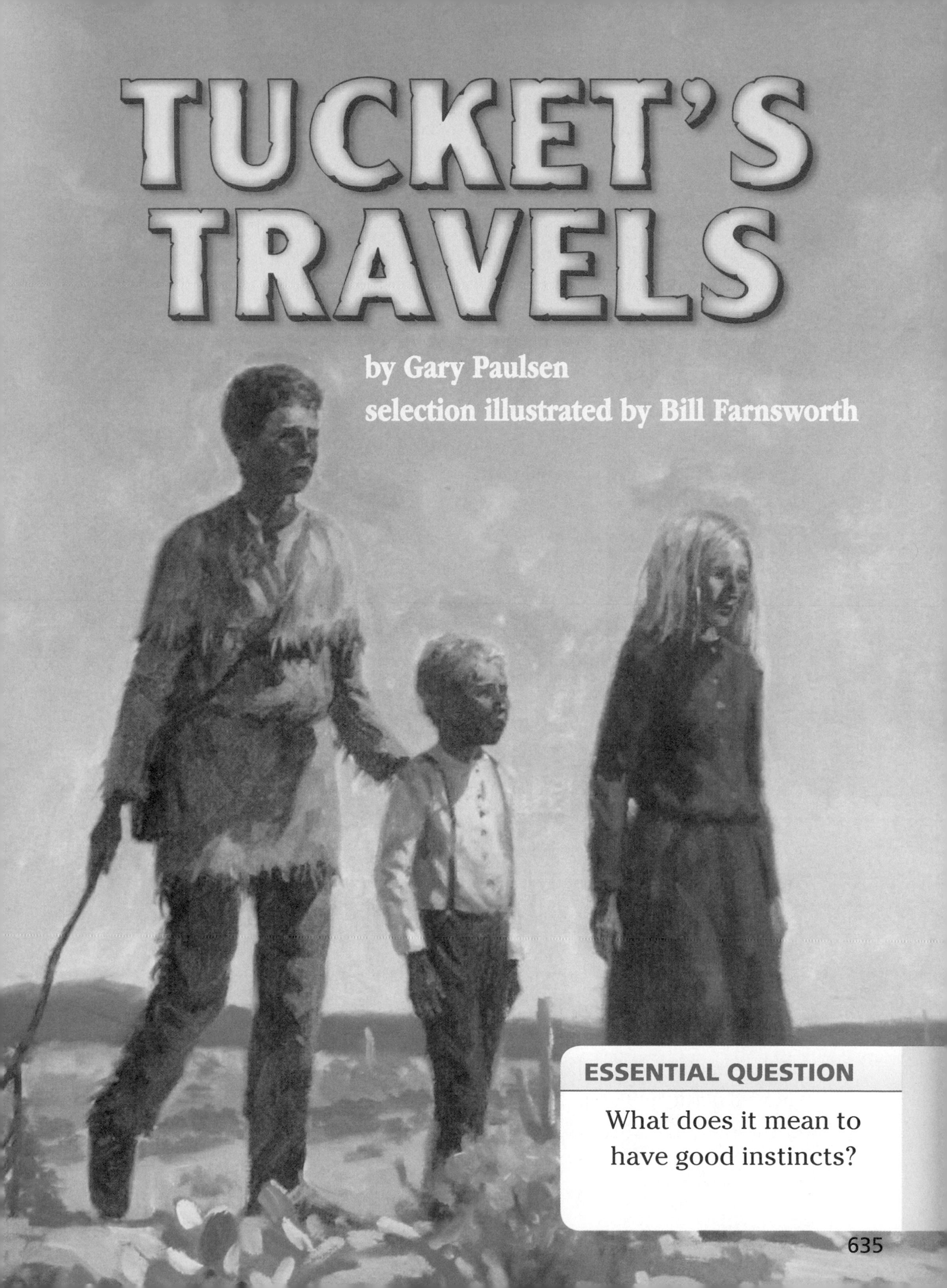

ESSENTIAL QUESTION

What does it mean to have good instincts?

If there was one thing Francis Tucket knew with certainty it was that death was close to taking them.

Dawn was coming and here he was, a fifteen-year-old boy in charge of two children, walking across a sunbeaten, airless plain that seemed to be endless. Francis, Lottie and Billy had no food or water or any immediate hope of getting any, and at any moment a dozen or two of the dirt-meanest men Francis had ever seen in a world *full* of mean men could come riding up on them and . . .

He didn't finish the thought. There was no need. Besides, in surviving Indian fights, blizzards, battles and thieves, he had learned the primary rule about danger. It would come if it would come. You could try to be ready for it, you could plan on it, you could even expect it, but it would come when it wanted to come.

Lottie and Billy understood this rule too. He had found them sitting in a wagon on the prairie all alone. Their father had died of cholera (KAHL ur uh) and their wagon train had abandoned the family, afraid of disease. Lottie had been nine then, Billy six. Francis hadn't thought he and the children would stay together long—after all, he had to keep searching for his own family. He'd been separated from them a year before, when Pawnees had kidnapped him from the wagon train on the Oregon Trail. But Francis and Lottie and Billy—well, they were used to each other. They stuck together. Unlike Francis and Jason Grimes, the one-armed mountain man.

Jason Grimes had rescued Francis from the Pawnees and taught him how to survive in the West on his own. Then they'd parted ways.

Until last night. Last night when Grimes had helped them to escape from the Comancheros (koh mahn CHEH rohs). The Comancheros were an outlaw band, ruthless, terrifying, inhumanly tough. To escape, Grimes had had to take the packhorses Francis and Lottie and Billy had been riding and lead them off empty, hoping the Comancheros would follow his tracks westward while the three children headed north on foot in the dark of night.

It was a decent plan—it was their *only* plan—and it seemed to be working. As Francis and the two children had moved north in the dark, they had seen the Comancheros ride past them after Mr. Grimes, tracking the horses. The Comancheros had missed the footprints of the children, partly because it was hard to see them and partly because Francis made Lottie and Billy walk in each other's footprints. He came last, brushing out the trail with a piece of mesquite behind him.

But luck was the major factor in the plan. If the Comancheros caught Grimes or even got within sight of him they'd know that Francis and the children weren't with him. They'd turn and come back for the children. Children meant real money because they could be sold or traded into slavery.

Francis knew that brushing out the tracks would only work in the pitch dark of night. In daylight the brush marks themselves would be easy to follow.

"I'm tired." Billy stopped suddenly. "I think we've gone far enough."

Francis frowned. When Francis had first met Billy, the boy wouldn't say a word. And now he'd gone from never talking at all to complaining.

"If they catch us they'll skin you," warned Lottie. "Now keep walking. If we don't keep moving they'll be on us like dogs, won't they, Francis? On us just like dogs . . ."

Lottie loved to talk, would talk all the time if she had the chance, seemed to have been talking since Francis had found her in that wagon. Lottie would explain every little detail of every little part of every little thing she was talking about so that not a single aspect of it was missed, and she sometimes drove Francis over the edge. Now, as Billy started moving again, Francis picked up the pace, pushed them as hard as they could stand it and then harder, and Lottie didn't have breath left to speak.

Dawn brought the sun and the sun brought heat. Francis and the children were bareheaded and the sun quickly went to work on them. Billy wanted to complain, especially as the morning progressed and there was no water and the sun rose higher and became hotter, but Francis drove them until Billy began to weave. Then Francis picked Billy up and carried him piggyback, mile after mile, then yard after yard, and finally, step after step.

ANALYZE THE TEXT

Sequence of Events What steps do Francis and the children take to escape the Comancheros during the night? What is happening now that it is day?

Lottie saw it first.

"There," she said. "See the spot?"

Francis was near dead with exhaustion. He had hardly slept at all for the two nights before and had been used roughly by the Comancheros in the bargain. He was close to the breaking point as he said, "What spot?"

"There. No, more to the right. On the horizon. It's trees. I'm sure of it. A stand of trees."

They had seen many mirages—images of trees and water that were not there. But Francis looked where she was pointing and saw it instantly. He stopped and set Billy down. The boy was asleep, and he collapsed in a heap, still sleeping. "You're right! Trees. And trees mean water."

He turned and studied the horizon. He hadn't been able to look up when carrying Billy and he was shocked now to see a plume of dust off to the west and south. It was at least fifteen miles away, against some hills in the distance. It was so far away that it seemed tiny, but Francis knew it was probably caused by riders, many riders.

Lottie saw him staring.

"Could it be buffalo?" She watched the dust. "A small herd?"

Not here, Francis thought. Not here in this dust and heat with no grass and no water. Buffalo wouldn't be that stupid. "Sure. It's buffalo."

"You're lying." She sighed. "I can tell when you're lying to me, Francis Tucket. It's them, isn't it?"

Francis said nothing but his mind was racing. So the riders were heading back eastward. But why would they be coming back so soon? Had they caught Grimes already? If so they'd be looking for the children. Or had they given up the chase or just seen Grimes and found that he was alone and turned back, still looking for the children? They might miss the tracks . . .

He knew this was a vain hope. There hadn't been a breath of wind to blow the dust over the brush marks he'd left, and undoubtedly they had men who were good trackers, men who were alive because they could track mice over rocks. So the Comancheros would find them and then . . . and then . . .

He looked to the trees, which were about two miles away. He could carry Billy there. They could get to the trees in time. Then what? The riders would keep coming back until they came to the place where Francis and the children had turned off, about nine miles back. They would see the marks and turn and start north. Nine miles. The horses would be tired but they would make ten miles an hour. They had to ride maybe twenty miles back to the turn and then nine or ten miles north after the children. He let the figures work through his tired brain. Maybe four hours but more likely three. The riders would be on them in three hours.

Francis and Billy and Lottie would need an hour to make the trees and then . . . and then nothing.

It would all just happen later. They'd get him and take the children and nothing would have changed except that a few horses would be very tired and he, Francis, would be dead.

And as for what would happen to Lottie and Billy—his heart grew cold. But there was something else back there, more than just the plume of dust. There was a cloud. At first it was low on the horizon and showed only as a gray line, so low that Francis almost didn't see it. But it was growing rapidly, the wind bringing it from the west, and as it grew and rose he could see that it was the top edge of a thunderhead.

It didn't *look* like salvation, not at first. He had seen plenty of prairie thunderheads but as he watched it he realized two things.

One, it was growing rapidly, roaring along on the high winds, coming toward them at a much faster rate than the horses of the Comancheros. Two, it would bring rain.

642

Rain that would ease their thirst and cool their burning bodies and, far more important, rain that might wipe out their tracks, erase everything they had left behind them.

Still, it was a race, and nothing was sure. The clouds had to keep coming to beat the horsemen to where the children's tracks turned north. And it had to rain.

If the clouds turned off or didn't beat the Comancheros or didn't leave rain, then distance was all the children had. They needed to get to the trees and build some kind of defense.

Francis picked up Billy, who was still sound asleep and seemed to weigh a ton. He set off at a shambling walk, abandoning the tedious brushing in their race to get to the trees. Lottie shuffled ahead, carrying Francis's bag. She was wearing a ragged shift so dirty it seemed to be made of earth. Her yellow hair was full of dust. Francis wore buckskins, but the children only had what was left of their original clothing and what they'd managed to pick up along the way.

We're a sight, Francis thought. A ragtag mob of a sight.

He looked at the trees and they didn't seem any closer.

He looked at the cloud and it was still building, though it seemed to be heading off slightly to the south.

He looked at the dust plume and it was still moving on the same line eastward, getting ready to cross their trail.

He looked back to the trees and thought, I would absolutely kill for that old mule we had. But the mule had been taken by the Comancheros.

ANALYZE THE TEXT

Author's Word Choice What vivid verbs and adjectives does the author use to show the terrible circumstances these characters are in?

They reached the trees just as the edge of the clouds caught up with them.

"Ten more feet and I would have died," Lottie whispered, and sank to the ground.

Francis dropped Billy like a stone—the boy fell without awakening—and studied their location. It was a meandering dry streambed with a row of stunted but leafy cottonwoods on each side. There were also stands of salt cedar, thick and green, and while no water was evident the streambed seemed moist. Francis knew there was water beneath the surface or the trees would have been dead.

"Lottie, scoop a hole there, at the base of that rock."

"You want to start digging, why don't you just go ahead? I have more important things to do than scrape at the old ground."

"Water." Francis was so dry he croaked. "Dig down and let it seep in."

"Oh. Well, why didn't you say so?" Lottie knelt by the rock and started digging in the loose sand with her hands. When she was down two feet, she yelped.

"Here it is! Just like you said, coming in from the sides. Oh, Francis, it's so clear, come see." She scooped some up and drank it. "Sweet as sugar. Come, try it."

Francis knelt and cupped his hand and drank and thought he had never tasted anything so good. But he stopped before he was full.

The wind was picking up now, blowing hard enough to lift dust and even sand, and he could no longer see the dust from the riders. The wind was blowing at the coming thunderheads and he smiled because even if it didn't rain there was a good chance the wind would fill in and destroy their tracks.

By now the thunderhead was over them, dark, so huge it covered the whole sky, and the wind had increased to a scream.

ANALYZE THE TEXT

Figurative Language A **metaphor** is a description that compares one thing to another thing without using *like* or *as*. What metaphor does the author use on this page to describe the sound of the wind? Explain the metaphor's meaning.

"Over here!" Francis yelled to Lottie. "Beneath this ledge." Incredibly, Billy was still asleep. Francis grabbed the boy and shook him until his eyes opened. "Get over by that rock ledge. Everything is going to break loose—"

A bolt of lightning hit so close Francis felt it ripple his hair, so close the thunder seemed to happen in the same split instant, and with it the sky opened and water fell on them so hard it almost drove Francis to his knees. He had never seen such rain. There seemed to be no space between the drops; it roared down, poured down in sheets, in buckets. Francis couldn't yell, couldn't think, couldn't breathe. He held Billy by the shirt and dragged him in beneath the ledge that formed the edge of the streambed, away from the trees and out of the wind.

Lottie was there already and they huddled under the overhang just as the clouds cracked again and hail the size of Francis's fist pounded down. One hailstone glanced off the side of his head and nearly knocked him out.

"Move in more," he yelled over the roar of the storm. "Farther back—*move!*"

He pushed against Billy, who slammed into Lottie. They were already up against the clay bank beneath the ledge and could not go farther in. Francis's legs and rear were still out in the hail and took a fearful beating. He doubled his legs up but even so the pain was excruciating and though the large hailstones quickly gave way to smaller ones, his legs were immediately stiff and sore.

The streambed filled in the heavy downpour. Luckily they were near the upstream portion of the storm and so avoided the possibility of a flash flood—which would have gouged them out of the overhang and taken them downstream to drown. As it was, the water came into the pocket beneath them and turned the dirt to mud and soon they were sitting in a waist-deep hole of thick mud and water. And just as soon, in minutes, the rain had stopped, the clouds had scudded away and the sun was out, cooking the mud dry.

Aching, Francis pulled himself into the sun. The children crawled after. Water still ran in the stream but was receding quickly. The hot sun felt good, and Francis wanted to take his buckskin shirt off to hang. But he knew that if he didn't keep wearing it the shirt would dry as stiff as a board.

He straightened slowly, working the pain out of his legs. He looked to the west and smiled.

There would be no tracks after *that*.

Dig Deeper

How to Analyze the Text

Use these pages to learn about Sequence of Events, Figurative Language, and Author's Word Choice. Then read "Tucket's Travels" again to apply what you learned.

Sequence of Events

Writers of historical fiction often structure their plots as a **sequence of events**. They present the events in chronological order, or time order. This structure helps clarify the relationships between events. One event leads to another, and excitement builds until the story reaches its conclusion.

To indicate the sequence of events, authors may use signal words and phrases such as *last night*, *then*, *now*, and *later*. Look back at page 644. In the sentence "They reached the trees just as the edge of the clouds caught up with them," the phrase *just as* tells you that the two events happened at the same time.

As you track the sequence of events, keep in mind that this story contains a **flashback**. Which part of the text interrupts the story's main action to describe events that happened at an earlier time? How does this scene affect the story's structure?

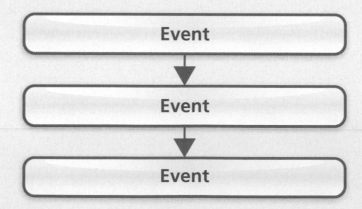

Event

↓

Event

↓

Event

RL.5.4 determine the meaning of words and phrases, including figurative language; **RL.5.5** explain how chapters, scenes, or stanzas fit together to provide the overall structure; **RL.5.10** read and comprehend literature; **L.5.5a** interpret figurative language in context

Figurative Language

One type of figurative language used by writers is **metaphor**. A metaphor compares two unlike things, showing how they are similar in some way. Metaphors do not use the word *like* or *as*. Instead, metaphors say that one thing is another. For example, "The plane was a graceful silver bird overhead" describes an airplane by comparing it to a bird.

Author's Word Choice

To make readers feel and see the action of a story, authors rely on powerful, **vivid words**. These kinds of words paint a picture for readers of what is happening. Look back at page 647. Instead of saying that the rain *fell* down, the author uses the verb *roared*. This choice of verb helps readers visualize a powerful storm and imagine the sound of the rain.

Your Turn

RETURN TO THE ESSENTIAL QUESTION

 Turn and Talk Review the selection with a partner to prepare to discuss this question: *What does it mean to have good instincts?* As you review the story, discuss words and phrases that help explain what kinds of instincts Francis has about safety and danger.

 Classroom Conversation

Continue discussing "Tucket's Travels" by using text evidence to explain your answers to these questions:

1. Why wasn't Francis entirely comfortable with the plan to evade the Comancheros?

2. Was Billy truly aware of the danger that they were in? Why or why not?

3. What roles did skill and luck play in the outcome of the story?

COMPARE STORY SETTINGS

Use a Venn Diagram In the story, the action takes place in two settings—a desert-like plain and a small stand of trees. With a partner, complete a Venn diagram that compares and contrasts these two settings. Look for details in the story that describe the physical features, the dangers, and the advantages of each setting. Share your diagram with the class.

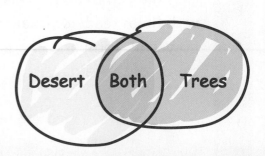

Desert   Both   Trees

WRITE ABOUT READING

Response As event follows event in "Tucket's Travels," readers wonder what will happen next and whether the characters will solve their conflict. Write a paragraph in which you explain how the events build on one another until the moment the storm clouds burst and the footprints are washed away. Be sure to include quotations and other evidence from the text that show how the author leads to this climax and resolution.

Writing Tip

Before you write, complete a story map to help you remember the events in the story. Review your draft to decide whether you need to expand, combine, or shorten sentences to clarify your ideas for your readers.

Go Digital

COMMON CORE **RL.5.1** quote accurately when explaining what the text says explicitly and when drawing inferences; **RL.5.3** compare and contrast characters, settings, or events, drawing on details; **W.5.9a** apply grade 5 Reading standards to literature; **W.5.10** write routinely over extended time frames and shorter time frames; **SL.5.1a** come to discussions prepared/explicitly draw on preparation and other information about the topic; **L.5.3a** expand, combine, and reduce sentences

✓ **GENRE**

Technical text explains a process, procedure, or job in detail.

✓ **TEXT FOCUS**

Characteristics of Technical Text A technical text includes facts and domain-specific words and phrases that provide readers with a deeper understanding of the topic. A technical text might also include detailed diagrams that illustrate important concepts.

COMMON CORE

RI.5.10 read and comprehend informational texts; **L.5.6** acquire and use general academic and domain-specific words and phrases

Wild Weather

by Laura Townsend

What's the weather like where you are? Sunny and warm? Snowy and cold? Is a storm predicted? Have you thought about the weather at all today?

Meteorologists, or scientists who study weather, always think about the weather. They also observe, measure, and record its changing patterns. Their goal is to better predict what the weather will be, especially when storms are about to strike.

What Causes Weather?

When predicting weather, scientists study air masses. An air mass is a large body of air with the same properties, such as temperature, air pressure, and water vapor.

A colder air mass doesn't mix well with a warmer air mass, and that can cause stormy weather! Cold air is heavier than warm air, so it pushes underneath a warm air mass. When warm air moves into a cold air mass, however, the opposite action occurs. Warm air is lighter, so it rises above the cold air.

Changes in the weather occur because air masses are always on the move. The area where two air masses meet is known as a *front*. When a warm air mass is moving into an area, it's called a warm front. When a cold air mass moves in, that area is called a cold front.

Scientists also study air pressure to predict the weather. Air pressure is the weight of air pressing down on you. High air pressure causes the weather to stay calm, but if air pressure begins to drop, watch out—this can lead to really wild weather!

Warm Front: Warm air is lighter, so it lifts above a cold air mass.

Cold Front: Because cold air is heavier, a cold front pushes a warm air mass upward.

KEY

■ warm air ■ cold air

What Causes Hurricanes?

Hurricanes affect the weather in the United States each year. Beginning as tropical disturbances, some storms continue to gain force and size. Once their wind speeds reach 74 miles per hour, the huge, rotating storms are officially labeled hurricanes.

A hurricane forms over warm ocean waters. Its winds begin to circle around an area of low air pressure, creating clouds and thunderstorms. More warm, wet air gets pulled upward, causing the storm to become larger and stronger. Wind speeds build, air pressure drops, and the storm keeps strengthening because of the warm, wet air feeding it. Eventually, a dangerous hurricane is born.

Pushed ahead of a hurricane, the ocean's surface may rise up to 33 feet higher. These *storm surges* can be as wide as 100 miles and can smash into shorelines like bulldozers. If a hurricane comes ashore, it brings heavy rain, flooding, and powerful winds, causing damage to property and harm to people and animals.

A hurricane may be as wide as 300 miles. It can travel thousands of miles and last for more than a week. Once it reaches cooler seas or moves across land, however, the hurricane loses its energy source. As a result, it begins to weaken.

A Look at a Hurricane

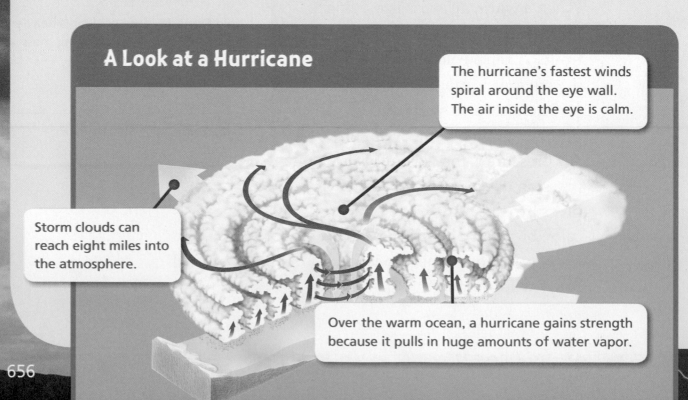

The hurricane's fastest winds spiral around the eye wall. The air inside the eye is calm.

Storm clouds can reach eight miles into the atmosphere.

Over the warm ocean, a hurricane gains strength because it pulls in huge amounts of water vapor.

What Causes Thunderstorms?

About 45,000 thunderstorms occur around the world every day, bringing rain, wind, lightning, thunder, and sometimes hail. These powerful storms develop when air masses of different temperatures come together.

Thunderstorms begin to form as warm, humid air rises rapidly. Then a cold front or strong winds push under the warmer air mass. As the rising air begins to cool, clouds take shape, heavy with water droplets and even ice crystals. Strong winds blow both upward and downward within the cloud. Finally, rain begins to fall, pulling cool air down with it. Strong electric charges build up at the bottom of the cloud, causing lightning and thunder.

While violent, these powerful storms are usually over within about an hour. Because the rain and cooler air prevent warm air from continuing to rise into the clouds, most thunderstorms will move away quickly.

When extremely strong thunderstorms occur, meteorologists become concerned about the possibility of another severe weather event—a tornado. Tornadoes form in less than one percent of all thunderstorms, but when they hit, they can destroy everything in their path.

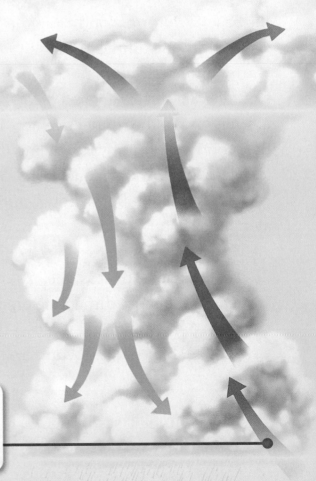

Large amounts of warm air are pushed upward, forming a thundercloud. These upward movements of air, called updrafts, can reach speeds of 62 miles per hour.

What Causes Tornadoes?

A violent, twisting column of air racing across the plains may be exciting to see in a movie, but few people want to see one in real life. Some tornadoes generate the fastest winds on Earth. Their wind speeds may reach over 300 miles per hour.

Tornadoes form when winds spin a funnel, or column of air, at the base of a storm cloud. Rapidly rising air in the funnel pulls warm, humid air into it. The fast-spinning air creates an area of low air pressure in the funnel's center. Due to the low pressure, air on the ground continues to rush into the funnel and to join the cloud above. The swirling funnel begins to lengthen. If conditions are right, the funnel touches down, and the tornado begins to move along the ground.

These violent storms typically have narrow paths of destruction; nevertheless, their routes may cover many miles. Tornadoes are more difficult to predict than other storms. However, with advanced weather tracking, meteorologists are now better able to warn people and give them time to take cover.

cool air

warm air

spinning funnel cloud

Sudden changes in wind direction and speed create a violently spinning funnel that may become a dangerous tornado.

As meteorologists continue to learn about weather patterns, they will be able to more accurately predict the paths that storms may take. This means less chance of loss of life and property. With better forecasting, people have more time to prepare, so wild weather doesn't have to be so scary!

Compare Texts

Compare Protective Instincts Think about Francis in "Tucket's Travels" and Travis in "Old Yeller" (Lesson 7). In what similar ways do the two characters confront challenges and help the children for whom they feel responsible? With a partner, review both selections and compare and contrast the characters. Use the characters' actions to draw inferences about protecting children in dangerous situations. Be sure to support your ideas with quotations and text evidence.

TEXT TO SELF

Write About Weather The selections in this lesson describe extreme weather conditions. Think of a time when you experienced extreme weather, such as a storm or a heat wave. Describe in a few paragraphs how it affected you or others around you. Explain what you or others did to adapt to the conditions.

TEXT TO WORLD

Present Information With a partner, use a combination of resources to research how to survive extreme weather events such as hurricanes or tornados. From your research, create a safety brochure with information, supply lists, and helpful illustrations. Then present your brochure to a group.

COMMON CORE **RL.5.9** compare and contrast stories in the same genre on their approaches to themes and topics; **RI.5.7** draw on information from print and digital sources to locate answers or solve problems; **W.5.2a** introduce a topic, provide an observation and focus, group related information/ include formatting, illustrations, and multimedia

Grammar

Correct Uses of the Verbs *be* and *have* The verbs *be* and *have* can be used as **main verbs** or **helping verbs**. As you have learned, a verb and its subject must agree in number. *Be* and *have* are **irregular verbs.** You must change the forms of the verbs *be* and *have* in special ways to achieve **subject-verb agreement.**

Subject	Form of *be*		Form of *have*	
	Present	**Past**	**Present**	**Past**
Singular Subjects:				
I	am	was	have	had
You	are	were	have	had
He, She, It (or singular noun)	is	was	has	had
Plural Subjects:				
We	are	were	have	had
You	are	were	have	had
They (or plural noun)	are	were	have	had

 **Rewrite each sentence below on a sheet of paper. Use the correct form of *be* or *have* shown in parentheses.**

1 Francis (is, are) a skilled tracker.

2 He (has, have) survived battles and blizzards.

3 (Are, Is) you familiar with his story?

4 Lottie and Billy (is, are) the children in his care.

5 They (has, have) no one else to look out for them.

Remember to use the correct forms of *be* and *have*. When you write, make sure you keep the verb tenses consistent so your paragraphs make sense.

Shifting Tenses	Consistent Tenses
The thunderstorm has frightened the children, and they took shelter.	The thunderstorm has frightened the children, and they have taken shelter.

 Connect Grammar to Writing

As you revise your editorial this week, pay special attention to the verbs in your sentences. Look for inappropriate shifts in verb tenses and correct them.

COMMON CORE **W.5.1a** introduce a topic, state an opinion, and create an organizational structure; **W.5.1b** provide logically ordered reasons supported by facts and details; **W.5.1c** link opinion and reasons using words, phrases, and clauses; **W.5.1d** provide a concluding statement or section; **W.5.4** produce writing in which development and organization are appropriate to task, purpose, and audience

Opinion Writing

✔ **Voice** An **editorial** is a type of persuasive writing that includes a writer's opinion about a current issue or news story. An editorial with a strong voice causes readers to feel, think, or act in a certain way. A good editorial will also have a clear topic and an opinion that is supported by logically ordered reasons.

Dan drafted an editorial for his school newspaper about the school's severe weather plan. Then he added transitions to link opinions and ideas more effectively.

Writing Traits Checklist

✔ **Ideas**
Did I introduce the topic clearly and state my opinion?

✔ **Organization**
Did I order my reasons logically and support them with facts and details?

✔ **Sentence Fluency**
Did I use transitions effectively to link opinions and reasons?

✔ **Word Choice**
Did I use precise words?

✔ **Voice**
Does my writing show that I have strong feelings about the topic?

✔ **Conventions**
Did I use correct spelling, grammar, and punctuation?

Revised Draft

It is true that our school has a good plan
for severe weather, ~~but~~ However, that does not mean
it's the best we can do. Students have many
good ideas to share, ~~and~~ With our help, the school could be
a safer place. All we need is a chance to be heard.

Be Prepared

by Dan Morse

A change in weather can catch people by surprise. When weather becomes dangerous, it is important to be prepared. Our school has severe-weather drills to practice what to do in an emergency. These drills are good, but I think we could do more to be prepared and to keep everyone safe.

We are young people, but we can still have good ideas about weather safety. I think each class should have a time when students can share ideas. We might say that drills should happen more often or that every class should elect a weather-safety expert.

Students could also share ideas about how teachers might help students after severe weather hits. If the building is damaged, students want to know what to expect. Will we all go to a safe place in the building? How will we get home? Knowing what to expect might make us feel less afraid.

It is true that our school has a good plan for severe weather. However, that does not mean it's the best we can do. Students have many good ideas to share. With our help, the school could be a safer place. All we need is a chance to be heard.

Reading as a Writer

What transitions did the writer use to link his opinions and reasons? Where in your writing can you connect ideas more clearly?

In my final paper, I used transitions to link my opinions and reasons. I also checked to see that I had used *be* and *have* correctly.

✓ TARGET VOCABULARY

astonished
nerve
bared
banish
reasoned
envy
spared
margins
deserted
upright

Vocabulary Reader | Context Cards

Meet the Ojibwa

COMMON CORE L.5.6 acquire and use general academic and domain-specific words and phrases

Vocabulary in Context

1 astonished

People may be astonished at seeing wild animals. The sight can be amazing.

2 nerve

He was scared, but this boy worked up the nerve, or courage, to handle the snake.

3 bared

This lion opened its mouth and bared its teeth. Everyone could see its fangs.

4 banish

The leader of a wolf pack will banish a defeated challenger. The loser must leave.

Go Digital

▶ Study each Context Card.

▶ Use a thesaurus to determine a synonym for each Vocabulary word.

5 reasoned

Scientists reasoned, or logically figured out, how to assemble these fossil bones.

6 envy

People may watch seals with envy. They are jealous of the seals' swimming ability.

7 spared

This cat played with the mouse but spared its life and did not harm it.

8 margins

You can sometimes see deer standing in fields at the margins, or edges, of the woods.

9 deserted

A baby bird that is all alone may seem deserted, but its mother may be nearby.

10 upright

Meerkats stand upright, or straight up, to keep a lookout for nearby predators.

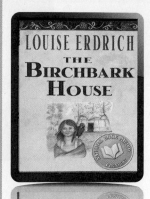

Read and Comprehend

Go Digital

☑ TARGET SKILL

Theme Every story has a **theme**, or message, that runs through it. The main character's actions and responses to challenges can help you determine a story's theme. As you read "The Birchbark House," use a graphic organizer like this one to record details about the main character, Omakayas. Then ask yourself what theme the text evidence suggests.

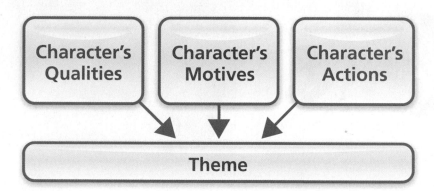

Character's Qualities

Character's Motives

Character's Actions

Theme

☑ TARGET STRATEGY

Infer/Predict As you read "The Birchbark House," use text evidence to figure out what the author means or what might happen later in the story. **Inferring** can help you better understand a story's characters, **predict** what they might do, and determine how their actions relate to the theme.

COMMON CORE

RL.5.2 determine theme from details/summarize

Traditions

Every culture has traditions, or special ways of doing things that have been handed down through the generations. The selection you are about to read features some traditions and teachings from the Ojibwe culture.

The Ojibwe lived on the shores of the Great Lakes until United States expansion forced most of them out in the mid-1800s. They lived in dome-shaped homes called wigwams, which were supported by saplings and covered in birchbark. During the growing season, the Ojibwe lived together in large groups. In winter, these villages were abandoned for smaller hunting camps. "The Birchbark House" takes place in the early summer, when an Ojibwe girl picking strawberries encounters two bear cubs.

ANCHOR TEXT

✓ TARGET SKILL

Theme Analyze characters' actions and feelings to determine the story's theme.

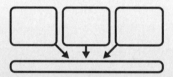

✓ GENRE

Historical fiction is set in a real time and place in the past. As you read, look for:
▶ realistic characters and events
▶ details that show the story took place in the past

COMMON CORE **RL.5.2** determine theme from details/summarize; **RL.5.7** analyze how visual and multimedia elements contribute to the meaning, tone, or beauty of a text; **RL.5.10** read and comprehend literature

MEET THE AUTHOR

Louise Erdrich

Louise Erdrich is a member of the Turtle Mountain Band of Ojibwe. While she was growing up in North Dakota, her father often recited memorized poetry to her and her six siblings. She was inspired to write *The Birchbark House* while she and her mother were researching their own family history.

MEET THE ILLUSTRATOR

S.D. Nelson

When he was young, S.D. Nelson's Lakota/Sioux mother told him traditional Coyote stories. Now he is a storyteller. He is the author-illustrator of many books for young readers, including *Coyote Christmas, Gift Horse, Quiet Hero,* and *The Star People,* winner of the Western Writers of America Spur Award.

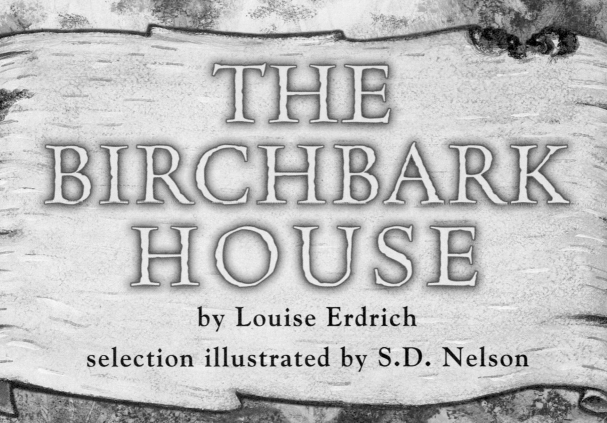

THE BIRCHBARK HOUSE

by Louise Erdrich

selection illustrated by S.D. Nelson

ESSENTIAL QUESTION

How can traditions influence a person's thoughts and feelings?

Omakayas (oh MAHK ay ahs) is returning home from an errand. She carries scissors for her mother and a lump of sweet maple candy for herself. Both the scissors and the candy are rare and valued items in her Ojibwe village in 1847. She is not eager to return home to the chore of tanning a moose hide and to her older sister, Angeline, who made fun of her earlier in the day. Her feelings are hurt, and she wants nothing but to be respected by Angeline.

Before she went back on the trail, Omakayas rinsed off the old candy lump in the lake. It came out beautifully, creamy-golden, translucent and grainy-dark. And sweet. She started walking, her treasure now wrapped in a leaf. As she walked, Omakayas thought. There was no way to share such a tough nut of sweetness. How would she divide it? Omakayas decided she did not want to cause trouble at home. Furthermore, it suddenly made sense to her that at least one person in the family should get the full effect of the maple sugar. She would pop the whole thing into her mouth. All at once! This would save problems. Aaaaah. The lump was delicious, tasting of spring sweetness and the inside of trees. Besides, Omakayas reasoned, as she walked contentedly along, the taste of the sugar would save her from eating every one of the berries she was sure she would find on the path.

Omakayas's feet moved slower and even slower yet. For one thing, the moose hide waited. For another, she was still angry with her older sister, and didn't want to see Angeline. She could still feel that sister foot pressing hateful on her back. If only there were some way to impress Angeline, cause her envy, make her say, "Can I have some of those berries, please, please, please?" You can be sure, Omakayas thought, her face taking on a faraway, haughty expression, she would be slow in answering! Yet the worst of it was this: her sister was usually on her side, helping her plan tricks on the other children in the village or gathering new ferns or snaring rabbits, visiting the grave houses looking for sugar or food left for the spirits, tossing off her clothes to swim with her. And to have her older sister laugh at her hurt Omakayas so much inside that she both wanted Angeline to smile in surprise, to be proud, to envy her, and to feel rotten and be sorry forever. So Omakayas took the slow way back looking for odaemin (oh DAY mihn), little red heartberries, in the sunny margins of the woods near the ground.

She carefully removed the hard lump of sweetness from her mouth, stuck it back in its leaf just inside the pocket of her dress. Just as the taste of maple sugar faded along her tongue, she bent over, pushed back delicate leaves, and found masses of plump red little berries. Ah! One, two, three. She'd eaten a huge handful. Another. She grinned, thinking that she'd allow her sister to return with her to plunder them, but only if Angeline changed her ways.

All of a sudden, a rustle and then a thump in a bush ahead made Omakayas freeze. A long moment passed as she stared through the dark leaves. Suddenly, *crash!* Two bear cubs burst from the bush and rushed pell-mell, tumbling head over heels straight for her. They came on in such a hurry that they didn't see Omakayas until they were nearly in her lap, and then, with comical looks of shock, they tried to stop themselves. One flew flat on its face, bumping its nose and squealing. The other twisted in midair and landed in a heap on the ground, shaking its head in confusion at Omakayas.

The bear boys looked at her. Slowly, she put out her open hand filled with heartberries. Curious, the cubs jumped forward, lost their nerve. They scampered backward, and then crept forward shyly again. The smaller cub seemed slightly bolder and sniffed at Omakayas's hand.

The bear cub took one berry, then jumped away in seeming fright at its own bold act. But the taste of the berry seemed to banish fear. The two now tumbled at her, growling, mock-ferocious. Their long pink tongues touched up every berry from her hands, eagerly flicking them from her fingers as fast as she could pick. They seemed to like the game. It could have gone on for hours, that is, until she stood upright. Then they tumbled backward in alarm. Their chubby bottoms rolled them over like playing balls, and she laughed out loud. She realized they had thought Omakayas was their own size. They were astonished the same way Omakayas had been the first time she saw the trader Cadotte unfold a seeing glass, something he called a telescope, a long shiny tube that grew in his hands.

She bent down again.

"Ahneen, little brothers," she said to them kindly, and they came forward.

She looked around. No mother bear. Omakayas was well aware that she shouldn't stay so close to these cubs, but after all, they seemed deserted. She looked around again. They were orphans! Perhaps the mother bear's skin was now draped across old Tallow's bed, although she hadn't heard about a recent kill. But still, no mother bear in sight. And these little ones so hungry. Wouldn't her big sister be thrilled when Omakayas returned with these two new brothers! Eagerly, Omakayas began to plan out her triumphant walk back to the house. She would enter the little clearing with the cubs, one at her heels and one before her. Everyone would make way, impressed. She would lead the bear cubs around the fire four times before she presented one of them to Angeline, who would look at her with new respect.

There was no warning. One moment Omakayas was wiggling a leafy stick, making it move on the ground so the cubs would jump on it, biting fiercely. Then next moment, she found herself flipped over on her back and pinned underneath a huge, powerful, heavy thing that sent down a horrible stink. It was the sow bear, the mother. Breathing on her a stale breath of decayed old deer-hides and skunk cabbages and dead mushrooms. Owah! The surprising thing was, Omakayas realized later, that although she had no memory of doing so, she had the scissors out of their case and open, the sharp ends pointing at the bear's heart. But she didn't use them as a knife. She knew for certain that *she should not move*. If the bear began to bite and claw, she would have to plunge the tip of the scissors straight in between the bear's strong ribs, use all of her strength, sink the blade all the way in to the rounded hilt and then jump clear, if she could, while the bear went through its death agony. If she couldn't get clear, Omakayas knew she would have to roll up in a ball and endure the bear's fury. She would probably be clawed from head to foot, bitten to pieces, scattered all over the ground.

Until the mother bear made the first move, Omakayas knew she should stay still, or as still as possible, given the terrified jumping of her heart.

674

ANALYZE THE TEXT

Visual Elements What do you notice about this story's illustrations? How do the illustrations add to the beauty of the text?

For long moments, the bear tested her with every sense, staring down with her weak eyes, listening, and most of all smelling her. The bear smelled the morning's moose meat stew Omakayas had eaten, the wild onion seasoning and the dusty bit of maple sugar from old Tallow stuck to the inside of her pocket. How she hoped the bear did not smell the bear-killing dogs or the bear claw that swung on a silver hoop from Old Tallow's earlobe. Perhaps the bear smelled the kind touch of Grandma and Mama's bone-and-sprucewood comb, her baby brother's cuddling body, the skins and mats she had slept in, and Little Pinch, who had whined and sobbed the night before. The bear smelled on Omakayas's skin the smell of its own cousin's bear grease used to ward off mosquitoes. Fish from the night before last night. The berries she was eating. The bear smelled all.

Omakayas couldn't help but smell her back. Bears eat anything and this one had just eaten something ancient and foul. Hiyn! (HY n) Omakayas took shallow breaths. Perhaps it was to take her mind off the scent of dead things on the bear's breath that she accidentally closed the scissors, shearing off a tiny clip of bear fur, and then to cover her horror at this mistake, started to talk.

ANALYZE THE TEXT

Author's Word Choice Authors use **sensory details** that make readers feel what is happening in a story. Which details of the bear encounter make you feel Omakayas's fear?

"Nokomis," she said to the bear, calling her grandmother. "I didn't mean any harm. I was only playing with your children. Gaween onjidah (gah WEEN ohn jee dah). Please forgive me."

The bear cuffed at Omakayas, but in a warning manner, not savagely, to hurt. Then the bear leaned back, nose working, as though she could scent the meaning of the human words. Encouraged, Omakayas continued.

"I fed them some berries. I wanted to bring them home, to adopt them, have them live with me at my house as my little brothers. But now that you're here, Grandmother, I will leave quietly. These scissors in my hands are not for killing, just for sewing. They are nothing compared to your teeth and claws."

And indeed, Omakayas's voice trembled slightly as the bear made a gurgling sound deep in her throat and bared her long, curved yellowish teeth, so good at ripping and tearing. But having totaled up all of the smells and sifted them for information, the bear seemed to have decided that Omakayas was no threat. She sat back on her haunches like a huge dog. Swinging her head around, she gave a short, quick slap at one of the cubs that sent it reeling away from Omakayas. It was as though she were telling them they had done wrong to approach this human animal, and should now stay away from her. Omakayas's heart squeezed painfully. Even though it was clear her life was to be spared, she felt the loss of her new brothers.

ANALYZE THE TEXT

Theme How does Omakayas respond during the mother bear encounter? How do her reactions relate to the theme of this story?

"I wouldn't ever hurt them," she said again.

The little cubs piled against their mother, clung to her. For a long moment the great bear sat calmly with them, deciding where to go. Then, in no hurry, they rose in one piece of dark fur. One bear boy broke away, again tried to get near Omakayas. The other looked longingly at her, but the big bear mother abruptly nosed them down the trail.

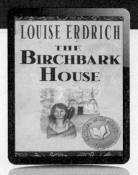

Dig Deeper

How to Analyze the Text

Use these pages to learn about Theme, Author's Word Choice, and Visual Elements. Then read "The Birchbark House" again to apply what you learned.

Theme

In "The Birchbark House," Omakayas reacts quickly when she encounters the bears. How a main character responds to challenges or conflict can help you determine theme. **Theme** is the central message or idea of a story.

Authors may state some character traits directly. Often, however, the reader must make inferences about a character's qualities based on descriptions of his or her appearance, thoughts, and actions. These clues help you identify and understand the story's theme.

Look back at page 671 in "The Birchbark House." How does Omakayas react to having her feelings hurt by her sister? Think about how her reaction—and what she does as a result—relates to the theme of the story.

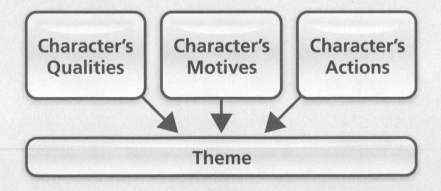

RL.5.2 determine theme from details/summarize; **RL.5.7** analyze how visual and multimedia elements contribute to the meaning, tone, or beauty of a text; **RL.5.10** read and comprehend literature

COMMON CORE

Author's Word Choice

Authors carefully choose words to help their readers understand what is happening in a story. Reread the first sentence at the top of page 678. It is easy to imagine why Omakayas's voice trembles when the mother bear makes "a gurgling sound deep in her throat" and opens her mouth to show "long, curved yellowish teeth." The author's **word choice** provides a clear impression of what Omakayas hears and sees.

Visual Elements

When you analyze a text, it is important to consider how visual elements affect your understanding. **Visual elements** may include photos, graphics, and illustrations. "The Birchbark House" is accompanied by illustrations that show Omakayas interacting with her natural surroundings and highlight the power of nature. Think about how these illustrations add to the beauty of the text.

Your Turn

Turn and Talk Review the selection with a partner to prepare to discuss this question: *How can traditions influence a person's thoughts and feelings?* As you discuss, take turns reviewing and elaborating on the key ideas in your discussion.

 Classroom Conversation

Continue your discussion of "The Birchbark House" by using text evidence to answer these questions:

1. How does Omakayas react when her feelings are hurt by her sister?

2. How do Omakayas's feelings about her sister relate to her experience with the bears?

3. What details from the story show Omakayas's knowledge of her environment?

TALK ABOUT THEME

List and Discuss Omakayas forms a special bond with the bear cubs. She shares her berries with them and imagines taking them home. What does her interaction with the bears show about her? How does it relate to the theme of the story? Discuss these questions with a partner, and work together to make a list of text evidence that supports your answers.

WRITE ABOUT READING

Response How do the descriptions of Omakayas's thoughts and actions provide clues about her character? Write a paragraph describing the author's characterization of Omakayas. Include text evidence such as quotations and details that help you make inferences about Omakayas's traits, such as her courage or her respect for nature.

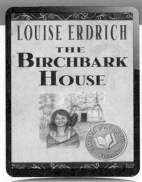

Writing Tip

Be sure to cite specific evidence from the text to develop your ideas and support your analysis. Double-check any quotations or paraphrases for accuracy.

COMMON CORE **RL.5.1** quote accurately when explaining what the text says explicitly and when drawing inferences; **RL.5.2** determine theme from details/summarize; **W.5.2b** develop the topic with facts, definitions, details, quotations, or other information and examples; **W.5.9a** apply grade 5 Reading standards to literature; **W.5.10** write routinely over extended time frames and shorter time frames; **SL.5.1a** come to discussions prepared/explicitly draw on preparation and other information about the topic; **SL.5.1c** pose and respond to questions, make comments that contribute to the discussion, and elaborate on others' remarks

INFORMATIONAL TEXT

Four Seasons of Food

✓ GENRE

Informational text, such as this photo essay, gives facts and examples about a topic.

✓ TEXT FOCUS

Procedural Information A text may include procedural information such as a recipe—a set of directions for preparing something to eat or drink.

Four Seasons of Food

by Joyce Mallery

Think about what your life would be like if you had to grow and find everything that you ate. That is exactly what the Ojibwe people did for centuries.

Between 1817 and 1854, most Ojibwe moved to, or were forced to move to, reservations. Before that, they lived in an area extending from the shores of the Great Lakes to the plains of North Dakota. The Ojibwe who lived along the margins of the Great Lakes gathered wild rice, made maple syrup, and hunted game to eat. However, the seasons of the year dictated what they hunted and gathered.

Spring The Ojibwe gathered roots and ate plants such as leeks and fiddleheads. By late spring, they began tapping maple trees. The sap was boiled to make sugar, syrup, and candy.

Summer The Ojibwe gathered berries and grew vegetables such as squash and beans. The women and girls began storing food for the winter. They reasoned that they would need extra food in the cold months ahead.

Fall The Ojibwe harvested wild rice from nearby lakes. Typically, the men steered a canoe through the upright reeds. Then the women knocked the grains of rice from the plants into the canoe.

An Ojibwe woman collects maple sap from a tapped tree.

An Ojibwe woman uses one long stick to bend the rice plants and the other stick to knock the grains into the canoe.

Making Ojibwe Wild Rice Breakfast

This recipe combines several traditional Ojibwe ingredients. You will be astonished by how good this sweet and nutty breakfast dish tastes.

Ingredients:
Wild rice
Raisins, blueberries, or raspberries
Maple syrup
Milk (optional)

Directions:
Ask an adult to cook the rice.
Add the fruit and maple syrup to the rice.
Add milk if you want.
NOTE: If you want to eat the dish cold, cook the rice the night before.

Make enough for everyone. Anyone left out will surely feel envy when they see you eating this delicious treat.

Winter Summer camps were deserted in winter. New hunting spots were sought. Imagine the nerve that men needed to hunt deer and moose with just a bow and arrows. A hunter had to banish fear if a wolf bared its teeth and attacked. His life depended on it.

Almost no part of an animal was spared. The women dried the meat, made clothes from hides, and made tools from bones.

All parts of an animal hunted for food were used. Here, an Ojibwe woman scrapes a hide, preparing it to be made into clothing.

Compare Texts

TEXT TO TEXT

Discuss Similar Topics Both "The Birchbark House" and "The Black Stallion" (Lesson 20) explore ideas related to animal behaviors and instincts. In a small group, compare and contrast Omakayas's and Alec's experiences with wild animals. Then compare and contrast the themes of the stories. Use quotations, details, and evidence from both texts to support your ideas. Ask and answer questions to clarify everyone's thoughts.

TEXT TO SELF

Imagine the Past If you lived in an Ojibwe village in the 1800s, what modern conveniences would you miss most? What aspects of life during that time would appeal to you? Explain your thoughts in a short essay.

TEXT TO WORLD

Translate the Message The photo essay "Four Seasons of Food" gives information about what life was like for the Ojibwe, who grew or gathered their food. Imagine a documentary film on the same topic. Compare and contrast how the photo essay and the documentary film would use words, images, graphics, or sound to present their message. What would you do to translate the text's message about the Ojibwe culture to film?

COMMON CORE **RL.5.1** quote accurately when explaining what the text says explicitly and when drawing inferences; **RL.5.2** determine theme from details/ summarize; **RL.5.9** compare and contrast stories in the same genre on their approaches to themes and topics; **W.5.1a** introduce a topic, state an opinion, and create an organizational structure; **W.5.1d** provide a concluding statement or section; **SL.5.1c** pose and respond to questions, make comments that contribute to the discussion, and elaborate on others' remarks

Grammar

What Are the Perfect Tenses? You have already learned the simple verb tenses: past, present, and future. English has another group of tenses called the **perfect tenses.** All perfect-tense verbs include *has, have,* or *had* as a helping verb. A verb in the **present perfect tense** includes *has* or *have* as a helping verb. A verb in the **past perfect tense** includes *had* as a helping verb. A verb in the **future perfect tense** includes *will have* as a helping verb.

Sentence	Tense of Verb
Two bears have tumbled into the berry patch.	present perfect tense
Omakayas had picked some berries minutes earlier.	past perfect tense
Soon the mother bear will have found her cubs.	future perfect tense

Try This! Copy these sentences onto a sheet of paper. Circle each verb. Then label the verbs as present perfect, past perfect, or future perfect tense.

1. Now the mother bear has captured Omakayas.

2. That huge, smelly bear had surprised Omakayas.

3. Apparently the bear had eaten something foul earlier.

4. Omakayas has kept calm somehow.

5. In a few minutes the mother bear and her cubs will have left the area.

You know that regular verbs add *-ed* when used with *has*, *have*, or *had*. You must add a special ending to irregular verbs used with *has*, *have*, or *had*. Use the correct forms of regular and irregular verbs when you write sentences in the perfect tenses.

Incorrect	Correct
A baby bear has ate some berries.	A baby bear has eaten some berries.
Omakayas had gave them to the cub.	Omakayas had given them to the cub.
By tonight, Omakayas will have telled her story many times.	By tonight, Omakayas will have told her story many times.

 Connect Grammar to Writing

As you revise your response to literature, correct any perfect-tense verb usage errors you find. Forming and using the perfect tenses correctly will help make your writing clear.

W.5.1a introduce a topic, state an opinion, and create an organizational structure; **W.5.1b** provide logically ordered reasons supported by facts and details; **W.5.1c** link opinion and reasons using words, phrases, and clauses; **W.5.1d** provide a concluding statement or section; **W.5.10** write routinely over extended time frames and shorter time frames

Opinion Writing

✔ **Organization** Writing a **response to literature** allows you to share your opinion about a character in a story. It is important to include reasons for your opinion, and facts and details that support those reasons. Decide which reason will come first, second, and third. The order should be logical so that your audience can follow along easily.

Carleasa wrote a response to literature to share her opinion about Omakayas from "The Birchbark House."   When she revised her draft, she made sure that her ideas were in a logical order and that they were linked by transitions when necessary.

Writing Traits Checklist

✔ **Ideas**
Did I express the traits, feelings, or motives of a character?

✔ **Organization**
Did I put my reasons in logical order?

✔ **Sentence Fluency**
Did I vary the structure of my sentences?

✔ **Word Choice**
Did I use transition words to link reasons and support?

✔ **Voice**
Did I clearly state my opinion about a character?

✔ **Conventions**
Did I use correct spelling, grammar, and punctuation?

Revised Draft

"The Birchbark House" is a story about a girl named Omakayas. Omakayas is a character I can relate to and admire because she is smart and brave. She must use her instincts and good judgment to survive when a protective mother bear finds her playing with two young cubs.

Omakayas

by Carleasa Dutton

"The Birchbark House" is a story about a girl named Omakayas. She must use her instincts and good judgment to survive when a protective mother bear finds her playing with two young cubs. Omakayas is a character I can relate to and admire because she is smart and brave.

Like Omakayas, I have an older sister I argue with sometimes and want to impress. When Omakayas meets the cubs, she imagines bringing them home with her and showing them off to her older sister. That is something I might have thought about in her position, too.

Omakayas believes the cubs are orphaned, but their mother soon appears. Omakayas does not let her fears take over. The mother bear pins her to the ground, but she stays calm and is able to escape. Most people would scream and panic. I admire Omakayas's courage.

I like stories that feature characters I can relate to. In the case of Omakayas, I also admire the way she deals with a dangerous situation. Though she is from a different place and time, I would enjoy being her friend.

Reading as a Writer

Carleasa made sure the reasons she used to support her opinions were arranged logically. Are there reasons or ideas in your writing that should be rearranged?

In my final paper, I used transition words to link ideas. I also made sure that any perfect-tense verbs were used correctly.

Vocabulary in Context

✓ TARGET VOCABULARY

dominated

extending

sprawling

hostile

acknowledged

flourished

residents

prospered

acquainted

decline

Vocabulary Reader

Context Cards

L.5.4c consult reference materials, both print and digital, to find pronunciation and determine or clarify meaning

1 dominated

Herds of cattle once dominated the plains. They were often the biggest thing in sight.

2 extending

This cowgirl wears chaps extending, or reaching, from the hips to the ankles.

3 sprawling

This cowboy rides his horse over the vast and sprawling range.

4 hostile

A farmer who is hostile, or unfriendly, to cattle ranchers can use fences to stop cattle drives.

NO TRESPASSING

Go Digital

▶ Study each Context Card.

▶ Use a dictionary or a glossary to verify the meaning of each Vocabulary word.

5 acknowledged

This rodeo cowboy acknowledged, or recognized, his fans with a smile.

6 flourished

Cattle were driven to towns near rail lines. These towns flourished and grew rich.

7 residents

When cowboys were not living on the trail, they were residents in the ranch bunkhouse.

8 prospered

A cowboy who has prospered, or succeeded, may buy fancy boots and a hat.

9 acquainted

Cowboys get to know one another on cattle drives. They become well acquainted.

10 decline

Because there has been a decline in cattle drives, there are fewer cowboys today.

Read and Comprehend

✅ TARGET SKILL

Text and Graphic Features   In "Vaqueros: America's First Cowboys," you will see headings, captions, and other **text features** the author uses to organize information. You will also see **graphic features**, such as maps and photographs, that highlight and show relationships between important ideas. Use a graphic organizer like the one below to record information about the text and graphic features in the selection.

Text or Graphic Feature	Location and Purpose

✅ TARGET STRATEGY

Summarize When you **summarize**, you use your own words to tell about the main ideas and details in a text. As you read the selection, pause now and then to summarize key points. Doing so will improve your understanding and help you remember what you read.

RI.5.2 determine two or more main ideas and explain how they are supported by details/summarize; **RI.5.3** explain the relationships between individuals/events/ideas/concepts in a text

The West

California, Texas, and other parts of the American West were once controlled by Spain. As a result, many terms associated with cowboys are from the Spanish language. By the early 1800s, however, Spanish control of the region was declining. Mexico won its independence from Spain in 1821. Texas, California, Arizona, and other states later gained independence from Mexico and joined the United States.

The huge expanses of land in the West were ideal for cattle ranching. "Vaqueros: America's First Cowboys" explains the vaqueros' essential role in managing the cattle ranches.

ANCHOR TEXT

VAQUEROS

George Ancona

George Ancona grew up in Coney Island, New York, where his father practiced photography as a hobby. Ancona says that "as a photographer, I can participate in other people's lives…producing something that can be shared and has a life of its own." He has created books about horses and helicopters, cowboys and carnivals, migrant workers and murals. Ancona's book *Charro* tells about the fascinating culture of Mexican horsemen and their rodeo-like *charrería*.

✅ TARGET SKILL

Text and Graphic Features
Use text and graphic features to better understand ideas and information in the selection.

✅ GENRE

Informational text gives facts and details about a topic. As you read, look for:

▶ text features, such as headings, that organize information and help explain the topic

▶ photographs and captions

▶ domain-specific words that help you better understand the topic

COMMON CORE **RI.5.2** determine two or more main ideas and explain how they are supported by details/ summarize; **RI.5.10** read and comprehend informational texts; **L.5.5b** recognize and explain the meaning of idioms, adages, and proverbs

 Go Digital

VAQUEROS

America's First Cowboys

by George Ancona

ESSENTIAL QUESTION

What kinds of lessons were learned by people who lived in the old West?

Imagine: five hundred years ago there were no cows or horses in North and South America. Thousands of years earlier there had been horses, but they disappeared. Since there were no cows, there were no cowboys. Of course, today there are cowboys. It is all because of Christopher Columbus.

The Journeys

After his voyage to the Americas in 1492, Christopher Columbus returned to Spain. He told the Spanish king and queen of the riches to be found in the paradise he discovered. He described the native people who lived there. The royal couple agreed to more voyages. They needed gold to help pay for their expanding empire.

The following year, Columbus returned to the West Indies. He brought seventeen ships loaded with over a thousand settlers, horses and cattle. The ships dropped anchor at an island they named Hispaniola (ees pah NYOH lah). Today the island is shared by Haiti and the Dominican Republic.

For the next twenty-five years Spanish ships sailed in and out of Hispaniola. The Spaniards explored and conquered the nearby islands. The native islanders were enslaved. Thousands died of smallpox, a terrible disease for which they had no resistance. As the islanders disappeared, they were replaced by the settlers and their animals.

Christopher Columbus landing on the island of Hispaniola, 1493

Hernán Cortés brought horses back to the mainland of North America.

In 1503, Hernán Cortés (ayr NAHN kor TEHS), a Spanish adventurer, arrived in the West Indies. He spent several years helping to conquer Cuba. Then in 1518, Cortés set out with a fleet of six ships to explore the nearby coast to the west. On board were five hundred men and sixteen horses strong enough to carry a man in full armor.

The ships dropped anchor near where the port of Veracruz, Mexico, is today. The Totonac people who lived there welcomed Cortés. They offered to help him conquer the hostile Aztec empire that had long dominated them. Cortés did so in two years. He claimed all the lands in the name of the Spanish king. He called the land New Spain.

It wasn't long before the Spanish conquerors brought more livestock to the colonies. The animals were allowed to graze on the open grasslands. Many took off into the wilderness, forming large herds of wild horses and cattle.

The Expanding Colony

The Spanish king rewarded Cortés and his soldiers with gifts of land. Throughout New Spain they built ranches called *haciendas* (ah SYEHN dahs) and prospered.

Accompanying the soldiers and settlers were Catholic missionaries. They had come to convert the native people. They moved north, building missions and churches along the California coast, extending the lands of New Spain.

In 1540, Francisco Vázquez de Coronado (VAHS kehs day koh roh NAH doh) organized an expedition into the northern territories. Coronado was searching for the legendary Golden Cities of Cíbola (SEE boh lah). Along with the men and supplies he brought five hundred longhorn cattle to supply meat and hides.

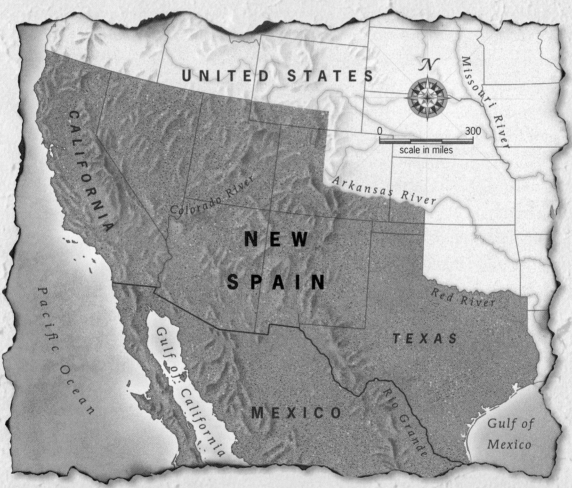

Review the map. What water sources run through the area known as New Spain?

An early vaquero lassoes a steer.

The expedition never found the city of gold. However, it did introduce the first longhorns to what is now the American Southwest. From those first five hundred longhorns, ten million had spread across the Texas plains by the 1800s.

The soldiers and priests of New Spain were already acquainted with raising cattle in Spain. Many were skilled horsemen. Even so, they needed help in rounding up the livestock on their sprawling lands.

At that time it was against the law for any native person to ride a horse. But the ranchers and priests needed help. They taught the native converts to ride and use the *lazo* (LAH soh), or lasso, a looped rope. These men who worked with horses and cattle were called *vaqueros* (vah KAY rohs). In Spanish, the word means "cow-men." With the vaqueros, a new culture took root in the west. It lives on today.

> ### ANALYZE THE TEXT
>
> **Main Ideas and Details**
> Summarize the sections "The Journeys" and "The Expanding Colony" on pages 698–701. What is the main idea of each section? What details does the author use to support these main ideas?

Coronado introduced the longhorn.

701

A herd of mustangs

A Way of Life

The vaquero's job was to keep tabs on cattle in the wild and round them up. It took many vaqueros to surround a herd so that it could be moved to the hacienda. These roundups are called *rodeos* (roh DEH ohs) in Spanish. Rodeo comes from a verb that means "to go around."

The vaqueros were also needed to capture the wild horses that flourished on the prairies and valleys of the large haciendas. The vaqueros called the horses *mesteños* (mehs TAY nyohs), a word that would become "mustangs."

Vaqueros spent most of their lives in the saddle, riding hard, in all kinds of weather. At night they sat around the fire where they cooked their meals. They told stories and sang songs about their lives. Then they rolled up into their ponchos to sleep. From California to Texas, native vaqueros were acknowledged to be the best horsemen in the world.

An early vaquero with his lariat

Doing the Job

A vaquero had to cope with a rough landscape and harsh weather. He needed the right tools to do his job.

Vaqueros wore wide-brimmed hats called *sombreros* (sohm BRAY rohs). *Sombra* (SOHM brah) means "shade" in Spanish. The sombrero protected vaqueros from the burning sun.

A vaquero also wore *chaparreras* (chah pah REH rahs) or chaps. These were leather leggings, worn over trousers. They protected the vaquero from cactus, thickets of wild brush, and rope burns.

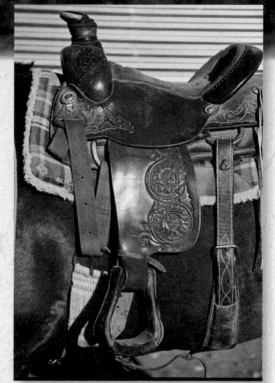

A modern saddle

The horses belonged to the owner of the hacienda. The vaquero, however, owned the saddle that he put on the horse. The saddle had to be comfortable for both horse and rider. The vaquero's feet slid into two wooden stirrups that hung from the saddle.

A vaquero's most trusted tool was his lasso, also known as the lariat. Often a vaquero would have to gallop after a runaway steer. He would toss the loop of the lariat around the steer's horns, neck, or foot. Then he would wrap the rope around his saddle horn and rein in his horse. This would hold the steer or bring it to the ground.

Once the herds were together they calmed down and began to graze. Mounted vaqueros would separate the calves from their mothers to brand them with the hacienda's mark.

The Vaquero Legend

In 1821 Mexico won its war of independence from Spain. All of New Spain became the independent nation of Mexico. The northern lands of Mexico, however, were difficult to govern. Many American immigrants crossed into the territory that would one day become Texas. Soon there was a large population of Americans in Texas. In fact, they outnumbered the Mexican residents who lived there for generations.

With the Americans came changes in the culture of the vaquero. Even the word changed. When the Americans tried to say *vaqueros* it came out "bukera." Later the word became *buckaroo*. It was only after 1860 that men who worked with cattle were called cowboys.

Cowboys continued the culture of the vaquero.

In 1836 Texas declared itself independent from Mexico. Nine years later it joined the United States. Then, in 1847, Mexico lost a war with the U.S. As a result, it lost its northern lands. They would become the states of California, Nevada, Utah and parts of Arizona, New Mexico, Colorado and Wyoming.

After the end of the Civil War, the vaqueros were joined by freed slaves and young men from the east. These newcomers wanted a new life in the wide-open spaces. They had to learn what the vaqueros had been doing for centuries.

The large ranches needed many men to manage the huge herds of cattle on the vast prairies. Cattle drives would take weeks to travel from ranches to railroads. From there, the cattle traveled to the markets in eastern and western cities.

Cowboy movies were among the first movies made.

The invention of barbed wire made it possible to build fences to keep cattle in pastures. The vaquero was not needed to ride the wide-open spaces. Long cattle drives became unnecessary. The decline of the vaquero began.

Yet the vaquero's traditions did not fade from the American imagination. At the turn of the century the cowboy became the hero of the west. Books, magazine stories, and the early movies featured the brave exploits of the American cowboy.

ANALYZE THE TEXT

Text and Graphic Features
Identify the photos, illustrations, map, captions, and headings that the author uses on pages 698–705. What do these features help you understand about the vaqueros?

A horse rears, throwing its rodeo rider.

Celebrating Traditions

Today the arts and skills of the vaquero can be seen in two countries. They appear in the *charrerías* (chah ray REE ahs) of Mexico and the rodeos of the United States. Both vaqueros and cowboys pride themselves in their skills. They keep alive the traditions and cultures of their past.

On September 14th, Mexicans celebrate *El dia del charro*. It is a holiday of parades, church services, music and *charrerías*. The charrería is a rodeo where vaqueros can exhibit their skills. They perform with *charros* (CHAH rohs) and *charras* (CHAH rahs), gentlemen and women riders. The men dress in their elegant silver-buttoned outfits and large sombreros. The women wear the traditional dress of the *China Poblana* (CHEE nah poh BLAH nah).

Many of the events performed in rodeos and charrerías are similar. Both may include riding a bucking horse or bull and getting thrown off, for example. But like the first vaqueros, the riders are ready. There is an old saying in the corrals. It goes: "There's never been a horse that can't be rode. There's never been a cowman who hasn't been throwed."

The grammar may not be right, but the idea is pure cowboy.

ANALYZE THE TEXT

Adages The author uses an **adage**, or a traditional saying, in the third paragraph on this page. Why do you think he chooses to end the selection this way? What do you think the author means when he says "the idea is pure cowboy"?

Dig Deeper

How to Analyze the Text

Use these pages to learn about Text and Graphic Features, Main Ideas and Details, and Adages. Then read "Vaqueros" again to apply what you learned.

Text and Graphic Features

Informational texts such as "Vaqueros: America's First Cowboys" often include text and graphic features. **Text features**, such as titles and headings, help to organize a text. They also make it easier for readers to find important information. **Graphic features** include photographs and illustrations, such as maps or charts. These features support or explain complex ideas in the text. Briefly looking over the text and graphic features before you begin to read can help you understand what a selection will be about.

Look back at page 698. The italicized text at the top of the page makes a connection between Christopher Columbus and the cowboys. This note helps readers to see how the events and ideas in the first sections of the text are related to those that follow.

Text or Graphic Feature	Location and Purpose

 COMMON CORE **RI.5.2** determine two or more main ideas and explain how they are supported by details; summarize; **RI.5.3** explain the relationships between individuals/events/ideas/concepts in a text; **RI.5.10** read and comprehend informational texts; **L.5.5b** recognize and explain the meaning of idioms, adages, and proverbs

Main Ideas and Details

In informational texts such as "Vaqueros: America's First Cowboys," several **main ideas** are developed. These main ideas relate to the overall main idea of the selection. To identify a main idea, think about what point is being supported by the **details** in the paragraph or section. For example, on pages 702 and 703, the facts and descriptions support the idea that vaqueros played a vital part in the success of large ranches.

Adages

"Good things come in small packages" and "Don't judge a book by its cover" are **adages** that warn people not to underestimate something or someone because of outer appearances. Adages are familiar sayings that pass on easy-to-understand advice. Authors may include adages in nonfiction texts to interest readers and to show them what they can learn from the information presented.

"If at first you don't succeed, try, try again."

Your Turn

Turn and Talk Review the selection to prepare to discuss this question: *What kinds of lessons were learned by people who lived in the old West?* After discussing this question with a partner, summarize your key points and share them with the class.

Classroom Conversation

Continue your discussion of "Vaqueros: America's First Cowboys" by using text evidence to explain your answers to these questions:

1. What qualities did a vaquero need to be successful?

2. What specific event led to the decline of the vaqueros?

3. Why does the cowboy lifestyle and tradition still appeal to many Americans?

WHAT DOES IT MEAN?

Look It Up In the selection, the author uses domain-specific words, or terms directly related to the topic of vaqueros, including *lariat, mustang, sombrero, chaps,* and *ponchos.* Look up these words (or others you find in the text) in a print or digital dictionary. Then write a new sentence for each word. Share your sentences with a partner.

WRITE ABOUT READING

Response Although the lives of the vaqueros changed over time, they had a lasting effect on America. Write a paragraph in which you explain what changes the vaqueros went through and why they had a strong influence on culture in the United States. Use specific details, direct quotations, and other text evidence to support your explanation.

Writing Tip

As you write your explanation, be sure to use precise language. Include some of the domain-specific vocabulary about vaqueros that you learned in the selection.

COMMON CORE **RI.5.2** determine two or more main ideas and explain how they are supported by details/summarize; **W.5.2d** use precise language and domain-specific vocabulary; **W.5.9b** apply grade 5 Reading standards to informational texts; **SL.5.1a** come to discussions prepared/explicitly draw on preparation and other information about the topic; **L.5.4c** consult reference materials, both print and digital, to find pronunciation and determine or clarify meaning

POETRY

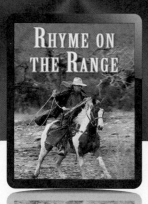

RHYME ON THE RANGE

☑ GENRE

Poetry uses the sound and rhythm of words to suggest images and express feelings in a variety of forms.

☑ TEXT FOCUS

Imagery Poets create vivid descriptions in their poems by using words and phrases that appeal to the senses.

RL.5.10 read and comprehend literature

Go Digital

RHYME ON THE RANGE

Cowboy poetry flourished in the 1800s when ranches and farms dominated the American West. These poems, which were sometimes sung, cover subjects like the sprawling landscape, hostile weather, and the loneliness of cowboy life.

The Cowboy's Life

Poet unknown, from *Songs of the Cowboys*

The bawl of a steer
To a cowboy's ear
Is music of sweetest strain;
And the yelping notes
Of the gray coyotes
To *him* are a glad refrain.

For a kingly crown
In the noisy town
His saddle he wouldn't change;
No life so free
As the life we see
Way out on the Yaso range.

The winds may blow
And the thunder growl
Or the breeze may safely moan;
A cowboy's life
Is a royal life,
His saddle his kingly throne.

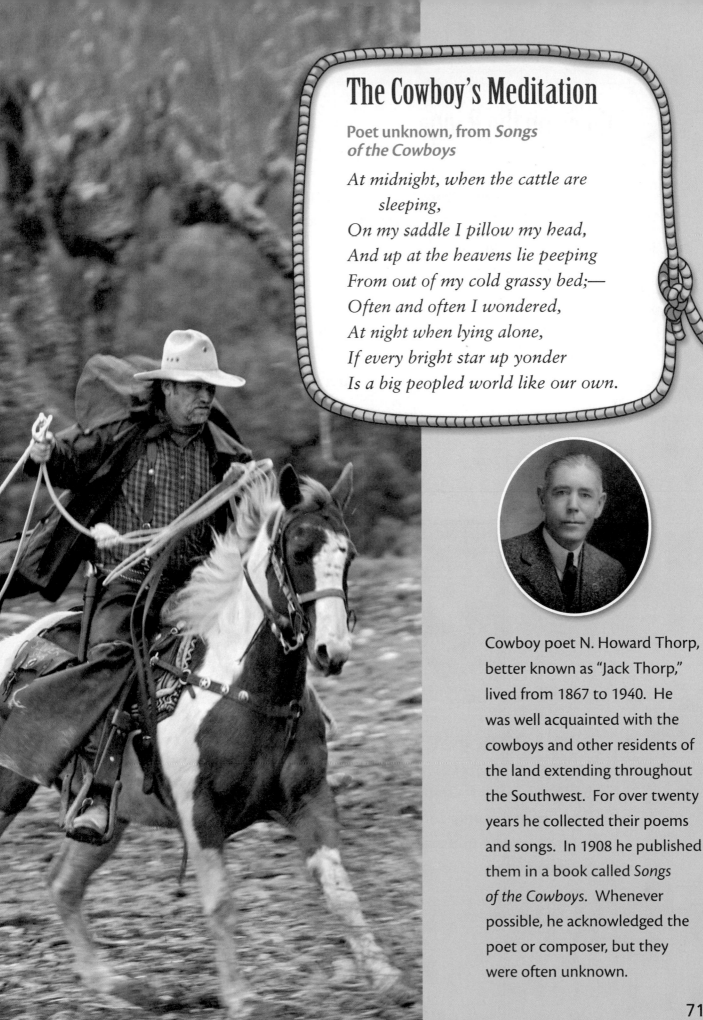

The Cowboy's Meditation

Poet unknown, from *Songs
of the Cowboys*

At midnight, when the cattle are
    sleeping,
On my saddle I pillow my head,
And up at the heavens lie peeping
From out of my cold grassy bed;—
Often and often I wondered,
At night when lying alone,
If every bright star up yonder
Is a big peopled world like our own.

Cowboy poet N. Howard Thorp,
better known as "Jack Thorp,"
lived from 1867 to 1940. He
was well acquainted with the
cowboys and other residents of
the land extending throughout
the Southwest. For over twenty
years he collected their poems
and songs. In 1908 he published
them in a book called *Songs
of the Cowboys.* Whenever
possible, he acknowledged the
poet or composer, but they
were often unknown.

Home on the Range

by Brewster Higley

Oh, give me a home where the Buffalo roam
    Where the Deer and the Antelope play;
Where never is heard a discouraging word,
    And the sky is not clouded all day.

Home, home on the Range
    Where the Deer and the Antelope play,
Where never is heard a discouraging word,
    And the sky is not clouded all day.

I love the wild flowers in this bright land of ours,
    I love the wild curlew's shrill scream;
The bluffs and white rocks, and antelope flocks
    That graze on the mountains so green.

Write a Cowboy Poem

The cowboy lifestyle eventually went into a decline, but cowboy poetry has still prospered. Today, Cowboy Poetry Week is celebrated every April during National Poetry Month.

Review the poets' uses of imagery. Then write your own cowboy poem or song. Try to use imagery in similar ways.

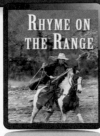

Compare Texts

TEXT TO TEXT

Compare Poems With a partner, take turns reading each poem aloud. Discuss the sound of each poem, describing its rhythm and rhyme. How do these sound effects help bring out each poem's meaning? Then look at the language and imagery used by the speakers in the poems. Think about how each speaker expresses ideas about a topic. Explain how these elements contribute to the theme of each poem. Share key ideas from your discussion with the class.

TEXT TO SELF

Imagine Being a Vaquero Would you have enjoyed being a cowboy or cowgirl in the 1800s? What aspects of life during that time would you have liked or disliked? Explain your ideas in a short composition. Support your opinions with quotes and other text evidence from "Vaqueros."

TEXT TO WORLD

Connect to Social Studies "Vaqueros" gives information about cattle ranching. Work with a partner to research the impact cattle ranching had on the history of the western United States, using print and digital sources. Share your findings with the class in a brief presentation.

COMMON CORE **RL.5.2** determine theme from details/summarize; **W.5.1a** introduce a topic, state an opinion, and create an organizational structure; **W.5.7** conduct short research projects that use several sources to build knowledge through investigation; **SL.5.4** report on a topic or text, or present an opinion, or recount an experience/speak clearly at an understandable pace

Grammar

 Go Digital

Easily Confused Verbs Some pairs of verbs have such closely related meanings that they are easily confused. Most of these verbs are **irregular verbs**. A few are **helping verbs**. By studying the meanings of both verbs, you can avoid using the wrong one in your speaking and writing.

Easily Confused Verbs			
can	able to do	**may**	allowed to do by someone or fairly likely to do
sit	to lower yourself onto a seat	**set**	to place an item onto something
teach	to give instruction to someone	**learn**	to receive instruction from someone
lie	to recline on something	**lay**	to put an item carefully on top of something
rise	to get up or to stand up	**raise**	to lift something up

Try This! Work with a partner. Tell which sentences have verbs that are used incorrectly. Say each of these sentences, replacing the incorrect verb with the correct one.

1 The young cowboy sets in his saddle.

2 "We will learn you how to rope a steer," the vaquero says.

3 "I can capture cattle already," the cowboy replies.

4 The cowboy raises from his saddle and throws the rope.

5 Then he falls off his horse and lays on the ground.

716

You know that some pairs of verbs have meanings that are related but different. These verbs are easily confused with each other. When you proofread your writing, it is important to pay special attention to these verbs.

Incorrect Verbs	**Correct Verbs**
I lie the saddle on my horse gently. He rises his head and turns to look at me. I jump up, set on his back, and give him a nudge. We're ready to go.	I lay the saddle on my horse gently. He raises his head and turns to look at me. I jump up, sit on his back, and give him a nudge. We're ready to go.

 Connect Grammar to Writing

As you edit your persuasive argument this week, look closely at each sentence for mistakes made with easily confused verbs, such as those above. Using verbs correctly is an essential part of good writing.

W.5.1a introduce a topic, state an opinion, and create an organizational structure; **W.5.1b** provide logically ordered reasons supported by facts and details; **W.5.1d** provide a concluding statement or section; **W.5.4** produce writing in which development and organization are appropriate to task, purpose, and audience; **W.5.10** write routinely over extended time frames and shorter time frames

Opinion Writing

✔️ **Organization** When writing a **persuasive argument**, begin with a point that you would like to prove to an audience. This point is called your **claim**. It is your position, or opinion, on a topic. Once you have decided on a position, build an argument using reasons that are supported by facts, details, and examples.

Sara drafted a persuasive argument about the importance of keeping traditions alive. Later, she presented her claim more clearly. Use the Writing Traits Checklist below as you revise your writing.

Writing Traits Checklist

✔️ **Ideas**
Did I give reasons for my opinion and support them with facts, details, and examples?

✔️ **Organization**
Did I provide a strong concluding paragraph?

✔️ **Sentence Fluency**
Are all of my sentences complete and correct?

✔️ **Word Choice**
Did I use persuasive words?

✔️ **Voice**
Did I show my interest in the subject?

✔️ **Conventions**
Did I use correct spelling, grammar, and punctuation?

Revised Draft

Think of what the world would be like if there were no traditions. There might be no art, music, or holidays. ~~Traditions are important.~~

In "Vaqueros: America's First Cowboys," we read that being a vaquero is a tradition that goes back over a hundred years.

It is important for people to celebrate their heritage and keep traditions alive.

Keeping Traditions Alive

by Sara Luna

Think of what the world would be like if there were no traditions. There might be no art, music, or holidays. It is important for people to celebrate their heritage and keep old traditions alive.

In "Vaqueros: America's First Cowboys," we read that being a vaquero is a tradition that goes back over a hundred years. There are still cowboys today because they teach their skills to young people. If no one cared to keep this tradition alive, we would only be able to read about vaqueros in books or watch them on TV.

Many traditions are kept alive because a lot of people work together to celebrate them. For example, all the grades at my school work on a culture parade every year. It takes many months to plan and to make the floats. If only one grade worked on it, we wouldn't be able to finish on time.

It can be fun to start a new tradition in your city or with your friends, but old traditions are very important. They teach us about our history and about other cultures. They also show us the importance of working together.

Reading as a Writer

What does Sara do to express her ideas clearly? How can you clarify your opinion and make your argument more persuasive?

In my final paper, I used facts, details, and examples to support my claim. I also made sure I arranged my reasons in a logical order.

Vocabulary in Context

✓ TARGET VOCABULARY

mishap

rustling

lectured

beacon

torment

surged

disadvantage

balked

quaking

fared

Vocabulary Reader

Horses in North America

Context Cards

COMMON CORE **L.5.4c** consult reference materials, both print and digital, to find pronunciation and determine or clarify meaning

---

① mishap

These hikers took a wrong turn by accident. They were lost due to the mishap.

② rustling

A rustling in nearby brush can worry you. Look for the sound's cause, and stay calm.

③ lectured

This ranger lectured, or explained, about the importance of staying on the trail.

④ beacon

A tall object in the distance can serve as a beacon to guide you to a familiar area.

Go Digital

▶ Study each Context Card.

▶ Use a dictionary or a glossary to help you pronounce each Vocabulary word.

5 torment

This girl suffered torment, or distress, because she couldn't find her homework.

6 surged

After this river surged, or swelled, over its banks, hikers had to find a new trail.

7 disadvantage

Losing the trail was a disadvantage, or handicap, to finding camp before dark.

8 balked

This woman balked, or refused to move, after realizing she was lost.

9 quaking

You may start quaking, or trembling, when you're lost. Your body expresses fear that way.

10 fared

Once he was rescued, this boy slept and ate. He fared, or progressed, better after that.

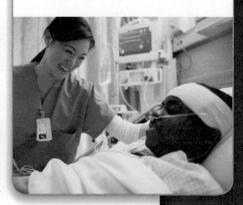

Read and Comprehend

☑ TARGET SKILL

Cause and Effect As you read "Rachel's Journal," identify events that are related by **cause and effect**—one event leading to another. Causes might include natural events or the decisions that characters make. Look for more than one effect for each cause. Also look for how each cause and effect helps to build the plot and structure of the story. Use a graphic organizer like the one shown below to record these causes and effects.

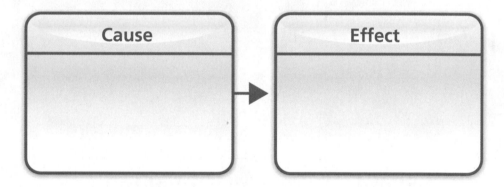

Cause	Effect

☑ TARGET STRATEGY

Analyze/Evaluate As you read "Rachel's Journal," identify causes and their effects by **analyzing** the events in the story. Ask why they happen or how they influence other events. Then **evaluate** what you learn from understanding these relationships.

RL.5.5 explain how chapters, scenes, or stanzas fit together to provide the overall structure

Pioneers

In American history, pioneers were people who settled in western parts of the country during the eighteenth and nineteenth centuries. These pioneers traveled by wagon, moving their belongings and their livestock hundreds of miles over rugged terrain. When they finally arrived, they had to build their own homes and farms. Then they struggled to survive in a harsh environment. For many, however, achieving their dream of starting a new life was worth it.

In "Rachel's Journal," the narrator and her family are traveling a route known as the Oregon Trail in a wagon. Her journal tells of the many challenges that the group encounters.

ANCHOR TEXT

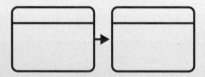

✓ TARGET SKILL

Cause and Effect Analyze causes and effects to better understand relationships between events in the story.

✓ GENRE

Historical fiction is a story whose characters and events are set in a real period of history. As you read, look for:

▶ a setting that was a real time and place in the past

▶ details that show the story took place in the past

▶ realistic characters

COMMON CORE **RL.5.4** determine the meaning of words and phrases, including figurative language; **RL.5.6** describe how a narrator's or speaker's point of view influences how events are described; **RL.5.10** read and comprehend literature; **L.5.5a** interpret figurative language in context

724

MEET THE AUTHOR

Marissa Moss

Marissa Moss "always kept a notebook as a girl and loved to read those of others." To try to make Rachel's voice sound real, she relied on her own childhood memories and read "firsthand accounts written by pioneers at this time—mostly women and children."

MEET THE ILLUSTRATOR

Megan Halsey

As a child, Megan Halsey took piano lessons, but rather than practice, she colored in the sheet music! To this day, she loves to color and cannot play the piano. As an adult, she took a children's book illustration class. She knew right away that she wanted to be a children's book illustrator. Since then, she has illustrated more than forty children's books.

Rachel's Journal

THE STORY OF A PIONEER GIRL

by Marissa Moss

selection illustrated by Megan Halsey

ESSENTIAL QUESTION

Why would a pioneer traveler record events in a journal?

It has been two months since Rachel's family left Illinois in a wagon train bound for good farmland in California. During the long ride, Rachel spends time with her brothers Ben and Will, as well as Frank and Prudence, children from other families in the wagon train. She writes about their adventures in her journal.

May 10, 1850

Pa says we are taking the Oregon Trail until it splits and we veer south for California. Now we are following the Platte River. The sight of the broad river and the bluffs is restful, but the dust kicked up by all the stock is not. Especially when our wagons are in the rear—then it is so thick, I can barely see past our own teams. But I found a way to escape the heat and dirt of the main road. All along the trail there are narrow cut-off paths. Pa says they were made and used by Indians and hunters. These cut-offs run diagonally to the road and are often by shady creeks, so they are pleasant to walk along. Since they always lead back to the trail, there is no need to fret about getting lost. The boys have to drive the stock, so they have no choice but to eat dust, but I take the younger children with me, and we have great fun, picking berries and wildflowers and wading in the creeks.

May 16, 1850

Today I had my first adventure. We had been walking on the cut-off for 2–3 hours, traveling upstream into a deep canyon. The trail was not only out of sight, but out of earshot as well. I liked feeling alone, but Emma fretted that we were lost and the twins were tired, whining that a jouncing wagon ride would be better than tramping on. I tried to cheer everyone by singing "Turkey in the Straw" when we heard a rustling in the bushes. Something much larger than a turkey—Indians! Frank pulled out his little knife, all fierceness, but I hushed him and went to look for myself. (All quaking inside, I admit, but I could not let _them_ see that!) And what should I see when I parted the bushes with trembling hand? The moist snout of a very content ox, chomping on leaves. Somebody must have lost him. If it _had_ been an Indian, Frank declared, he would have protected us. I hope we have no such need.

That was just the beginning of our adventure. When the cut-off reached the trail, there was no sign of our train, either ahead or behind. There was nothing for it but to continue on the cut-off in the hopes of coming out ahead of our wagons soon. On and on we walked. Frank and Emma never complained, nor did little Caroline, but those twins whined worse than the mosquitoes. Still we found no wagons. The sun set, the buffalo wolves started in to howl, and it was too dark to see the trail before us. I would have sat down in the darkness and cried, but I had to take care of the others. Then I recalled what Ben had said about looking for a high view point if you get lost, so I urged everyone up a hill before us. It was not very high, but we were rewarded with the sight of 3 campfires. Since our train is not large, we headed for the smallest one, going straight across country. We barged through brambles and sloshed through creeks, but we always kept that light in view, like the beacon of a lighthouse.

At last I was greeted with the welcome sight of Prudence nibbling bacon. I could not help but embrace her, though she did not appreciate my smudged arms and dress. In fact, she was so startled by our abrupt appearance, she screamed as if we were ghosts or Indians.

Mrs. Arabella Sunshine, Mrs. Elias, and Mother were first joyous, then mad. In between hugging me and scrubbing my face, Mother scolded. Now I cannot take cut-offs after the noon break. That means swallowing dust in the hottest part of the day. At least we still have the mornings.

The bacon and coffee smelled wonderful!

May 23, 1850

Now we are not permitted ever to walk along the cut-offs! Not that we got lost today—something much more exciting happened. Once again we were out of sight of the train, singing as we strolled, when an Indian brave came riding straight at us. I was so amazed to see a true Indian, I forgot to be frightened. We all stood staring at him (though Frank once again reached for his knife—I hissed at him to leave it be, no sense <u>asking</u> for trouble). The twins hid behind my skirt, and the others huddled around me when the brave rode up to us and leapt off his pony. You could have heard a pin drop! He stepped toward me and said something, then held his hand straight out. I did not know what else to do, but shake it, so I did. And that was exactly what he wanted! He offered his hand to each child. Even Frank shook it, grinning so broadly his mouth looked like he had swallowed an ear of corn whole.

The brave knew some English, and he clearly thought we were lost. He asked if I knew where our wagon was. I nodded yes. Satisfied that we were not in trouble, he got back on his pony, waved good-bye, and rode off. It was all over in two shakes of a lamb's tail. After all the horrible stories we had heard about Indians, we had a story of our own to tell and a pretty funny one at that. Only somehow when the adults heard of our meeting, they were not amused. Instead they lectured us on all the awful things that <u>might</u> have happened. And so the cut-offs are forbidden from now on.

ANALYZE THE TEXT

Figurative Language Authors sometimes use **hyperbole**, or exaggeration, to make a point or to describe something. For example, Rachel says, "You could have heard a pin drop." What does this tell you about how quiet it was when the brave approached the children?

My shoes are so caked with mud, they are more mud pie than footwear.

It's hard keeping this journal dry— I do my best..

May 30, 1850

It has rained for days, which has the benefit of keeping down the dust but the disadvantage of turning the trail into an enormous puddle. Despite our cover claiming to be watertight, everything is soaked through. The Platte is swollen and wild. I am relieved we do not have to ford it. Pa says we will reach the government ferry tomorrow.

Sunbonnets are definitely _not_ meant for rain, unless you find a sopping curtain before your face desirable—I do not!

The prairie is so low and the sky so close that in a storm you feel the clouds pressing down on you.

June 7, 1850

Yesterday was the first time I truly felt scared. Getting lost, howling wolves, Indians—nothing compares to the fury of this river! We arrived at the ferry only to discover that it had broken loose of its moorings when the rains started. Some men finally retrieved it, but it took so long that an enormous line of wagons waited ahead of us to take the ferry. The man said it would be 3 <u>weeks</u> before our turn came. Mr. Elias warned that we were already behind schedule and such a long delay would surely mean crossing the Sierra Nevada Mountains in the snow. No one wants to suffer the fate of the Donner Party, frozen and starving in the mountains. Mr. Elias determined that we should take the wagons off their wheel beds and raft them over the river. The current was swift and the banks like quicksand, but there was no other way. Both Sunshine families balked at the danger and refused to go first. Mr. Elias offered to cross, but he has young children, so Pa suggested we go. Mother's face was drawn tight, but she nodded. Ben and Will stayed behind to drive the stock over, so Pa, Mother, and I each took a pole to make our way across. The waves were high and it was hard to keep from tipping. Twice I almost fell in. The second time I lost my pole and clung on to the wagon hoops, not much help to anyone after that. Somehow we landed. My knuckles were white from holding so tightly to the hoops, but Mother's face was even paler. What a relief to be on land again!

The worst part was trying to avoid the sandy islands in the middle of the broad river. I could not steer worth a bean.

ANALYZE THE TEXT

Point of View The author uses first-person point of view to tell this story. How does it affect the way the crossing of the river is described?

The others followed with no mishap. (And Frank declared that he was not scared, not a bit. I do not credit that!) Only the stock still had to be driven over. Ben and Will, along with Samuel, John, Daniel, and Jesse, rounded up all 115 head of cattle and drove them to the river, but they refused to go in. They had no idea of the dangers of the Sierras, but they could plainly see the dangers of the Platte. Three times the boys gathered the cattle together only to have them split and stampede at the water's edge. It was getting dark, and it looked like we would have to camp on opposite shores when Will decided he had stood enough, he would <u>make</u> those cattle cross. He rode next to Bo, the lead herd ox, and just as the stubborn animal reached the banks, Will leapt from his horse onto Bo's back, clung to his horns, and, kicking and screaming, drove that ox into the river. And it worked! Bo started swimming across and all the stock followed. Safe on the other side, Will jumped off Bo and looked back to see his own horse foundering in the water. His foreleg had gotten tangled up in the loose reins. Will rushed into the water to free his horse just as a clap of thunder split the sky open. Lightning flashed with an eerie brightness followed by pitch black and the deafening roll of thunder.

In the dark we could not see Will, but his horse clambered safely onto shore. When the next lightning flashed, Pa cried out that Will had made it to a sandbar in the river. Whether he was dead or alive, no one could say, and while the storm raged, no one dared swim out to rescue him.

ANALYZE THE TEXT

....

Cause and Effect There are several factors that cause Will to become stuck on the sandbar in the river. What are they?

732

That was a miserable and awful night! It was total confusion— thunder booming, oxen bellowing, children crying, men shouting, as light as day one minute, as dark as a cave the next. Add to that the torment of not knowing how poor Will fared and feeling utterly helpless to do anything for him. All we could do was huddle together, a pile of drenched human rags, as the men worked blindly to control the stock.

At dawn the storm quieted, and Pa rushed into the churning river and brought back Will's limp body. He was so pale and still, I thought sure he was dead. Pa started rubbing him down. When at last he opened his eyes, the whole company cheered. He was alive! I have never been so proud—nor so scared.

I never thought I would be so happy to see the sun rise.

June 15, 1850

We took some days' rest to wash everything and dry it out, to put the wagons back together and repair them, to coddle Will and return him to his usual good health. We are fortunate no one drowned in that crossing. There are several new graves of men who died that way, and we heard that in a wagon train near ours, a woman was killed by lightning. Will has always claimed to live a charmed life, and now I believe him.

June 20, 1850

A different kind of storm passed by us today—a herd of buffalo. It was as if the river had leapt out of its banks and taken solid form to chase us down. A thick cloud of dust surged toward us, then there was a tremendous noise, an earthly thunder. We could see their shaggy backs rising and falling like a great wave. Nothing could turn back such a force, so we hastily pulled the wagons close together while the boys drove the stock away—for once a cow or an ox is caught up in a buffalo stampede, it is gone for good, part of a new wild herd.

The buffalo hooves raised such a cloud of dust that though I tried to hold in my breath, my throat and tongue were coated with grit. I could taste them pounding past! The cloud was so big, it blotted out the sun like a buffalo eclipse.

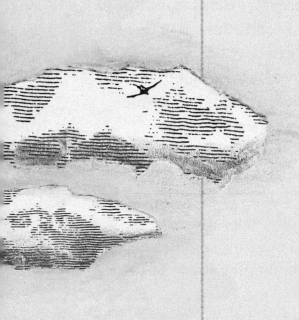

We cowered in the wagons and watched them come closer and closer. Mother tried to keep me back, but I wanted to see them as best I could. After all, if they plowed into us I would not be any safer in the middle of the wagon than in the front. So I poked my head out into the whirling dust storm. I could see their rolling eyes and flaring nostrils, but Will must have brought us some of his charmed luck, and the massive beasts thundered <u>by</u> and not <u>through</u> us. I have seen cattle stampede, but this was different—buffalo are so big and so wild. I wished I could run after them.

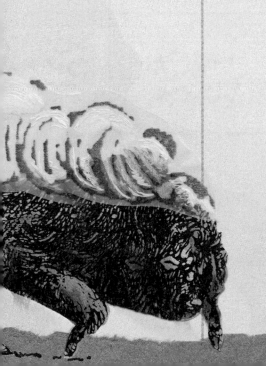

Dig Deeper

How to Analyze the Text

Use these pages to learn about Cause and Effect, Figurative Language, and Point of View. Then read "Rachel's Journal" again to apply what you learned.

Cause and Effect

"Rachel's Journal" describes how Rachel's actions lead to adventure on the Oregon Trail. In historical fiction, as in real life, events are often related as causes and effects. A **cause** is an event that makes something else happen. An **effect** is something that happens because of an earlier event. Some causes lead to more than one effect. Some effects have more than one cause.

Recognizing causes and their effects can help readers see connections between events, better understand characters and themes, and even predict what might happen next. Look back at the scene on page 726. The dust from the trail causes Rachel to travel on the cut-off path. This effect—traveling on the cut-off—then causes other events to happen, shaping the story's structure.

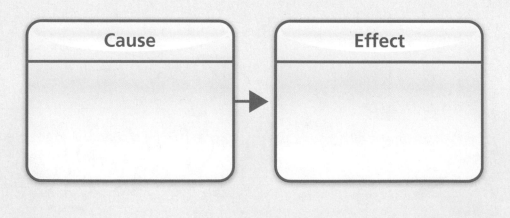

Cause		Effect
	→	

RL.5.4 determine the meaning of words and phrases, including figurative language; **RL.5.5** explain how chapters, scenes, or stanzas fit together to provide the overall structure; **RL.5.6** describe how a narrator's or speaker's point of view influences how events are described; **RL.5.10** read and comprehend literature; **L.5.5a** interpret figurative language in context

Figurative Language

The author of "Rachel's Journal" uses **figurative language**—words and phrases that go beyond their literal meanings—to create vivid descriptions. **Hyperbole**, an exaggeration used for dramatic effect, is one kind of figurative language. Another kind is **simile**, a comparison between two unlike things that uses *like* or *as*: "Her laughter was as shrill as a siren." A third is **metaphor**, a comparison that says one thing is another: "His smile was a ray of sunshine."

Point of View

The **point of view** of this story is first-person. Pronouns such as *I, me, my,* and *we* signal this point of view. Rachel is telling the story through her journal, in which she records what happens to her as well as her thoughts and feelings. This point of view means that readers see the action and other characters through Rachel's eyes.

Your Turn

 Turn and Talk Review the selection to prepare to discuss this question: *Why would a pioneer traveler record events in a journal?* As you discuss this question in a small group, build on each other's responses and then summarize your group's key points.

 Classroom Conversation

Continue your discussion of "Rachel's Journal" by explaining your answers to these questions:

1 What text evidence supports the idea that Rachel is a good narrator for this story?

2 What events would you write about if you kept a journal?

3 How does the setting of the story affect what happens and how characters react to events?

TALK ABOUT ILLUSTRATIONS

Analyze Drawings With a partner, look closely at the illustrations in "Rachel's Journal." Then discuss these questions: *How do the illustrations help you better understand the story's setting and events? What tone, or attitude toward the characters and events, do the pictures convey? What do you learn about Rachel through the illustrations?*

WRITE ABOUT READING

Response In real life, Rachel would have taken her journey by wagon more than a hundred years in the past. Her experiences and surroundings were quite different from our modern ones, and yet her journal entries are easy to relate to. What might modern readers have in common with Rachel? Write a paragraph about whether Rachel is similar to modern girls her age. Use details and other evidence from the text to support your opinion.

Writing Tip

Before writing your paragraph, identify your reasons and find examples to support each one. Use transitions to show how the reasons and their supporting details are connected.

Go Digital

COMMON CORE **RL.5.6** describe how a narrator's or speaker's point of view influences how events are described; **RL.5.7** analyze how visual and multimedia elements contribute to the meaning, tone, or beauty of a text; **W.5.1b** provide logically ordered reasons supported by facts and details; **W.5.1c** link opinion and reasons using words, phrases, and clauses; **W.5.9a** apply grade 5 Reading standards to literature; **SL.5.1a** come to discussions prepared/explicitly draw on preparation and other information about the topic

WESTWARD TO FREEDOM

WESTWARD to FREEDOM

by Tracy Moncure

To many African Americans in the 1800s, the West meant freedom, independence, adventure, and the good life. For those who wanted to leave behind memories of slavery, the West offered a chance to start a new life. The trip west was not easy. Travelers risked danger and mishap. Every rustling of the brush might signal a threat. After the torment of slavery, however, African American pioneers were up to the challenge.

MILESTONES IN THE WESTWARD MOVEMENT OF AFRICAN AMERICANS

1835   **1850**

1848 Southwest and California are acquired.

1849–1852 Up to 4,000 African Americans join the California Gold Rush.

From Mountain Men to Settlers

African Americans were part of United States westward expansion from the start. York, William Clark's "manservant," was a valued member of the Lewis and Clark expedition in 1803. Mountain men such as James Beckwourth (1798–1866) were early settlers of the Wild West. Some historians believe that as many as one in four cowboys was African American.

Other African Americans built homes, started cities, or upheld the law. In 1889, the Indian Territory opened to settlers. African Americans surged over the tall grasses of the Oklahoma plains. They built more all-black towns in Oklahoma than in all the rest of the country. Bass Reeves (1838–1910) was a U.S. Marshal in the Indian Territory. People thought of him as being tough but fair. Outlaws must have started quaking in their boots when they heard his name.

1863 Emancipation Proclamation frees slaves in the Confederacy.

1877-1879 Benjamin "Pap" Singleton helps African Americans settle in Kansas.

1889 African Americans join the Indian Territory land rush.

1865   **1880**   **1895**

1861-1865 Civil War

1868 Fourteenth Amendment grants citizenship to African Americans.

741

Helping Others on the Path to Freedom

Many African American pioneers became successful in business. They often used their wealth to help others find better lives.

Biddy Mason (1818–1891) traveled with her owner to California in 1847. Her owner balked at giving her freedom. So a judge lectured him, saying that California was a free territory. Later, she owned land in Los Angeles. She became the city's richest citizen. She used her wealth to help those in need.

Clara Brown (1800–1885) also began her life enslaved. After some time, she overcame this disadvantage and fared well. She gained freedom and became the first African American woman to settle in the Colorado gold fields. She started a laundry business. She invested in mines, too. A beacon of hope to freed slaves, she helped many people move to the West.

A regiment of African American cavalry, known as "Buffalo Soldiers," stand next to their horses.

Compare Texts

Compare Texts About Pioneers Many people traveled west in the 1800s. Their reasons for going and their experiences were alike in some ways and different in others. With a partner, complete a Venn diagram comparing the characters in "Rachel's Journal" with the African American pioneers in "Westward to Freedom." Examine why they went west, what happened to them, and what personal qualities helped them survive.

TEXT TO SELF

Evaluate Figurative Language The author of "Rachel's Journal" uses hyperbole, or exaggeration, to help describe the children's encounter with an Indian brave. With a partner, discuss how this and other uses of figurative language in the text help you better understand Rachel's experiences or feelings. Make a list of the figurative language you find, and interpret the meaning of each.

TEXT TO WORLD

Compare Texts About African American History Review "Westward to Freedom" and "Pea Island's Forgotten Heroes" (Lesson 9). Look for several main ideas in each selection and the details that support each idea. Then, in a small group, compare and contrast the two selections. Focus on the view of African Americans in history that each selection conveys. As you discuss, provide quotes and other evidence from both texts as support.

COMMON CORE **RI.5.1** quote accurately when explaining what the text says explicitly and when drawing inferences; **RI.5.2** determine two or more main ideas and explain how they are supported by details/summarize; **RI.5.9** integrate information from several texts on the same topic; **SL.5.1a** come to discussions prepared/explicitly draw on preparation and other information about the topic; **L.5.5a** interpret figurative language in context

Grammar

Comparative and Superlative Forms A **comparative adjective** compares two people, places, or things. Add *-er* to a short adjective, or use *more* before a long one, to make its comparative form. A **superlative adjective** compares more than two people, places, or things. Add *-est* to a short adjective, or use *most* before a long one, to make its superlative form. The adjectives *good* and *bad* have special comparative and superlative forms.

Adjective	Comparative	Superlative
young (short adjective)	younger	youngest
beautiful (long adjective)	more beautiful	most beautiful
good	better	best
bad	worse	worst

Many adverbs have comparative and superlative forms. Use the word *more* in front of an adverb to make a **comparative adverb**. Use *most* in front of an adverb to make a **superlative adverb**.

Adverb	Comparative	Superlative
cheerfully	more cheerfully	most cheerfully

 **Work with a partner. Identify each comparative and superlative adjective and adverb.**

1. Wolf howls made the night seem scarier.

2. The lead ox behaved the most stubbornly of any animal.

3. I was more afraid of the thunder than of the lightning.

4. That river crossing was the worst situation ever.

5. Will acted more bravely than anyone else.

You can sometimes make comparisons, sentences, or ideas in your writing clearer by using comparative and superlative forms of adjectives and adverbs.

Less Clear	Clearer
I am eight years old. I have a sister and a brother.	I am eight years old. I have an older brother and an older sister. My sister is the oldest of us all.

 ## Connect Grammar to Writing

As you revise your response essay next week, look for opportunities to make your ideas clearer by using comparative and superlative forms. Make sure you use the correct forms when writing comparative or superlative adjectives or adverbs.

Opinion Writing

Reading-Writing Workshop: Prewrite

✔ **Organization** A **response essay** often requires that you state an opinion about a topic. When writing a response to literature, support your opinion with reasons and details from the text.

Kira thought about her answer to this prompt: *Does the journal format of "Rachel's Journal" tell the story better than a traditional narrative would have? Why or why not?* First, she made notes. Then, in a chart, she restated her opinion, listed her strongest reasons, and included supporting details.

Use the Writing Process Checklist below as you prewrite.

 Writing Process Checklist

▶ **Prewrite**

☑ Did I state my opinion clearly?

☑ Did I give at least two good reasons?

☑ Did I list details from the story to support my reasons?

Draft

Revise

Edit

Publish and Share

Exploring a Topic

Opinion: The journal format is better for this story.

Reason: It focuses on the writer's feelings and has a personal touch.

Reason: It is a good way to tell about a journey.

Reason: It shows Rachel's voice.

Opinion: The journal format is better for this story.

Reasons	Details
The journal format allows Rachel to share her story as if she is a reporter taking detailed notes about settings and events.	• Platte River, bluffs, cut-offs, Indian brave, buffalo, oxen, Rachel's family, members of wagon train
The journal format helps readers imagine what a real pioneer girl would sound like.	• mud-caked shoes, washing and drying things out, repairing wagons • sayings: "worth a bean," "two shakes of a lamb's tail," "I do not credit that" • words: "fret"

Reading as a Writer

How did Kira make her reasons stronger when she created her chart? What reasons or details could be made stronger in your chart?

When I made my chart, I strengthened my reasons by adding details from the text to support them.

Lewis and Clark

A SURPRISE REUNION

☑ TARGET VOCABULARY

expedition
tributaries
trek
barrier
despite
fulfilled
range
techniques
resumed
edible

Vocabulary
Reader

Context
Cards

River Travel

COMMON CORE **L.5.6** acquire and use general academic and domain-specific words and phrases

Vocabulary in Context

1 expedition
Adventurer Edmund Hillary led an expedition to climb Mount Everest.

2 tributaries
This creek is one of the tributaries, or small branches, of a larger river.

3 trek
These hikers are on a week-long trek through a national park.

4 barrier
Thick vegetation forms a barrier in the jungle. Explorers must cut through the obstacle.

Go Digital

▶ Study each Context Card.

▶ Use a thesaurus to find a word to replace each of the Vocabulary words.

5 despite

Despite the blazing heat, these pioneers crossed the prairie.

6 fulfilled

This astronaut fulfilled his lifelong dream of going to the moon.

7 range

Jim Bridger explored the mountain chain known as the Rocky Mountain range.

8 techniques

This hiker knows different techniques, or methods, for starting a campfire.

9 resumed

After resting, this boy resumed his bike ride. He felt ready to ride again.

10 edible

Hikers need to know which berries are edible and which ones they must not eat.

Read and Comprehend

☑ TARGET SKILL

Main Ideas and Details As you read "Lewis and Clark," look for the **main ideas**, or most important points, that the author presents. Notice the **details**—such as facts, examples, and quotations—that explain or support each main idea. Use a graphic organizer like the one shown below to record main ideas and supporting details.

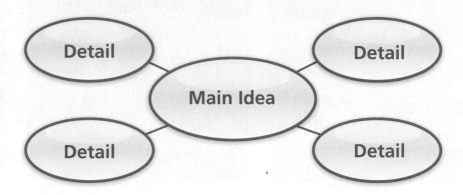

☑ TARGET STRATEGY

Monitor/Clarify As you read "Lewis and Clark," **monitor**, or pay attention to, how well you understand the main ideas. Reread parts of the text or look for text evidence to **clarify**, or clear up, confusing details.

RI.5.2 determine two or more main ideas and explain how they are supported by details/summarize; **RI.5.3** explain the relationships between individuals/events/ideas/concepts in a text

750

PREVIEW THE TOPIC

Exploration

President Thomas Jefferson bought the Louisiana Territory from France in 1803. He knew the area was immense, but he didn't know much else about it. He sent Lewis, Clark, and their Corps of Discovery to chart the region. Jefferson hoped they would find a major waterway that ships could use to sail from one coast to the other. Although they never found such a passageway, the expedition made valuable contacts with many Native American communities. The Corps also studied the territory's natural features, animals, and plant life.

This selection is based on journals kept by the explorers. As you read it, you will learn more about the day-to-day challenges they faced and the excitement they felt as they moved west.

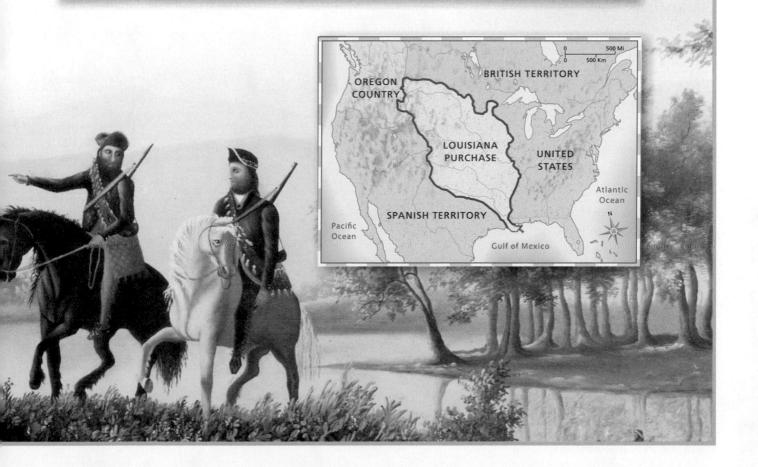

ANCHOR TEXT

✅ TARGET SKILL

Main Ideas and Details
Determine the main ideas of the text. Find details that support the main ideas.

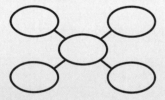

✅ GENRE

Narrative nonfiction tells about people, events, or places that are real. As you read, look for:

▶ factual information that tells a story

▶ features such as photographs and captions

▶ events in time order

COMMON CORE **RI.5.2** determine two or more main ideas and explain how they are supported by details/summarize; **RI.5.3** explain the relationships between individuals/events/ideas/concepts in a text; **RI.5.10** read and comprehend informational text

 Go Digital

MEET THE AUTHOR

R. Conrad Stein

R. Conrad Stein knew from the time he was twelve years old that he wanted to be a writer. After serving as a Marine, he studied history at the University of Illinois. A few years after he graduated, his background in history helped him get assignments writing history books for young readers. He has published more than eighty books; many of them are biographies or are focused on history. Stein believes his job is to express the drama of historical events.

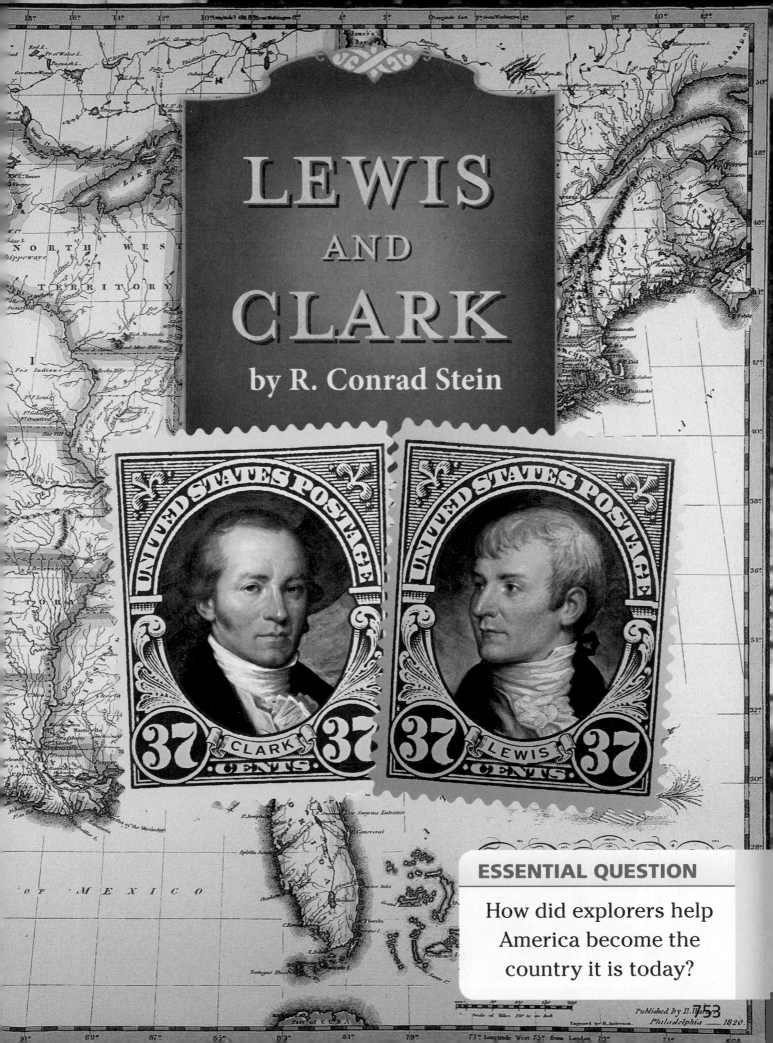

LEWIS
AND
CLARK

by R. Conrad Stein

ESSENTIAL QUESTION

How did explorers help America become the country it is today?

In 1803, President Thomas Jefferson doubled the size of the United States after completing an agreement with France called the Louisiana Purchase. He had acquired the vast Louisiana Territory west of the Mississippi River. Jefferson decided to form an expedition through the unexplored Territory to the Pacific Ocean. He asked Meriwether Lewis to lead a group called the Corps of Discovery. Lewis chose William Clark to help him as co-leader. In 1804, Lewis and Clark began their journey from St. Louis, Missouri. They traveled through the Great Plains and then stopped for the winter season. A trader and his wife, a Native American named Sacagawea (sak uh juh WEE uh), joined the expedition when it resumed its journey in April 1805.

Lewis considered the Mandan (MAN duhn) Indians' stories about huge bears to be fanciful tales until one of the explorers was chased by a grizzly bear.

754

The Great Falls of the Missouri River were a beautiful sight, but also were difficult to travel around.

William Clark had perhaps the best eyesight of any crew member. On May 26, he saw the outline of a great mountain range to the west. In the next few days, all of the explorers could see the snow-covered Rocky Mountains on the horizon. The sight was inspiring as well as troubling. The explorers knew that they would have to find a way to cross the incredible barrier.

Before they could cross the Rockies, the Corps of Discovery faced the Great Falls of the Missouri River in present-day Montana. Here the river tumbled down a bluff that was as high as a modern six-story building. The roar of the water was deafening. Lewis called it, "the grandest sight I ever beheld." But the waterfall meant that the explorers had to carry their boats and supplies up steep cliffs before they could set out again on quieter waters upstream. Traveling around the falls took the party twenty-four days, and left everyone exhausted.

Sacagawea quickly proved to be a valuable asset to the expedition.

Carrying her baby boy on her back, Sacagawea won the admiration of the crew. She carefully scanned the riverbank to find edible roots and fruit. These foods provided a welcome relief from the customary diet of meat and water. And in the mountain country, the Missouri River became a crooked stream that split into many small tributaries. Sacagawea pointed out landmarks that she remembered from a journey as a slave child, and she helped the captains choose the correct river branches on which to travel.

Soon the members of the party began to wonder why they had not yet seen any Shoshone (shoh SHOH nee) or other American Indians. They had seen signs of Indian settlement—hunters' trails and abandoned campsites—but since they left the Mandan and Hidatsa (hee DAHT suh) villages, the Corps of Discovery had not encountered any other people at all.

ANALYZE THE TEXT

Explain Historical Events What does the author do to make historical events easy to understand? How does this help you see relationships between the events and people described in the text?

In mid-August, Meriwether Lewis, hiking ahead of the party with a few other explorers, came upon three Shoshone women and several children. Lewis had carried an American flag in his pack for just such a meeting.

He waved the banner and walked slowly toward the group. One of the children fled. The women sat very still as if frozen with fear. Lewis explained that he was an explorer, and the women led him to their village.

The Shoshone were a small tribe who were almost always at war with their powerful neighbors, the Blackfeet. They had never seen white people, but constant warfare made the Shoshone suspicious of all outsiders. Lewis hoped to buy horses from the tribe. Now that the rivers had all but disappeared, he needed horses to cross the peaks of the Rocky Mountains. But the chief, Cameahwait (kuh MEE uh wayt), would not part with any of the animals. Lewis did persuade Cameahwait to send a few Shoshone to find Clark and the rest of the party and bring them to the village.

At first, the Shoshone were cautious of Lewis and Clark, but the explorers soon realized that they were fortunate to encounter the Indians.

The next morning, Clark and the others arrived at the village, and a meeting was held with Chief Cameahwait. Sacagawea prepared to serve as the translator. When the meeting began, Sacagawea stared intently at the chief. Then she broke into tears of joy. Lewis wrote, "She jumped up, ran, and embraced him, and threw her blanket over him, and cried profusely." Sacagawea recognized Cameahwait as her brother, whom she had not seen in six years. Cheers and laughter rose from the village. The Shoshone hailed Sacagawea as a lost daughter who had come home.

On September 1, 1805, the Corps of Discovery left the Shoshone territory. Chief Cameahwait not only provided the party with horses, he also gave them a guide to show them the best route through the mountains. Crossing the Rockies proved to be a difficult ordeal. The trails were too rugged to ride on, so the party walked and used the horses as pack animals.

The expedition crossed the Rockies on foot, using the horses to carry their equipment and supplies.

ANALYZE THE TEXT

Primary Sources The author uses a primary source, a direct quote from Lewis's writing, in the first paragraph. What can you conclude about Lewis from his words?

Upon reaching the Clearwater River Valley, the expedition built new canoes to continue their journey west.

In mid-September, a blinding snowstorm struck. Even the Shoshone guide got lost. Worst of all, the once-abundant wild game could not be found on the high mountain peaks. The explorers were forced to kill some of their pack animals for meat. The explorers' journals report that the men laughed out loud when they finally crossed the mountains and reached grasslands on level terrain.

The Lewis and Clark expedition emerged from the Rocky Mountains into the lovely valley of the Clearwater River in present-day Idaho. The waters were so clear that the river bottom and schools of fish were visible despite the river's depth. In the Clearwater country, Lewis and Clark abandoned their pack horses and built new canoes. They reasoned that the streams on this side of the Rockies would all eventually flow into the Columbia River, the major river of the Pacific Northwest. American Indians called the Columbia River the *Ouragon* or *Origan*. The land around it was later called the Oregon Territory.

Traveling the rivers, the voyagers met the Nez Perce (NEZ PURS) Indians, who taught them valuable techniques for building and sailing log canoes. Less friendly were the Chinook (shih NOOK), who drove hard bargains when trading for goods. But encountering the Chinook meant that the Pacific Ocean was not far away. One of the Chinook wore a black navy coat that he may have bought from a North American or European sailor.

A dismal rain pelted the travelers in early November as they sailed down the Columbia River. They made a camp near an Indian village and spent a restless night. On the morning of November 7, 1805, the rain stopped and the fog cleared. A chorus of shouts suddenly went up from the camp. William Clark scribbled in his notes, "Ocean in view! O! the joy." On the horizon, still many miles to the west, lay the great Pacific Ocean. Upon seeing the ocean, some of the explorers wept, and others said prayers of thanksgiving.

The explorers experienced some difficulty in dealing with the Chinook Indians, but their encounter brought signs that the Pacific Ocean was near.

The explorers saw the Pacific Ocean for the first time near present-day Astoria, Oregon.

But arriving at the Pacific Ocean did not end the Lewis and Clark expedition. The party still had to return home to St. Louis. President Jefferson had provided Meriwether Lewis with a letter of credit guaranteeing payment to any ship captain who would take the explorers to the eastern coast. The party made a winter camp at the mouth of the Columbia River near present-day Astoria, Oregon, and kept a watch for ships. No vessels were spotted. Finally, on March 23, 1806, the crew broke camp and began the long trek east toward St. Louis.

To the explorers, the six-month return journey seemed to be easier than their first journey because they knew what to expect in the river and mountain country. When the crew reached the Mandan village, they said good-bye to Sacagawea and her husband and continued back to St. Louis.

On September 23, 1806, the Lewis and Clark expedition arrived safely back in St. Louis, Missouri, where their journey had begun more than two years earlier. The travelers had gone a distance of just less than 4,000 miles (6,400 km) from St. Louis to the mouth of the Columbia River and back. But the twisting rivers and mountain trails meant that the Corps of Discovery had actually covered about 8,000 miles (13,000 km) on the history-making trip. Throughout the explorers' travels, they encountered more than fifty American-Indian tribes.

The journals kept by Captains Lewis, Clark, and several members of their expedition have been compiled into many published accounts since the journey ended in 1806.

The expedition returned with numerous samples of plant and animal life that had never before been seen by American scientists. Before the expedition, President Jefferson had hoped that the explorers would find a broad river that ships could use to sail directly to the Pacific Ocean. Lewis and Clark failed to find such a river, and the expedition was final proof that an inland waterway in North America did not exist.

From St. Louis, Lewis and Clark traveled to Washington, D.C. Almost every town they passed through brought out bands to welcome them as heroes. In Washington, D.C., the explorers delighted President Jefferson with tales of grizzly bears and high mountain passes. The president said, "Lewis and Clark have entirely fulfilled my expectations....

The world will find that those travelers have well earned its favor."

To Meriwether Lewis and William Clark, the mission itself was their greatest reward. Traveling through virtually unexplored lands was an exhilarating experience that they would cherish for the rest of their lives. Although they faced many dangers, the thrill—not the peril—of the expedition bursts from the pages of the journals they kept. As Lewis wrote the day he left the Indian village to enter the Western wilderness, "I could but esteem this moment of my departure as among the most happy of my life."

ANALYZE THE TEXT

Main Ideas and Details What is the main idea of the text on this page? What is the selection's overall main idea? Identify the key details that support it.

Dig Deeper

How to Analyze the Text

Use these pages to learn about Main Ideas and Details, Primary Sources, and Explaining Historical Events. Then read "Lewis and Clark" again to apply what you learned.

Main Ideas and Details

The **main idea** is what a text is mostly about. In addition to the overall main idea, paragraphs and sections of a text also have their own main ideas. Each main idea is supported by **details**. These details may be facts, examples, descriptions, quotations, or other types of text evidence.

Sometimes main ideas are stated directly. At other times, **implied** main ideas must be inferred from the information given. To find an implied main idea, readers ask themselves what point all of the details in a paragraph or section support. On page 757, the main idea is implied. Readers have to read carefully and make inferences based on text evidence to understand it.

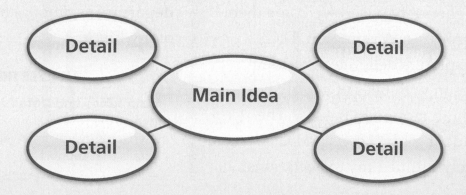

RI.5.2 determine two or more main ideas and explain how they are supported by details/summarize; **RI.5.3** explain the relationships between individuals/events/ideas/concepts in a text; **RI.5.8** explain how an author uses reasons and evidence to support points; **RI.5.10** read and comprehend informational texts

Primary Sources

Authors of narrative nonfiction often rely on **primary sources** for details and information about people and events. Primary sources are materials created by someone who witnessed or took part in the event he or she is describing. Throughout "Lewis and Clark," the author refers to the expedition members' journals. From these primary sources, the author uses quotations and information to support his points.

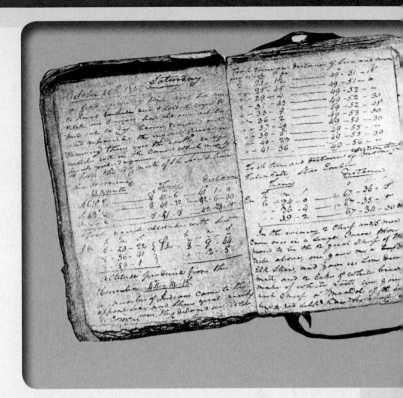

Explain Historical Events

In most of "Lewis and Clark," the author presents **events** in sequence, helping readers understand the experiences of expedition members. The last part of the text, however, examines the significance of the explorers' accomplishments. It shows how individual events on the journey are related to the greater historical purpose of the expedition. Look for relationships between events in a historical text to understand what happened, when it happened, and why.

Your Turn

RETURN TO THE ESSENTIAL QUESTION

Turn and Talk Review the selection to prepare to discuss this question: *How did explorers help America become the country it is today?* Discuss the question in small groups. As you present your ideas, be sure to relate them to what others in the group have said.

 Classroom Conversation

Continue your discussion of "Lewis and Clark" by using text evidence to explain your answers to these questions:

1. Why was an expedition to explore the Louisiana Territory necessary?

2. Why was Sacagawea's role in the expedition important?

3. How does the author make Lewis and Clark seem like real people instead of just historical figures?

ALL IN THE DETAILS

List It Think about the words, descriptions, and examples the author uses when he refers to the explorers Lewis and Clark. With a partner, create a list of these details. Use quotation marks to show the details that you quote directly from the text. Discuss what you learn about the explorers from your list. Then analyze what the details show about the author's feelings toward the two men.

"Traveling around the falls . . . left everyone exhausted."

"Lewis had carried an American flag in his pack for just such a meeting."

WRITE ABOUT READING

Response One word that could describe the Lewis and Clark expedition is *eventful*. The group met one challenge after another in their quest to reach the Pacific Ocean. Write a paragraph in which you explain what happened on the expedition and why it was a great achievement. Support your ideas with quotations, details, and other text evidence.

Writing Tip

Use sequential order to organize your paragraph. Be sure to include words and phrases that describe each event.

COMMON CORE **RI.5.1** quote accurately when explaining what the text says explicitly and when drawing inferences; **W.5.9b** apply grade 5 Reading standards to informational texts; **W.5.10** write routinely over extended time frames and shorter time frames; **SL.5.1a** come to discussions prepared/explicitly draw on preparation and other information about the topic; **SL.5.1c** pose and respond to questions, make comments that contribute to the discussion, and elaborate on others' remarks

PLAY

A SURPRISE REUNION

By Byron Cahill

Cast of Characters

Narrator
Chief Cameahwait
Captain Meriwether Lewis
Captain William Clark
Sacagawea
Shoshone Scout

☑ GENRE

A **play,** like this dramatic adaptation, tells a story through the words and actions of its characters.

☑ TEXT FOCUS

Dialogue and Theme

Dialogue is lines of text in a play that stand for the words spoken by the characters. Because much of what happens in a play is conveyed through dialogue and interactions between characters, these elements are used to establish the play's theme.

COMMON CORE **RL.5.2** determine theme from details/ summarize; **RL.5.10** read and comprehend literature

 Go Digital

Narrator: It is August of 1805 in the camp of the Shoshone. The main party of the Lewis and Clark Expedition is making its way back to Captain Lewis's group. While Shoshone scouts are out searching for them, Lewis is asking the chief, Cameahwait, for help.

Lewis: Chief Cameahwait, won't you please reconsider parting with a few of your horses? They would be a great help to us in crossing the western mountain range.

Cameahwait: (*Firmly*) No, stranger. You could be allies of the Blackfoot.

Lewis: We simply seek passage to the other side of these mountains.

Cameahwait: So you say, but despite your words, you are intruders in my lands.

Lewis: I give you my word. We mean the Shoshone no harm.

Cameahwait: We Shoshone judge others by their actions, not by words alone. We have lost much in war. I myself lost a sister years ago.

Shoshone Scout: (*Entering with Clark and Sacagawea*) Cameahwait, we have brought the strangers to you. We found them camped near one of the tributaries of the river.

Lewis: (*Relieved*) Captain Clark! Sacagawea! It is good to see you safe.

Clark: Everyone is in good health, Meriwether, thanks to the edible plants Sacagawea found and her excellent techniques for preparing them.

Lewis: Good! Sacagawea, perhaps you can convince Cameahwait that our journey can be resumed much sooner if he agrees to trade with us.

769

Clark: Sacagawea? What is wrong? You are shaking!

Narrator: Sacagawea does not answer. She gazes at Cameahwait, then rushes into his arms and throws her blanket around his shoulders, weeping loudly.

Sacagawea: (*Through her tears*) Brother! It is you, is it not?

Cameahwait: It is not possible! You were taken. Are these men your captors?

Sacagawea: No! I am a free woman. I am helping them on their journey. My husband and child are outside with the rest of the group.

Cameahwait: (*Surprised*) Husband? Child?

Sacagawea: Yes, Brother! You are an uncle! These men are friends!

Cameahwait: Then let distrust no longer be a barrier between us, Captain Lewis. I promise you horses for your journey, and one of my best guides. My promise will be fulfilled after we celebrate my sister's return to her tribe!

Narrator: With the help of Cameahwait, the Lewis and Clark Expedition safely completed its trek through the dangerous terrain of the Rocky Mountains. They arrived at the shores of the Pacific Ocean just three months later.

Compare Texts

Compare Presentations of Events With a partner, review the play and the account of Sacagawea's reunion with her brother in "Lewis and Clark." Discuss the ways in which the portrayal of the event in both versions is the same and different. Identify the author's purpose in both texts and explain how the purpose affects the way the event is described. Summarize your key points and share them with the class, supporting your ideas with evidence and quotations from each text.

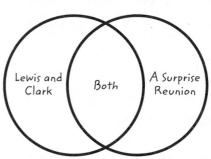

Lewis and Clark | Both | A Surprise Reunion

Write a Story Write a short story about a key event that happened after Lewis and Clark left St. Louis, Missouri. Include sensory details, appropriate language, and dialogue. Read your story aloud to a small group, using different voices, facial expressions, and gestures to add interest and convey feeling.

Connect to Social Studies Use print or online sources to research the Louisiana Purchase. Take notes on the new facts you learn about this historic land purchase. Then discuss those facts with a partner.

COMMON CORE **RI.5.9** integrate information from several texts on the same topic; **W.5.3a** orient the reader by establishing a situation and introducing a narrator or characters/organize an event sequence; **W.5.3b** use narrative techniques to develop experiences and events or show characters' responses; **W.5.3d** use concrete words and phrases and sensory details; **SL.5.6** adapt speech to contexts and tasks, using formal English when appropriate to task and situation

Grammar

What Is a Contraction? A **contraction** is a word formed by joining two words into one shorter word. An **apostrophe** (') takes the place of the letter or letters that are dropped to make the shorter word. You can combine some verbs with the **negative** word *not* to make contractions. You can also combine personal pronouns with verbs such as *is*, *are*, *have*, *had*, and *will* to make contractions.

Examples of Contractions Made with Verbs Plus *not*			
do not	don't	were not	weren't
does not	doesn't	will not	won't
is not	isn't	has not	hasn't

Examples of Contractions Made with Pronouns Plus Verbs			
I am	I'm	I have	I've
he is	he's	he has	he's
you are	you're	you have	you've
they are	they're	they have	they've
you will	you'll	you had	you'd

Try This! **Rewrite each sentence below on a sheet of paper. Replace each pair of boldfaced words with a contraction.**

❶ The expedition **will not** be an easy trip.

❷ **It is** likely that supplies will run short.

❸ However, that **does not** mean we should be afraid.

❹ **We will** find people along the way who can help us.

❺ **I am** sure the experience will be a great adventure!

When using a contraction, put the apostrophe in the correct place. In a contraction with a pronoun and a verb, make sure the verb agrees in number with the pronoun. When using a contraction with *not*, avoid including another "no" word and creating a double negative. Finally, avoid using the contraction *ain't*.

Contractions

Incorrect	Correct
Chief Cameahwait **don't** speak English. Sacagawea is able to translate. **She're** able to help the explorers borrow horses from the Shoshone.	Chief Cameahwait **doesn't** speak English. Sacagawea is able to translate. **She's** able to help the explorers borrow horses from the Shoshone.

 Connect Grammar to Writing

As you edit your response essay, make sure you have used and written contractions correctly. Be sure to correct any contraction errors you find.

W.5.1a introduce a topic, state an opinion, and create an organizational structure; **W.5.1b** provide logically ordered reasons supported by facts and details; **W.5.1d** provide a concluding statement or section; **W.5.5** develop and strengthen writing by planning, revising, editing, rewriting or trying a new approach; **W.5.10** write routinely over extended time frames and shorter time frames

Opinion Writing

Reading-Writing Workshop: Revise

✔ **Word Choice** When you write your **response essay,** use strong verbs and adjectives to help make your points clear. Support your opinion and reasons with good examples, and provide a conclusion that readers will find memorable.

Kira used her chart to draft a response to the prompt, *Does the journal format of "Rachel's Journal" tell the story better than a traditional narrative would have? Why or why not?* Then she revised her essay to strengthen her topic sentence and her conclusion.

Use the Writing Process Checklist below as you revise your writing.

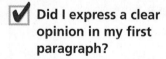

Writing Process Checklist

Prewrite

Draft

▶ **Revise**

✔ Did I express a clear opinion in my first paragraph?

✔ Did I include strong reasons for my opinion?

✔ Did I use good examples to explain my reasons?

✔ Is my conclusion strong and convincing?

Edit

Publish and Share

Revised Draft

"Rachel's Journal" is a story about a young

pioneer. ~~I like its journal format.~~ Sometimes

you even forget you are reading fiction!
When she writes in her journal,
Rachel is like a reporter taking notes on

her life.

Because the story is written in the main character's journal, it feels very realistic.

Good Storytelling

by Kira Delaney

"Rachel's Journal" is a story about a young pioneer. Because the story is written in the main character's journal, it feels very realistic. Sometimes you even forget you are reading fiction!

When she writes in her journal, Rachel is like a reporter taking notes on her life. She writes about what she sees, what she does, and the people she meets. She describes the Platte River, cut-offs, and buffalo. She also writes about her family. Sometimes she writes about everyday chores such as washing and drying things out and repairing wagons.

The journal format makes it easy to imagine what a real pioneer girl would sound like. Rachel uses words that sound old-fashioned, such as *fret*. She also uses sayings that people don't use much in the present time, such as "worth a bean" and "two shakes of a lamb's tail."

The journal format is the perfect choice for this story. It makes readers feel close to Rachel and makes it easy to see the settings, events, and people through her eyes. It seems like we could be sitting next to her on the wagon.

Reading as a Writer

How did Kira make her response essay more convincing? Where can you strengthen your essay to make it more convincing?

In my final paper, I made my topic sentence and my conclusion stronger. I also used strong adjectives to convey my thoughts.

Test POWER

Read the passages "In Honor of Grandmother" and "Welcoming Grandfather." As you read, stop and use text evidence to answer each question.

In Honor of Grandmother

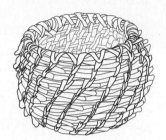

Julie couldn't help feeling jealous as she watched her older sister work. Minna's skillful hands wove the thread and bundles of pine needles into tidy coils to form a basket. As it took shape, the basket began to look just like the baskets their grandmother used to make.

Julie picked up one of her favorite photographs of her grandmother, taken in the last year of Grandmother's life. In this picture, Grandmother was holding a beautiful pine needle basket that she had made. The picture always reminded Julie of what a thoughtful and talented person her grandmother had been and how much she missed her.

The school the girls attended was holding a multicultural festival at which students were invited to share special family customs. Julie and Minna wanted to share something from their Cherokee background, and the pine needle baskets seemed like the perfect choice. Baskets had an important role in Cherokee culture. The Cherokee wove baskets from materials found in nature and used the baskets for gathering food and for storing various items.

By the following week, Minna had completed her basket, but Julie had barely begun to weave hers. She realized she was not skilled enough to complete even a single basket in time for the festival. "Minna, what am I going to do?" Julie cried in despair. "I won't have anything to share!"

Minna always tried to smooth Julie's ruffled feathers. "Maybe you can think of something else," she suggested kindly. "Why don't you look through some of Grandmother's keepsakes and see if you can come up with another idea?"

---

 1   What does the phrase *smooth Julie's ruffled feathers* mean within the context of the passage?

RL.5.1 quote accurately when explaining what the text says explicitly and when drawing inferences; **RL.5.2** determine theme from details/summarize; **RL.5.4** determine the meaning of words and phrases, including figurative language; **RL.5.9** compare and contrast stories in the same genre on their approaches to themes and topics

Julie went to Grandmother's old room, where it was so easy to remember Grandmother's hands always busy at work as she told her granddaughters fascinating stories. Julie opened a dresser and quietly went through a drawer that still held Grandmother's favorite possessions. Julie set aside some beautiful woven belts and small baskets. Then she picked up a bright green folder and leafed through the papers inside it. Suddenly she cried, "Look, Minna, I've found a project that's perfect for me! Grandmother left directions for using ribbon and pine needles to make a picture frame. This is something I know I can do well!"

Minna smiled encouragingly as Julie set to work on her frame, carefully threading the ribbon and pine needles. She used green and blue ribbons because those had been Grandmother's favorite colors. When she was finished, she put the photograph of her grandmother in the frame. Julie was looking forward to displaying her work at the festival, and she knew Grandmother would have been proud.

 2 What is the theme of this passage?

Welcoming Grandfather

"Edgar, you need to get busy and move the rest of your things into Hector's room today," Mrs. Valdez reminded her oldest child.

"Mom, you know that room is going to be way too cramped for both of us," Edgar complained for the twentieth time. Mrs. Valdez sighed in frustration. She had explained many times to her three children that their grandfather, almost eighty years old, needed help now with chores like cooking and laundry.

Since Grandmother had passed away a year ago, Mrs. Valdez had been caring for Grandfather. Together they had decided that it would be easier for everyone if Grandfather moved in with their family. Mrs. Valdez had explained to the children that everyone would benefit from this arrangement. Grandfather would help the family by being home with the children after school, and Mrs. Valdez and the children would also be there for Grandfather if he needed help.

Lupita and Hector, the younger Valdez children, were excited about having Grandfather come to live with them. Only Edgar was unhappy. He preferred things the way they were, and he definitely did not want to share a room with his inquisitive little brother!

On Friday night, after Grandfather had moved in, Edgar hardly spoke during dinner. Grandfather did not seem to notice as he entertained everyone with stories about his childhood. If Edgar hadn't been so grumpy, he would have enjoyed the stories as much as Lupita and Hector did.

 How have things changed for Edgar and his family since his grandmother passed away?

"When I was growing up, the whole family always sat down together for our evening meal," Grandfather said. "Everyone would take turns telling the others about what we had done during the day. I would like to follow that same custom here, if everyone agrees."

"I think that's a lovely idea," said Mrs. Valdez, and Hector and Lupita nodded in agreement.

"I'd like to start," Grandfather continued, "by thanking each of you for allowing me to move into your home. I would especially like to thank you, Edgar, for giving up your room for me. I know this is a big change and must be difficult for you." Edgar felt his face turning red with embarrassment over the fuss he had made.

After dinner, Grandfather offered to do the dishes. Edgar wanted to do something to make Grandfather feel welcome. "How about if you and I do them together, Grandfather?" he said.

 How are the themes and topics of these two passages similar, and how are they different?

Glossary

This glossary contains meanings and pronunciations for some of the words in this book. The Full Pronunciation Key shows how to pronounce each consonant and vowel in a special spelling. At the bottom of the glossary pages is a shortened form of the full key.

Full Pronunciation Key

Consonant Sounds

b	**b**i**b**, ca**bb**age	l	**l**id, need**le**, ta**ll**	th	ba**th**, **th**in
ch	**ch**ur**ch**, sti**tch**	m	a**m**, **m**an, du**mb**	_th_	ba**the**, **th**is
d	**d**ee**d**, maile**d**, pu**dd**le	n	**n**o, sudd**en**	v	ca**v**e, val**v**e, **v**ine
f	**f**ast, **f**i**f**e, o**ff**, **ph**rase, rou**gh**	ng	thi**ng**, i**nk**	w	**w**ith, **w**olf
		p	**p**op, ha**pp**y	y	**y**es, **y**olk, on**i**on
g	**g**a**g**, **g**et, fin**g**er	r	**r**oar, **rh**yme	z	ro**s**e, si**z**e, **x**ylophone, **z**ebra
h	**h**at, **wh**o	s	mi**ss**, **s**auce, **sc**ene, **s**ee		
hw	**wh**ich, **wh**ere			zh	gara**g**e, plea**s**ure, vi**s**ion
j	**j**u**dg**e, **g**em	sh	di**sh**, **sh**ip, **s**ugar, ti**ss**ue		
k	**c**at, **k**i**ck**, s**ch**ool				
kw	**ch**oir, **qu**ick	t	**t**ight, stopp**ed**		

Vowel Sounds

ă	p**a**t, l**au**gh	ŏ	h**o**rrible, p**o**t	ŭ	c**u**t, fl**oo**d, r**ou**gh, s**o**me
ā	**a**pe, **ai**d, p**ay**	ō	g**o**, r**ow**, t**oe**, th**ough**	û	c**i**rcle, f**u**r, h**ear**d, t**er**m, t**ur**n, **ur**ge, w**or**d
â	**ai**r, c**a**re, w**ea**r	ô	**a**ll, c**au**ght, f**or**, p**aw**		
ä	f**a**ther, k**oa**la, y**a**rd	oi	b**oy**, n**oi**se, **oi**l		
ĕ	p**e**t, pl**ea**sure, **a**ny	ou	c**ow**, **ou**t	yŏŏ	c**u**re
ē	b**e**, b**ee**, **ea**sy, p**ia**no	ŏŏ	f**u**ll, b**oo**k, w**o**lf	yōō	ab**u**se, **u**se
ĭ	**i**f, p**i**t, b**u**sy	ōō	b**oo**t, r**u**de, fr**ui**t, fl**ew**	ə	**a**go, sil**e**nt, penc**i**l, lem**o**n, circ**u**s
ī	r**i**de, b**y**, p**ie**, h**igh**				
î	d**ear**, d**eer**, f**ie**rce, m**ere**				

Stress Marks

Primary Stress ´: bi•ol•o•gy [bī **ŏl´** ə jē]
Secondary Stress ´: bi•o•log•i•cal [bī´ ə **lŏj´** ĭ kəl]

aspect

Aspect comes from the Latin prefix *ad-* ("at") and the Latin word root *specere*, which means "to look." A *spectator*, which comes from the same word root, is a watcher. A *prospect*, which is something that is looked forward to, comes from the prefix *pro-*, "in front of" or "before," and *specere*.

attract

Attract comes from the Latin prefix *ad-* ("toward") and the Latin word root *trahere*, "to pull or to draw." The English word *tractor*, a vehicle that pulls another vehicle or object, also comes from *trahere. Contract*, an agreement between two or more parties, comes from the Latin prefix *com-* ("together") and *trahere. Retract*, which means "to take back," comes from the Latin prefix *re-* ("again") and *trahere.*

A

ac·knowl·edge (ăk **nŏl´** ĭj) *v.* To recognize: *They were **acknowledged** as experts in science.*

ac·quaint·ed (ə **kwānt´** ĭd) *adj.* Familiar or informed: *People **acquainted** through mutual friends develop meaningful relationships.*

a·dapt·ed (ə **dăp´** tĭd) *adj.* Fitted or suitable, especially for a specific purpose: *A dog's claws are **adapted** for digging.*

ad·mit (ăd **mĭt´**) *v.* To acknowledge or confess to be true or real: *He **admitted** that I was right.*

ad·van·tage (ăd **văn´** tĭj) *n.* A beneficial factor or feature: *Museums and libraries are some of the **advantages** of city life.*

an·noy·ance (ə **noĭ´** əns) *n.*
1. Something causing trouble or irritation; a nuisance: *His tummy ache was a minor **annoyance**.*
2. Irritation or displeasure: *He swatted at the mosquito in **annoyance**.*

ap·pren·tice (ə **prĕn´** tĭs) *n.* A person who works for another without pay in return for instruction in a craft or trade: *The blacksmith's **apprentice** was trained to make horseshoes.*

as·pect (**ăs´** pĕkt) *n.* A way in which something can be viewed by the mind; an element or facet: *The doctor reviewed all **aspects** of the patient's history.*

as·suming (ə **soo ming**) *conj.* If; supposing: ***Assuming** our guests arrive on time, we'll have dinner at 6:00.*

as·ton·ish (ə **stŏn´** ĭsh) *v.* To surprise greatly; amaze: *It **astonished** me that we finished our project on time.*

at·tract (ə **trăkt´**) *v.* To cause to draw near; direct to oneself or itself by some quality or action: *Crowds were **attracted** to the beautiful beach.*

au·thor·i·ty (ə **thôr´** ĭ tē) *n.* A person or an organization having power to enforce laws, command obedience, determine, or judge: *City **authorities** closed the street for repairs.*

a·vail·a·ble (ə **vā´** lə bəl) *adj.* Capable of being obtained: *Tickets are **available** at the box office.*

B

back·ground (**băk´** groŭnd´) *n.* A person's experience, training, and education: *Math knowledge is a perfect **background** for jobs in science.*

balk (bôk) *v.* To stop short and refuse to go on: *My pony **balked** at the gate and would not jump.*

ă **rat** / ā **pay** / â **care** / ä **father** / ĕ **pet** / ē **be** / ĭ **pit** / ī **pie** / î **fierce** / ŏ **pot** / ō **go** /
ô **paw, for** / oi **oil** / oo **book**

ban·ish (**băn´**ĭsh) *v.* To drive out or away; expel: *Banish such thoughts from your mind.*

bare (bâr) *v.* To open up to view; uncover: *The bear opened its mouth and bared its teeth at the wolf.*

bar·ri·er (**băr´** ē ər) *n.* Something that blocks movement or passage: *Cows crossing the road are a barrier to traffic.*

bea·con (**bē´** kən) *n.* A light or fire used as a warning or guide: *The flashing beacon on the lighthouse warned the ship that it was nearing the coast.*

beam (bēm) *v.* To smile broadly: *The baseball player was beaming after he made the game-winning play.*

beck·on (**bĕk´** ən) *v.* To signal (a person), as by nodding or waving: *The principal beckoned us to her office.*

ben·e·fit (**bĕn´** ə fit) *n.* Something that is of help; an advantage: *The field trip was of great benefit to the students.*

bon·dage (**bŏn´** dĭj) *n.* The condition of being held as a slave or serf; slavery or servitude: *The slaves were held in bondage.*

bound (bound) *v.* To leap, jump, or spring: *The deer was bounding into the woods.*

brace (brās) *v.* To give support to; make firm; strengthen: *The camper is bracing a tent with poles.*

bran·dish (**brăn´**dĭsh) *v.* To wave triumphantly or threateningly: *She came home, brandishing the award she received at school.*

bru·tal (**brōōt´** l) *adj.* Cruel; ruthless: *The enemy launched a brutal attack.*

bun·dle (**bŭn´** dl) *v.* To dress (a person) warmly: *She made sure to bundle up before heading out in the snow.*

bun·gle (**bŭng´**gəl) *v.* To manage, do, or handle badly: *He bungled dinner when he didn't follow a recipe.*

beacon

C

cal·cu·late (**kăl´**kyə lāt´) *v.* To find by using addition, subtraction, multiplication, or division: *They calculate the number of supplies needed before starting the project.*

ca·reer (kə **rîr´**) *n.* A profession or occupation: *She is considering a career in medicine.*

check (chĕk) *v.* To stop or hold back: *The defenders were in charge of checking the opposing offense during the soccer match.*

clam·my (**klăm´** ē) *adj.* Unpleasantly damp, sticky, and usually cold: *My feet feel clammy in wet boots.*

col·lapse (kə **lăps´**) *v.* To fall down or inward suddenly; cave in: *Part of the roof collapsed after the fire.*

ōō b**oo**t / ou **ou**t / û c**u**t / û f**u**r / hw **wh**ich / th **th**in / *th* **th**is / zh vi**s**ion / ə **a**go, sil**e**nt, penc**i**l, lem**o**n, circ**u**s

col·lect·ed (kə lĕk′ tĭd) *adj.* In full control of oneself; composed; calm: *He did his best to stay cool and collected when making his speech.*

com·mo·tion (kə mō′ shən) *n.* A disturbance or tumult: *The argument created a commotion in the hall.*

com·pe·ti·tion (kŏm pĭ tĭsh′ ən) *n.* A test of skill or ability; a contest: *The soccer match was a competition between two talented teams.*

competition

com·pli·ment (kŏm′ plə mənt) *n.* An expression of praise, admiration, or congratulation: *She gave me a compliment.*

con·cen·trate (kŏn′ sən trāt′) *v.* To keep or direct one's thoughts, attention, or efforts: *It's hard to concentrate on my homework when the television is on.*

con·duct (kŏn′ dŭkt) *n.* The act of directing; management: *The coach was responsible for the team's conduct.*

con·serve (kən sûrv′) *v.* To protect from loss or harm; preserve: *Conserving energy is important.*

con·ta·gious (kən tā′ jəs) *adj.* Spreading by direct or indirect contact: *Her desire to win the team relay was contagious.*

con·tent·ment (kən tĕnt′ mənt) *n.* The condition of being content; satisfaction: *Cats purr with contentment when they are satisfied.*

con·trar·y (kŏn′ trĕr′ ē) *adj.* Stubbornly opposed to others; willful: *Little children often become contrary when they need a nap.*

con·tri·bu·tion (kŏn′ trĭ byōō′ shən) *n.* Something that is given: *We made contributions of food to the poor.*

cramped (krămpt) *adj.* Confined and limited in space: *A family of four lived in a cramped little apartment.*

crit·i·cal (krĭt′ ĭ kəl) *adj.* Extremely important or decisive: *The surgeon performed a critical surgery.*

D

de·bate (dĭ bāt′) *n.* A discussion or consideration of the arguments for and against something: *The class held a debate to discuss the fairness of the school dress code.*

de·cline (dĭ klīn′) *n.* The process or result of going down in number or quality: *Some people think the neighborhood is in decline.*

ă rat / ā pay / â care / ä father / ĕ pet / ē be / ĭ pit / ī pie / î fierce / ŏ pot / ō go / ô paw, for / oi oil / ōō book

dec•or•ate (dĕk´ ər āt´) *v.* To furnish with something attractive, beautiful, or striking; adorn: *The students **decorated** the auditorium with flowers for graduation.*

del•i•ca•cy (dĕl´ ĭ kə sē) *n.* A choice food considered with regard to its rarity, costliness, or the like: *When my family travels, we always taste the local **delicacy**.*

de•mol•ish (dĭ mŏl´ ĭsh) *v.* To tear down completely; level: *They **demolished** the old building.*

de•pend•ent (dĭ pĕn´ dənt) *adj.* Relying on or needing the help of another for support: *Plants are **dependent** upon sunlight.*

de•scend (dĭ sĕnd´) *v.* To move from a higher to a lower place or position; go or come down: *The hikers **descended** from the top of the mountain.*

de•sert•ed (dĕ zûrt´ ĭd) *adj.* Left alone; abandoned: *The girl felt **deserted** when her friends walked away from her.*

de•spite (dĭ spīt´) *prep.* In spite of: *Lewis and Clark traveled to the Pacific **despite** the unknown land.*

des•ti•na•tion (dĕs´ tə nā´ shən) *n.* The place to which a person or thing is going or is sent: *The **destination** of that package is written on the label.*

de•struc•tion (dĭ strŭk´ shən) *n.* The condition of having been destroyed: *The tornado caused great **destruction**.*

de•tect (dĭ tĕkt´) *v.* To discover or determine the existence, presence, or fact of: ***Detecting** the smell of smoke could save your life.*

de•te•ri•o•rate (dĭ tîr´ ē ə rāt) *v.* To make or become inferior in quality, character, or value; worsen: *The moisture is **deteriorating** the cover of the old book.*

de•vel•op (dĭ vĕl´ əp) *v.* To bring into being: *The author **developed** the book's plot gradually.*

dex•ter•i•ty (dĕks tĕr´ ĭ tē) *n.* Skill or grace in using the hands, body, or mind: *A silversmith with **dexterity** can make beautiful pots.*

di•min•ish (dĭ mĭn´ ĭsh) *v.* To make or become smaller or less: *The store's supply of clothing is **diminishing** because of the clearance sale.*

dis•ad•van•tage (dĭs´ əd văn´ tĭj) *n.* A circumstance or condition that makes it harder to do something or to be successful: *A **disadvantage** of river transportation is its slowness.*

dis•com•fort (dĭs kŭm´fərt) *n.* A lack of comfort or ease: *The **discomfort** caused by her tight shoes made it difficult to run.*

destruction

Destruction comes from the Latin prefix *de-* ("off" or "down") and the Latin word root *struere*, which means "to construct." Related words are *structure*, "something that is constructed," and *instruct*, "to teach," which come from the same Latin word root.

---

o͞o b**oo**t / ou **ou**t / û c**u**t / û f**u**r / hw **wh**ich / th **th**in / *th* **th**is / zh vi**s**ion / ə **a**go, sil**e**nt, penc**i**l, lem**o**n, circ**u**s

dis•tract (dĭs trăkt´) v. To draw (the attention, for example) away from something: *The noise* **distracted** *the students in the library.*

dis•turb (dĭs tûrb´) v. To intrude upon; bother: *The visitors were* **disturbing** *the musician's practice.*

dom•i•nate (dŏm´ ə nāt´) v. To have controlling power or occupy a commanding position over: *The mayor* **dominated** *the town hall meeting.*

dwarf (dwôrf) v. To cause to look or seem smaller: *The cruise ship* **dwarfed** *the fishing boat.*

E

ed•i•ble (ĕd´ ə bəl) adj. Safe to eat: *James was surprised to learn that some flowers are* **edible.**

e•di•tion (ĭ dĭsh´ ən) n. The entire number of copies of a book or newspaper printed at one time and having the same content: *Today's* **edition** *of the paper is sold out.*

ef•fec•tive (ĭ fĕk´ tĭv) adj. Having an intended or expected effect: *The vaccine is* **effective** *against the flu.*

ef•fi•cient (ĭ fish´ ənt) adj. Acting or producing effectively with a minimum of waste, expense, or unnecessary effort: *High gas mileage makes this car an* **efficient** *vehicle.*

el•e•ment (ĕl´ ə mənt) n. A part of a whole, especially a fundamental or essential part: *The novel is a detective story with one* **element** *of a science fiction story.*

e•lite (ĭ lēt´) or (ā lēt´) adj. Relating to a small and privileged group: *The athletes were the* **elite** *stars of the sports world.*

em•bark (ĕm bärk´) v. To set out on an adventure; begin: *The sailors* **embark** *on an ocean voyage.*

em•bar•rass (ĕm băr´ əs) v. To cause to feel self-conscious or ill at ease; disconcert: *Not knowing the answer to the question* **embarrassed** *me.*

en•dan•gered (ĕn dān´ jərd) adj. Nearly extinct: *The* **endangered** *animals were put in a preserve.*

en•thu•si•as•tic (ĭn thōō zē as´tĭk) adj. Full of or showing a strong interest, excitement, or admiration: *She is* **enthusiastic** *about going to summer camp with her friends.*

en•vy (ĕn´ vē) n. A feeling of discontent at the advantages or successes enjoyed by another, together with a strong desire to have them for oneself: *I was filled with* **envy** *when I saw their new car.*

ep•i•sode (ĕp´ ĭ sōd) n. An incident that forms a distinct part of a story: *The story was divided into six* **episodes** *for television.*

ă rat / ā pay / â care / ä father / ĕ pet / ē be / ĭ pit / ī pie / î fierce / ŏ pot / ō go / ô paw, for / oi oil / ōō book

ev•i•dent (ĕv´ ĭ dənt) *adj.* Easy to see or notice; obvious: *From the dark clouds, it was **evident** that it would soon rain.*

ex•cep•tion (ĭk sĕp´ shən) *n.* The act of leaving out or the condition of being left out: *All of our guests have arrived, with the **exception** of two.*

ex•pe•di•tion (ĕk´ spĭ dĭsh´ ən) *n.* A group making a journey for a specific purpose: *The **expedition** cheered when they reached the top of Mt. Everest.*

ex•tend (ĭk stĕnd´) *v.* To stretch out; reach: *We saw a clothesline **extending** from the tree to the house.*

F

fac•tor (făk´ tər) *n.* Something that brings about a result: *A willingness to work hard is an important **factor** in achieving successes.*

fare (fâr) *v.* To get along; progress: *How are you **faring** with your project?*

fea•ture (fē´ chər) *v.* To give special attention to; offer prominently: *The exhibit will **feature** Native American pottery.*

fe•ro•cious (fə rō´ shəs) *adj.* Extremely savage; fierce: *The tiger's **ferocious** roar frightened the deer.*

fit•ful (fĭt´fəl) *adj.* Starting and stopping: *During the storm, the wind blew in **fitful** gusts.*

flour•ish (flûr´ ĭsh) *v.* To do well; prosper: *Their business **flourished** and they became rich.*

foe (fō) *n.* An enemy, opponent, or adversary: ***Foes** of the new city dump met to fight the plan.*

for•mal (fôr´ məl) *adj.* Structured according to forms or conventions: *The board of directors met in a **formal** meeting.*

for•mu•la (fôr´ myə lə) *n.* A method of doing something; procedure: *The teacher gave us the **formula** for writing a good research paper.*

fran•tic (frăn´ tĭk) *adj.* Very excited with fear or anxiety; desperate; frenzied: *She was **frantic** with worry.*

ful•fill (fŏŏl fĭl´) *v.* To carry out: *Sharon **fulfilled** her responsibility when she finished cleaning her room.*

G

gor•geous (gôr´ jəs) *adj.* Dazzlingly beautiful or magnificent: *The snowcapped mountains were **gorgeous** in the sunset.*

ferocious

ōō **boo**t / ou **ou**t / û **cu**t / û **fu**r / hw **wh**ich / th **th**in / *th* **th**is / zh vision / ə **a**go, sil**e**nt, penc**i**l, lem**o**n, circ**u**s

household

Household is made up of *house*, meaning "a building made for people to live in," and *hold*, meaning "possession."

identical

Identical comes from a Latin word meaning "identity," the physical and personality characteristics that make up who a person is. Other English words relating to someone's identity come from the same Latin word root: *identity*, of course, *identify*, and *identification*.

inflate

grad·u·al·ly (**grăj´** ōō əl lē) *adv.* Occurring in small stages or degrees, or by even, continuous change: *The water level in the lake changed gradually.*

grant (grănt) *v.* To give or allow (something asked for): *The teacher granted us permission to leave early.*

guar·di·an (**gär´** dē ən) *n.* A person or thing that guards, protects, or watches over: *Courts act as guardians of the law.*

gush (gŭsh) *v.* To flow forth suddenly in great volume: *Water gushed from the broken pipe.*

H

heave (hēv) *v.* To lift with effort or force: *We had to heave the furniture onto the moving truck.*

hes·i·tate (**hĕz´** ĭ tāt´) *v.* To be slow to act, speak, or decide: *We hesitated about whether to go over the rickety bridge.*

hon·ored (**ŏn´** ərd) *adj.* Proud to be given special respect or a special opportunity: *I felt honored to represent our class in the school talent show.*

hos·tile (**hŏs´** təl) *adj.* Not friendly: *Don't give me such a hostile look.*

house·hold (**hous´** hōld´) *n.* The members of a family and others living together in a single unit: *Every household has its own rules.*

I

i·den·ti·cal (ī **dĕn´** tĭ kəl) *adj.* Exactly equal and alike: *We're riding identical bicycles.*

im·merse (ĭ **mûrs´**) *v.* To involve deeply; absorb: *She immersed herself in her character for the school play.*

im·press (ĭm **prĕs´**) *v.* To have a strong, often favorable effect on the mind or feelings of: *The worker impressed his manager and was promoted.*

im·print (ĭm **prĭnt´**) *v.* To make a mark or pattern on a surface by pressing or stamping: *The company's logo was imprinted on its products.*

in·cred·i·bly (ĭn **krĕd´** ə blē) *adv.* In a way that is hard to believe: *The winner of the race ran incredibly fast.*

in·flate (ĭn **flāt´**) *v.* To cause to expand with air or gas: *She inflated the tires on her bicycle.*

in·flu·en·tial (ĭn´ flōō **ĕn´** shəl) *adj.* Having or exercising influence: *Our city has an influential newspaper.*

in·sight (**ĭn´** sīt) *n.* The perception of the true nature of something: *The movie critic's review had brilliant insights about the meaning of the movie.*

in·te·ri·or (ĭn **tîr´**ē ər) *n.* An inner part; inside: *The carvings appear on the interior walls of the cave.*

ă rat / ā **pay** / â **care** / ä **father** / ĕ **pet** / ē **be** / ĭ **pit** / ī **pie** / î **fierce** / ŏ **pot** / ō **go** / ô **paw, for** / oi **oil** / ōō **book**

in•ter•rupt (ĭn tər **ŭpt´**) v. To do something that hinders or stops the action or conversation of; break in on: *I was about to finish my joke when my brother* **interrupted** *me.*

in•tim•i•date (ĭn **tĭm´** ĭ dāt) v. To fill with fear; to frighten, or discourage: *The rough water* **intimidated** *us in our light canoe.*

is•sue (**ĭsh´** ōō) n. A subject being discussed or disputed; a question under debate: *The senator spoke about the* **issue** *of reforming campaign laws.*

K

keen (kēn) adj. Acute; sensitive: *The* **keen** *eyes of the owl help him to see at night.*

L

lack (lăk) v. To be without: *The neighborhood* **lacked** *streetlights.*

launch (lônch) or (länch) n. The act of starting or setting into action: *The company was ready for the* **launch** *of its new research program.*

lec•ture (**lĕk´** chər) v. To give an explanation or a scolding: *My father* **lectured** *me about going out after dark.*

leg•en•dar•y (**lĕj´** ən dĕr´ ē) adj. Very well-known; famous: *Paul Revere's ride is* **legendary.**

lunge (lŭnj) v. To make a sudden forward movement: *She was* **lunging** *for the ball.*

M

mag•nif•i•cent (măg **nĭf´** ĭ sənt) adj. Outstanding of its kind; excellent: *Jackie Robinson was a* **magnificent** *athlete.*

mar•gin (**mär´** jĭn) n. An edge or border: *Weeds grew around the* **margins** *of the pond.*

mar•vel (**mär´**vəl) v. To be filled with surprise, astonishment, or wonder: *He stared at the ocean,* **marveling** *at its vastness.*

mas•ter (**măs´** tər) v. To become the master of; bring under control: *He* **mastered** *a foreign language.*

ma•ture (mə **tyŏŏr´**) or (mə **tŏŏr´**) or (mə **chŏŏr´**) v. To grow older: *Most puppies* **mature** *into full-grown dogs in a year or two.* adj. Having reached full growth or development: *A* **mature** *redwood can be hundreds of feet tall.*

men•tal (**mĕn´** tl) adj. Occurring in or done in the mind: *Good writing creates a* **mental** *image for the reader.*

midst (mĭdst) or (mĭtst) n. The middle position or part; the center: *They planted a tree in the* **midst** *of the garden.*

ōō b**oo**t / ou **out** / û c**u**t / û f**ur** / hw **wh**ich / th **th**in / *th* **th**is / zh vi**s**ion / ə **a**go, sil**e**nt, penc**i**l, lem**o**n, circ**u**s

mim·ic (**mĭm´** ĭk) *adj.* Acting as an imitation: *A snowman is a **mimic** person.* *v.* To resemble closely; simulate: *Children often **mimic** the mannerisms of their parents.*

min·i·mum (**mĭn´** ə məm) *n.* The smallest amount or degree possible: *We need a **minimum** of an hour to make dinner.*

mi·rage (mĭ **räzh´**) *n.* An optical illusion in which something that is not really there appears to be seen in the distance: *In the desert we saw **mirages** that looked like lakes.*

mis·hap (**mĭs´** hăp´) *n.* An unfortunate accident: *The trip ended without a **mishap**.*

mock (mŏk) *v.* To treat with scorn or contempt; deride: *I felt bad for Tom while his brother was **mocking** him.*

N

nerve (nûrv) *n.* Courage or daring: *It took all my **nerve** to talk to the new student in our class.*

numb (nŭm) *adj.* Deprived of the power to feel or move normally: *The boy's toes were **numb** with cold.*

numb

Numb comes from the Old English word *niman*, which literally means "to take." When you are numb, you cannot feel or move normally; feeling has been taken from you.

O

ob·ject (əb´ **jĕkt´**) *v.* To be opposed; express disapproval: *We **objected** to the loud noises downstairs.*

ob·vi·ous (**ŏb´** vē əs) *adj.* Easily perceived or understood; evident: *Large football players have an **obvious** advantage.*

of·fi·cial·ly (ə **fish´** əl lē) *adv.* By or in a way relating to an office or post of authority: *The winner was **officially** declared.*

op·po·nent (ə **pō´** nənt) *n.* A person or group that opposes another in a battle, contest, controversy, or debate: *The two runners were **opponents** in the race.*

or·di·nance (**ôr´** dn əns) *n.* A statute or regulation, especially one enacted by a city government: *The **ordinance** requires that every dog be on a leash.*

or·gan·ize (**ôr´** gən īz´) *v.* To put together or arrange in an orderly, systematic way: *She was told to **organize** her messy room.*

o·rig·i·nal (ə **rĭj´** ĭ nəl) *adj.* Existing before all others; first: *Virginia is one of the **original** thirteen colonies.*

out·fit (**out´** fit´) *v.* To equip: *The campsite was **outfitted** with a tent and a grill.*

ă rat / ā pay / â care / ä father / ĕ pet / ē be / ĭ pit / ī pie / î fierce / ŏ pot / ō go / ô paw, for / oi oil / o͞o book

P

pace (pās) *n.* Speed of motion or progress: *I love the fast **pace** of city life.*

par·tic·u·lar (pər tĭk´ yə lər) *adj.* Separate and different from others of the same group or category: *The painter wanted the walls a **particular** shade of blue.*

peal (pēl) *n.* A loud burst of noise: *A **peal** of thunder frightened the baby.*

perch (pûrch) *n.* A branch or rod on which an animal can sit: *The cat climbed to the highest **perch** to avoid the dog.*

per·son·al·ly (pûr´ sən əl lē) *adv.* In person or by oneself; without the help of another: *I thanked her **personally.***

per·suade (pər swād´) *v.* To cause (someone) to do or believe something by arguing, pleading, or reasoning; convince: *He tried to **persuade** them to come with us.*

pic·ture (pĭk´ chər) *v.* To form a mental image of; visualize; imagine: *He **pictured** himself winning the bike race.*

pierc·ing (pîr´ sĭng) *adj.* Loud and shrill: *The **piercing** sound of the alarm woke me up.*

plunge (plŭnj) *v.* To thrust, throw, or place forcefully or suddenly into something: *The farmer **plunged** the pitchfork into the hay.*

pre·lim·i·nar·y (prĭ lĭm´ ə nĕr´ ē) *adj.* Prior to or preparing for the main matter, action, or business; introductory: *The architect showed **preliminary** sketches for a building.*

pres·ence (prĕz´əns) *n.* The fact or condition of being present or near: *The crying child was comforted by his mother's **presence**.*

press·ing (prĕs´ ĭng) *adj.* Demanding immediate attention; urgent: *Hunger is one of the world's most **pressing** problems.*

pre·vi·ous·ly (prē´ vē əs lē) *adv.* Before something else in time or order: ***Previously**, the girls lived in New Orleans.*

prim·i·tive (prĭm´ ĭ tĭv) *adj.* Simple or crude: *A log cabin is a **primitive** type of house.*

pro·ce·dure (prə sē´jər) *n.* A way of doing something or getting something done, often by a series of steps: *To conduct a science experiment, he had to follow a **procedure**.*

prod (prŏd) *v.* To stir to action; urge: *She continually **prodded** him to do his homework.*

pro·duce (prə dōōs´) *v.* To create by mental or physical effort: *It takes time to **produce** a painting.*

primitive

ōō b**oo**t / ou **ou**t / û c**u**t / û f**u**r / hw **wh**ich / th **th**in / *th* **th**is / zh vi**s**ion / ə **a**go, sil**e**nt, penc**i**l, lem**o**n, circ**u**s

G11

pro·hib·it (prō hĭb´ ĭt) *v.* To forbid by law or authority: *The pool rules prohibit diving in the shallow end.*

pros·per (prŏs´ pər) *v.* To be fortunate or successful; thrive: *The man prospered after graduating from college.*

pro·vi·sions (prə vĭzh´ ənz) *n.* Stocks of foods and other necessary supplies: *Soldiers at war are given provisions.*

pub·li·ca·tion (pŭb lĭ kā´ shən) *n.* An issue of printed or electronic matter, such as a magazine, offered for sale or distribution: *The school's monthly publication is very informative.*

provisions

Q

quake (kwāk) *v.* To shiver or tremble, as from fear or cold: *I was so frightened that my legs were quaking.*

qual·i·fy (kwŏl´ ə fī´) *v.* To make eligible or qualified, as for a position or task: *She received high grades, qualifying her for the Honor Society.*

quiv·er (kwĭv´ər) *v.* To shake with a slight vibrating motion; tremble: *Her voice quivered with excitement when she talked about her birthday party.*

R

range (rānj) *n.* An extended group or series, especially a row or chain of mountains: *The Rocky Mountain range is in the western United States.*

re·al·i·za·tion (rē əl ĭ zā´ shən) *n.* The act of realizing or the condition of being realized: *The realization that he lost his wallet panicked him.*

rea·son (rē´ zən) *v.* To use the ability to think clearly and sensibly: *I reasoned that I should stay inside because it was raining outside.*

re·bel·lious (rĭ bĕl´ yəs) *adj.* Prone to or participating in a rebellion: *The rebellious farmer fought in the Revolutionary War.*

re·cite (rĭ sīt´) *v.* To repeat or say aloud (something prepared or memorized), especially before an audience: *The players recite the Pledge of Allegiance before each game.*

rec·ord (rĕk´ ərd) *n.* The highest or lowest measurement known, as in sports events or weather readings: *Death Valley holds the record for least rainfall in a year in the United States.*

reg·u·late (rĕg´ yə lāt) *v.* To control or direct according to a rule or a law: *Rangers regulate park activities.*

re·peal (rĭ pēl´) *v.* To withdraw or cancel officially; revoke: *The Senate voted to repeal the law.*

ă **rat** / ā **pay** / â **care** / ä **father** / ĕ **pet** / ē **be** / ĭ **pit** / ī **pie** / î **fierce** / ŏ **pot** / ō **go** / ô **paw, for** / oi **oil** / o͞o **book**

rep•re•sen•ta•tive (rĕp´ rĭ zĕn´ tə tĭv) *n.* A person who acts for one or more others: *Rob and Peter were elected as class representatives.*

re•quire (rĭ **kwīr**´) *v.* To be in need of; need: *Practice is required for a person to become better at a sport.*

re•sem•ble (rĭ **zĕm**´ bəl) *v.* To have similarity or likeness to; be like: *Some house cats resemble cougars.*

res•i•dent (rĕz´ ĭ dənt) *n.* A person who lives in a particular place: *Residents of the building had to leave because the power was out.*

re•spon•si•bil•i•ty (rĭ spŏn´ sə **bĭl**´ ĭ tē) *n.* Something that one is responsible for; a duty or obligation: *The two cats are my responsibility.*

re•store (rĭ **stôr**´) *v.* To bring back to an original condition: *The carpenter wanted to restore the old building.*

re•sume (rĭ **zo͞om**´) *v.* To continue: *Classes resumed after school vacation.*

re•treat (rĭ **trēt**´) *v.* The act or process of withdrawing, especially from something dangerous or unpleasant: *Patriots forced the Hessians to retreat from battle.*

rev•o•lu•tion (rĕv´ ə **lo͞o**´ shən) *n.* The overthrow of one government and its replacement with another: *The goal of the American Patriots during their revolution was to overthrow British rule.*

rhyth•mic (rĭ***th***´mĭk) *adj.* Of or having a movement, action, or condition that repeats in regular sequence: *The rhythmic sound of the drums had a calming effect.*

romp (rŏmp) *n.* Lively or spirited play: *The girls took their dogs for a romp in the park.*

rou•tine (ro͞o **tēn**´) *n.* A series of activities performed or meant to be performed regularly; a standard or usual procedure: *They were delayed by the guards' routine of checking their passports.*

ru•mor (**ro͞o**´ mər) *n.* A story or report, usually spread by word of mouth, that has not been established as true: *I heard a rumor that Peter is moving to China.*

rur•al (**ro͞or**´ əl) *adj.* Of, relating to, or characteristic of the country: *Farms are found in rural areas.*

rus•tle (**rŭs**´ əl) *v.* To make a soft fluttering sound: *A rustling in the woods scared me away.*

rural

---

o͞o b**oo**t / ou **ou**t / û c**u**t / û f**u**r / hw **wh**ich / th **th**in / *th* **th**is / zh vi**si**on / ə **a**go, sil**e**nt, penc**i**l, lem**o**n, circ**u**s

S

sal•va•tion (săl vā´ shən) *n.* Someone or something that saves or rescues: *The spring was the* **salvation** *of the thirsty traveler.*

sav•age (săv´ ĭj) *adj.* Ferocious; fierce: *The* **savage** *tigers hunted their prey.*

scan (skăn) *v.* To examine (something) closely: *She* **scanned** *the report card.*

se•cre•tive (sē´krə tĭv) *adj.* Inclined to secrecy; tending to keep secrets: *We had to be* **secretive** *while we planned the surprise party.*

se•cure (sĭ kyoŏr´) *v.* To cause to remain firmly in position or place; fasten: *We* **secured** *the ship's hatches.*

seep (sēp) *v.* To pass slowly through small openings; ooze: *Cold air could* **seep** *in through the cracks.*

shake (shāk) *v.* To make uneasy; disturb; agitate: *She was* **shaken** *by the bad news.*

shat•ter (shăt´ ər) *v.* To break into pieces by force; smash: *The* **shattered** *glass was unfixable.*

shift (shĭft) *v.* To move or transfer from one place or position to another: *She* **shifted** *the heavy basket in her arms.*

shim•mer (shĭm´ ər) *v.* To shine with a subdued, flickering light: *The* **shimmering** *candle could be seen in the darkness.*

shoul•der (shōl´ dər) *v.* To place on the shoulder or shoulders for carrying: *The dad* **shouldered** *the boy so he could see over the crowd.*

shuf•fle (shŭf´ əl) *v.* To walk slowly, while dragging the feet: *I* **shuffled** *my feet because I was so tired.*

snug (snŭg) *adj.* Fitting closely: *A bicycle helmet should be* **snug**, *so it doesn't fall off.*

spare (spâr) *v.* To show mercy or consideration to: *I* **spared** *your feelings by not telling you about the problems.*

spe•cial•ty (spĕsh´ əl tē) *n.* A special pursuit, occupation, talent, or skill: *His* **specialty** *is portrait painting.*

sprawl•ing (sprôl´ ĭng) *adj.* Spreading out in different directions: *I looked over the* **sprawling** *meadow.*

squal•ling (skwôl ĭng) *n.* Loud crying: *The mother stopped her baby's* **squalling** *by singing him to sleep.* *adj.* Crying loudly: *They found the* **squalling** *kitten under a bush.*

squash (skwôsh) *v.* To beat or flatten into a pulp; crush: *He was* **squashing** *the peach on the pavement.*

shattered

ă rat / ā pay / â care / ä father / ĕ pet / ē be / ĭ pit / ī pie / î fierce / ŏ pot / ō go / ô paw, for / oi oil / ŏŏ book

stag·ger (stăg´ər) *v.* To move or stand unsteadily, as if carrying a great weight; totter: *Carrying the large boxes, she **staggered** clumsily.*

stall (stôl) *v.* To slow down or stop the process of; bring to a standstill: *The traffic **stalled** because of the accident ahead.*

strain (strān) *v.* To work as hard as possible; strive hard: *The boy **strained** to lift the heavy bag.*

strat·e·gy (străt´ə jē) *n.* The planning and directing of a series of actions that will be useful in gaining a goal: *General George Washington came up with a **strategy** for the battle.*

stride (strīd) *n.* A single, long step: *The giraffe took long **strides**.*

strug·gle (strŭg´əl) *v.* To make strenuous efforts; strive: *She **struggled** to stay awake.*

stunt·ed (stŭn´tĭd) *adj.* Slowed or stopped abnormally in growth or development: *The **stunted** tree did not grow because there was no water.*

sum·mon (sŭm´ən) *v.* To call forth; muster: *The smell of turkey **summons** memories of past Thanksgiving dinners.*

sup·posed·ly (sə pō´zĭd lē) *adv.* Seemingly: *Until she lied, she was **supposedly** my friend.*

surge (sûrj) *v.* To move with gathering force, as rolling waves do: *The crowd **surged** forward.*

sur·vey (sər vā´) or (sûr´ vā´) *v.* To look over the parts or features of; view broadly: *We **surveyed** the neighborhood from a hilltop.*

sus·pense (sə spĕns´) *n.* The state or quality of being undecided or uncertain: *The movie left us in **suspense**.*

sweep·ing (swēp´ĭng) *adj.* Moving in, or as if in, a long curve: *The castaways waved to the rescue plane with **sweeping** gestures.*

T

tech·nique (tĕk nēk´) *n.* A procedure or method for carrying out a specific task: *Jason learned **techniques** for carving wooden toys.*

te·di·ous (tē´ dē əs) *adj.* Tiresome because of slowness, dullness, or length; boring: *He didn't like math, so he thought the lecture was **tedious**.*

tem·po·rar·y (tĕm´ pə rĕr´ ē) *adj.* Lasting, used, serving, or enjoyed for a limited time; not permanent: *The man was given a **temporary** license until he could get a permanent one.*

ten·ta·tive (tĕn´ tə tĭv) *adj.* Not fully worked out, concluded, or agreed on: *The publisher created a **tentative** production schedule.*

suspense

The word *suspense* comes from the Latin prefix *sub-*, meaning "from below," and the Latin word root *pendere*, "to hang." A *suspension* bridge is a bridge on which the roadway hangs from cables. The related word *depend*, which means "to rely on" or "be determined by," comes from the Latin prefix *de-*, "down from," and *pendere*.

ōō b**oo**t / ou **ou**t / û c**u**t / û f**u**r / hw **wh**ich / th **th**in / *th* **th**is / zh vi**s**ion / ə **a**go, s**i**lent, penc**i**l, lem**o**n, circ**u**s

thumb (thŭm) *v.* To scan written matter by turning the pages with the thumb: *She **thumbed** through the magazine.*

tor·ment (tôr´ mĕnt´) *n.* Great physical or mental pain: *I was in a state of **torment** listening to the teacher explain the homework assignment.*

trans·fer (trăns fûr´ *or* trăns´fər) *v.* To cause to move from one place to another: *She **transferred** money into her savings account.*

trek (trĕk) *n.* A long, hard journey, especially on foot: *Settlers made the **trek** to the West.*

trib·u·tar·y (trĭb´ yə tĕr´ ē) *n.* A river or stream that flows into a larger river or stream: *People enjoy boating on **tributaries** of the Mississippi River.*

typ·i·cal·ly (tĭp´ ĭ kəl lē) *adv.* In a way that is usual for a kind, group, or category: ***Typically**, school begins early in the morning.*

U

un·doubt·ed·ly (ŭn dŏu´ tĭd lē) *adv.* Beyond question; undisputedly: *He was **undoubtedly** glad he made it to the meeting on time.*

un·e·vent·ful (ŭn´ ĭ vĕnt´ fəl) *adj.* Having no significant events: *The trip was **uneventful**.*

u·ni·form (yōō´ nə fôrm´) *adj.* Being the same as another or others: *He built the porch out of planks of **uniform** length.*

u·nique (yōō nēk´) *adj.* Being the only one of its kind: *The puppy had a **unique** mark on his back.*

un·i·son (yōō´ nĭ sən) or (yōō´ nĭ zən) *n.* At the same time; at once: *The rowers must work in **unison** to win.*

un·ob·served (ŭn´ əb zûrvd´) *adj.* Not seen or noticed: *We crept up the walkway **unobserved**.*

up·right (ŭp´ rīt´) *adv.* Straight up: *I taught my dog to sit **upright** and beg for a biscuit.*

urge (ûrj) *v.* To entreat earnestly and repeatedly; exhort: *The coach continues to **urge** us to stay in shape over summer vacation.*

V

vain (vān) *adj.* Having no success: *Firefighters made a **vain** attempt to save the burning building.*

var·y (vâr´ ē) *v.* To be different or diverse: *His diet will **vary** from day to day.*

veg·e·ta·tion (vĕj´ ĭ tā´ shən) *n.* The plants in an area or region; plant life: *There is little **vegetation** at the North Pole.*

uni-
The basic meaning of the prefix *uni-* is "one." It comes from the Latin prefix *uni-*, which in turn comes from the Latin word root *unus*, "one." The word *unicorn*, a mythological one-horned horse, comes from *uni-* and the Latin word root *cornu*, "horn." *Uniform, unique, unison,* and *unicycle* all have "one" in their definitions.

vegetation

ă rat / ā pay / â care / ä father / ĕ pet / ē be / ĭ pit / ī pie / î fierce / ŏ pot / ō go /
ô paw, for / oi oil / ōō book

view·point (**vyōō´** pŏĭnt´) *n.*
A position from which something
is observed or considered; a point
of view: *From the **viewpoint** of
the British, their navy was the
best.*

vil·lain (**vĭl´** ən) *n.* A wicked or
very bad person; a scoundrel:
*The evil brothers were the
villains of the movie.*

vi·o·la·tion (vī ə **lā´** shən) *n.*
The act or an instance of breaking
or ignoring or the condition of
(a law or rule) being broken or
ignored: *She was fined for traffic
violations.*

W

wheel (hwēl) *v.* To turn or whirl
around in place: *She **wheeled**
to see what had made the loud
sound behind her.*

wob·ble (wŏb´ əl) *v.* To move
unsteadily from side to side: *The
old table **wobbled**.*

villain
The meaning of
villain has changed
over the centuries.
The word comes
from the Latin word
root *villa*, which
means "country
house." It originally
meant a peasant
or serf who lived
in the country. It
gradually changed
to mean a person
with coarse feelings
or a foolish person,
and then a wicked
person.

ōō b**oo**t / ou **ou**t / û c**u**t / û f**u**r / hw **wh**ich / th **th**in / *th* **th**is / zh vi**s**ion / ə **a**go,
sil**e**nt, penc**i**l, lem**o**n, circ**u**s

Acknowledgments

The Birchbark House written and illustrated by Louise Erdrich. Copyright © 1999 by Louise Erdrich. Reprinted by permission of Hyperion Books. All rights reserved.

Can't You Make Them Behave, King George? by Jean Fritz, illustrated by Tomie dePaola. Text copyright © 1977 by Jean Fritz. Illustrations copyright © 1977 by Tomie dePaola. Reprinted by permission of Coward-McCann, a division of Penguin's Young Readers Group, a member of Penguin Group (USA). Inc., and Gina Maccoby Literary Agency.

Cougars by Patricia Corrigan, illustrated by John F. McGee. Copyright © 2001 by Northword Press. Reprinted by permission of T & N Children's Publishing.

Dangerous Crossing by Stephen Krensky, illustrated by Greg Harlin. Text copyright © 2005 by Stephen Krensky. Illustrations copyright © 2005 by Greg Harlin. All rights reserved including the right of reproduction in whole or in any form. Reprinted by permission of Dutton Children's Books, a member of Penguin's Young Readers Group, a division of Penguin Group (USA) Inc., and The Gersh Agency.

Darnell Rock Reporting by Walter Dean Myers. Copyright © 1994 by Walter Dean Myers. Reprinted by permission of Random House Children's Books, a division of Random House, Inc.

"Deanie McLeanie" by Walter Dean Myers. Copyright © 1994 by Walter Dean Myers. Reprinted by permission of Miriam Altshuler Literary Agency.

"Disturbed, the cat" from *The Penguin Book of Japanese Verse* (1967). Translated by Geoffrey Bownas and Anthony Thwaite. Reprinted by permission of Geoffrey Bownas.

"The Dog Newspaper" from *Five Pages a Day: A Writer's Journey* by Peg Kehret. Text copyright © 2005 by Peg Kehret. Reprinted by permission of Albert Whitman & Company and Curtis Brown, Ltd.

El Diario de Elisa by Doris Luisa Oronoz. Text copyright © by Doris Luisa Oronoz. Reprinted by permission of the author.

Everglades Forever: Restoring America's Great Wetlands by Trish Marx, photographs by Cindy Karp. Text copyright © 2004 by Trish Marx. Photographs copyright © 2004 by Cindy Karp. Reprinted by permission of Lee & Low Books, Inc., NY, NY 10016.

Excerpt from *The Black Stallion* by Walter Farley. Text copyright © 1941 by Walter Farley. Text copyright renewed © 1969 by Walter Farley. Reprinted by permission of Random House, Inc. and the Walter Farley Family Trust.

Excerpt from "Man Na Meri" from *Quest for the Tree Kangaroo: An Expedition to the Cloud Forest of New Guinea* by Sy Montgomery, photographs by Nic Bishop. Text copyright © 2006 by Sy Montgomery. Photographs copyright © 2006 by Nic Bishop. Reprinted by permission of Houghton Mifflin Harcourt Publishing Company.

"Genius" from *A Dime a Dozen* by Nikki Grimes. Copyright © 1998 by Nikki Grimes. Reprinted by permission of Dial Books for Young Readers, a division of Penguin Young Readers Group, a member of Penguin Group (USA) Inc. All rights reserved.

"Good Sportsmanship" from *All in Sport* by Richard Armour. Copyright © 1972 by Richard Armour. Reprinted by permission of Geoffrey Armour.

"James Forten" from *Now Is Your Time! The African-American Struggle for Freedom* by Walter Dean Myers. Copyright © 1991 by Walter Dean Myers. Reprinted by permission of HarperCollins Publishers.

"Karate Kid" by Jane Yolen from *Opening Day: Sports Poems*, published by Harcourt Brace & Co. Copyright © 1996 by Jane Yolen. Reprinted by permission of Curtis Brown, Ltd.

"LAFFF" by Lensey Namioka from *Within Reach: Ten Stories* edited by Donald P. Gallo. Copyright © 1983 by Lensey Namioka. Reprinted by permission of Lensey Namioka. All rights reserved by the author.

Lewis and Clark by R. Conrad Stein. Copyright © 1997 by Children's Press®, a division of Grolier Publishing Co., Inc. All rights reserved. Reprinted by permission of Scholastic Library Publishing.

Lunch Money by Andrew Clements. Text copyright © 2005 by Andrew Clements. Reprinted by permission of Simon & Schuster's Books for Young Readers, a division of Simon & Schuster's Children's Publishing Division, and Writers House, LLC, acting as agent for the author.

"A Package for Mrs. Jewls" from *Wayside School is Falling Down* by Louis Sachar, illustrated by Adam McCauley. Text copyright © 1989 by Louis Sachar. Illustrations copyright © 2003 by Adam McCauley. Reprinted by permission of HarperCollins Publishers.

Off and Running by Gary Soto. Text copyright © 1996 by Gary Soto. Reprinted by permission of the author and BookStop Literary Agency. All rights reserved. Jacket cover reprinted by permission of Random House Children's Books, a division of Random House, Inc.

Old Yeller by Fred Gipson. Copyright © 1956 by Fred Gipson. Reprinted by permission of HarperCollins Publishers and McIntosh & Otis, Inc.

"The Princess and the Pea" from *The Starlight Princess and Other Princess Stories* by Annie Dalton, illustrated by Belinda Downes. Text copyright © 1999 Dorling Kindersley Limited. Illustrations copyright © 1999 by Belinda Downes. Reprinted by permission of DK Publishing, Inc.

Rachel's Journal written and illustrated by Marissa Moss. Copyright © 1998 by Marissa Moss. All rights reserved. Reprinted by permission of Houghton Mifflin Harcourt Publishing Company and the Barbara S. Kouts Agency.

"Rockett Girls" from *Double Dutch: A Celebration of Jump Rope, Rhyme and Sisterhood* by Veronica Chambers. Copyright © 2002 by Veronica Chambers. Reprinted by permission of Hyperion Books for Children and the Sandra Dijkstra Literary Agency. All rights reserved.

"A Seeing Poem" from *Seeing Things* by Robert Froman, published by Thomas Y. Crowell, 1974. Copyright © 1974 by Robert Froman. Reprinted by permission of Katherine Froman.

Storm Warriors by Elisa Carbone. Copyright © 2001 by Elisa Carbone. Cover illustration copyright © 2001 by Don Demers. Reprinted by permission of Alfred A. Knopf, an imprint of Random House Children's Books, a division of Random House, Inc.

Credits

Photo Credits

Illustration